By Noble Things She Stands

By Noble Things She Stands

She Stands

The Fiction of Gwendoline Keats/Zack

—— *by* ——

CARL WELLS

authorHOUSE

AuthorHouse™
1663 Liberty Drive
Bloomington, IN 47403
www.authorhouse.com
Phone: 1 (800) 839-8640

Scripture quotations marked NASB are taken from the New American Standard Bible®, Copyright © 1960, 1962, 1963, 1968, 1971, 1972, 1973, 1975, 1977, 1995 by The Lockman Foundation*. Used by* permission.

Scripture quotations marked KJV are from the Holy Bible, King James Version (Authorized Version). First published in 1611. Quoted from the KJV Classic Reference Bible, Copyright © 1983 by The Zondervan *Corporation.*

Published by AuthorHouse 09/22/2015

ISBN: 978-1-5049-2370-5 (sc)
ISBN: 978-1-5049-2391-0 (e)

Print information available on the last page.

Any people depicted in stock imagery provided by Thinkstock are models, and such images are being used for illustrative purposes only. Certain stock imagery © Thinkstock.

This book is printed on acid-free paper.

For Gwendoline Keats/Zack, with
admiration and love. "'God guved me thee.'"

But he who is noble devises noble things,
and by noble things he stands.

Isaiah 32:8

TABLE OF CONTENTS

INTRODUCTION

This mixture of realism based on close observation with the symbol-making imagination is very like the quality that we call genius.

> Anonymous reviewer of *Life Is Life*,
> "The Academy," June 25, 1898

Gwendoline Keats was an English writer (b. 1865, d. ?). She wrote under the pen name Zack, though there seems never to have been any mystery as to her identity. She was born Oct. 4, 1865, at Port Hill—a gracious country home—near the small town of Northam, Devonshire, in the southwestern portion of England. The Library of Congress catalog lists her date of death as 1910, which means she died at the young age of 44 or 45. There is, however, uncertainty as to her date of death. She may have died as late as 1934. We will discuss this vexing question in the proper place.

Her first published story, "Widder Vlint," appeared in the November 1896 issue of "Blackwood's Magazine." She had just turned 31 in early October of that year. Having one's first published story appear in "Blackwood's" was pretty similar to having a debut in "The New Yorker" in our day. That may be an exaggeration, but only slightly so. Percy Bysshe Shelley, Samuel Taylor Coleridge, George Eliot, and Thomas de Quincey were among the authors published by "Blackwood's." Joseph Conrad's *Heart of Darkness* first appeared in "Blackwood's" in 1899, slightly more than two years after Zack's "Widder Vlint."

Her publishing career was brief, but fertile in its brevity—although her books were short. Her first book, *Life Is Life: And Other Tales and Episodes*, appeared in 1898. Then followed, in rapid succession, four other books of fiction: *On Trial* (1899), *The White Cottage* (1901), *Tales of Dunstable Weir* (1901), and *The Roman Road* (1903).

No more books followed in the seven years—or possibly even 31 years!—until her death. This silence, from an author who had been so diligent, seems at first glance to be at least unusual. But there is a reasonable explanation which we will discuss in Chapter 5. The world has mostly ignored Zack for 110 years. I suppose it can patiently wait through a few chapters to find out more about why she stopped writing books which no one today is reading anyway.

I think the books of Gwendoline Keats/Zack deserve a much wider audience. Alas, I have no scholarly credentials. I am not a critic or a professor. But I have read a lot of books, good and not so good, in my lifetime. I think Gwendoline Keats is a writer who should be and can be appreciated by readers as long as books are read. Her style and attitudes toward life will not appeal to every reader. But I think a significant percentage of readers will respond with gratitude to discover her books. Right now she is almost forgotten, but she deserves to have a niche in world literature.

Don't believe me. Don't trust me. Like Zaphod Beeblebrox, I'm "'just this guy, you know?'"[1] Read Zack's books for yourself. There are copies for sale at Amazon.com, and no doubt many other places.

Buy one of her books and read it. The best place to start is her first book, *Life Is Life*. Any of the following three would also work. (A hint: *The Roman Road* is not her best book, in my opinion and in the opinion of a few early critics as well; read any of the other four first.) Send me an insulting letter or email if you think I've led you astray.

Actually, you can avoid investing money in an author you've probably never heard of, and still see if she is worth reading. All five of Zack's books can be read for free on the Internet. You can read these entire books for zero expense. All you have to do is push the buttons on your keyboard. There is a bit more about this in Appendix VI.

---

[1]Douglas Adams, *The Restaurant at the End of the Universe* in the collection entitled *The Ultimate Hitchhiker's Guide*, Avenel, New Jersey, Wings Books, 1996 [original date of publication of *The Restaurant at the End of the Universe* is 1980], Chapter 2.

The title, *By Noble Things She Stands*, is taken from Isaiah 32:8, Revised Standard Version. "But he who is noble devises noble things, and by noble things he stands." That quote provides the epigraph to this book. There is an intrepid nobility to the character of Gwendoline Keats. She stands by noble things, and has devised noble books.

Chapters 1 through 5 each discuss one of her books, in chronological order of publication. Chapter 6 sums up what we know about Zack and her books.

Appendix I is a prayer.

Appendix II lists some of the reviews Zack's books elicited.

Appendix III explains how this book came to be written.

Appendix IV gives a bit more information on Gwendoline Keats and her family.

Appendix V briefly discusses Zack's letters to the writer May Sinclair.

Appendix VI discusses the current availability of Zack's five books.

Appendix VII briefly lists ten authors whose books are worth taking with you if you were stranded on a desert island. We'll see if Zack makes the list.

Appendix VIII discusses the future of Zack studies.

Then come acknowledgements, and finally a listing of my other books.

Nineteen of the photographs appear due to the kind permission of Andy and Beverley Keats. I wrote this book expecting all along that at most I would have a cover photograph of Gwendoline Keats. It is a great joy to me to be able to include the nineteen photographs of Gwendoline and her family in this book. Thank you, Mr. and Mrs. Keats!

The photograph of Port Hill was taken by Penny Portman and is used due to the kind permission of Michael and Penny Portman, current owners of Port Hill. The watercolor of Port Hill is by Tim Scott Bolton, and is used due to his kind permission and to that of the Portmans. Thanks to the three of you! I think seeing the stately birthplace of Gwendoline Keats adds greatly to our understanding of this true daughter of Devon.

Brad Herndon gave me much help and good advice in regard to the photographs. I don't think I would have figured out how to get the photographs into the book, without his guidance, and the book would have been vastly worse without the photos. If any other people become interested in Gwendoline Keats/Zack, they will have reason to thank my frequently sapient friend Brad Herndon that they are able to see those photographs

----

Warning!

As I describe each of Zack's novels and stories, inevitably I give away the plot of each and every one. I don't see any way around it. So, don't read this book. Or, rather, read Zack first, then come back to *By Noble Things She Stands* afterward. Perhaps you could read just enough of this book to have your interest in Zack piqued. That may cause you to invest some time, effort, or money, in obtaining one of Zack's books.

CHAPTER 1

Life Is Life: And Other Tales and Episodes

> "Ah, lad," she answered, "when a thing *is*, what does us gain by saying it isn't?"
>
> "But it's a dreary philosophy," he protested.
>
> "What do the ills of life matter if us faces 'em courageous?" she answered; but her old, tired voice trembled, for of life and life's ills she was somewhat weary.
>
> Zack, *Life Is Life*

Zack's first book was a masterwork. If she had published no other book than *Life Is Life: And Other Tales and Episodes*, she would deserve to be remembered with respect. Happily, her following books proved that *Life Is Life* was no fluke, but rather was simply the first offering of an artist of unique gifts.

Life Is Life is in some sense a microcosm of her work as a whole. The subjects and themes she deals with here reappear in her other books. There is considerable use of Devonshire dialect in some of the stories. There is the emphasis on facing reality without self-deception. There is the understanding that uneducated people of the lower classes are just as much people as are the upper classes—neither more nor less so. There is an anti-collectivist spirit, or to phrase it more positively, what we might call a pro-freedom or a pro-responsibility spirit. There is a recognition that evil really does exist, and is powerful in some people. There are coincidences which seem completely improbable, unless we grant Zack's apparent premise that God is always acting in the affairs of men and women. There is humor, often of the dark variety. There is a love of beauty. The style is Zack's style. Here at once we are introduced to the real Zack.

Zack's connection to the God of the Bible deserves a paragraph of its own! There seems to be a belief in a God whose ways are above our ways, but who is approximately the Christian God. I don't want to assume too much. Whether Zack was a Christian is not a question that can be answered hurriedly, or probably ever answered with finality by those of us down here below. We will try to chip away at this question as we discuss her books, always trying to remember that it is God Himself who has the final dispensation of our souls. There is a God in her books, and He is a good God and is present rather than distant, but He takes the exceedingly long view in His dealings with us: He gives us what He thinks we need, rather than what we would prefer to have.

James MacArthur wrote, "For a first book, one is also struck with the maturity of thought and life which marks these pages."[2] This is true. Gwendoline Keats, age 33 in October of 1898, the year the book was published, was already a mature thinker. She has strong and very individual ideas about how the world is put together. One might quarrel with those ideas—or admire rather than quarrel—but even those wanting to quarrel would recognize that they were reading a strong-minded woman quite willing and able to think for herself.

Zack's first published story was "Widder Vlint," in the November 1896 issue of "Blackwood's Magazine." She reached age 31 on October 4 of 1896. Six more of her stories appeared in "Blackwood's" through 1898. All seven of those stories and five more make up the contents of her first book, *Life Is Life*, which was published by Blackwood's in 1898. The price of the book was six shillings.

The American edition was put out by Charles Scribner's Sons. Sidney Colvin told Charles Scribner about Zack's stories, and the New York publisher "wrote immediately to Messrs. Blackwood and arranged for the publication of the book"[3] in the U.S. Thus Zack, from the start of her book publishing career, was published in the United States as

---

[2]James MacArthur, "The Light That Burns Upward," "The Bookman," Sept., 1898, pp. 45-46 in a review stretching from p. 44 to p. 47.

[3]Unknown reviewer, "A New Story Writer," "The Critic," July 1898, Vol. 3, p. 70.

well as in England. The price of the American edition was $1.50. In fact all five of her books eventually were published in America by Charles Scribner's Sons, and all were selling for $1.50 each when her final book was published in 1903.

However, given the copyright laws of the time (or the lack thereof), we probably should not be surprised to hear that an American company published the book without Zack's permission. She wrote her friend and fellow writer May Sinclair in October of 1898, "I see too that another firm has published the book in America—which is a bad lookout for Scribner & myself."[4] If we try to look on the bright side of the situation, at least this is an indication that Zack's book had attracted enough attention that a publisher hoped to make some money by issuing his own edition of the work.

Zack occasionally gives footnotes explaining the meaning of some of her words. As I quote her, I will instead include the footnote in brackets at the appropriate place in the text, with her name indicating that the explanation came from Zack. In a few places I have added my own explanation of words, in brackets, in which case I will give my initials.

I will discuss the stories in the order in which they appear in the book.

"Life Is Life"

The title story is the first in the book, and is by far the longest. It checks in at about 117 pages in the Books For Libraries Press edition of 1969 which I own. It's more than twice as long as the next longest story in the collection, and ten times as long as some of the stories.

---

[4]Zack letter to May Sinclair, Oct. 4, 1898. Oct. 4 was Zack's 33rd birthday; she does not mention that fact in her letter to May.

For her initial appearance before the reader of her first book, Zack chose wisely, for the story, "if longer, it could not well be stronger."[5] This was not a unanimous opinion, however. One reviewer groused at the "inanity" of the title, and others also carped at the concept that life is life. The story and the book as a whole were considered depressing by some. Zack was even pictured by one reviewer as the sort of person who "extracts pain from everything . . . casting her dark mantle over all who approach."[6]

Between the claim that the story "could not well be stronger" and the perceived "inanity" there is an unbridgeable gap. The reader will have to decide for himself where Zack fits in his universe of writers.

It is certainly true that Zack often deals with dark events. Some readers are likely to be—as some readers were three generations ago—put off by the often unhappy events portrayed.

But within the darkness of the stories, the very real light she gives us shines all the brighter.

Put me down on the side of those who find the title "Life Is Life" to be perfect. The title summarizes Zack's view of the world in three words: life must be faced squarely, head on, with no self-deception. Yes, life contains events of great sadness and great evil. It is our duty, but also our privilege, to face life honestly.

"Life Is Life" is a story containing cruel physical violence, a story in which the imperfect but admirable young hero suffers an irreversible disaster of the sort that is among the most terrible human beings can undergo, a story of sudden death, of lingering death, of hopeless despair, of rape, of murder, of possible damnation. And yet for all that it is a story of tender love, of courage in the face of evil, of bone-jarring honesty in facing frightening reality. It is a story of considerable depth of thought concerning the relationship of God and man, and a story which subtly points the way to the reconciliation of the classes.

"Life Is Life" opens in rural northern Devonshire in the southwestern portion of England. It opens, in short, in Zack's home country: she was born near Northam in rural northern Devonshire. Young (fourteen) Humphrey, grandchild of the Squire of Thursby Chase, is talking to

---

[5]Unknown reviewer, "'Zack.,'" "The Academy," June 25, 1898, p. 689.
[6]Unknown reviewer, "The Nation," Oct. 20, 1898, p. 299. The ellipsis is mine.

Wilkie, an old poacher, about the somewhat mysterious circumstances of Humphrey's birth. Approximately twelve years ago Wilkie had been taken for poaching and therefore had been on the scene at Thursby Chase when Dick Atter, the servant to the Squire's son (Captain Thursby), returned from Australia. Atter put the baby Humphrey in the hands of the Squire, saying that Captain Thursby was dead, but that the 2-year old baby was ""'a Thursby, an' a ginelman.'""

Then Atter disappeared. The Squire made use of detectives, but on their failing to turn up anything he had accepted Humphrey as his grandchild and had raised him as such.

All these long ago doings, well known as they are to him, are endlessly fascinating to Humphrey. Humphrey, whatever the secret of his birth, is unquestionably becoming a young gentleman, in his bearing, conversation, and attitudes. He is "a well-built lad enough, broad at the shoulders, slim at the hips, the face keen, sensitive, with a promise of will in the cut of the chin." He dislikes "'hitting below the belt,'" and, though it costs him an effort, he apologizes to Wilkie when he (Humphrey) finds himself in the wrong.

In this opening scene in her first published book, we find already one of the strengths of Zack. She understands fully that gentlefolk and simple folk are both people. Humphrey is a young gentleman and Wilkie is of a class far below him, but Wilkie easily holds his own as a person, in both intelligence and dignity, in their conversation. At the same time there is no denial that class differences exist. Wilkie himself says, "'ther ba a trustdrawsomeness about real ginelfolks that makes a man unusual truthful.'" A key word in the sentence is "real," but real gentlefolk do exist.

In this first scene, we also are introduced to another recurring facet in the writings of Zack: her use of Devonshire dialect in the speech of some of her characters. It can be quite difficult to understand—and at times deeply moving, as we will see. It is the speech of her home country, and she knew it well.

Humphrey has grown to be a very young man by the time of the next scene. The mystery of his birth is still much on his mind. He tells the Squire that he fears he is not the Squire's grandchild. "'The truth means a great deal to me, sir,'" he says to the older man. Moreover, he not only believes that it is possible that his mother is still alive, he also dreams of earning the money to pay the debts on Thursby Chase, which the Squire fears "'must all come to the hammer'" one day in the not too distant future. Humphrey is awkward at revealing the depth of his emotion in regard to both his mother and his love for Thursby Chase. He intends to go to Australia. His grandfather tries to discourage him; for one thing the Squire realizes that Humphrey is much too sanguine about his own abilities and maturity. But Humphrey will go. Thus ends Part I, "Chiefly Concerning the Man Atter."

We jump abruptly to New South Wales, Australia for Part II, "The Man Atter." A strike of shearers and "rouseabouts" is on. Humphrey is a laborer, but not one of the strikers. Captured by four of the strikers, he is taken before the strikers' leader, Bullocky Dick. Humphrey is wearing a "ragged jumper and tarred moleskins," and is not feeling heroic—"he felt something much nearer akin to fear"—but looks and is a gentleman: "his quiet bearing distinguished him as belonging to a different class from his tormentors." When asked why he is "'skulking'" in not joining the other strikers, Humphrey says, "'I do not believe in strikes.'" For this he is thrown into the creek.

Pulled out, he is addressed by Bullocky Dick.

> "Well, you long-tongued, corn-stalking son of a kangaroo," he said, "have you had enough of preaching, or do yer want another dose of the creek?"
>
> Tearing and plunging in Humphrey's chest a great sob rose, he fighting it back to silence, as he would have fought a devil; for Bullocky was watching, tracking the sob with triumphant scorn, and, when it broke bonds, stuttering out, kicked him very, very softly, in the way he would, when not drunk, have toed out his contempt on a woman.
>
> The boy staggered to his feet. "You cowardly cur," he cried, "I will never give in to you."

Bullocky Dick strikes him above the heart, and Humphrey is knocked in the creek with a snag tearing at his face. He is dragged out of the creek. Is he dead? 'Another man came forward, knelt down, raised the boy's eyelids, dropped them, and exclaimed, "Not dead;—blinded!"' Everyone runs or rides off, leaving Humphrey unconscious on the bank.

We are sometimes told that there is an operating principle in life that "no good deed goes unpunished." It is a sarcastic exaggeration, of course, but at times—certainly not always—there is more than a grain of truth to it. Here we see a similar principle operating. Humphrey bravely has stood alone, on principle refusing to join the strikers. He has refused to follow a multitude in doing evil (Ex. 23:2). His reward is to be blinded. It is an horrifically sad irony—but it is one we sometimes do see in how life is played out.

Blindness is one of the most horrible fates one can be forced to endure. But that is exactly the fate apparently given to our hero. And, it is the fate given to many people on the earth. There is no way we can pretend that physical blindness does not exist. Why does it exist? God permits it. He could stop it. He does not. He has, in Zack's story, permitted the blinding of the courageous, admirable young hero.

Hours later, Bullocky Dick returns alone, and finds that Humphrey has regained consciousness. Bullocky Dick props Humphrey against a tree. Humphrey, grateful, asks the name of his helper. "'In the old country they called me Dick Atter,' said Bullocky at last.' Humphrey is delighted. "'A man called Dick Atter once did me a great service," he exclaimed eagerly. "I've always wanted to meet and thank him.'" Humphrey wonders if it is possible that this is the Dick Atter he has wanted to find. Humphrey explains that he is the son of Captain Thursby, and that he had been taken home to Devonshire by Dick Atter. It is "'pleasant'" to meet Atter at last.

Humphrey says that he is "'blind now, but it can't be permanent. A fellow's career isn't destroyed quite so easily—eh, Atter?'"

Atter has been silent all this time. Finally,

> Atter burst into a loud, terrible laugh. "Yer ain't no bloody Thursby," he exclaimed; "you're my son, and I've blinded yer."
> "You lie in your throat!" cried Humphrey, and fainted, his head striking Atter across the chest as he fell forward.

Two days later Atter, still leading the strikers, cruelly whips a trooper's mare across the eyes. The maddened animal eventually is drowned in the creek, directly as a result of Atter's vicious action. Two days ago he blinded Humphrey, possibly at the same creek; now he has struck at the eyes of a defenseless mare, causing her death. The mare's situation was much like Humphrey's; Atter apparently has not changed. A few minutes later Atter throws a piece of mulga (wood native to Australia) at the trooper who had been thrown from his mare, striking the man in the head; he falls.

Atter rides away from his companions back to his own camp. Humphrey lies sleeping, flies swarming around his bandaged face. Atter arrives and switches the flies away. Atter sits smoking a pipe and switching, while Humphrey sleeps.

At last Humphrey awakes. Humphrey wants to get to a hospital, and also to get away from Atter. He also wants and demands an explanation as to the circumstances of his own birth. Atter at first refuses to give an explanation, but at last tells what had happened.

With the constantly repeated refrain of "'wot's a wuman?—wot's one wuman more than another?'", or in words very similar, Atter tells his story, speaking more to "some invisible auditor" than to Humphrey.

Atter had seen Humphrey's mother, for the first time, on board ship on the voyage to Australia. She was too poor to afford the first class fare of the ladies, but she was herself a lady nevertheless. Atter, a servant to Captain Thursby, felt a "'line'" between the woman and himself—an uncrossable line. He brooded about this line. Captain Thursby finally sees the poor lady, helps her slightly, and only occasionally talks to her a bit; she falls to thinking of him, the observant Atter sees. There was no line between Captain Thursby and the poor lady, but then nothing of the romantic sort occurred between them, either, and Captain Thursby went up country on arrival in Sydney.

Atter quits the captain's service, saying ""There ain't no masters and servants in this country; you go your way and I'll go mine.""

Atter stayed around Sydney because of his infatuation with the poor lady, who grows poorer. One afternoon he follows her to a lonesome spot. The line is still between them and he can't approach her. Then it comes to him that the poor lady is thinking of Captain Thursby. In the passage below the ellipsis is Zack's.

"and wi' that the line melted like wax. I rose to my feet and coomed towards her, and her rose to her feet too, and us stood looking at one 'nother. I reckon my face was a devil's face, for her got sheet-white; but her stood there terrible quiet and proud, and the line came atween us agin, cutting me off. And when I felt that the line was atween us agin, I swore to break it and her. 'Cap'en Thursby is dead,' sed I, and her fell at my feet as one wi' the life knocked out from her—" He stopped abruptly, and wrenched apart his shirt at the throat. "Then 'twas," he said, "then 'twas . . . my brain and heart seemed to burst; but her was mine, and the line might work its will. Wot's a wuman? Wot's one blanked wuman more than another? Wot's a wuman, any way?"

Atter hides and watches the woman come to consciousness. She is unaware that she has been raped.

The months pass and Atter keeps track of the woman. She continues to be "'poor—workus poor,'" but she keeps her integrity. She got a job, but four months later she was turned out into the streets. We are left to infer that the reason for her losing her position was that her pregnancy had begun to show. Atter went to a woman he knew, told her the truth about what had happened, and the woman took in the lady and cared for her. The child was born, at which the woman was content, because she had gone mad and considered herself to be Captain Thursby's wife, the child his child.

Two years pass. Atter happens to be on the scene when Captain Thursby is gored by a bullock. Dying, Captain Thursby asks Atter to take a message to the Squire for him. The captain's watch and chain are wrapped up and given to Atter. Atter goes back to Sydney, and is told that the woman is dying and has asked for him. He cursed her and said he wouldn't go near her, but is unable to follow through. Reluctantly, he finds himself standing in her presence:

"she called me, and I was fo'ced to come. She was lying propped up wi' pillys, the child aside her, and death most nigh as near; the sheets was blanked coarse, and her bit o' night-shift nort to speak of, but, damn yer, it only made the breeding in her show the more. 'Atter,' she said, 'take him back to his people and tell them he is a Thursby and a gentleman,'—then she sorter tried to hold yer towards me, and fell back dead. So I took yer to the old Squire and sed wot her told me; her thought you was a Thursby—maybe her knows better now. But wot's a wuman?—wot's one wuman more than another?—wot's a wuman, any way?"

Humphrey, horrified, tries to escape from Atter, but fails. However, Atter is captured by police troopers just then. "Atter made no effort to escape, but stood stone-still, staring at his son's face, with its expression of sudden joy, of great elation."

The police trooper Atter had hit with the thrown mulga wood has died. Atter is tried for manslaughter, convicted, and is sentenced to three years' hard labor. He accepted the sentence with "callous indifference." His murder of the trooper does not haunt him: "between him and the memory of other misdeeds there stood a dead woman, and into his fierce, passionate heart had come a fierce, passionate need of her forgiveness." "Remorse, like cancer," eats into his heart, but he, though "racked by conscience, scarce understood that he had sinned."

Atter is dying. The prison chaplain asks if anyone's forgiveness would make Atter happier. "'Forgiveness!'" repeated Atter, glancing at him in astonishment—"wot the blanky blank should I want with forgiveness; I ain't done nothing to be ashamed of. I've alles acted the man.'" The chaplain smiled and made no further suggestion.

The chaplain is one of several nameless characters we see sketched in a few lines who not only move the story along by their actions, but who also demonstrate an admirable character. In his recital to Humphrey, Atter mentioned the woman, no doubt of very low social class, who took in the pregnant victim of Atter's rape, and cared for her. Here we have the chaplain, in his three paragraphs of action, showing insight and wisdom. Later we will come upon a nameless doctor of fascinating character, and I will discuss him in the proper place. There are horrors in some of the things Zack writes about, but there are also people we can admire. This, I would contend, is an accurate presentation of life as it is really lived by us in the world.

The chaplain, well able to think for himself, brings Humphrey to Atter. The chaplain leaves the two alone. Atter is elated that Humphrey has come. Humphrey confesses to Atter that he, Humphrey, has been a "'mucker'" since he parted with Atter. The Squire has sent him some money—the enormous sum of £5,000—under the continuing belief that Humphrey is his grandson. Humphrey has speculated with that money and lost it all. Atter tells him to go home to England and keep on being a gentleman, but Humphrey has already written the truth of his birth to the Squire, for "'Clinging to a name that was not mine would not make me a gentleman.'"

Humphrey, however, wants to be a gentleman—but a gentleman in the sense of doing right, rather than in some more artificial sense. "'The Squire said once," he exclaimed, "that as long as a man is a man, he, for one, wouldn't ask more of him.'" Humphrey, in having taken the Squire's money under false pretenses, has not kept his record clean, and knows it, but he plans to act more honorably in the future. Atter scorns such a definition of being a gentleman.

Atter falls to talking aloud to himself. He reiterates that he has nothing to be ashamed of in his life. On two issues, however, he would "'like to make things right'": the woman and her son. He "'hadn't sorter speshil wanted to hurt 'em, either o' 'em; but I sent her mad, I blinded him—mother and son, mother and son.'"

Humphrey reminds Atter that Atter had not blinded Humphrey intentionally, and says that he, Humphrey, is not beaten yet.

> "Yer ain't beaten yit," Atter answered, "but yer won't niver make things right wi' me."
>
> "Atter," exclaimed the boy, "I could if it weren't for her."
>
> "Her," repeated Atter, and his voice was infinitely sad— "her, her, her; her comed atween me and herself, her comes atween me and her son; her was niver mine tho' I held her in my arms; and when I reckoned to have her body and soul, her stud away from me—her stud away from me."
>
> "Atter, Atter," said the boy, "Atter, Atter."
>
> "Ay, Atter, Atter," the man repeated, "Atter, Atter; Atter 'twas wi' yer from the fust, Atter 'twill be wi' yer to the end."
>
> "Father," said the boy huskily.
>
> In hesitation the words came stuttering forth. Atter's heart stopped a beat to listen, and then slammed back against his ribs, the whole man rocking in the unreality of his own happiness. He put out his hands in trembling hesitation, then, conquered by all-mastering desire, drew the boy to him, up against his breast; and within the breast his heart clanged and throbbed as some imprisoned engine. Gripped close in his father's arms,

inert from pity, sundered from him by repulsion, the son's mind groped in agonising longing for some link that should be an ennobling bond of union.

"Father," he said, "shall we not lead straighter lives because of *her?*"

The great engine within Atter's breast strained more wildly against its imprisonment.

"Her cudn't change me when her was alive; her'll never do it now her's dead," he answered. "No, no, I'll bide as I am: when my time comes for loosing ropes and slipping the stock-yard rails, I reckon hell 'ull about do me—a place where a man can curse free and fight for his own, come God, come devil,"—and so saying, his heart burst bonds, his grip on his son relaxed, and with a sob he fell back dead.

"Humphrey, Son of Atter" is the third and final part of the story. Humphrey, having buried Atter, returns to his lodgings, where he tears up an unopened telegram. He leaves the house, and wanders into "one of the poorest quarters of the town." He hears a man whistling happily over his job of fixing a broken umbrella. The man is blind—has been blind twenty years. When Humphrey asks, "'You have a wife dependent on you?'", "'Well,' replied the man, with a slow smile, "us puts it that way, though maybe the truth is t'other end about.'" Humphrey wonders at the man "acknowledging so lightly a galling dependence."

The man relates the accident that blinded him—"'one of they things that there ain't no speshil reason why they should happen, but happen they does'"—with great good humor, claiming that "'now there ain't one day in seven that I notices there's anything wrong with my eyes at all.'"

Humphrey asks to be taken on as an apprentice to umbrella mending, to the astonishment of the man. Humphrey says he could pay for his food and lodging for the first few months. The man's wife joins them from inside the house, and we learn her husband's name as she warns him to be careful. "'Don't you be after doing nothing rash, Joe,' she exclaimed in a harsh, high-pitched tone. 'The young man's a step above us; he's stood behind counters—I can see that by the look of his hands.'"

When his wife goes to make tea, Joe confides an interesting fact.

"I used to give her the strap one time," he continued, lowering his voice; "that was when I could see, the same as the rest. Now the strap hangs on the nail aside the dresser, and I find her acts a sight more reasonable wi'out it. A woman is a queer thing—more heart than sense; but the sense her has carries her tarnation far on the right road."

At tea, "strangely content," Humphrey renews his request to work under Joe, "'on trial.'" (Zack's next book would be titled *On Trial*.) "He had a sudden longing to be near this man, who was blind, and whom he suspected of being happy." Joe is willing, and his wife half-reluctantly agrees. She shows Humphrey what would be his room, where he exhibits great clumsiness of movement, to the woman's distress. However, his "'soft-tongued'" manner thaws her a little, and when he asks if they are friends, she finally answers, "'I shall mother 'ee my own way.'"

Humphrey returns to his current lodgings, where his landlady greets him with a letter from Squire Thursby. Humphrey refuses to let her read it to him, and takes it from her. By himself in his room, he sobs at his blindness.

The next week Humphrey moves in with Joe and his wife, and begins learning to repair umbrellas. He incurs the woman's wrath by the wet messiness of his room. She sternly sends him up to clean it, and Joe intercedes for him. "'Well,' said Joe, 'I reckon he's a gintleman, and ain't bin used to taking notice.'" The woman soon follows Humphrey to his room. The room is still a mess, but Humphrey is so forlorn the woman holds her tongue, gives him his tea, and leaves. She returns to find he has rubbed the wet floor dry with one of his shirts, to the woman's despair. But she offers these words of commiseration: "'You ain't niver bin taught better,'" she answered. "I warrant you've bin fine and spoiled in your time; but then the Almighty seed for Hisself that you needed a dressing, or He would never have brought 'ee to the pass He has.'" Humphrey is unable to hide a half sob, and she comforts him. "'Ah, lad, us have all got to go through wi' it,' she said. 'Life's life.'" We don't have the choosing of our burdens, she says, "'us must fit 'em to our backs as best us can.'"

The days passed slowly away, and little by little Humphrey found what Joe called "the feel o' his fingers." Other things he learned of greater value; unperceived by himself his views of life were altering, and he realised dimly that a position of dependence might still be compatible with self-respect. Perhaps he was able to look at the subject with less bias, because he could now earn sufficient to support himself; and, having escaped being dependent, recognised that another might be justified in submitting to so galling a position.

One day Joe complains of a sore throat. Humphrey takes him to see a doctor. Another consultation, with three doctors, follows; Joe returns home, leaving Humphrey to talk to the doctor. The prognosis: throat cancer, which means "'Loss of voice first, starvation afterwards.'" "'What a hell of suffering this world is!'" Humphrey exclaims. The doctor makes no comment to that. He tells Humphrey that someone must tell the wife, so that she can break the truth to Joe, and he suggests that Humphrey do it. He protests vigorously, saying "'She has been so awfully good to me,'" at which the doctor replies, "'Well, and isn't that—? eh?—'"

The doctor, with a few words and a few silences, has been established for us as a man of practical wisdom and kindness. How much honest thought and generosity of spirit are expressed in the words "'Well, and isn't that—? eh?—'" of Zack's nameless doctor! Humphrey sees the man's point, and agrees to talk to Joe's wife.

The next day, in Joe's absence, Humphrey tells her.

> "Mother," he said (he had taken to calling her mother), "I have something to tell you."
>
> "Well, lad," she answered, "say on."
>
> A great knob rose in his throat. "It's about Joe's illness," he said.
>
> She dropped her work, and looking up at him, "Yer ain't going to tell me nothing bad o' it?" she exclaimed anxiously.
>
> He knelt down and put his arms round her. "Oh, mother!" he answered, "it is the old terrible thing, life's life."
>
> She gave a little abrupt cry. "He ain't to be took from me; it ain't that?" she said, "it ain't that?"

But it is that, and she fully understands that cancer of the throat means that Joe will be first without the ability to speak, then starved. "'Oh, Joe, my pore Joe, the Almighty must have been fair mazed wi' the joys o' heaven when He reckoned such suffering nought compared to it.'" Humphrey consoles her as well as he can, then leaves the house.

Joe, very tired, returns home. He and his wife talk. Only in the course of this conversation will he learn the full extent of his predicament.

"I reckons us won't set eyes on the Old Country again, mother?"

She did not answer.

"You've bin a good wife to me," he said.

"Nought to speak of," she answered, her voice breaking.

"Ay, but you have," he said. "I was reckoning to myself this arternoon 'twas a poor day when I put the strap to yer."

"It hangs on the nail now," she exclaimed, half to herself.

"Ay, and let it."

"I've spoke my mind to the rest o' 'em, but you was alles my master, Joe," she said.

"There ain't no disputing I've layed it into 'ee at times," he answered, with a half smile.

"I've slept the easier for it. I've known your mind when maybe I shud niver have known my own."

"Well, well," he exclaimed, "they days be done."

She turned away, and taking up the loaf began cutting the bread. "I've nought but a bit o' dripping for 'ee to-day," she said; "they ain't paid me for the washing yet along, and I was niver no friend to debt."

"You're right there, mother," he answered; "and I likes a bit o' dripping turn about."

"There have bin times when us cudn't git either," she said.

"Yes," he replied, smiling across at her—"us have bin fo'ced to fare scanty now and agin; but ther, hard times haven't hurt us."

"You was alles a well-plucked un, Joe," she said.

"Us fared and fared alike, mother, and I reckon, God willing, us 'ull do it till the end."

"Ay, God willing," she said, and her voice broke.

"Wot's come to 'ee, mother?"

"Joe, Joe," she answered, putting her arms around his neck, "God ain't willing. 'Tis just that; 'tis just that."

"Wot makes 'ee take on so?" he asked anxiously. "Yer ain't kept it from me that you're ill?"

She drew him close to her. "Oh, Joe!" she exclaimed, "'tis yerself that is sicker than you reckon."

He did not answer, but putting up his hand stroked her faded hair: the tears coursed down her red freckled face, God wot she was ugly enough; but she had a heart to love with, and what greater gift has He given to man or woman yet?—what greater, though the symbol be a crown of Thorns, a Cross, and the steep steps of Calvary?

"Ay, mother," he exclaimed at last, "ain't us alles said as how life was life?"

"Life's life," she answered; "but oh, Joe, lad, 'tis hard to live it."

The "grisly disease" drove Joe "along the road to death at a right merry pace, so that he had reached his destination before he had half realised the direction in which he had been hurried." With Joe dead, his former customers found Humphrey "a passable makeshift," so that he had plenty of employment.

At least three critics quoted with admiration from a large part of the next portion.

Seated on the broken doorstep, repairing the ribs of some neighbour's broken gingham, his heart would swell with homesickness, and a terrible longing for the people he had known and loved in childhood take possession of him. Then the umbrella would drop from his hand, and his blind eyes fill with visions of his English home; the crude street noises around him would hush themselves, and the lop-lop of the river, as it humped its way over brown pebbles, become audible: he watched it wind through the Thursby meadows where the big elms lolled and sunned themselves, past the gorse-covered hills, and the shuffling woods in their spring coat of beech-green. He saw again the long green alleys of the Chase, played in its old-world gardens, where old-world flowers dozed with drooping heads as if dog-tired of blooming. Watching, the boy's heart would swell with homesickness, and he would creep up-stairs to the little attic, fling himself upon the bed, and sob like the fool that he was. The woman marked the traces of tears on his face, but made no comment; and the days crept on, each much as the other.

Humphrey and Joe's widow get along with the loving affection of a son and his mother. One day the woman finds three unopened letters from England in Humphrey's coat pocket. Convinced by her urging, Humphrey finally asks her to read them. Before she does, though, Humphrey gives her a brief summary of his life, including his speculating with Squire Thursby's money after he already knew that the Squire was not really his grandfather. "'I wrote to my grandfather, I mean—you understand—and owned up, and these letters are in answer to mine.'"

Then, his head leaning on her knee, Humphrey hears the brief first letter read. The ellipses are mine. "'"My dear boy, . . . Did I not always tell you you were a young fool? . . . Come home at once, and give me the pleasure of telling you so in person. Enclosed find a draft for a hundred pounds.—Yours affectionately, JOHN THURSBY.'"'

Humphrey is moved, "fighting with a lump in his throat," and is silent at first. While Humphrey gathers his thoughts to make a verbal response to this letter, the woman gives a most astonishing soliloquy on education and the state. She has admired the Squire's brief letter.

"Just as I've said many a time," she continued, running her fingers through the boy's hair with a slow mechanical movement, "the fewer the words, the fuller the sense; that's what comes o' bein' eddicated. Eddication, mark me, is the shortest way there; not that I hold wi' things as they are nowadays, when every frog busts hisself out trying to be took for a bull: there's more in eddication than book-larning, whativer the State may say to the contrary. But there, I ain't no speshil friend to the State,—as I've said to Joe many a time, the State is taking a deal more on itself than becomes it; 'twas all very well in the old days, when it was content wi' the making o' roads and suchlike, but when it takes into its head that the pudding in my pot is the same size as my neighbour's, I thank it to let well alone. It wasn't long after Joe was took ill that I heard that radical jumbuck William Harness a-telling him, 'Us ain't got no masters now,' says he, 'the State is master now.' 'An' a poor exchange,' I sed; 'if I am to have a master, let him be o' flesh and blood the same as meself.' 'Women ain't got no right understanding in such matters,' ses he. 'No, nor men either, if the laws be a token,' ses I; 'why, if I had my will, I'd disinfranchify the whole lot o' ye!' 'You're jealous 'cos you ain't got no vote yirself, Missus,' ses he. 'Women have their dues the same as the rest,' sed I, 'tho' maybe their first right should be to stand aside and hold their tongue.' 'I'm with 'ee there, Missus,' ses he. Well, well," she added, folding up her spectacles, and putting them in the work-basket, "if ther wasn't no laws, ther 'ud be a sight more unemployed: wot wi' the making o' 'em and setting o' 'em in acting they gives a deal o' amusement to the men; and, bless 'ee, a man likes his bit o' play the same as a chile. Many's the time I've said to Joe, 'Take a man to pieces and you'll find he's a chile at heart.'"

Humphrey says he doesn't want to go home because he has failed in everything. Joe's widow tells him, "'And as to failing, ther's two kinds of failing, I reckon: the failing to do what us have marked out for ourselves, and the failing to do what the Almighty has laid down for us; many's the time in missing the first us follers the last, unconscious.'"

Humphrey asks her if she would come with him if he went back to England, but she says she has "given up wearying for the Old Country.'" Humphrey says "'I couldn't leave you, mother, I love you so.'" However, she knows he is hungering for his own people, and persuades him to go. He swears he will return to her, but she tells him to leave swearing alone: "'I ain't no friend to rash promises.'"

"I don't believe you care for me after all," he said, in a hurt voice.

"You are terrible much a chile, lad," she answered, bending and kissing him.

"If I leave you, tell me something better than 'life's life,'" he said, drawing her face close to his own.

"Ah, lad," she answered, "when a thing *is*, what does us gain by saying it isn't?"

"But it's a dreary philosophy," he protested.

"What do the ills of life matter if us faces 'em courageous?" she answered; but her old, tired voice trembled, for of life and life's ills she was somewhat weary.

Again he drew her face down towards his own.

"Mother," he asked, "did you say life's life when first you knew Joe loved you?"

"Ay, on my knees I said it."

"God bless you for having lived!" cried the boy.

"Oh, lad, lad," she answered, "I was never for denying the Almighty was the Almighty."

Thus ends "Life Is Life." Humphrey clearly is planning to return to the Devonshire home and the "grandfather" he loves (and who loves him, despite well knowing that Humphrey is not truly his grandson by blood). The woman, his "mother," will not go with him. He plans to return to her. But will he return? She has told him not to make rash promises. Could he make the long, expensive trip back to Australia, just to visit her? Perhaps. We don't know what will happen, beyond the fact that we expect Humphrey to return to Devonshire for the moment. We are left with a few loose ends. That, Joe's widow might tell us, is life. Things are seldom as neatly organized as we might like.

In fact, life contains incredibly much that we don't like. We don't like to have Atter rape the woman who fascinated him. We don't like to see her driven mad by her situation. We don't like Humphrey to be blinded. We don't like Atter to kill the trooper and the mare, or to have blinded his own son. We don't like Joe to have lost his sight twenty years before we meet him. We don't like Joe to die of throat cancer.

Zack has set herself a challenging but important task in this story. Why, she asks, do terrible things happen? She does not shy away from the answer. God is sovereign, and does what He wants. Modern man tells us that things happen by chance. Zack has a different answer. Things happen because God arranges them so. He could have stopped Humphrey from being blinded. Instead, Humphrey loses his sight. Joe's widow tells us that God saw that Humphrey "needed a dressing." That is strong meat for us readers! But the theological question won't go away because it is a difficult question. If God really is in control of world history, then ultimately Humphrey was blinded because God permitted that to happen. This answer frustrates us. We don't want Humphrey to be blinded because God permitted it, or worse, because He saw that Humphrey "needed a dressing,'" and thus intentionally brought about the blinding. But if God is truly God as the Bible teaches, then He is indeed in control of all events of world history.

No wonder modern man asks to be excused from believing such difficult things! The Christian, however, has to face these questions squarely. In real life, such horrible events as Zack describes, really do happen. Our Christian faith must take all of reality into account—and all of reality includes many terrible things. People get raped. People get blinded. These things happen daily, around the world. We must deal with reality as it exists, not as we wish it existed.

Part of the answer for us, Zack is saying, is simply to face the truth with courage: "'when a thing *is*, what does us gain by saying it isn't?'" And, "'What do the ills of life matter if us faces 'em courageous?'" But Zack does not pretend that this courage is easy. Joe's widow speaks those wise words, but her voice trembles, "for of life and life's ills she was somewhat weary."

Another part of the answer for us, is that the ills of life are not all there are. There are good things, noble things. We see a woman tend to Atter's victim. We know nothing about the woman. But she acts to help another woman, no doubt a woman of a social class above her own. We see the chaplain bring Atter together with his son as Atter nears death, exactly what both men need. We see Humphrey confess to the Squire his crime in speculating with money he knew was not rightfully his, we see him confess to the Squire his knowledge that he is not the Squire's grandson. We see Humphrey call Atter "'Father'"—the same Atter who raped his mother. We see Atter, on the brink of hell as he supposes (and perhaps quite rightly supposes), in an ecstasy of joy to have his son acknowledge him as father. We see Joe dealing with his handicap with cheerfulness. We see the love of Joe and his wife toward one another. We see the doctor shepherd Humphrey toward responsible behavior toward Joe and his wife. We see the Squire demonstrating love toward a young man he knows is *not* his natural grandson. We see Humphrey affectionately treating Joe's widow as his mother, and we see the mother/son love between the two, although they are not related by birth.

So the ills of life, and the good things of life, are entertwined, in Zack's world. The key thing for us, is to face life honestly and courageously, not lying to ourselves about how reality is put together. It is a lesson difficult to learn in any era. It is a lesson especially needed by us, in a time when lying and self-deception are rampant.

Some of the ideas expressed in this story are pretty unusual, even astonishing. At least five come to mind.

1/Who dares to criticize striking workers in our era? We have dishonestly given unions a free pass, morally. In the movie "F.I.S.T.," striking union truckers waylay and beat the so-called "scabs" to the great approval of the film score and the director. This, we are supposed to think, is the brave strikers acting to protect their jobs. While in reality, what it is, is bullies beating up on men who want to earn a living at a wage agreeable to them and to their employers. Free men are being beaten by collectivist bullies, and this is supposedly wonderful. And what we see in the fictional film, only reflects the attitude of most of our largely collectivist culture.

Zack's thought runs along a different track on this issue. Humphrey does "'not believe in strikes.'" He sees himself as a free man, and he wants to work. He and his employer will set his wage, agreed between the two of them. Humphrey courageously defies the collectivist bullies, and as a result is tormented and eventually blinded. To do the right thing can be costly. But Zack understands very well that on this issue, Humphrey has indeed acted with responsible courage.

Zack stands outside the spirit of our age. She doesn't sentimentalize striking workers. She sympathizes with the individual doing the right thing. Will this be another reason why she will never find a large audience?

Perhaps, but there will always be a handful of people who are not collectivists emotionally. Those people will find a kindred spirit in Zack—if they ever know she exists. Moreover, our age is dying—as well it should. Our collectivist culture is marked for death. It is impossible to know for sure what will rise out of the ashes, but there is at least a chance that a reChristianized culture will arise somewhere if not everywhere—a culture which respects the person who wants to do the right thing rather than follow a multitude to do evil.

My own interest in the topic of unions is very personal. My grandfather on my mother's side was an immigrant to the United States from Italy. He worked in the steel mills of Gary, Indiana. When it came time to strike, my grandfather refused to do so. He became a scab. My mother had just been born. Her crib was under a window of the house. When my mother was approximately one week old, her mother changed the location of the crib away from under the window. That night (or morning?) a brick came through the window where the crib previously had rested, no doubt through the generosity of the brave strikers attempting to punish my grandfather for his lack of solidarity with their cause. My mother might have been killed or seriously injured. Dick Atter in the 1890s throwing his piece of mulga wood at a trooper and killing him, or throwing Humphrey into the creek and blinding him, is the direct ancestor of the conscienceless striker bullies of 1919 of Gary, Indiana.

Why did my grandmother move the crib at just the right time? Chance? Or God's providential control? I prefer to think it was the latter.

2/The comments on Joe having taken a strap to his wife are also astonishing. Joe regrets having ever beaten his wife. She responds in a remarkable way. She says the strap hangs there now—in other words beating is still an option—and that when she had been beaten she had known her husband's mind when she wouldn't have known her own. She has slept the easier for having had the strap put to her.

Zack is not recommending wife beating. (Read her story "Mary Amelia Spot" in *Tales of Dunstable Weir* for proof of this.) It is just that Joe's wife is so remarkably objective in looking back on their life together, that she is able to see that there were things she gained by being beaten! Try running that idea by the next hundred people you meet, and see how many are in sympathy with it.

Joe beating his wife is a thing of the past, and Joe himself now knows that it should not be done. But Joe's wife makes a subtle point—one we are unlikely to agree with entirely, but one in which we can see what she is getting at and one which we can at least respect to some extent.

I am not of the pro-wife beating camp. In fact, I think that if we ever have Christian republics, Christian monarchies, Christian democracies, or Christian something elses, men who beat their wives should be beaten in turn—several times more severely than they beat their wives. There is ample scriptural warrant for that (Deut. 25:1-3, etc.), and it is only our pallid antinomian Christianity which refuses to defend women as biblical Christianity requires. But I see what Joe's wife is getting at, and it makes me like her even more as a person who can think for herself with unusual objectivity.

3/Joe's wife admires the Squire's letter, and sees it as a fruit of education, but she also knows that there is more to education than book-learning. Moreover, she immediately criticizes the modern State (Zack capitalizes the word) as "'taking a deal more on itself than becomes it.'" Making roads she sees as a valid responsibility of the State, but for the State to try to take from some people to give to others, is not the State's proper business. She would rather have a flesh and blood master than have the State for a master. This is one thoughtful and original woman. The spirit of our age runs exactly contrary to her: the State is going to do everything for us. The State is going to feed us, provide us with education, give us health care, pay for our retirement, give us money for not working, give us money for not growing crops, subsidize our crops if we do grow them, pay us for having illegitimate children, bail out needy millionaire bankers when their investments go sour, and so on, endlessly. But, as I said a few paragraphs earlier, the collectivist culture is doomed. The scam can go on only a few years or decades longer. Joe's wife was right. The mostly uneducated poor woman of low social class understood that the State was taking on itself more than it had a right to take on. We are learning that hard fact as our culture implodes.

4/Joe's wife says voting and making laws is something men (children at heart) do in playing the way children play. When we see how much harm men do in their voting and making laws, we are scarcely likely to call it playing. But we also see that moral infants are running our nations. Moral infants vote, and moral infants rule. Joe's wife was wise to be skeptical about the value of the vote. Women gaining the vote is no advancement over men only voting. A Hillary Clinton or a Nancy Pelosi are as mindless and unprincipled as a Bill Clinton or a George W. Bush. When we want to be adults, we will begin to have laws that reflect an adult attitude. Until then, Joe's wife is completely correct in sensing the fraudulence behind the democratic principle.

5/Joe's wife was "'niver no friend to debt.'" Here again we see someone living in opposition to the spirit of our age. The meal she is preparing is "'nought but a bit o' dripping'" as opposed to something more substantial (and more costly). The reason was that she had not yet been paid for the washing she had done. Rather than run into debt for a food purchase, she serves a meal lacking in prestige.

This elicits two thoughts from me, one slightly critical of Zack, and one the reverse. It seems to me that it would be unlikely that Joe and his wife are living so close to the line of absolute destitution that the failure to be paid immediately for the most recent washing done, would force them to go into debt in order to purchase a meal. Joe works diligently and is paid for his work. His wife works diligently and is paid for her work. Humphrey is paying rent for his room and board. The woman clearly is a careful housekeeper who avoids debt. Given her personality as it is presented, we can be quite certain she was no spendthrift. Rather, she is a woman who will constantly put aside money for a rainy day—rainy days which she has experienced in the past, so that she knows they really do happen. Why then does she have no money for a regular meal rather than "'a bit o' dripping'"? I think she does have the money. I think what has happened is that Zack has wanted to say something about the foolishness of debt, and has put those words in the mouth of Joe's wife. The words are completely in accordance with the character of Joe's wife. Where I think Zack goes wrong is that her character's personality—consistently portrayed as it is throughout the story—would have assured that there would have been no need to go into debt for their meal, because plenty of saved money would have been on hand. They would not have been well-to-do people with bales of pounds laid away, of course. But Joe's wife would have had plenty of cash in hand. Homer nodded. Or rather, Zack nodded here, in her desire to say something useful about the danger of debt.

And on that point, I am grateful to see that once again Joe's wife (and Zack herself, I am guessing) are standing in opposition to the disastrous spirit of our age. As individuals, as nations, in fact almost as a planet taken as a whole, we have been trying for a long time to live largely by means of debt. Rather than pay for something we want with money, we borrow so that we can live beyond our true means. This is not to say that all borrowing is foolish. A key question to ask is, are we paying back the debt as quickly as possible? And a second key question is, are we absolutely committed to paying what we owe, no matter what? The answer to both these questions, far too often, is no. We want a lifestyle beyond our means. And if we find it inconvenient to repay our debts, well, too bad for the debt-holder. We seem to feel entitled.

As a nation, the U.S. will never pay its debts. We will, some time in the future, near or slightly beyond near, default on our debts. Meanwhile, we even steal from our creditors, by creating money out of thin air, so that the money we pay back (whether as interest or as principal) does not really repay in full the value of the money as it was loaned to us. It is a cowardly and thieving way to live, unworthy of an honorable people. But then, we are not an honorable people. Check out how readily we as individuals abscond with our neighbors' money by declaring bankruptcy, and we can begin to understand how our nation became the irresponsible debtor it has become. What the U.S. is, most other nations seem similarly to be. We are a world living on debt—until default wakes us up to the fact that financial reality actually does exist, no matter how much we wish it didn't exist. Lots of people are going to get hurt. Is it good to hurt other people by not paying them what you owe them?

Joe's wife, Joe, and Zack want to live in the real world. Life is life. Debt is irresponsible. Pretending it isn't, does us no good. To live within one's means is honorable and noble.

One of the most fascinating aspects of "Life Is Life" is the way it deals with class differences. Class, I think, is something which instinctively interested Zack. She deals with the topic at some length in this long story, and also elsewhere in her books. The longest story in *Tales of Dunstable Weir*, "The Hall and He," has a fascinating take on how class operates in the lives of several characters.

Zack herself was of a very high social class. She was born into a prominent family. Her grandfather was an admiral (William Abraham Keats). Her grandfather's uncle (thus Zack's great-uncle) was an admiral (Sir Richard Goodwin Keats). Her stepfather was a vice-admiral and justice of the peace (Edward Charlewood). Admirals tended to run in the family! Her childhood home Port Hill was stately, described in *Kelly's Directory of Devonshire & Cornwall 1883* as "among . . . the principal" (my ellipsis) "villas and country houses scattered over the hilly grounds" which make the "approach to Northam from the Bideford road" "highly picturesqe." The family had seven servants.

Beyond her birth into a high social class, her literary interests and her writing propelled her into the intellectual aristocracy of her time.

Her friends and acquaintances were nationally prominent people—editors, translators, writers. George Meredith, the famous novelist, visited her for tea—and he asked to come again.[7]

She was conscious that her own social position was high. In one of her letters to her friend the novelist May Sinclair, we read this sentence: "It must have been vile, squabbling with your landlady—one always feels degraded if one loses ones temper with anyone in that class of life."[8] Zack knew she herself was not in "that class of life," but was rather in a much higher social class.

In "Life Is Life," Dick Atter is very conscious of his own lower social class. There was a "'blanked line atween'" him and the poor lady, which made him unable to approach her as an equal. She was poor, yes—indeed was more poverty-stricken than Atter himself—but she was a lady, and he was a servant. Atter resents being a servant to Captain Thursby, and takes the first opportunity to split with him. Atter never says anything to indicate that the captain had mistreated him. The captain tries to make the split with Atter take place in a friendly manner, but in the captain's presence Atter tears the captain's card and spits on it. When Atter trails the poor lady to a lonely spot, it is the fact that he imagines the lady is thinking of Captain Thursby that finally drives him to break the line between the two—and to rape her. He is a man for whom class envy is an obsession.

The child born of this rape is delivered to Squire Thursby with the lie that he was the son of Captain Thursby. Humphrey is raised by the Squire as if he really was the Squire's grandson. Humphrey undeniably becomes a gentleman in bearing, character, and attitude—one worthy of being the Squire's grandson, and worthy of being the son of his poor but ladylike mother. Then Humphrey discovers that he is not the son of Captain Thursby after all, but rather the son of the lower class Dick Atter. It is a blow to him, but he does not stop being a gentleman in attitude. While he is appalled at the truth of his situation, he eventually works up the courage to call Atter "'Father.'"

---

[7]Zack letter to May Sinclair, Sept. 13, 1899. Zack writes: "Had afternoon tea with George Meredith last Monday, it was awfully interesting but rather nervous work—he asked me to come again."

[8]Zack letter to May Sinclair, October 1898?.

Atter, the father of Humphrey via rape, feels an ecstasy of love to have a son call him Father. Even that does not call Atter to want to lead a "'straighter'" life; hell will do for him, he decides. He dies, leaving his gentleman son fatherless, motherless, and no longer of the family of Squire Thursby.

Humphrey still had felt himself to be a Thursby, however, and had speculated with the Squire's £5,000 when he knew he had no right to the money. (Being a gentleman is no guarantee that one will always act like a gentleman!) Humphrey then belatedly returns to doing the right thing, and returns to acting as a gentleman should, as he confesses his sin to his "grandfather." Then he sets about to earn his living, and does so, although it is not a large living. His mother had been poor but a lady; now Humphrey is poor but a gentleman.

Joe and his wife are working class people, poor, poorly educated. Among them Humphrey flourishes. Joe's example of hard work, cheerfulness, and generosity of spirit, is very good for Humphrey. In Joe's wife he finds a mother. His birth mother was a poor lady, and he never knew her. His new mother is of the working class.

She is poor, slightly educated, and has some opinions at which Humphrey smiles, and is definitely of the working class. But the situation is more complex than that. One could never call Joe's widow a lady. But she has ideas which we can only describe as aristocratic in the best sense. She may be poor and uneducated, but she thinks for herself. She wants the State to be restrained, for people to make their way without asking the State to steal for them. That includes, she seems to hint, not asking the State to provide education for people. She is skeptical of the value of voting. She knows debt is dangerous.

The working class woman is also in some sense an aristocrat.

The Squire is a gentleman to the core. He has raised Humphrey as his grandson, and the truth of Humphrey's birth does not change the Squire's love for Humphrey. He will continue to acknowledge Humphrey as part of his family.

Humphrey is in the middle of all this. His true father was a lower class rapist. His birth mother was a lady, dirt poor. His "grandfather" is a gentleman of the propertied class, a Squire. Joe's wife/widow is his new "'mother,'" working class but with aristocratic ideas. What is the key tying Humphrey both to his "grandfather" and to his new mother? Both the Squire and the woman have "a heart to love with" and both are moved to love not in some gooey antinomian way that denies God. No, both love generously—the Squire able to love a young man who is not of his blood and who has lost £5,000 of the Squire's money, while at the same time telling Humphrey quite accurately that Humphrey has been a young fool. The woman loves and mothers Humphrey in her own way which includes very high ideals concerning freedom and responsibility. Humphrey loves his "grandfather" and will return to him. He also loves his lower class "'mother'" and promises to return to her.

I think Zack, whether she knows it or not, has pointed us to the way to the reconciliation of class differences: love and noble principles. Humphrey, in speculating and losing the £5,000, did very wrong. That was not the act of a gentleman. In confessing his sin to his "grandfather," and in struggling to earn his own living as best he could by repairing umbrellas, he has moved back in the right direction. Squire Thursby, in turn, shows a nobility of spirit in accepting Humphrey as his grandson despite full knowledge of Humphrey's true parentage. God, in putting Humphrey in Joe's household, has given Humphrey the mother he never knew because of her early death. A few weeks ago Humphrey had no family at all. He now has two families, both excellent—one represented by the Squire, one represented by Joe's working class widow. It will be his job to act in a worthy manner deserving of the respect of both families. It takes courage. It can be done, but it is not easy, as Zack well knows: Joe's widow proclaims her determination to face the ills of life with courage, "but her old, tired voice trembled, for of life and life's ills she was somewhat weary."

Here is one more criticism of part of the plot of "Life Is Life." I think it is unlikely that Squire Thursby would send Humphrey £5,000.

There are two problems here. The Squire is concerned that his property as a whole may all have to be sold off. The sale of one part of the property will raise a significant sum—£5,000, as it turns out. But would the Squire not use some of that money to defend the rest of his property (which is in danger of coming to the hammer), rather than send so large a sum away from Thursby Chase to Humphrey?

Secondly, the Squire knows well that Humphrey has an exaggerated opinion of his (Humphrey's) abilities and common sense. He predicts that Humphrey would lose "'every penny'" of any large sum of money sent to him. Humphrey, a sort of prodigal son (Luke 15:11-32), wants the money now rather than waiting until he is twenty-five, so as not to miss out on good opportunities in Australia. Eventually the money comes to Humphrey in Australia (long before he is twenty-five), and he duly loses "'every penny'" just as the Squire predicted.

One possibility: Zack may have been consciously retelling the story of the prodigal son. The prodigal son's father was a good man, but he acquiesced in his son's foolish request. The Squire is a good man, but he also acquiesces in a foolish request.

In any case, the amount of money sent to Humphrey is not really important. The important thing is that Humphrey spent the money when he knew he had no right to it. If the Squire had sent Humphrey a much smaller figure—say 100 pounds—as a way of supporting him and making sure he was provided for until he found his way in Australia, the principle would be the same. Humphrey would still have been at fault for keeping money he now knew was not his by right, because he now knew the Squire was not really his grandfather.

The plot of "Life Is Life" was criticized by some reviewers. In her letters to May Sinclair, Zack could be very dismissive of her own work. This attitude I am guessing was a factor of several different things: 1/ an objectivity that often (if not always!) permitted her to accept adverse criticism without complaining; 2/the desire that any wounded author feels to not appear to be a whiner, no matter how hurt one may truly be; 3/a genuine humility; 4/an inner confidence that she had her own literary path to follow and that it was the right path. This was one strong-willed, quite individual woman. And she was right: the path she followed was a good one. The criticisms of others could be accepted, because she knew she was doing what she could do and had to do— something that nobody else could do.

So when Zack tells May Sinclair, in regard to *Life Is Life* as an entire book, that "You are rather an impulsive fool to think so much of it—there are not above ten pages of good stuff in the whole book &

that is not saying much"[9] she is trying to maintain a suitable humility, but in her heart of hearts she must have known better. She must have known that she had written a remarkable book with a great deal of very "good stuff" in it.

In regard to the plot of the story "Life Is Life," Zack says this: "However, I fully agree with the critics, who say that the plot of Life is Life is melodramatic & absurd, only what they don't all see, (but some of them feel unconsciously) is that the characters are alive."[10]

It is not necessarily true that the plot is absurd. The coincidences can seem unlikely, yes, but there are no coincidences in a world in which God is sovereignly acting to bring about events.

But what Zack is exactly correct about is that "the characters are alive." The major characters such as Wilkie the poacher, the Squire, Humphrey, Atter, Captain Thursby, the poor lady, Joe, Joe's wife live and breathe before us: we see them and know them. Their personalities are strong and individual. The same can be said of some of the minor characters—we would recognize them if we met them.

It is also very insightful for Zack to recognize that even some of those critics who didn't understand that "the characters are alive," nevertheless felt such a fact unconsciously. True again.

I have quoted extensively from the story. But there is much more worth quoting. Insights into human nature, and colorful writing, abound. A constant of Zack's writings is her use of humor, and "Life Is Life" has its share. Her humor reminds me most of the humor of Fyoder Dostoyevsky. The humor of both writers seems to well out of life itself. Life is funny/strange and funny/humorous, and frequently the two go together. The humor can be dark, but it is there. Humor is so frequent in her books that it is part of what makes Zack uniquely Zack, and it is a humor that flows steadily out of the real, often dark, humor of real life.

"Life Is Life" is one of Zack's major stories, and not just because of length alone. The critic who said it "could not well be stronger" had it right. The story shocks or at least surprises. Some critics seemed to be depressed by it. Apparently the more hopeful things are readily missed

---

[9]Zack letter to May Sinclair, unknown date but almost certainly some time in 1898.

[10]Zack letter to May Sinclair, July 21, 1898.

by some readers. The story challenges and moves the reader. A reader whose first Zack story is "Life Is Life" may be somewhat in the position of the explorer who meets his first eight-foot tall Martian. The explorer may be a little uncertain at what is taking place at that meeting, and a bit apprehensive. The Martian is friendly, however, and the explorer will eventually look back on their meeting with gratitude, and with admiration for his unique companion.

"The Failure of Flipperty"

Once again we are back in Australia. One reviewer wrote that Zack's Australian stories "testify indubitably an experience gathered overseas."[11] This was an insightful guess. Zack had indeed been in Australia as a visitor to her family. Her three brothers "all lived their adult life in Australia."[12]

Keats family letters indicate that Gwendoline Keats was to go to Australia with her brother Fred (who was returning to Australia) in April of 1887 (when she would have been 21 1/2). And she was definitely in Australia in 1888—probably having indeed accompanied Fred in 1887 as planned. There is a photo album, no longer in Keats family hands, which is inscribed "Gwendoline Keats/1888." The National Gallery of Australia describes it as containing South Australian and Port Said views by an unknown photographer. Mrs. Beverley Keats says that the photos were not taken by Gwendoline herself, but that they were purchased by her. Some fortunate person owns a photo album previously owned by Gwendoline Keats—probably a name that currently means little or more likely nothing to the current owner![13]

In one of her letters to May Sinclair, Zack wrote, "Just read my first Australian review—they don't seem able to make out whether I am an

---

[11]Unknown reviewer, "The Academy," "'Zack.,'" June 25, 1898, p. 689.

[12]Email letter to me from Mrs. Beverley Keats, Mar. 27, 2013.

[13]Email letter to me from Mrs. Beverley Keats, July 29, 2014.

Australian or not, which is a bit of a compliment."[14] That would indeed be a compliment—Zack's Australia seemed pretty close to the real thing to at least one Australian reviewer.

"The Failure of Flipperty" is the third longest story in the book, at 22 pages. It is a story that attracted little individual recognition from reviewers. However, *The International Library of Masterpieces, Art, and Rare Manuscripts, Volume 18* (of 30), published in 1899 and limited to 1000 copies, included this story on pp. 6756-6766. Their brief introduction to the story, which says she was born about "1868" (really 1865) mentions that besides her stories, "Miss Keats has written two plays." This is one of the rare mentions of the plays of Gwendoline Keats. The plays seem never to have been produced, and are currently lost.

Despite the lack of attention from the reviewers, it is a very good story. *The International Library* may have been on to something by including it in a collection of masterpieces. The now forgotten Gwendoline Keats is in there with Henry James, Thomas Jefferson, Sarah Orne Jewett, Samuel Johnson, Ben Jonson, her namesake John Keats, and several other names still read and remembered today.

In the three characters of Buster, the nameless long-legged digger, and Flipperty, we have personalities strong enough to carry a novel—or perhaps even a series of novels. Due to the distinctive characters and to humor of both darker and lighter types, and to its hard-edged end, the story is memorable.

The story opens on an Australian liner steaming west. Two boys meet on deck for the first time. Buster is "short, broad, with red hair and ears agape." Flipperty, "who looked about eleven, was slim, his face small and finely drawn, with a straight, determined little nose, the brow and eyes giving an impression of width and imagination."

They converse. Flipperty is heading for the Teetulpa goldfield to help his brother Philip dig for gold. Buster is scornful: "'why, you look as if you had sat on a high chair all your life and fed the poor out of a long spoon.'" But only once has Flipperty given anything to the poor. What did he give, Buster asks. Though he goes white at having the

---

[14]Zack letter to May Sinclair, postmarked Oct. 4, 1898. As also noted in a footnote above, Zack does not mention in this letter that Oct. 4 was her 33rd birthday.

fact come out, Flipperty tells the truth: "'It was a flannel petticoat.'" A further fact comes out: Flipperty is a girl.

"Cracky!"
"Do you think it very wrong?"
"What, to be a girl?"
"No; to pretend to be a boy?"
"The police will nab you as sure as an egg."
"Philip won't let them; I'm not afraid."
"They will dress you in yellow and black like a wasp, and paint you all over arrows—solemn Dick. I've seen pictures of thieves in a book."
"I'm not a thief," indignantly.
"What are you, then?"
"I'm just a girl, who hates being a girl because girls are stupid cooped-up things; so I ran away from home, and now I'm a boy, and I will never be a girl again; so there."

When Buster suggests that the letter Flipperty wrote to Philip will have gone wrong, 'Flipperty's eyes filled with angry tears. "I hate you," she said, passionately, "you red-headed, mean-minded, supposing thing."'

Buster is surprised at the vehemence of Flipperty's response, and offers two bites of his apple in placation; Flipperty is able to take "a small sobby bite." They go to Buster's cabin, where he shows her an old broken pistol, and offers to lend it to her. She doesn't take it, although Buster continues to press her to take it.

"You will be glad of it," he said, "even if it doesn't go off—sleeping at night with a nugget under your head and murder all around. Why, Flipperty, I daresay you will have to kill a man yourself."
"No," she answered with decision; "I shall let him off. But come and look at the sea, and think of sharks."
"Yes," said Buster. "I wish some one would tumble in, don't you? only a baby, you know, or the boatswain—the cross one with the swivel eye."
"We'd save them," cried Flipperty, flushing; "and nearly get drowned ourselves, and the boatswain would entreat us to ask questions ever afterwards."
"Yes," chimed Buster; "and the captain would let us steer the ship, and beg us to eat more at dessert."

Buster teaches Flipperty the word So-la. Flipperty says "'It sounds rather empty.'" "'That's being a man,' he answered.'

Flipperty says if Philip doesn't meet her tomorrow she will go to Teetulpa to find him. Buster wonders what Philip will say when he sees her, and Flipperty has a ready answer. Clearly she has been thinking on this topic from the start of her adventure and even before, and her answer seems to contain the moral center of the story.

> Her eyes filled with tears. "He will say, 'Flipperty, it would have been braver to have stayed at home.' I knew that all along. I tried and tried, because I did want to be brave and grow like Philip, only somehow I never can be brave when he's not there. Philip is quite different from you and me. He doesn't think much of big grand deeds, like the Crusades and that; he says that small, dull, stay-at-home things are harder to do, and ever, ever so much nobler. Why, he even thinks learning to sew noble if you don't like it: of course it isn't noble for the smooth-haired girl."
>
> But Buster was not interested. "Let us steal dessert from the steward," he said.

The next morning, Flipperty is forced to exclaim to Buster that Philip hasn't come to greet the steamer. "'No more he has,' echoed Buster; "but perhaps he's found a nugget and is afraid to leave it.'" Flipperty begins to cry and clings to Buster's arm.

> "Don't cry," he said. "See," and he produced a large nobby green apple from his pocket; "how much do you bet that I can't get this apple into my mouth at one go?"
>
> She was put into the tender: looking up at the great vessel to say good-bye to Buster, the "So-la" died on her lips. The boy's face was a dull purple hue, his mouth wide open, and tightly wedged inside was the nobby apple: a compassionate passenger led him away, and Flipperty saw Buster no more.

With that, Part I ends. Flipperty will see Buster no more, perhaps to the dismay of both Flipperty and the reader.

Flipperty takes the train to Teetulpa, then climbs aboard a coach for the gold fields. A long-legged digger teases Flipperty—he doesn't know

Flipperty is a her—but admires his (her) spunk. Flipperty explains why Philip hadn't met her.

"Buster thinks that Philip has found a nugget already; that's why he didn't meet me. You see he would have to defend the nugget."

There was another roar of laughter, and Flipperty blushed painfully.

"Nuggets ain't so easy found, youngster," the long-legged digger answered. "Fever terrible bad at the diggin's, I hear," he said, turning to his companions. "See a man alive and hearty one morning; the next week yer go into his tent, and there he is lying with his face as black as my hat."

"Why black?" Flipperty asked.

"Flies," he answered, shortly.

They arrive at Teetulpa. The nameless long-legged digger takes Flipperty under his wing, and helps her find out where Philip might be. Philip is reportedly down with fever. The digger escorts Flipperty to a tent, where they do indeed find Philip—delirious with fever. The digger says he will try to find the doctor.

Then he went out, leaving Flipperty alone with Philip. She lay down beside him, placed her cheek against his cheek, and her small, thin arms clasped his broad shoulders. The sun sank and swept the long shadows into one uniform grey-black mass; then the moon rose, and its soft light stole across the great plain, making the blue bush look quite soft: it fell, too, on the brother and sister. The hours crept by, but the long-legged digger did not return, nor did Philip wake. The grey light of dawn shivered in the east, and Flipperty realised that Philip had grown strangely cold: she drew the blanket close, and pressed her own little form nearer to him. Then day broke, and as the great plain reddened beneath the sun a vast crowd of flies rose from the ground and entered the tent.

Flipperty gave a shriek of agony: myriads had settled on Philip's face.

The doctor arrives and covers dead Philip's face with his coat. He tries to lead Flipperty away, but she refuses to go. Later the doctor returns with two other men. They are bringing a coffin made out of old packing cases with "'five prize medals'" painted across the side. One of the men is the long-legged digger, with "a look of shame in his face." He tells Flipperty, "'God strike me for a damned hound,' he said, 'but I got drunk and forgot yer.'" They bury Philip; "Flipperty flung herself down on the spot beneath which Philip lay buried." She is again left alone.

Later in the day the digger returns with another man. The digger, we find from his words, finally knows that Flipperty is a girl rather than a boy. Probably he found out from his companion.

> Raising Flipperty in his arms, he held her out towards the stranger.
> "Her be yer pup, ain't her?" he asked.
> "I'm her stepfather."
> "Wall," said the long-legged digger, slowly, "her's sleeping now; maybe her'll wake soon enough," and he turned on his heel and left them.

There the story abruptly ends.

There are several elements to this story, and somehow Zack makes them all work together. The first part features the delightful conversation of the children. Their talk together is entertaining—colorful, blunt, funny, impolite but direct, and fully engaging. The children are not completely in touch with reality, of course, and we are invited to laugh at them. But we are also laughing with them. And at the same time that we are being treated to humor, we are also learning to see both of them as complete human beings, and as admirable ones. To a certain extent we begin to see Buster's deeper and better side, as when he placates Flipperty with an offer of part of his apple, when he brightens in reaction to Flipperty's praise of him, and when he tries to encourage the crying Flipperty by putting all of an apple into his mouth at once. There is plenty of bottom to Buster, if we could only get to know him better. Beneath his rough exterior there is in Geoffrey Chaucer's phrase a "parfit, gentil knyght" ready to burst forth with deeds of courage and kindness.

Flipperty we learn to know also. We see her courage fighting her fear, her honesty in admitting that Philip will say it would have been braver to have stayed at home, we see her love and admiration for her brother.

Part II takes us to a harsher world. The land is hard: arid, with bones and rotting flesh dotting the landscape. Flipperty's companions are also mostly rough. If the physical environment is rough and her companions rough, an even more rough reality meets Flipperty: her beloved brother is dying. Within hours her brother's body is cold and dead against her.

Even in the second part of the story, there is humor, but it is of the darker sort, appropriate to the setting. In seven words, Zack describes Flipperty's companions on the coach. "They smoked, swore, spat—spat, swore, smoked." When a non-paying passenger is thrown off the coach by the conductor, the ex-passenger lay "swearing so fearfully that the wonder was that he held together." When the doctor begins quoting Philip's burial service from memory, he says, "'And they shall rest from their labours'" only to be interrupted by "'A damned good thing, too'" from the long-legged digger.

Here again we see Zack's consciousness that the various classes are living in the same world at the same time, and are not as separate as we often imagine. The relationship between the long-legged digger and Flipperty is a reminder of class interconnectedness. Their relationship is far from an ideal or idealized relationship, for the brutal truth of the matter is that the digger lets Flipperty down by getting drunk and forgetting to get the doctor—though we guess that Philip was doomed in any case. But earlier, when the digger was helping Flipperty, Zack tells us "She put her small hand into his rough one, and the man's great fingers, scored with purple scars from the barcoo rot, closed over them." It is an affecting scene, believable and heartening.

Flipperty has failed, and hence the title of the story. Reality was too much for her and her happy daydreams of living with Philip and mining gold with him. There we are left by Zack; one brief incident has been painted for us. With poignancy and with grim honesty, Zack has shown us Flipperty with her arms around her dying, then dead brother, and has shown us the black flies resting on the dead Philip's face. As the long-legged digger says, "'her's sleeping now; maybe her'll wake soon enough.'" Flipperty must wake to reality.

"The Busted Blue Doll"

The book's third and final Australian story is "The Busted Blue Doll," which checks in at just 10 pages. Most reviewers ignored this story, although one reviewer thought both it and "The Failure of Flipperty" to be remarkable. A second reviewer said he carried away "a fragrant memory of reverence for the poor Italian" whose actions the story recounts.

This is a brief, stark story, perhaps an incident or an episode rather than a tale.

We are shown a deserted mine; the name "'Battista" is scrawled over a grave. Battista had come to Australia from Italy, to hunt gold, carrying with him an image of the Madonna. We already know that Battista is dead, but now we are told more of his story. We return to his early days searching for gold: "the thought came to him that there where the ray fell he would dig for gold, and the idea comforted him: it seemed as if the Blessed Virgin herself had deigned to point out a way of escape from this strange and homeless land."

He works hard, but because he had neglected to obtain a license, his claim is jumped by an American. When Battista understands what has happened, he begs the Madonna image to bless his knife and goes to fight the American. The American, like Battista, has courage, and they fight; the American escapes and apparently decides against further chance of sudden death, for he sells the mine to Termater Bill "for three long drinks and a new swag."

Termater Bill goes to talk things over with Battista, who insists the mine is his. Termater Bill offers reasonable terms for the lease of the mine, but Battista ignores him. Much time passes, and no gold is found. Battista retains faith in the gold-finding abilities of the Madonna, but finally there

> had come into Battista's heart a great weariness of waiting, and he had flung himself down before the image of the Madonna and wept.
>
> And the little blue-and-gold figure had stared out into the gathering darkness with its blank meaningless smile as vacant and as indifferent as before.

Termater Bill comes back again, and Battista assures him fiercely that there's gold in the claim. Termater Bill spits and agrees, but comes back the next day with a suggestion that Battista dig in a somewhat more promising part of the claim. Bill suggests that Battista not rely too much on the "'jumpt-up blue doll,'" which looks "'jest as if her was kinder larfin' at yer; her ain't no mug that busted doll, I'll lay to that.'" But Battista says Bill doesn't understand.

A few weeks later a bush-fire sweeps the land, and Termater Bill returns to the mine to find Battista's dead body. Battista's grave is dug. A man suffering from delirium tremens offers to fight Battista. (As stated previously, I will incorporate Zack's footnotes into the body of the text.)

> But the dead man lay still and paid no heed to him.
> Termater Bill said he reckoned the company wud 'low him to say a few words.
> The company 'lowed him.
> Some of the men sat down on the mullock-heaps and began to fill their pipes; others stood about; and one, a jackeroo [Lately arrived colonist.—Zack], took off his hat and then rather sheepishly put it on again.
> Termater Bill cleared his throat and spat into the open grave. "Life," he said, "was a jumpt-up quare thing: there wa' they who bottomed payable dirt [*Bottom payable dirt*=find sufficient gold to pay working expenses.—Zack] fust go off, an' thar wa' they who—didn't." He was silent for a moment, and rubbed his face with his sleeve. "But," he continued, "maybe out thar," and he pointed vaguely towards a patch of sunset sky, "across the Divide, they finds colour." [*Find colour*=find gold.—Zack] He ceased speaking, and the men puffed away at their pipes in silence: at last some one suggested that it was time for the corpse to "turn in."

Battista is lowered into his coffin-less grave. "They shoveled back the earth rather gingerly, avoiding the dead man's face; but, after all, it had to be covered the same as the rest." That men covering a dead body would gingerly want to avoid covering a man's face is an insight into human nature typical of Zack. That such covering is unavoidable, is equally typical of her.

The other men stroll back towards the camp, leaving Termater Bill alone.

> He went to Battista's hut and peered through the half-shut door: there in the corner the little blue-and-gold image stared, smiling down inscrutable, indifferent. Long the man gazed back on it; then with sudden determination he entered the hut, and taking Battista's coat from a bench, covered the small figure, then lifting it in his arms, carried it out and flung it down the deep shaft.
>
> But under the gum-trees Battista lay still, silent, satisfied. The years went on, the bottom of the shaft filled with water, and the mullock slipped back into it with a heavy splash; the windlass rotted and grew green, and some one stole the bucket and hide rope; far, far below in the valley the sweet-scented wattle burst into tufted yellow balls, and the blue mists lay on Omeo.

Thus the story ends, with time and nature winning, as they always do. Battista's day and personality are forgotten, as life moves on.

"The Busted Blue Doll" is another story of human failure. Battista fails to find gold, and dies. His faith in the powers of the Madonna proved misplaced. But, in Zack's worldview, failure is never exactly what we might think it is. Life is "'a jumpt-up quare thing'"; some are fortunate, some are not. As Termater Bill senses, there is a providential hand which disposes; man only proposes. As Bill says, perhaps those who don't find gold on this side of life, have more success after death—perhaps "'across the Divide, they finds colour.'" That is, perhaps the men who cross over into death without having found gold or any other form of success, find gold or some better form of joy on the other side.

So even in failure we can see that there might be hope. This, it seems to me, applies to Zack herself. She had her day of moderate success and recognition—doing somewhat better than Battista in that regard, although she was never wildly successful—and now the years have moved on and she is as forgotten as Battista and his failed mine, while the beautiful world, with its "sweet-scented wattle" and its "blue mists," remains. I would guess that of people who read books, not one in a thousand, perhaps not one in a hundred thousand, has ever even heard of Zack, let alone read her books. Life has some surprises, however, and perhaps Zack will yet find "colour" among reading people on this side of the grave. What she found across the Divide after death, is a matter of intense interest, but we will find out for sure only when we join her.

After Battista's death, we are told that he lay "satisfied." It is a striking word for a man supposedly beyond the ability to feel anything good or bad, and it inclines us to hope that he did indeed find color across the Divide, despite his failure on earth.

Battista has too little individuality for us to know him deeply. He is homesick, determined, brave, not fortunate, mostly silent, and superstitious. We know him well enough to sympathize with him, and we hope that he did indeed find color across the Divide.

The best character in the story is Termater Bill. He is a humorous and entertaining man, but there is a deal of substance to his character. He seems to be a very fair-minded man. Rather than attempt to stand on the strict letter of the law in regard to the ownership of the mine, he generously offers to negotiate reasonable terms with Battista, who after all is the one who has put in the work in developing the mine. Even when Battista fails to respond to this offer, Bill simply lets Battista and time go forward, perhaps unconsciously but wisely aware of the biblical reminder that "'Sufficient unto the day is the evil thereof'" (Matt. 6:34, KJV). Why worry about legal technicalities when there is no gold yet to quarrel over? If Battista had struck gold, one feels confident that Bill would have been able to work out an arrangement that left both men financially well off. And there is a thoughtful philosopher inside Bill—he is a man who looks at life and wonders, if he doesn't know. His comments at the burial of Battista are worthy of respect. His disposal of the figure of the Madonna into the mineshaft is not something that happens without thought. Yes, he throws the "'busted blue doll'" into the failed mineshaft. But he wraps the figure in Battista's coat before he does so. Battista failed; the doll failed to help him. Battista has died; the Madonna figure should go to its grave as well, wrapped in the coat of the man it did not help, into the mine at which the man worked so hard in expectation of the Madonna figure's blessing. May they both rest in peace.

"The English Girl's Christmas Presents"

This story represents Zack's only German story, in all her writings. The brief story of 7 plus pages takes place in the German town of Dresden. It attracted very little notice among reviewers, but it seems to me to be a superb story.

The plot is simple. A nameless English girl is spending time alone in Dresden just at the Christmas season. She is staying at the pension of two "very old, very poor German ladies" named Fraülein Käthe and Fräulein Marta. She is the only boarder. The two ladies had not yet begun their Christmas preparations. When the nameless English girl pays her first week's rent, the ladies have enough money to buy coal.

When Fräulein Marta goes out to make some purchases, the English girl accompanies her. Marta's eyes glow at the countless Christmas trees for sale, but it seems that this year they are not going to have a tree. She is delighted also at the Christmas cake showing in a confectioner's window. There is, she says,

"no time like Christmas. It heals the heart through the eyes."

She stood a moment in front of a stall and fingered some brilliant coloured stuffs lovingly with her worn hands. "My sister," she said, "would call such colours vulgar, but I love the bright things. You," she continued, turning to the girl, "you will have lots of Christmas presents, no doubt. Ach, what it is to be young! We—we shall have many gifts, too: Christmas is for the old and young alike."

The English girl expected no presents, but she did not say so: she felt a little ashamed at her friendless condition, and as the days went on the feeling increased. She gathered from the conversation of the two sisters that they, on their part, were assured of being almost overburdened with gifts.

But then, as they said, "Christmas is Christmas, and one takes the little things and one gives them in the same spirit."

The girl lay awake at night and counted the people who might possibly send her a present; she could think of only two, and the more she thought about the matter, the more certain she became that this year they would neglect to do so. The moment came when she would have telegraphed to them, "For Heaven's sake send me a present"—but Christmas Eve had already arrived.

Reduced to despair, she determined at last to buy herself a number of presents, and tell the sisters that they had been given to her by friends. She bought things that she needed,—pins, sealing wax, string: then the thought struck her that, should either Fräulein Käthe or Marta ask to see the contents of such parcels, they would certainly fail of being impressed. So she went out a second time and tried to look at the shops with their eyes, and buy things that they would think beautiful. On her return she hid her purchases deep down in her trunk. She was still on her knees before the box when Fräulein Marta entered. The girl blushed, shame-faced; the Fräulein seemed also a little discomposed.

The sisters will be dining with friends tomorrow; the English girl also says she will be dining with several friends. They wish each other Merry Christmas, the girl "with a sob in her throat."

On Christmas day the girl receives a number of letters and parcels— which she had posted to herself the day before. "She laid them in a conspicuous place on the table, but the two Fräuleins seemed occupied with their own affairs, and did not glance that way."

On Christmas evening the girl goes out.

Leaving the road for a narrow foot-track, she pierced deeper into the solitude. A great self-pity fell upon her,—she sobbed because every one in the whole world was more happy than she: even the two Fräuleins had friends; they were not obliged to buy presents for themselves,—and she sobbed again. High up in the sky the moon kicked a way through the heavy clouds, but the stars were hidden. Suddenly the girl heard voices; unnoticed by herself she had approached a summer-house. She drew nearer, and, peering in, saw the two sisters. Far away in the town the Kreutz Kirche clock tolled nine.

Fräulein Marta sighed. "Are you cold, sister?" she said. "In another half hour we might go home."

"Ah yes, in another half hour; but what shall we do if she asks to see the presents?"

"Perhaps she may not ask; I was careful not even to glance at hers." The girl stole away, and, hurrying back to the house, lifted the presents out from the trunks and wrote on them Fräulein Marta and Käthe's names, then, making them into one big package, went out again into the night. The snow fell softly upon her as she stood in the street waiting for the two sisters to return home. At last she saw them cross the Platz, their thin figures bent, as if they were afraid of the white light that the snow flung back upon them. They cast a fugitive look round, before entering their house. The door clanged close on their heels, the echo ringing down the street. For a moment the girl stood and listened to it, then moving away, she found a dienstman, gave him the parcel containing the presents, and told him to deliver it at the pension. When she returned later, Fräulein Marta called her into the dining room. "Sehen Sie nur," she said, pointing at the presents that lay unpacked upon the table; "Christmas is Christmas for old and young alike."

That is the end of "The English Girl's Christmas Presents."

Getting by with a little help from my friends, as the Beatles sang, I am told that "Sehen Sie nur" means something like, "Just look" or "Just see" or "Just you see." There seems to be no indication that the sisters understand that the presents came from the English girl.

My preference would be that Zack had translated the German words herself, so that we could be sure of the meaning—but she didn't. I would contend that her artistry would have been higher here if she had given us the meaning in English, so that we can be certain of the sisters' response. And she should not expect us to know German in order to understand that response.

I was hoping, but it seems to be a vain hope, that Fräulein Marta was saying something like "Look what you've done." That would indicate that the sisters understood that the presents came from the English girl. We have gone through pages of lying on the part of all three characters. The German ladies have been lying to the English girl, and she has been lying to them. In Zack's moral universe, and I would contend in God's universe as it really exists, lies are not good; truth is good. I think it would be good for all concerned if the German ladies did indeed understand that it was the young English girl who has given them the gifts. But unfortunately the text does not permit us to have strong confidence that the sisters do indeed understand exactly what has happened. Rather, there seems to be a loose end in regard to the sisters' understanding—and loose ends are often typical of Zack's stories, as they are typical of life.

Fräulein Marta may not understand that the presents came from their boarder, but she is correct that Christmas is for old and young alike—for the old ladies and for the young English girl. The old ladies have received beautiful Christmas presents when they expected no presents at all. The young English girl is more blessed yet. She has been pretending to have friends with whom to spend Christmas evening, pretending to have gifts which others have sent her. It is not a very honorable way to proceed, obviously. Wandering the streets on Christmas night, swamped with self-pity, she discovers she is not the only lonely, more or less friendless person. The very people she has been lying to in order to impress, are almost as friendless as she is. Käthe and Marta have each other, but little else. The blessing for the English girl is to come out of her self-pity and to have the opportunity to do a generous act for the sisters. Her experience here testifies to the truth of Christ's statement that ""It is more blessed to give than to receive,"" which Paul quotes (Acts 20:35).

Hers is an act especially appropriate for Christmas. Jesus Christ was born and died, in order that sinful people would receive the generous and undeserved gift of eternal life. How appropriate that we give gifts at Christmas time. Christians are the recipients of the greatest gift of all. How fitting that we imitate our Savior by giving gifts to others during the Christmas season especially. (And at other times as well!) The young English girl had lost sight of the meaning of Christmas to a certain extent. She was so focused on her own somewhat solitary situation, as to lose sight of the situation of others. She has even missed the numerous hints that the two fräuleins are experiencing a poverty-stricken Christmas season. It takes what can only be described as a near miracle, to wake her up.

What are the odds that the English girl, wandering the streets, would come to the very place where the German ladies were hiding out before their return home? Dresden we can be sure was not a small town, even in the 1890s. And that she would hear them speaking in a matter that explained all, without them seeing her? The odds are astronomically against, of course. But Zack was never dismayed by odds. There are no coincidences, in her world: God could turn events however He wanted them, to bring about the results He intended. God apparently had a generous intention of giving the English girl a lesson—and a chance to be greatly blessed—and He put her where He needed her to be to carry out His intention. He also wanted the German ladies to be blessed. If it took an unlikely coincidence, well, it's His universe, after all.

Some readers may be offended by such "coincidences"—others will grant Zack the right to her own worldview, and will not mind at all. Since my own view is that God is in providential control of world history, I can swallow just about any supposedly unlikely coincidence without undue stress.

It is fascinating to note that even the dishonesty of the English girl allows the blessing to both her and to the ladies to be increased. At first the English girl, in her attempt to trick the ladies, buys herself practical gifts only. On second thought she realizes the ladies are unlikely to be impressed by such gifts, at which point she buys beautiful things to give herself in her attempt to pretend that such gifts came from her friends. Then when the English girl awakens from her blindness and self-pity, she has beautiful things to give to the ladies—to their advantage and to hers! It seems that the Supreme Ironist, as God is sometimes called, had a trick or three up His sleeve. Not every irony, it seems, is painful to undergo.

One thing that adds interest to our reading of "The English Girl's Christmas Presents" is the fact that Gwendoline Keats herself spent time in Dresden. I don't know how long she was there, but she was there long enough for the following incident to occur. It has come down to us in Keats family lore. It will clarify things to point out that my Keats family correspondent Mrs. Beverley Keats tells us Gwendoline "probably was better known in the family as Gwenda."

> Gwenda at one stage gave a party for her "arty" friends at the Dresden Opera House. The artist Friedrich Anton Otto Prolss was present and he was captivated by her beauty, and he painted her portrait dated 1892. This portrait is still in the family.[15]

It is interesting that Zack, whether her stay in Dresden was long or short, was able to come up with enough "'arty'" friends to be able to give a party at the Dresden Opera House. From her letters to May Sinclair, we sense that Zack was a woman who enjoyed interacting with other artistic people. The picture of her that arises is of a woman who did

---

[15]Email letter to me from Mrs. Beverley Keats, Mar. 27, 2013.

not need the constant companionship of other people, but who enjoyed being with people quite often. She may have been mostly solitary, without often being lonely. She had, it seems clear, an intense inner life.

I would not have guessed that she was the party giving type. A few friends gathered together would seem more her style. And maybe that is what the "party" really amounted to in reality.

It is good to hear that Prölss (1855-1934) was captivated by her beauty! The photographs of Zack that have come down to us do not seem to indicate that she was physically beautiful in the usual sense. She tends to appear to be somewhat austere and unsmiling, seemingly plain. We sometimes run into people we would never call beautiful, yet who are undeniably attractive. This well could have been the case with Gwendoline Keats. Prölss, in the presence of the living Gwenda, thought enough of her to paint her portrait. In it she almost smiles, if not quite.

Mrs. Keats also says that apparently Gwenda had to arrange for her brother Thorold to pay for the painting.[16] Christ tells us, "'the laborer is worthy of his wages'" (Lk. 10:7). We would not expect Gwendoline Keats/Zack to write her stories and give them away for nothing, so we can not be surprised that Prölss wanted to be paid for his portrait of Gwenda Keats. He is still remembered today, and his paintings continue to be sold internationally. Some of his works can be viewed on the Internet. It is good to know that the original painting remains with the Keats family.

The young (age 26-27 in 1892) Gwenda was able to gather a party of friends at the Dresden Opera House, but she may well have found time to be lonely as well! Perhaps the experience of the "English Girl" was in some sense her experience, at least in terms of feelings if not exactly in the details of the story. If she did feel some loneliness and self-pity, she took the raw materials and, as an artist does, transmuted them into something beautiful and moving. "The English Girl's Christmas Presents" is a lovely story.

----

[16]Email letter to me from Mrs. Beverley Keats, Feb. 13, 2014.

"The Red-Haired Man's Dream"

The second longest story in the book is "The Red-Haired Man's Dream"; it is 56 pages long and is a story of high quality. For so long a story, it attracted surprisingly little individual notice from the reviewers. One thought it sentimental, another saw "no spark of merit" to it, while a third felt the story was powerful, technically well written, and giving evidence of ability to write a longer work, but "tainted with modernity."

"The Red-Haired Man's Dream" is a cautionary tale, one of two stories by Zack set in Italy. While the background is an Italian village, the three major characters are all English, all of whom are of what we might call approximately the well educated middle class or perhaps upper middle class.

The story opens with two English girls—young women—getting off a train and being driven to the Italian mountain village of Olevano in the Hernican Mountains. The older girl is Jess, who says she was born in a "'queer old grey stone house on the border of Exmoor.'" "'I learnt to love those moors, with their look as if the peace of God had settled on them and couldn't be rubbed off.'" But she has no desire to go home. Her home was sold years ago when her parents died, and she hates the past. The younger girl is Roch. We will find out eventually that she is very beautiful. Rochfort was a Keats family name. Zack's father, for example, was William Rochfort Keats. Also Zack's younger brother was named Arthur Rochfort Keats. Zack has turned her father's and brother's name into the name of Jess' beautiful friend.

As they reach their lodging (the Albergo) late at night, they are met by "a tall, gaunt young Englishman" with "a tumbled mop of red hair." He is taking a thorn out of a kitten's paw. He notices that Jess is lame, "and that she looked tired and sad," and goes for the padrona for them. He will remain the Red-haired Man, nameless, as some of Zack's major characters do.

The next morning Roch, "fresh and charming," finds the Red-haired Man apparently sleeping, with a two-year old child on his chest. She makes faces at the child, to its delight, and when she dances a jig, the child loses its balance and rolls down the bank to come to rest at Roch's feet. The Red-haired Man has borrowed the baby from the

By Noble Things She Stands

washerwoman because, he tells Roch, "'Babies believe in things.'" "'They believe in themselves, in you, in the world in general.'" Roch tells him he is very "'*Young*,'" which he will not admit but which he has possibly considered himself.

While the two talk, the baby wanders away. Roch notices that the baby is missing, and begins to run after it, but the Red-haired Man quickly passes her and rescues the baby from a precipice. Roch is thoroughly frightened, and the man's face is "very white." A possible death or grave injury has been averted, but barely. Roch tries to take the baby from the young man, but he refuses to give him up.

> Roch looked at him, and then burst into a peal of laughter.
> "Well," she said, "the sooner that baby gives up believing in you the better." Then she proceeded on her way, leaving the Red-haired Man consumed with indignation.

A few days later the Red-haired Man joins Jess under the hotel loggia (open-sided roofed gallery).

> He glanced down as she leant back in the rocking-chair, remembering, with a pang of pity, that she was lame. It seemed to him that this lameness probably accounted for the bitter expression of her face: it was a strange, contradictory face; well-bred in detail, there was a certain nobility about the wide brow and full-couraged eyes, but the mouth, thin, hard, compressed, was the mouth of a middle-aged, disappointed woman. Yet the girl was young enough—twenty-two, at most. Looking at her, he found himself wondering whether the lips would grow full and soft if kissed: they were not the lips a man would feel much inclination to kiss—she was in so great need of love, the chances were she would never get it. He felt a great pity for her: a woman, he told himself, is not a woman unless she is loved—she remains a half-finished sketch of something she might be. Then Jess looked across at him and smiled,—her smile raised the veil between herself and him; for a brief moment he saw sheer down into her heart, and all that he saw was beautiful. He had a sudden sense of nearness, a belief that he had known this woman elsewhere.

In fact he has known her elsewhere. Here is another case of what we might call Zackian coincidence. It turns out that it was she whom, in the years when they were both children, he had made jump from a rock. That jump had lamed her for life, although the Red-haired Man had not known it at the time. (All this had taken place in Devonshire, which was of course where Zack herself was born and grew up.)

> "Then I am responsible," he said. It was horrible to him to be the indirect cause of suffering to any one.
>
> "No, no," she answered. "I should have jumped whether you had been there or not: the rock always had a fascination for me. Besides," she continued, trying to turn his attention from the subject, "it was the little book that I wanted. I remember in those days I had a ridiculous belief that in some book lay the secret of how to escape from unhappiness—though I am afraid that, as far as I am concerned, the secret has remained unanswered."
>
> He was full of bitter self-accusation. "I went back to school the next day and thought it was only a sprain. How could I have been such a fool!" he said.
>
> "Why should you have thought otherwise?" she replied. "Do you remember how good you were to me? You carried me almost all the way home. You were strong even in those days,"—she smiled at the involuntary recollection of him that rose before her, a lanky, grotesque, red-haired boy, but infinitely, awkwardly gentle.
>
> "And I have spoilt your life," he said.

But Jess tells him her lameness has "'had its good side,'" for it has encouraged people to do "'a hundred little acts of kindness'" to her. "'Don't you think," and she stopped a moment and smiled at him,— "don't you think," she continued, "that a little love is worth a lot of lameness? because if you don't, I do.'" She recalls that the only happiness of her childhood came from Nanny, her nurse. She tells him she believes in Fate, and is pessimistic. He, on the other hand, looks to the Future, and proposes a pact in which the two of them "'make a little grab at happiness.'" Jess agrees.

A few days later Roch buys a little pig named Felice, and goes walking with it tied to a string. Jess and the Red-haired Man follow more slowly, she on a mule. He prevents boughs from hitting her.

It was very pleasant to the Red-haired Man to wait upon this woman, to help her in some small way; his pulses beat with a big boyish happiness. He put his hand on the flap of the saddle: "A man is some use in the world when he can protect a woman. Why don't you need more protection?" he asked, his mouth expanding into one of its gigantic smiles.

She was so unused to being protected, her eyes filled with tears at the thought. When he saw the tears and the trembling of her lips, the strings of his heart vibrated like a resonant chord.

"Life has it's [there is an editing error here—the word should be its—CW] good things," he said, "though I don't believe you have tasted them yet."

She did not answer: she had a great longing for life's good things, but she was also afraid of them,—she was so certain that happiness had to be paid for with tears.

Felice, having escaped from Roch, begins eating the sketch books of two German artists. The Red-haired Man with considerable difficulty rescues the pig and the girl. Roch cheerfully rattles on, dominating the conversation. Her life has been much different from that of Jess. Roch says, "'Happiness is hereditary in our family—none of us can escape it.'" But light-hearted as she is, she values Jess.

"Dear Jess," she exclaimed, lightly, though there was a sound of tears in her voice, "how battered you will be when you reach heaven; but then, I am sure you will get there!"

The Red-haired Man's eyes rested on the two girls, but it was only Jess that he saw. "Yes," he told himself, "life so far had been hard to her, but it should not always be hard."

Roch glanced at him, and something in the expression of his face thrilled her strangely.

Another afternoon Jess and the Red-haired Man rest from a walk. He tells her he loves her. She says she believes he only pities her; he insists he loves her. She is afraid; "She loved him, but the intense happiness that his love would bring made her distrust its existence." She hates pity with a vehemence. Of his supposed love, "'It is a dream,'" she said, "'a desolate, deceiving dream.'" He feels a passion of tenderness toward her, and assures her it is no dream. Under his prodding, she admits that the joy she is feeling now is worth all her past and future pain.

> "Jess! Jess!" he exclaimed, turning to her, "tell me you are glad that you are lame."
>
> She smiled through her tears. "I am glad," she answered, "glad, glad."
>
> "See," he said, "see how rough the path is—I must carry you." He raised her in his strong arms. At the foot of the hill he put her gently down.
>
> "Dearest," he said, "it is good that we love each other." But she, trembling, answered nothing.
>
> The sun sank, and the stars shot out, rather reluctantly. "How strange," said Jess, at last, "that it is me you love and not Roch."
>
> "She is a child," he answered, smiling.
>
> "No, she is not a child," Jess said, "and she is very beautiful."
>
> He stooped and kissed her. "Is she?" he answered, indifferently. "I do not think I have ever noticed it. I believe I have always been looking at you."

Another day the Red-haired Man hears Roch talking to her pig. Eventually he laughs and she is alerted to his presence, and is momentarily but briefly angry. They talk—the Red-haired Man and Roch; not the pig—and Roch takes him to a pool of water so that the reflection can show him that his hair is red while hers is auburn. Looking in the pool, "His eyes rested on her face, lingeringly, then they followed the lines of her white throat till they rested on the soft curves that proclaimed her woman." He is dazed and speaks incoherently, finally rushing off. She watches him striding away, and exclaims that he must be mad.

> High up on the hill opposite she could see the Red-haired Man tearing along with great, wide-paced strides. She watched him a moment. "He's rough and gauche," she exclaimed; "he's not a bit clever; he has nothing that one really cares for or expects to find in a man; he's an unlicked cub—and yet—" she stopped short, and, returning to the pool, knelt down once more, peering again into its shadowy waters. "It would be very strange if he should be the first man who did not think me beautiful," she said at length.

In the next chapter Roch and the Red-haired Man rest after gathering flowers.

> He was supremely happy, and asked nothing more of life just then than to watch her deft, slim fingers rearranging the cyclamen. He had entered into that state of delight which at the same time arrests the mind and forces on it the impression that the faculties were never more keenly awake: he was certain that he had never lived, never come into full possession of himself, till that moment. Further than that he did not wish to analyse: possibly it may be a part of supreme happiness that we have neither the desire nor the capacity to analyse it.
>
> The soft warm air blew between them. She raised her eyes and smiled at him, he smiled back at her: as a sensitive plant trembles at the far-off tramp of horses, their hearts thrilled at the unperceived approach of love. Neither had any thought of being untrue to Jess.

Overhead clouds had been gathering. A flash of lightning hits, lighting up the sky. "The man and woman shrunk together, and in that blaze of light they read their own hearts." Silently they return to the Albergo.

A day or so later the Red-haired Man has borrowed the baby Pico again. He talks to it, saying, "never try and set the world to rights. It doesn't pay, old man—it doesn't pay.'" He tells the baby of Jess:

> "life has been hard down on her from the first, but she had plenty of pluck: she put her back up against the wall and faced it, till I came along and mulled everything. A man doesn't like to see a woman facing things too much, Pico; he wants to stand up beside her and hit out. You don't understand now, old fellow, but you will understand right enough by and by. Well, that's how I felt, only I thought there was something more. It doesn't matter what I thought, because, because—" he stopped short, and the baby crowed and thumped his friend's broad chest to emphasise approval of the story.
>
> "It was a dream," continued the Red-haired Man,—"a damned dream," he ended with a sob.
>
> But Pico's dream at that moment was to catch a big green beetle, so he crawled away on his own account and the man flung himself on his face. "Dreams are hell," he cried bitterly, "dreams are hell."

Returning to the Albergo that same day, he meets Jess. "Looking at her, remembering all the love he had promised, of which he had now none left to give, nothing but the pity that she so despised, his heart ached for her and himself."

She senses something wrong, and questions his love for her.

> "Your love is so much to me," she sobbed. "At first I couldn't believe that you loved me, I seemed so different from the kind of women men love; and now, if you took your love back, I would bear it, because it would be *you* who willed it back,—but oh, it would be hard, hard, hard."

He comforts her as best he can, "but the nearness of her bosom to his gave him no thrill, and he comforted her coldly." She asks for the child to be handed to her, "as if she was stretching out her hands toward motherhood." But he instinctively and fiercely refuses to give the child to her, and leaves her.

> She covered her face with her hands. "It is a dream, a dream," she cried, bitterly; "he is beginning to awake."
>
> And yet she could not believe it was a dream, even though she said it with her lips.

Later on in the same day (apparently) the Red-haired Man, racked by emotional pain, comes across Roch on the top of a hill. They look at one another silently; he sees that "her face was no longer that of a child, but of a woman."

He asks her to go away with him.

> Despair swept down upon her: it was all so strange, sudden, terrible,—she was so unaccustomed to facing the stern realities of life. Involuntarily she raised her eyes to his, seeking help; but manliness had forsaken him. He laid his hands upon her breast: the touch of his hands burnt her like fire; but her bosom was to him womanhood, and the soft, fresh joys of the bridal night.
>
> "Come," he said, "come, my beloved, you are mine; do I not possess you already?" and his hands slipped from her breast to her waist and soft rounded hips.
>
> She sprang back, and stood trembling like a tall flame.

Her coldness drives him away from her, and he does not return to the hotel that night. "The days lengthened into weeks, and the Red-haired Man did not return." Jess tries to convince herself that she has faith in his fidelity. Roch tells her that "'Love is full of pain and horror'" but Jess says "'love is most beautiful.'"

Jess refuses to leave the village, but Roch is to join her mother in Rome. On her last day in Olevano, Roch, carrying the baby Pico, walks to the small pool where the Red-haired Man had discovered her beauty. She discovers the Red-haired Man sleeping there. He sees Roch and the baby. Then he hears Jess limping on the path higher up on the hill, and hides himself. She retreats without having seen them.

> Roch and the Red-haired Man stood and stared each into the other's white face.
>
> "She must never know," they stuttered hoarsely, "she must never learn the truth."
>
> A great haste to be away came to the man—a great fear lingering.
>
> "I will go to her," he said; "but you—we must never meet again."
>
> "No," Roch answered, dully, "we must never meet again."
>
> "The diligence—you can leave Olevano today."
>
> His haste bruised her like stones. "Yes, I leave Olevano today."
>
> "You must never write."
>
> "No, I must never write."
>
> "And if we meet you in the street you must not know us."
>
> "If I meet you in the street I must not know you."
>
> "Swear!" he said, turning from her.
>
> "I swear."
>
> Then he fled hurriedly, and she, raising Pico in her arms, pressed the baby close up against her breast—for upon her there was a lust of motherhood.

Thus ends the "The Red-Haired Man's Dream."

There is a story, perhaps apocryphal, of what one leading Puritan said after the collapse of the Puritan hopes with the end of Cromwell's Protectorate: "God spat on our dream." God spat on the dream of the Red-haired Man. His dream had been to "'set the world to rights.'" Jess had been crippled, partly by his fault, and Jess had had little happiness in life despite having an admirable character. By loving her he will wipe out all her unhappiness and give her the joy she deserves in life.

But his love for her has come about through a mixture of self-deception and pity. In fact he is dreaming, but he discovers that "'Life is too real for dreams,'" that "'dreams are hell'" and are "'damned.'" Romantic love between the sexes must occur in a natural, unforced way. A sleepwalking dreamer trying to correct the foolish mistakes of Providence is taking more upon himself than he can handle.

If we define tragedy as a disaster which happens because of the moral flaws of someone, then this story may be in some sense a tragedy. The Red-haired Man is a good man, but his flaws are real. There is both "strength and weakness in his face." He is, as Roch says early on, "'*Young*.'" We tend to forget that youth may carry disadvantages, that sometimes age and experience guide us away from follies we need to avoid. He is "a man whose first tussle with facts was yet to come, and who was ignorant alike of the powers or passions that were slumbering in him." Although the episode with the wandering baby is treated in comic fashion by Zack, still it shows an immature carelessness in the Red-haired Man. This carelessness, joined with some of his virtues—his ability to pity, his shame at having been a partial cause of Jess' lameness, his desire to protect and comfort the weak—eventually combines with those virtues in a way which brings disaster for three lives.

The destructiveness of self-deception is constantly recurring theme in all of Zack's writings. The very title of the book we are considering, *Life Is Life*, hints at the danger of deceiving ourselves. In "The Red-Haired Man," the destructiveness of self-deception is very potent. The Red-haired Man is the first victim of his self-deception, for he ends up intending to marry a woman with whom he is not in love, and to lose a woman he does love and who loves him as well. His self-deception about his feelings toward Jess hurt him, and also hurt Roch. Jess will be hurt as well, if their marriage unfolds as we fear it might. Jess begins the story as a somewhat bitter person, but her unhappy past has at least taught her to avoid self-deception. She wisely distrusts the love of the Red-haired Man at first, calling it a "'desolate, deceiving dream,'" but the dream is too strong for her and she ends by trying to believe in his love, always burdened by a reservoir of fear behind her belief. The fear is reasonable, because she has indeed given in to self-deception. Her future is not promising. Apparently she will marry the Red-haired Man, but it is difficult to be too optimistic that she will find much happiness in her marriage. Eventually she will find out that the Red-haired Man has married her out of pity rather than because he was in love with her. This will devastate her.

The ending of the story is a grimly unhappy one, although both the Red-haired Man and Roch are trying to act for the best in regard to Jess. We may admire them for agreeing that they must never meet each other again. But the immediate future looks bleak for both of them, and for Jess. The Red-haired Man has sacrificed himself to marry a woman he pities rather than loves with romantic fervor. Jess is now living in a dream from which she may wake to find herself living in a nightmare. And Roch loses the man she loves. Probably the best decision on the Red-haired Man's part, rather than his self-sacrifice, would have been truth. Zack does not tell us her opinion of his decision to marry Jess. But in Zack's moral universe, truth, no matter how painful that truth may be, always works out better than does lying.

The Red-haired Man would have done better, in my opinion, to admit the truth to Jess. It would have hurt her, but it also would have been best for her to know the truth. Knowing her character as Zack has portrayed it, she would have risen to the occasion with greatness. She has already told the Red-haired Man that if he took his love back, she would bear it for his sake. It would be hard, but she would do it. This seems a true statement on her part; she is a brave and generous-spirited person. Moreover, such a brave renunciation on her part would further ennoble her character for the inescapable challenges of life which must come to her.

The marriage of the Red-haired Man and Jess is not necessarily doomed, although its prospects for success do not look good as the story ends. Romantic love is a wonderful thing, but there is also a kind of love which mirrors the love of God toward men: agape love. That is the type of love that actively seeks the good of another person, independently of whether or not feelings of affection are involved. Agape love encourages us to act lovingly toward people we don't necessarily even like. When we are seeking the best even for our enemies, we are imitating God who loved us when we were His enemies (Matt. 5:43-48). If the Red-haired Man can treat Jess with this active love, he may find that eventually his feelings of affection toward her will grow in a powerful fashion. We tend to love where we have invested our emotions. Jess is a good person with many good points to her character. If the Red-haired Man can treat her kindly and respectfully, he may eventually—slowly or quickly—find his romantic attraction toward her rekindled.

One doubts whether he can carry out this type of agape love, of course. But maybe he can. Maybe his weeks of disappearance were times he spent reasoning out what he must do, and he came to the conclusion that he could and would actively love Jess in their marriage. Is his understanding of Christian truth powerful enough for him to love Jess as he should when they are married? He has shown glimpses of such character, but has also show glimpses of the reverse. His determination that he and Roch must have no communication is of course very wise, showing that he knows he needs to avoid the temptation of her presence.

While we are left with uncertainty as to how their marriage will unfold, things do not look good. Here is another loose end. There is no, "They lived happily ever after." Nor is there, "Their lives were ruined completely." This is the uncertainty of life. What will happen in their marriage is another story—perhaps a novel that we readers will have to write ourselves.

Which is correct, then: is romantic love "'pain and horror'" or "'most beautiful'"? Zack shows us that romantic love can be beautiful when one loves and is loved, but that such love is a dangerous two-edged weapon, and when wielded in a self-deceiving dream, can grievously wound oneself and others.

Roch's chance for future happiness seems by far the best of the three. From a charming, humorous near-child, recklessly careening through life, she has matured, through suffering, into a woman capable of love. True, she loses the man she loves, but her character is uncompromised, she has acted as generously as she knows how to do in regard to her friend Jess, and one feels she will love again, this time with more maturity.

My sister Jill Byers responded to this story with some thoughtful comments. She believes that what the Red-haired Man felt for Roch was romantic attraction, not love in the agape sense. She points out that romantic attraction by itself is not enough to guarantee a happy marriage. A marriage to Roch, if it were based solely on physical attraction, would not turn out to be ideal. Jill believes there was a strong possibility that the marriage between Jess and the Red-haired Man could work out well. Jill thus leans toward the optimistic side concerning the future for these two.

In any case, my sister's response indicates that this is a story likely to elicit a variety of opinions from readers. It is a thought-provoking story.

Once again Zack has used a wild coincidence in constructing her story. That the Red-haired Man helped cripple Jess when they were both children, and that they meet again in an Italian village in their young adulthood is pretty far beyond the bounds of normal possibility. But this is what Providence has arranged. The story is not hurt by the coincidence. Rather, it is helped by it, once we grant Zack's angle of approach that life involves in part a series of tests sent by God.

Zack's view of sexual morality is not modern, if by modernity we mean that men and women can do whatever they please with their bodies whenever they want to, with no consequences for their choices.

We can only guess, without certainty, as to Zack's own religious beliefs. Her letters to May Sinclair give no evidence of church attendance. At one point she purchases, through May Sinclair, a christening robe for the new baby of her coachman—in fact she rejects May Sinclair's first purchase as not being of high enough quality, and has her buy a better robe! We are not told that Zack attended the christening, although she may well have done so.

Yet Zack seems to write from within the Christian tradition. It could be that she was so profoundly influenced by the Christian culture around her, that her ideas as expressed in her stories come across as largely Christian. She was a woman who was not afraid to put a supernatural element in her stories, as we will see later on, or as we may have sensed in reading about the providential "coincidences" that occur often in her writing.

If we cannot know positively that Zack considered herself to be a Christian, we can certainly see the influence of Christianity in her handling of sexual morality in this story and elsewhere. Her description of the Red-haired Man's touching of Roch in a sexual manner is a masterful piece of writing. She realistically portrays immodest behavior, but she does it modestly. And she makes it clear why this immodest behavior is occurring: "manliness had forsaken him." A man's true manliness will not allow him to behave in that fashion. That is the Christian view, at least, although it certainly is not the modern view, with its careless acceptance of all kinds of sexual immorality.

Once the Red-haired Man self-indulgently allows himself to behave immodestly toward Roch, Zack is well up to the task of describing the incident. There is delicacy but no prudishness in Zack. She was a writer called by one reviewer "more aggressively, more fiercely, virile even than Mr. Kipling," and she knows the power of sexual attraction. Sexual desire is a fact of life, and a lovely one, and a man's desire for a maid is a legitimate desire. When the Red-haired Man discovers Roch's beauty, "His eyes rested on her face, lingeringly, then they followed the lines of her white throat till they rested on the soft curves that proclaimed her woman." In fact the delicate loveliness of Zack's description is supreme. The writing here reminds me a bit of Jane Austen. Jane Austen had numerous oblique ways of indicating that women are built somewhat differently than men. Zack's description is similarly oblique, and delightful.

There is no hint that the Red-haired Man is acting dishonorably in being attracted to Roch's female physical beauty. But a man's sexual desire, like everything else of man's, can only be correctly used under the law of God. Given "free" reign, legitimate sexual desire can be transformed into a horrible lustfulness, and as C. S. Lewis says, "lust . . . disenchants the whole universe" (*That Hideous Strength*, Chapter 12; my ellipsis). Zack knows this truth very well, and hence her understanding that the Red-haired Man's touching of Roch's breast means that his manliness had forsaken him. Manliness is not lust; manliness is self-control which respects others. We rejoice to see Roch spring back away from such disrespectful behavior.

As is usual in Zack's stories, several sentences or phrases strike the reader as extraordinarily perceptive comments. We have quoted several passages, but I can't resist repeating her early evaluation of Jess: "she was in so great need of love, the chances were she would never get it." Indeed, the more desperately one needs to be loved, the less likely it is that one will attract the love of others. It is a true insight on Zack's part, but not one that falls into the hand automatically—it takes wisdom to see. The reader, led by Zack, learns something new, or finds the verbal expression of a truth he has only vaguely sensed before.

Here also we are tempted to speculate about Zack herself. Did she in some sense see herself as a Jess who would never be loved? When she was writing this story she was probably in her late twenties or early thirties. She may have sensed by then that she was unlikely to find a man to love her. We can guess that the 1890s were much like the 2010s—more worthy women than there were worthy men to deserve them. This is all speculation, of course. That's the price of being a writer of enormous talent and fascination—people will speculate about you. If she wanted to escape that she should have never published her five books. She is beyond being hurt by any of our guesses about her personal life. Her "full-couraged eyes" have been beyond the grave for (probably) about a hundred years, and have seen what they have seen. If she is in the Christian afterlife, we can be certain her physical beauty is astonishing there. She would laugh with delight at our speculation, perhaps.

One thing we can say with certainty: Zack never envied the beautiful. Some of her female characters are beautiful, but she doesn't automatically make them uninteresting or foolish characters because of their beauty. Roch is one example. She is ravishingly beautiful, but emerges as perhaps the most honest and honorable person in the story. If Zack may have seen herself as having "not the lips a man would feel much inclination to kiss," she didn't take revenge by making her beautiful females bad people.

Several other valuable insights into human nature could be cited. For just one more example, when the baby rolls down the bank, it "lay, a fat little lump of surprised, pleased alarm, at Roch's feet." That the baby could be both pleased and alarmed, seems odd at first glance, but such a combination is feasible in real life.

"The Red-Haired Man's Dream" is a dramatic and gripping story, and one of considerable value as a cautionary tale.

"The Stone Pine"

"The Stone Pine" is by a couple of pages the shortest of the twelve stories, being only about five full pages of text. The action takes place on the Mediterranean. It is a story which attracted almost no individual notice from the reviewers—one called it "merely a pretty prose idyll."

A "bare-legged, ragged boy" and an equally poor but perhaps slightly younger girl are goatherds beside the sea. "In front of the flock the boy walked, playing upon his reed pipe; the girl tripped content in the rear." The boy never looks back at the girl, but she doesn't mind, "for she was but nine summers old, and felt scant curiosity about herself or him."

The boys is contemptuous of the lagging goat 'the "Weary One,"' "calling it feeble-couraged and a woman. The maid, however, loved it." In the reed hut the pair live in, the boys sometimes comforts the girl, for which "She was grateful, as became her."

On the shore grows a Stone Pine, "as solitary as God." "Sometimes the girl wondered on the loneliness of the pine: was it God-lonely from being above men, their thoughts and ways?" The boy usually thinks of more manly things, but at times "he also tasted of loneliness and felt brief fellowship with the Pine."

> The years passed—the boy, reaching up towards manhood, becoming good to look on, so that when the maid walked behind the flock she ceased to gaze down on her knitting, but looked always at him. He did not glance back at her, because the whole wide world lay before him: besides, he had known her from a child, and, let her strive much or little, nothing but womanhood awaited her, a poor state of scant account.

One day the boy, or young man, becomes restless and wanders off; he sails away. After many weeks the still restless youth returns home. He finds the girl

> seated beneath the shadow of the Stone Pine. She rose to her feet, and they stood and looked at each other: he saw that she was beautiful, and the restlessness left his heart, so that he wondered.

A great fear fell on them both: the maid turned and fled, he following—though why she fled, or why he, who could have overtaken her, did not, neither of them knew.

Then at last her knees trembled, and she ran back to the Pine for shelter. But when the boy saw that she was afraid, he grew bold, took her in his arms, and kissed her on the lips—the Pine beside them glowing like a soul.

The brief story ends there.

Possibly the Stone Pine (always capitalized in the story) represents God. The Stone Pine is "as solitary as God," is "God-lonely," and twice glows like a soul. My guess is that Zack is indicating that God is overseeing the lives of the two young people as they grow up from childhood into young adulthood.

The boy and the girl—nameless and speaking no lines—seem to be symbols of all men and women. Zack's description of them shows them to be creatures of their class and country, but they represent all mankind. Boys and girls turn into young men and young women, and the indifference they feel for one another in youth turns into a sexual and romantic attraction with the coming of age; as they find each other the boy's restlessness ceases. And the solitary Stone Pine, silently looking on as God looks on, oversees it all. It is crucial to note that the solitary Pine, if it does represent God, is not emotionless. When the young man and the young woman kiss, we are shown "the Pine beside them glowing like a soul." God is pleased when a man and a maid find one another, I think Zack is saying.

As is typical of Zack, there are sharp and well expressed insights into the human condition. For example, we are told of the boy, "Yet there were moments when he also tasted of loneliness and felt brief fellowship with the Pine; moments when the beauty of all the earth seemed ripe, but in the harvest something lacking, though he knew not what it was, neither had met any one who could name it by name, the Pine also remaining silent." This is a lovely picture. The boy feels the earth ripe with beauty, but something is lacking in the harvest! He doesn't know what that is. But as the story ends, he has found the answer, and the silent Pine glows.

"The Storm"

With the completion of "The Stone Pine" half of the book's twelve stories have been told, but the first six stories contain about 72% of the pages of the book. However, it was the second half dozen of the stories which attracted most of the favorable attention of the reviewers. For most of the critics who liked some of *Life Is Life*, the beginning of the good writing comes with "The Storm."

It was the final six stories that one enthusiastic critic in the "British Weekly" spoke of when he mentioned "eighty pages, great pages, notable pages, unforgettable pages, pages sufficient to give the writer a reputation," and added that "there is not much to go along with them in English literature, not much with the same terrible, tearing, tearless passion." He said he would "pity anyone who could read those stories unmoved."[17]

Of the final six stories, the critical plaudits are split pretty evenly among four of the stories, with the fifth trailing a little bit. Only "At the Stroke of the Hour" fails to attract much attention.

So within the general critical unanimity that these six stories (or at least five of them) are superb, there was much room for disagreement on which of the stories really stand out. No clear-cut favorite arises; instead we have the individual stories being highly praised by several critics and not mentioned by others.

For one critic, "The Storm" was the most dramatic story in the book. The story's vividness and intensity drew considerable comment. It is short at about ten pages.

As the story opens, we hear that a gale has sprung up. Night has fallen on a seaside cottage containing three women and a baby. The husband of the woman with the baby is one of those at sea in the storm. Her companions are her sister-in-law and mother-in-law. As is so often the

---

[17]These comments appeared originally in the "British Weekly," and are quoted in a segment called Book Reviews Reviewed, with a subtitle of "Life Is Life," in "The Academy," July 23, 1898, p. 93.

case with Zack, we are dealing with poor, uneducated people. But they have characters that resonate for good or ill, as do people of any other class.

The old woman is worried that her son Joss is on the same boat with Rab Tapp, for Rab is of a disreputable character; she suggests that Rab should be cast out of the boat as Jonah was (see the brief biblical book of Jonah, especially chapter 1). Her sick daughter-in-law Nan protests vehemently at such words, but Nan's mother-in-law sternly rebukes her, saying, "'It ill becomes a mother with her first chile at breast to be taking such thought for furren men's lives.'"

But Nan isn't worried about her husband's safety.

> "Joss will not be drowned," replied her daughter-in-law carelessly. "What-for should he be drowned? Oh, my God!" she ended, with abrupt change of voice, as the hurrying scream of the storm wrenched its way through the cottage, "why did yer make the sea?" She flung herself back in the bed, and the child began once more to cry, but she paid no heed to it.

Martha, Nan's sister-in-law, comforts the baby; she says her own child "'was wonderful contentsome.'"

> "Your own chile!" exclaimed the harsh-voiced old woman. "Why, your own chile was born dead."
> "Her was never dead to me," Martha answered, gently. "I used to talk a deal to her lying there so close and trustful agin my heart. But now I sorter feel that if me and Jim had another chile, maybe 'twould be born dead."

Martha's husband Jim is brother to Rab Tapp. Nan has seen Rab Tapp only twice in her life, and when they met they didn't speak much to each other. The last time they met

> "you was sitting up in the front of the fire nursing the chile, and he just stood over again 'ee by the chimney piece, sorter thoughtful. 'Do you love it?' he axed, 'do you love it?'—but you didn't make no answer. Them were his words. Do you mind, Nan?"
> "Yes," said the girl, softly, "I mind."
> "'Twas a queer question I reckoned to put to a mother; but there, you ain't never been terrible took up wi' the chile."

"No."

"Maybe you didn't speak to him sorter tender afore you borned him—same as I did my little girl."

"No."

"Yet 'twor my chile that wor born dead."

Nan fiercely claims that her own baby was born dead too; after this astonishing statement she ignores the baby's call for the breast. Martha tells her mother to pray aloud for those at sea.

The old woman clasped her hands, worn with toil, knotted with age, and sank on her knees; her thin lips trembled, but no words broke from them. Wind and sea, as if in derision at her helplessness, burst into more hideous combat, and the thunder heaved its way through their clamour with a noise like the splitting of mountains.

"Oh God!" sobbed the woman, "he wor a good son to me—a good son to me." She was silent a moment, and the storm without upreared itself against the cliffs, rocking the cottage in its heavy embrace. "Oh God!" she burst forth again, "ye would have spared Sodom for the sake of ten righteous men, and 'twor a terrible big and wicked city—spare the boat cause o' Joss! I wouldn't have axed so bold if it wor a ship; but it's nought but a boat, mortal small and tiddleliwinkie, wi' only dree men an' a lad in it; and the lad's a decent lad come o' respectable church folk, no chappelites, a-setting o' theirselves up above their betters. Happen you're angered again Rab Tapp, and well you might be, for he's not over and above conspicuous in good works; still, he's young, and youth's larning time: but if ye be terrible set on cutting him off—and I'll not deny the temptation—then, O Lord God! speak to Joss through the mouth o' the winds, same as ye did the men o' Joppa, so that he shall rise and cast Rab forth into the deep, and the sea shall cease her raging."

Nan rages at her mother-in-law for reminding God of Rab's weaknesses, but the old woman defends her action.

"And shall I see my own son cast away for fear o' speaking out?" remonstrated the old woman, fiercely. "My first-born, that lay at my breast and milked me trustsome? Shame on you to think o' stranger folk afore your own wedded husband."

A heavy knocking comes at the door. When the door is unbolted, Joss stands there.

> "Nan," he cried, "sweetheart, woman, wife, God's given me back to 'ee!"
> "And Rab?" she said, hoarsely.
> "The sea has taken its toll—Rab's drowned," he answered.
> "'Twas he I loved!" she cried, and fell at the man's feet as dead.

That is the abrupt end of the story.

This is a story of considerable power. The three major characters, despite the constraints of space, are shown to us in their distinct characters. There is Nan, the sullen young wife, in her heart unfaithful to her husband, and indifferent to her child. There is the harsh old woman of stinging tongue. And there is Martha, a gentle woman whose husband is a failure, whose child has been born dead, and who quietly expects that if she has another child that it too will be born dead.

Off stage, at sea, the son, brother, and husband Joss, and the disrespectable Rab Tapp undergo the violence of the storm. The emotional storm in the cottage is just as great. A prayer is given, and the apparently favorable answer comes, but with consequences ironically unfavorable.

Zack seems to write the story without editorial comment on her characters. "They exist; this is what happens under the Providence of God; make of it what you will"; so at least she seems to be saying. It is up to the reader to bring his own religious/moral response as he reads the story.

This may be one of Zack's gloomiest stories, because we see little avenue of hope for any of the characters except possibly for Martha. And Martha is not optimistic about her future. Martha is sweet-natured and generous, but she expects that no living child will be born to her. We can only hope that she and her persevering but always failing husband Jim will indeed have a child that lives, and that they will make their way in a manner better than expected. Perhaps there is more hope here than appears at first sight. A persevering husband, and a sweet-natured and generous-spirited wife, would seem to have a good chance of winning through to a good life.

The other characters are in a much darker situation. Joss has survived near death to find his wife does not love him. The old woman knows her son is unwanted by his wife. And Nan, an uncaring mother, betrays her heart's disloyalty to her husband, and knows that the man she loves is dead. We can only conjecture what family misery will occur in future years, as a result of Nan's confession and (more importantly) as a result of the undisciplined heart which led her (inwardly) to desert her husband, and to ignore her child.

As usual with Zack, there are subtle insights into human nature. When Nan states her husband will not be drowned, she does so with considerable confidence. Why so confident? I think it is because she senses that God will not arrange matters so that Joss dies and Rab lives; she senses that God will not arrange things the way she prefers—and she is correct. Her instinct was right.

The attraction between Nan and Rab is perfectly portrayed. The two have met only twice, and then didn't speak much, yet Nan at least has fallen in love as a result of those two mostly silent, no doubt completely public meetings. For Zack, the romantic and/or sexual attraction between a man and a woman is an inescapable fact of life. Such things happen as they happen, under circumstances that might seem odd to bystanders. That the morally immature Nan lacked the strength of character to fight against so inappropriate a romantic love is a demonstrable fact, but meanwhile Zack realistically has shown us how quickly a person can be romantically attracted to a member of the opposite sex. Or, as my sister Jill Byers suggests, "romantically attracted" may be too generous an evaluation: perhaps the word lust describes Nan's feelings better.

The prayer of the old woman is perfectly suited to her character. The old woman prays with deep sincerity with her son's life at stake. The prayer shows us a very worried woman pouring out her heart to God as honestly as she can. The prayer is at once passionate, generous, ungenerous, and unintentionally humorous. The old woman is as generous as she can be to Rab Tapp, without forgetting that her own son Joss is the apple of her eye. The woman, despite her faults, prays a Christian prayer, and we mock her prayer at our own risk. She is right when she says, "'And shall I see my own son cast away for fear o' speaking out?'" We know that God can take prayers which are flawed, and make up the deficit in them Himself (Rom. 8:26-27, 34; Heb. 7:25). The biblical knowledge displayed by the old woman would put to shame that of most modern Christians, whether they be true believers or only professing.

God is perhaps the fourth major character in the story. It is His sea, which Nan wonders why He made, and the storm too is His. It is He who hears the old woman's prayer, and the answer is His. His answer is much in accordance with the old woman's suggestion: Joss lives, but Rab drowns. That ironic consequences also arrive will surprise no one who knows much about the character of God as portrayed by Zack.

For me this may be the gloomiest of Zack's stories, because the future prospects of her characters seem so dark. Even for Martha we have to work hard to manufacture a gleam of hope concerning the future. But it is a powerful and memorable story.

"At the Stroke of the Hour"

"At the Stroke of the Hour" is the only one of the final six stories which escaped much comment from the critics. One did say of it that "the youth of the old despairing pensioner lives and breathes before you," but most ignore it. Such a fate is very unjust, for it is a very good story, a quiet, serious story, deeply moving. It is another very short story, being only about seven full pages.

Like "The English Girl's Christmas Presents," "At the Stroke of the Hour" is a Christmas Eve story. As the story opens it is Christmas Eve, with deep snow and happy children. But for Sam Crag, Christmas this year is "out of joint." He has been clerk-sexton for fifty happy years, but the new young rector has dispensed with Crag's services.

The rector tells Crag that he has "grown too old for his work," and offers him one of the vacant almshouses along with a small weekly pension

> that he might totter to the grave without fear of starving by the way; but Crag, with the strange ingratitude of the poor, had declared he would have "none o' their charities," and when

remonstrated with had cursed the new rector to his face for "a snip of a currit."

So it had come about that sorrow on this Christmas Eve laid a heavy hand on Crag,

A man comes for the keys to the church, but when he sees Crag's tear splash on to the floor, the man retreats in pity and embarrassment, muttering that he will call "'termarrer.'" Crag goes to the church, extracts his pick and shovel, and walks to his wife's grave.

Forty years she had lain there, her baby at her breast—he had placed them in one coffin. "Her'll sleep quieter so," he said, and she had never stirred, but still slept on.

It had been Christmas Eve that she had died: he remembered that night well—the snow lay on the ground, and the moon shone full. The waits had been singing a Christmas hymn, and she had told him to open wide the window that she might hear more clearly, for the deafness of death was upon her. He had done so, and the words—

"Peace on earth, and mercy mild,
God and sinners reconciled,"

floated in through the falling snow, and she, hearing them, smiled and passed out to meet Him in whose praise they sang.

Crag begins to dig a grave beside that of his wife. Loony Jack, the village idiot—some claimed he "had the power of scenting death afar off"—watches Crag and burst into a wild, mocking laugh. Crag ignores him, finishes his digging, and returns to the church building. At the altar he remembers the circumstances of his wedding long ago.

It was at those same altar-steps that he, one morning in May, had knelt to be married; and now the memory of that day came back to him again. Once more he saw himself rise at dawn, and steal hand in hand with her, who so soon was to be his bride, across the quiet fields, where the blue mist hung sleepily. There, with none but the sky to see them, they had made a daisy chain. His part had been to kiss the daisies, hers to weave the flowers. The chain woven, she hung it around his hat, for a lad must needs look his best upon his wedding morning. Then they had stolen home, to meet again before the altar of the old church and swear to love and cherish each other till Death did them part. And Death had parted them; but now, he said to himself, Death should bring them together again. The clock in the tower gave a great whirring scream, preparatory to striking the hour.

"I'll do it on the stroke o' the hour," muttered the old man—"on the stroke o' the hour."

He prepares to hang himself, still envisioning his wife.

Then there came to him the knowledge that between the death that she he loved had died, and that which he would bring upon himself, there was a great gulf fixed. Thinking of it, he fell upon his knees. "Oh, God," he sobbed, "is the difference so mortal great, so mortal great?"

From out of the gloom of the church a voice answered, "Blessed are the dead that die in the Lord."

For one awful moment the man rose to his feet, then swayed, and fell forward on his face. Through the church rang peal after peal of discordant laughter. Loony Jack was playing at funerals; but Crag heeded him not, for he was dead.

Then with a whir the clock tolled twelve, and Christmas Day dawned upon the world.

Thus ends the brief story of seven pages.

Here the irony of Zack is a sweet irony: the man who digs his own grave will indeed fill that grave, but not by his hand in self-murder as he has originally intended. Providence is too kind to allow him to fix suicide's "great gulf" between him and his wife and all the other saints of God. The very idiots cry out in wisdom under that masterful Providence. "'Blessed are the dead that die in the Lord'" is a truth worthy of an angelic visitor, but it is spoken by Loony Jack "playing at funerals."

Crag's intention to commit suicide is stymied by God, and in that task it is very appropriate that God uses the love between Crag and his wife as a tool of warning. Crag dare not fix a gulf between himself and that woman whom he buried forty years ago. "Things hang together," as George Eliot says in *Middlemarch*, and the love of Crag for his wife, combined with the truth of the Scriptures being impressed upon him by the mercy of God, all go together to stay Crag's hand from the despairing but wrong deed he proposes.

But to Sam Crag, God's mercy is even greater. On the stroke of the hour which announces the anniversary of the birth of the Savior God, Crag, saved this night from a great sin purely by the mercy of God, is allowed to "'die in the Lord.'" That is, Crag is removed from his situation of no longer being able to work while existing on a pittance, and will be allowed to go to be with his wife. His body will rest in the grave he dug for himself on earth, but there will be, after forty long years, no more separation between Crag and the wife he remembers with so moving a tenderness.

At the risk of repetition, we should note that Zack sees the importance of each individual regardless of class. This is instinctive with her. It comes from deep within her. It must be something that somehow she began to learn from childhood on. Even when very young those somber eyes must have been drinking in the life around her, of her Devonshire neighbors high and low. She noticed things. One of the things she must have noticed, from early on, was that poor people were people, just as those of her own class were people. It is not a truth she has to strain to understand.

Moreover, the culture around her was Christian—perhaps more deeply Christian than we are likely to appreciate at first. Yes, no doubt it was a deeply flawed culture. But Christian ways of thinking had seeped into the life of the people to a remarkable extent—our culture could use some of that, and we won't whine if it is somewhat flawed; we'll take what we can get and be glad of it!—and Christian ways of thinking had seeped into Zack as well.

"Travelling Joe"

This is the fifth longest story in the book, checking in at about 16 pages. "Travelling Joe" was highly thought of by many reviewers. One thought it the best of her stories ("cannot be read unmoved by anybody"), while another echoed that comment very closely, citing especially "Travelling Joe" as among "pages of exquisite tenderness and beauty, pages that no one could read unmoved."

It is difficult to believe that many stories better than "Travelling Joe" have been written in the history of the earth. If I had only one story to place before a reader I was trying to persuade to take a chance on Zack, I would have to go with "Travelling Joe."

The story opens with old Zam Tapp peeling potatoes in his cottage; "lying in a truckle-bed was his grandson Travelling Joe, a boy of about nine years old, small, wizen, and partly paralysed."

> To the boy lying there, his heart full of the spirit of adventure, and his life bounded by the truckle-bed and the four walls of the small kitchen, the thought of heaven was of piercing interest; it haunted his dreams sleeping and waking, it was his New America, the land which he would one day explore. To him it never ceased to be a matter of regret that the Crystal Sea lay in front of the throne of God; he would have wished it might have been in what he called the "*dimmet* [Dusky, dim, full of shadows—Zack] part o' 'eaven"; a far border-land unknown to the angels, and where even the eye of God fell seldom.

Zam was probably christened Sam, but his name would have been pronounced Zam in the Devon dialect. We will continue to refer to him as Zam in our discussion. Zam reminisces about the death of his wife, and her skill at boiling potatoes ("'tetties'").

> "I reckon hur hand will ba moast out o'biling tetties by tha time I jines hur; but law, I doant complain, moast like tez zweet stuff they lives on up ther: I niver cud stomach zich stuff mezulf; but bless 'ee, glory hez tu be paid for the same ez tha rest."

The two discuss the nature of God.

> "The Laurd ba turribul mindful o' poor folk," the boy said, questioningly.
> "Ay, ay, lad," the old man answered, "ther ba a deal o' tha wuman about tha Almighty. Ha wull pramise 'ee an ill tarn if yer doan't mend; but Ha ba zlow tu lay it on—zlow tu lay it on."

Zam recounts the death of his wife, and her deathbed promise.

> "'I'll take it aisy, vather,' her zed, 'and the Laurd wull do the
> rast.' 'Eh! eh! moather,' I zed, 'Ha woan't forzake 'ee. Ha's bin
> a pore man Hiszulf, an' knaws what tiz not tu ba larned.' Hur
> smiled, but I zaw tha tears in hur eyes. 'I shall miss yer hand,
> vather,' hur zed, 'tha valley o' tha shader ba turribul dark.' 'The
> Laurd wull walk wi' 'ee, moather,' I zed, 'Hiz hand ba more
> restful than mine.' 'Eh, but vust along,' hur murmured, 'vust
> 'long'; then hur claused hur eyes and died quietvul. Hur wez
> mortal much a duman, poor zoul. Conzarvitive to tha end—
> conzarvitive to tha end."

Later Joe worries what might happen in the dimmet parts of heaven
when God's attention is elsewhere, but worse is his fear that men and
beasts alike will be too subdued in spirit in heaven. Will the lions that
stand before the throne of God ever roar? Zam begins by doubting that
they will, but when he sees the boy's disappointment, he adds

> "who can tull what the talking o' zich critters as thic wull be
> like—fearsome, no doubt."
>
> "And, grandfer," Joe exclaimed, with rising colour, "if lame
> Tom wez ther wi' hiz crutch now, and jest stepped on tha
> taw o' wan o' they baistesses, then ha wid talk mortal spiritty,
> grandfer, widn't ha?"
>
> "Eh, for zure, for zure, mortal spiritty, I'll be bound," Zam
> answered.
>
> The flush of excitement died out from the boy's face. "Moast
> like 'twull niver happen," he said, in a sorrowful voice; "up tu
> 'eaven things ba painful riglar."

Zam tenderly carries the boy in his arms, and at request speaks of
Joe's father Jim. He had been a handsome, good-hearted man, but wild,
and longing to travel the world. About half a year after his marriage to
Joe's mother, he had sailed for America; the ship had been lost with all
hands. His widow never forgave him. Joe's birth did not comfort her
for her husband's loss. She loved only Jim, and when he died, "'hur wi'
all hur pride wez fo'ced tu valler.'" Travelling Joe says his father was
"'mortal understandabul,'" with which Zam clearly agrees, but to which
Zam also adds, "'But not tu women-folk.'" Zam says to himself that Joe

has his father's spirit but that the Lord has arranged that Joe break no woman's heart with wandering.

About a week later Joe's uncle Ben Tapp arrives at the cottage. He has spent many years in America. Zam is absent. Ben Tapp comments on the oddity that Joe should be called Travelling Joe, saying the boy doesn't look very able to cover much ground. Joe explains that things will be different in heaven, that the only difference between Joe and other folk there will be that Joe is more rested.

> "'Dear Laurd,' I shall zay, 'I knaws what rasting ba like, and now I wid dearly like tu ba doing.'
>
> Just as Ben Tapp would have tortured any helpless animal that fell into his power, so now, as he looked down on the boy's eager, pathetic face, a desire came into his heart to crush out its happiness.
>
> "Thar ain't no such place as 'eaven, Joe," he said, leaning forward and placing his great hand on the child's cripple form; "'tis all darned rot—bunkum, as us says out in the States. And as for the Almighty that yer talk so slick about, tha bally old 'oss has kicked his last kick. Natur hez played low down on yer, Joe, and tied yer up to yar darned bed; but when Death gits hould of yer, ha wull tie yer a tarnation sight tighter, yer can bet yer bottom dollar on thet, Joker;" and the man burst into a laugh of coarse enjoyment.

From that moment a change came over Joe, he began to pine away, and the villagers said he was "'marked for death.'" Days pass. Martha Snykes drops by with a home remedy suggestion for him, and leaves. We are ready now for the end of the story. Joe asks his grandfather to carry him a bit, asking

> "tull me what the wordel ba like out ther,—ba it mortal wide?"
>
> "Ay, ay, lad," Zam answered, raising the dying child in his arms, "wide and lonezome, wide and lonezome."
>
> "But windervull full o' ditches," Joe said; "do 'ee jump they ditches, grandfer, when yer gaws tu and fraw tu wark?"
>
> "Naw, lad, I ba getting owld," Zam answered, "I moastly walks 'longzide."
>
> There was silence for a moment, and then Joe spoke. "Grandfer," he said, "do 'ee reckon thet they knaws more about 'eaven auver tu Merikey than they does yhere?"

"'Tiz tha tother zide o' tha wordel," the old man answered; "maybe they zees clearer ther."

"I ba mortal wangery [Tired—Zack], grandfer," Travelling Joe answered, sighing; "I reckon I cud zlape."

Zam laid the dying boy back in the old truckle-bed. "Shall I tull 'ee zommat from the Buk, lad?" he asked.

The child shivered. "Naw, grandfer," he answered, "I wid liefer bide quiet." He sank into a broken slumber, suddenly to awake with a start.

"'Tiz turribul dimmet," he exclaimed; "but," and his face brightened, "I zees things like ditches:" so saying, he died.

Thus ends the story of Travelling Joe.

I have quoted extensively from this remarkable story, but the temptation is simply to reprint the entire story and say here it is, read it for yourself. But even that might not solve all the difficulties for the reader, for the heavy dialect presents problems. One of the reviewers seems to have missed the point of the story. A person to whom I gave the story also misunderstood what had happened, and others have seemed unsure, and have suggested that the story (and Zack's works in general) would benefit from translating—something that plainly would not work. And when I read the book *Life Is Life* for the second time, I did not remember the story "Travelling Joe." Yet the second time through I was much shaken by the greatness of the story. Somehow, I had managed, the first time through, to read one of the finest stories in world literature without it making an impression on me. Perhaps my own problem that first time through was native stupidity, or careless reading, but the dialect really is heavy, and that was my first Zack book, so it was quite new to me. Despite the fact that Zack has used dialect off and on throughout the book, "Travelling Joe" marks the spot where it becomes very heavy. As one reads more and more of Zack, one begins more easily to understand what is being said. And while rereading is a necessity for understanding and appreciating any good writer, it may be especially necessary in Zack's case. The experience I had with "Travelling Joe" was not unique, though it was the most spectacular. Others of her stories have a way of hitting one on a second or third reading.

One of the reviewers noted that Zack had the gift of poignancy. That gift is surely prominent in this story. Another way in which the story is typically Zackian is that the pathos and the humor frequently come at the same time. One laughs and cries simultaneously. Also typical of Zack is the identification of ditches with Joe's heart's desire. Why ditches? Because Joe has spent his entire life being unable to walk and run. He wants ditches so that he can leap them! Zack shows us how something that may seem commonplace and even dull to most of us, can in fact be an attribute of heaven. It was not castles or streets of gold or gates made of pearl that Joe yearned for, but just ordinary ditches. We may find ourselves wondering if Joe and Zack are correct, and ditches are more wonderful than we had previously realized.

The story is unabashedly supernatural. There is nothing in the story to hint that Joe's dying vision of ditches is self-deception, or is in any way untrue. In fact, it seems possible that Zack has made a special point of showing that Joe's vision is exactly true, because not only have his earlier hopes of heaven's existence been dashed by Ben Tapp, but his grandfather has unconsciously reinforced Ben Tapp's statement by agreeing that people in America might see clearer than those in England. No, what Joe sees is not a self-deceiving hallucination; Joe's vision is not something self-induced by religious enthusiasm, but something surprising and unexpected to a boy dying for lack of hope. Joe is looking on the outskirts of paradise, and honestly reports what he sees there. That Joe is allowed to see ditches in a dimmet part of heaven is a measure of the titanic and very personal generosity of God.

As we have seen, Zack's characters inhabit a Christian culture. Zam Tapp is a good example. He is not a churchgoer and doesn't "'howld wi' zich things,'" and said "'thet ha didn't want no praicher to teach him tha way tu 'eaven; zalvation wez a kooris thing, and, like cream, let it alone and twid come to 'ee: meddle and praying widn't fetch it.'" These are some truly astonishing opinions for a man who seems very much to believe in the Christian afterlife. And in one of the quotes above we noted Zam's opinion that there is a great deal of the woman about the Almighty, in that He will promise one an ill turn but that He is slow to lay it on.

In discussing all this we have come to some very deep waters indeed. Is Zam a heretic heading for eternal death, or a Christian with some odd notions? It seems to me that only God can give us a definite answer.

The case may not be as clear cut as we might think. To try to answer at length would take us far afield. These questions should drive us to our Bibles to try to find out what the truth is.

In partial defense of Zam, we know that God is longsuffering. He does bring covenantal judgment, but He certainly does sometimes seem "'zlow tu lay it on—zlow tu lay it on.'" A passage like Hosea 11:8-9 reminds us how reluctant God is to lay it on. If He were in a hurry to lay it on, the American nation as a whole and probably most of the American church would have been destroyed decades ago.

The Bible speaks of God as masculine throughout. Still, the masculine God is the one who came up with the idea of woman, and the one who created woman—and females are astonishing creatures in many ways different from men. It is difficult to fathom how the masculine God even came up with the idea for woman. Again, these are deep waters.

Some of Zam's ideas may cause him to pay a price. His contempt for the church, for praying, and so on, may limit his ability to serve God and his grandson Joe. We can hope that the price to pay will not be eternal, but we will have to leave God to decide. Zam, of course, is a fictional character. But what of Gwendoline Keats herself? Did she have ideas about God that were wrongheaded? If she did, she too would have a price to pay. Again, we will leave God to decide how great that price should have been and was.

Where Zack herself stood on these issues is not easy to know for sure. I suspect she sympathized with Zam. That Zack has Zam repeat "'zlow tu lay it on'" seems to me one indication that Zam speaks for her. Repetition at key moments is a staple of Zack's style throughout her works. It seems an echo of the Bible's way of stressing something by repetition. For example, Christ begins sentences with the phrase "'Woe to you'" about eight times in a stretch of just seventeen verses in Matthew 23:13-29.

Others of Zam's ideas seem orthodox and even insightful. The Lord won't forsake his wife, he told her as she was dying; He will walk hand in hand with her through the valley of the shadow of death. Earlier, he tells Joe that Joe's grandmother will not break her wing, because "'there's nought promiscuous in 'eaven.'" God does not show us good things only in order to pull them away from us. The principle holds whether one talks about having wings like an angel, or something else. Whatever the wonders of heaven will be, they will work out to the blessing of God's people.

Typical of Zack is her recognition that evil exists in some people in a very large degree. Ben Tapp is not misguided, nor did he suffer a bad childhood which caused him to go wrong. He does evil because he is in a grumpy mood, but he also seems evil at the core. Ben Tapp's situation reminds us of the biblical injunctions against leading children astray (Matt. 18:6; Mk. 9:42). There are degrees of evil, of course. Ben Tapp does not strike or kill or sexually molest Joe. We will leave his final destiny to God to decide. But we can take warning from him that evil is very real. How easily we become bullies, and how easily we kill even children! The U.S. nation as a whole has spent many years killing children, and even Christians mostly shrug. The "collateral damage" from our bombs and drone strikes kills lots of children. At home we have killed 57,000,000 unborn children in a generation. We don't seem to be afraid to kill even children. We will find out the consequences when we stand before God.

Zack's presentation of Ben Tapp is brief but powerful. Zack could portray good but flawed men, or men evil but still human and individual. One example of the second type is Atter in "Life Is Life." He is a rapist and murderer, and blinds his own son as the unintentional result of an intentional act of bullying, but he is a real person. We even see gleams of potential in the man when he is deeply moved to hear his son call him "Father." Similarly, Zack vividly portrays Ben Tapp, who delights in crushing out the hope in the breast of a child. The man's few lines are spoken with a memorable forcefulness and vigor; if we met him among real people, in a few sentences we would know him. "'And as for the Almighty that yer talk so slick about, tha bally old 'oss has kicked his last kick.'" His language is colorful and clever.

It is fascinating, though, that Ben Tapp's cruelty seems in some sense to further the excellent plans of God. We are reminded that "God causes all things to work together for good to whose who love God" (Rom. 8:28). Ben Tapp has his innings, and kills the hope in Joe's heart, and indeed ends his will to live, ultimately driving him to the grave.

But there is something far more ultimate than Ben Tapp's evil heart. God is far more ultimate: Joe reaches the dimmet parts of heaven, and the ditches his adventurous heart longs for. Indeed, we can argue that, ironically (another sweet irony), Ben Tapp's cruelty has the effect of bringing Joe to great joy sooner than he otherwise would have reached it. Ben Tapp's evil heart has worked together with God's generous purpose to bring great good to Joe. We are reminded how serenely God controls world history. Joseph told his erring brothers, "'And as for you, you meant evil against me, but God meant it for good in order to bring about this present result, to preserve many people alive'" (Gen. 50:20; compare 45:5). Ben Tapp meant his cruelty for evil, but God turned his action to good use—for another Joseph, strangely!

"Rab Vinch's Wife"

"Rab Vinch's Wife" was very favorably mentioned by at least six critics. One thought it "the finest thing she has done," quoted it at great length (to almost half the space of his review), and ended by saying "This mixture of realism based on close observation with the symbol-making imagination is very like the quality that we call genius."[18]

At 16 plus pages "Rab Vinch's Wife" is slightly longer than "Travelling Joe," and is thus the fourth longest story in the book.

The story opens with a view of a cottage in Devonshire. The quiet is broken by Tummas Wulkie bringing in the exciting news that lame Tom has been arraigned or convicted on a charge of murder. The Squire at great expense has brought a doctor down from London to show that lame Tom is not quite right in his head, "'but tha jidge wez vor hanging, jidges baing paid vor zich, zo hanging it's ta ba.'" But the villagers believe others have been in on the crime.

Susan Finch says the law won't hang an innocent man. Wulkie says he saw the corpse three hours before the police, and that it was ringed

---

[18]Unknown reviewer, "The Academy, "'Zack,'" June 25, 1898, p. 689.

with footsteps that were not lame Tom's. However, the rain had washed the evidence away before the police could see it. Wulkie had refused to testify, telling his wife, "'tha law ba a catchy thing, an' like tother folk's turnips, best not meddled with.'" Wulkie suspects Josh Tuckitt of being involved, for he sailed for America the day after the murder. But Rab says Tuckitt is innocent, for Tuckitt was with him that night. Susan passionately rebukes Wulkie for his interfering comments which have elicited the information that Rab was with Tuckitt. Wulkie responds, "'a long tongue an' a short understandin' moast times run in couples; but ther wuman wez a kind o' extry thought o' tha Almighty's, an' uz all knaw thet tiz tha way o' zich things to cost a deal more than they ba worth.'" He leaves.

> The echo of the man's retreating footsteps died away, and the kettle seemed to hiss more loudly in the silence that fell upon the little kitchen. At last Rab spoke.
>
> "Hanging ba a mortal stuffy death," he said, hoarsely—"a mortal stuffy death."
>
> She knelt down beside him. "Twez an accident," she whispered; "yer ba thet strong 'ee doant alwiz knaw."
>
> "Yer ba a riglar dumman wi' yer haccidents, haccidents," he interrupted, with fierce contempt; "ain't I towld 'ee a skaur o' times thet 'twezn't no haccident."

Rab tells her that neither lame Tom nor Josh Tuckitt was involved. Susan tells Rab that she is with child, to which he responds tenderly. But a few seconds later she tells Rab that "'things dursn't bide ez they ba,'" angering him greatly. He suspects her of condemning him, and fiercely asks of what she is thinking.

> "I wez ony reckoning thet twezn't for nought thet our Lord coomed inter tha wordel feeble in body; twezn't for nought thet Ha let Simon o' Cyrene carry tha cross up tha steep hill to Golgotha; it bain't tha strong who's tu lane on tha wake."

She tells Rab, "'I widn't 'ave 'ee act contrary to tha best thet ba in 'ee,'" and says that lame Tom was as terrified as "'a poor dumb critter caught in wan o' yer snares.'" Rab is moved by this.

into his rugged passionate face there came a certain expression of nobleness. "Mayba I wull," he began; but she, following a train of thoughts of her own, interrupted him.

"Twid ba the zame ez if yer wez to let a chile die for 'ee," she said, in a slow, dreamy voice, speaking as one who had seen a vision.

He thrust her from him and rose to his feet: "Then I wull gi' mezulf up ta-marrer," he said; "but ez for 'ee," he added, with concentrated bitterness, "yer ba no wife o' mine from this hour," and he turned from her and climbed the rickety stairs that led to their bedroom.

Lying in bed beside his wife, he remembers the long ago day when he had promised to marry his wife, when she was only a little girl of six, in order to comfort her. "Then a sudden rush of tenderness came to him, and he put out his hand and touched her; but she had fallen asleep." At dawn Rab rises, bitterness and tenderness towards his wife still mixed.

"Mayba I widn't gaw for tu do lame Tom no harm," he said, "if her wezn't thet turribel meddlezome; tain't dying I ba a-feared of—I reckon I can die tha zame ez ony tother man; but I doan't want tu ba vustled [Fussed—Zack] inter it; but hurs a riglar wumman all-over, pushing 'ee t'wards 'Eaven wi' hur 'eart an' pulling 'ee back wi' hur tongue. But ther, tain't no good talking; mayba hur'll larn when 'tis too late."

He feeds his ferrets, tenderly handles his guns, ties the dog up, and leaves the cottage. "'I didn't reckon her wid zlape like thic," he said; "but ther, women be alwiz contrary.'" But on the way his wife catches up to him, as he is setting a snare for a hare. He assumes indifference, speaking to her of his hunting.

"Eh," he continued, drawing a deep breath, "but hares ba vantysheeny [Showy, handsome—Zack] baistesses; skaurs o' times I've ruckeed [Stooped down low—Zack] down behind a bit o' vuzz wi' tha moon a-glinting a-tap o' me and cock-leert [Dawn—Zack] jest on tha creep an' iverything thet quiet 'ee cud moast a-yhear tha dew a-valling; eh, an' I've 'ad tha gun a-zide o' me an' cudn't vire cuz they baistesses wez thic vantysheeny."

But she only saw that an animal caught in such a snare would be hung.

"Come away, Rab," she cried; "come away."

He looked down at the snare meditatively.

"Zome o' 'em," he said, half to himself, "makes a to-do, but moast die mortal quiet."

"O Rab! come away," she repeated in a voice of agony; "come away."

"Ba 'ee afraid I shull ba late for tha hanging?"

He rushes off, and later that day Susan learns that he had surrendered himself to the police. She is refused permission to see him. On her way home, "she heard a strange cry: the hare had been caught in the wire. Covering her ears with her hands she fled away, yet ever and ever the cry followed her."

At Rab's trial he gives no motive for his action, but states that the death was not accidental. "'Twezn't no haccident," he repeated; "I did it o' puppuss.'" The judge takes the black cap in hand, and asks Rab if there is any reason why he should not be sentenced to death.

Rab is silent, but Susan Finch breaks the silence. She says it may be against the law for her to testify for her husband, but the higher law of Nature requires her to speak, since she knows her husband to be innocent. She says that Rab is tempestuous at times, but his heart is "'tenderzome ez a chil's.'" As proof she points out that Rab had turned himself in rather than have lame Tom suffer unjustly.

"An' if yer ax me why ha hezn't stud up vrom tha vust an' zed it twez an haccident, then I tull 'ee it was becase I wez alwiz a-worritting o' him thet kept him to zilence. I wez alwiz a-axing questions, an' ha doan't like it, an' ha wants tu larn me. I've done a power o' thinkin' zince thickey marning Rab gi'ed hiszulf up, an' I've reckoned it all out. I wez too mortal anxious tu show him tha way, an' Rab ain't no wumman tu ba showed things. Ha likes tu do hiz right hiz own way—he doan't want no wan tu larn him; an' I wez alwiz a-zaying, yer dursn't do thic an' yer must do thet, zo ha ba jest a-larning o' me; but, O Rab!" she ended, in a voice of passionate entreaty, turning to him, "I've larned, I've larned; only tull 'em—*tull* 'em."

When the woman ceased speaking a silence fell upon the court, and the eyes of all there turned to the prisoner. Rab's harsh obstinate face had grown grey beneath the tanned skin; his lips, pressed one on the other with the grip of a vice, looked as if no power could ever force them to unclose: then his eyes met those of his wife, and with a convulsive effort he spoke. "'Twez done temperzome," he exclaimed, brokenly—"powerful temperzome; ha said thic thet wez baisteous o' hur," and Rab pointed with his hand in the direction of his wife. "Mayba," he continued, huskily, "if yer cud find Josh Tuckitt, ha cud make things look a bit better for me."

There the story ends.

It is a subtle story, true in its portrayal of human nature, and very moving. Rab and Susan Finch have a strong love for one another, but they still manage to get crosswise with each other. Both, it seems, are at fault. There's a shocker when we're dealing with human beings!

Susan is of course quite correct that religious truth and justice require that Rab step forth and declare the fact that lame Tom is innocent, and that the nameless man became a corpse by the hand of Rab. But she is also in the wrong because she should have known her husband better, and should have trusted him. Her nagging infuriates Rab. To him, Susan is a regular woman, pushing him toward heaven with her heart and yet pulling him back with her tongue. Susan's words about letting a child die for him are the last straw for the proud Rab.

Rab is also partly at fault. A word or two of explanation to his wife might have let her know his position and her own wrongheadedness, but he won't lower himself to explain. He prefers to teach her a lesson the hard way. So obstinate is he that when she has humbled herself before him at the trial, it seems for a moment that he is almost unable or unwilling to acknowledge the truth of his wife's words. Finally, with "a convulsive effort," he does manage to speak and to confirm the truth of her comments. It seems that, absent his wife's speech, he was quite ready to go to his death unjustly accused of murder, rather than let Susan's nagging cause him to speak the truth!

He is a man of pride—some of it of the good sort of pride, and some apparently the reverse. He is by no means a one-dimensional character. The dignity of his nature and behavior are very great. He loves his wife tenderly, even though he becomes so angry with her as to say she is no longer his wife. The news that lame Tom is wakesome touches his heart. If Susan had trusted him as she ought she might have known he would not let the innocent Tom die in his place. And so sensitive is Rab that sometimes he has been unable to fire his gun at hares because their beauty has struck him so mightily. He is a man of mixed parts, like all of us, but there is much that is impressive in his character. It is no surprise, though it may be ironic, that this tenderhearted but tempestuous man had been enticed into striking a man in order to defend the name of his wife.

Susan Finch's eleventh hour speech at the trial is believable and touching. Susan Finch is one of Zack's characters, of many such, who learns a hard truth, faces that truth squarely, and changes her ways as a result. Susan sees her error and, with humility, apologizes for it—not grudgingly, but with "passionate entreaty" she tells Rab that she has learned her lesson.

The future for these two people looks promising. Yes, Rab will probably have to serve a brief time in prison. But it will probably not be long. When Josh Tuckitt is brought back to England to testify, he will tell the truth of the incident which caused the nameless man's death. This will show that the man brought his own death upon himself. When you say something "'baisteous'" about a man's wife, you can expect consequences. Rab no doubt struck the man, but this is not exactly the same as intentionally trying to kill someone. My guess is that even in a fully biblical justice system, such a blow causing death would not be considered intentional murder. We can expect the court, apprised of all the facts, to be inclined toward mercy for Rab. So we can hope that within a few months, or perhaps at the outside within a few years, the couple will be reunited. They will raise their child together. "A cord of three strands is not quickly torn apart" (Eccl. 4:12). We are very hopeful that this family will live together well. The unnamed man's death at the hands of Rab will not be shrugged off easily, nor should it be. Still, having seen both the strengths and the weaknesses of Rab and Susan Finch, we can have a realistic hope that their marriage will endure and they will continue to learn to love one another, and their child, with growing practical wisdom.

Zack's use of symbolism, in the case of the snared hare, is straightforward. She is not trying to hide her meaning, but to make it accessible to the reader, and this she does impressively, as the reviewer quoted above noticed.

"Widder Vlint"

"Widder Vlint" was another story highly praised by at least half a dozen critics. One devoted almost half his review to quoting from it, and says that its "art rises to such a degree of perfection that it almost ceases to be art."[19]

This story marks the introduction of the character Zack as opposed to the author Zack. The narrator is no longer, as in all the other stories of the book, the omniscient author, but instead is the Devonshire villager Zack. However, Zack is not named in this story, and we only know it is him because the later book *Tales of Dunstable Weir* is entirely written by the character Zack. In that book he will turn out to be a character of considerable interest in his own right, but here in this story he is basically only a narrator, though even here his personality begins to show through.

This 11-page story is thus the only one of the book in which the dialect is total. Zack has waited until the next to the last story of the book to give us total dialect, no doubt a wise tactical move. She has given her readers time to get as used to the dialect as possible before giving them "Widder Vlint." One critic complained of the book as a whole that the dialect "makes many of their pages look as though written in a foreign tongue."[20] If the reader has the patience to struggle through the complete dialect of "Widder Vlint," he will discover a very good story.

"Widder Vlint" was the first published story of Gwendoline Keats/Zack. As noted earlier, it appeared in the November 1896 issue of "Blackwood's Magazine." She was 31 years old on Oct. 4, 1896. All honor to Mr. Blackwood for opening the pages of his magazine to a story totally in dialect—and that from an author completely unknown at the time.

---

[19]Unknown reviewer, "Literature," "Life is Life," July 30, 1898, p. 85.

[20]Unknown reviewer, "The Spectator," "A NEW STORYTELLER.," July 9, 1898.

Zack the character tells us that the Widder Vlint (the Widow Flint) is disrespected in the village because she has

> borned dree [three—C. W.] drunkards, tho' the naybours wez kind o' zorry vor hur now an' agin; an' when hur zon Josh wez drawed vrom hiz hoss an' brauk hiz neck, they jest zed that "wan o' the tu wez drunk," an' left folk to judge atween the man an' the mare.

Attracted by the enticing smell of fried bacon, Zack drops in to see the widow.

> I wez a kind o' relation o' Widder Vlint's, tho' I didn't make much o' it 'zept at mait [meat—C. W.] times an' zich, cuz o' hur baing so mortal disrespactit. It zeemed to me hur didn't take anuff count o' the 'pinion o' the vullage, hur wez thic turrible zet on her childer, women not 'aving no discarnment in zich things.

The Widder Vlint speaks of her children, though Zack the narrator tells us he had no special interest in the subject. She tries to find something good to say about each of her children, the first three of whom are dead. She struggles to find something good to say about Thomas, and finally mentions that he had a wonderful head of hair.

> "Pore lad! ha wez alwez a good lad to me; ha braut me the vurst shillun that iver ha arned, an' thin ha kinder tuk it back. Ha aimed high, did Tummas, tho' maybe ha didn't alwez raitch."

One can picture the "'good lad'" generously bringing his mother the first shilling he ever earned, then gently wheedling it back from her! One doesn't know whether to laugh or cry, or to do both.

Of Josh she remembers his enticing smile, and she recounts how she sat beside his dead body through the night of his death.

> "An' I kind o' thought ez how ha wez ez a little lad, I knawed ha hadn't alwez acted zactly vor the best zince he had grawed to be a man. The moon riz an' staled in upon him an' ha zmiled back at hur, an' twez a turrible pacevul zmile thic ha guved hur. An' thin ther coomed to me they words vrom the Buk, 'Gaw in pace, vor thy zins be vorguved to 'ee.' An' I vell a-sobbing,

quiet-like, cuz I didn't want to distarb him, pore lamb, but ha jest zmiled on. The pace o' the Laurd ain't like our pace, it ain't to be brauk, it ain't to be brauk."

Hur stapped short an' wan banging girt tear fell strat in the pan. I thort twez a mortal pity to spile good bacon zo, speshul ez Josh wez the biggest rapscallion thet ever walked; but I cudn't help baing a bit zorry vor the pore owld dumman, cuz 'tis the way wi' women to git turrible vond o' trash.

Jesse was the next to die. She called him "'hur little lad,'" though he was six feet tall and weighed close to fourteen stone (196 pounds). The Widder Vlint has only her son Dave left now, but he is fine upstanding lad; she says she has a deal to be thankful for.

Dave comes in from work just then, very thirsty with a thirst the tea doesn't fully answer. After tea, as they all sit close to the fire, Dave reminds his mother of the night Jesse, mad with drink, shot himself:

"an' I tooked pore Jesse's hand an' layed it atween yers an' mine, an' zwore thet I wid niver touch strong drink, an' if I had to die vor it I wid die game? Moather, moather," he ended up kind o' sharp like, "I reckon the drink 'ull have me yet."

The Widder Vlint eventually answers him

"Dave," hur zed, "do 'ee mind on the pore widdy wuman in the Buk, an' how she guved her mite to the Laurd, an' tho' ther wez urch [Rich—Zack] volks alongside o' hur ez guved gorgeus gufts, yit the Laurd Ha valleyed the mite moast. An' zo I reckon 'tiz wi' uz—'tain't wat uz does, but wat uz tries to do, that the Laurd vallys, an' thin Ha kind o' makes up the rast Hizsulf." But Dave ha ony gripped howldt o' the pore dumman more tight like. "Moather, moather," ha zed, "spose I shudn't die game?"

The Widder Vlint recounts how she became increasingly "'disrespactit'" as her sons died as drunkards one by one. Her comments on how the village shunned the funeral when Jesse died are heart-breakingly sad. When Dave asks if his mother surely would not have him die as a drunkard, we read,

"Dave," hur zed, "didn't I borne 'ee all, didn't 'ee all lay upon my brast, an' ain't 'ee all my childer, an' why shud wan gaw vor to make hiszulf higher than tothers?"

Dave ha drapped hiz head down on hur knay, an' the kitchen wez zilencevul.

At last ha lifted up hiz vace, an' twez a windervul pitying luk ha gived her. "Moather," ha zed, "I reckon uz zons 'ave brought 'ee a power o' zarrar [Sorrow—Zack]."

But hur answered kind o' random like. "Dave," hur zed, "God vorgive me an' make 'ee do wat iz vitty [right to do—C. W.]."

The story jumps to the next winter; the Widder Vlint becomes very ill. Zack and Dave are beside her. She asks first for a chapter from the Bible, but it is downstairs, and she has little time to spare, so she asks Dave to say a prayer instead.

"I ony knaws 'Our Vather' an' the Blessin', moather," he answered.

"Then I reckon 'tiz the Blessin' I wull 'ave," she zed; "'tiz a bootivul zaying, 'Vor wat us 'ave recaved'—zay on, lad."

"The Laurd make uz truly thankvul," Dave ended.

"An' uz 'ave ad' a deal to be thankvul vor, a deal," hur zed.

But Dave ha jest zat ther like a stone an' didn't zay naught.

"Zay, lad, zay," hur axed, kind o' painvul.

Thin ha took hur hands, mazing owld an' knotted hands they wez, ha tooked 'em in hiz an' ha kneeled azide the bed an' put his vace down agin hur heart.

"Moather, moather," he zed, "God guved me thee."

Hur only spoke wance after thic. "Lay me zide o' Jesse," hur zed; "I reckon the little lad 'ull be warmer along o' hiz moather."

There the story ends abruptly but suitably, as is typical with the author Zack.

God, for reasons of His own, has dealt the Widder Vlint a difficult hand to play. As we will learn in the next story, her husband and her husband's father were also drunkards. They died of drink. Now three of her sons have died as drunkards. She has become increasing disrespected in the village as a result. Now, in the last days of her life, she faces the knowledge that her last remaining son may also die a drunkard.

When Dave contemplates the drunkard's death which may await him, his mother tries to comfort him by saying that he need not make himself higher than the rest of the family. We can guess that she does not want seriously to draw Dave down to the level of his brothers, father, and grandfather. Rather, she wants to give him some species of consolation to fall back on in case he does fall. She ends by asking with humility that God forgive her, and that He make Dave do what is right.

Her humility before God, and her gratitude to Him, hold up as the brave woman lies on her deathbed. She and Dave combine to say the Blessing, or part of it, "For what we have received the Lord make us truly thankful." The words may seem at first glance inappropriate for a deathbed, but the fact is that they are exactly appropriate, for the Widder Vlint acknowledges ungrudgingly that they have a deal for which to be thankful. Dave's four words, "'God guved me thee,'" one of Zack the author's most haunting phrases, echo his mother's gratitude. Those four words form part of this book's dedication to Zack, for I believe God gave her to me, just as God gave Dave his mother.

"Dave"

The final story of the book, "Dave," follows "Widder Vlint" in time. The 11-page story attracted favorable attention from at least four reviewers. One cited it, with three others of the stories, for having "the life-stuff out of which great novels are created."

It is a moving story, again among the best Zack ever wrote.

The action begins in the White Lion Inn, with two men talking about Dave—the same Dave we just read about in "Widder Vlint." The older man says Josh Tuckett will never allow his daughter Phoebe to marry Dave, who is a drunkard.

> "Dave ain't no drunkard; he takes his glass and goes out. Dang him, I wish he wor."

The elder man leant forward and caught hold of the button of his companion's coat.

"Answer me this, Tummas Rod," he said, "didn't his father die o' drink?"

"Ay, sure."

"And his grandfather afore him?"

"Ay, certain."

"Bain't his three brothers lying in the churchyard at this very minnit reg'lar soaking the place wi' spirits; the grass niver growed casual over their graves the same as it did over t'other folks'."

"What's that got to do wi' Dave?"

"Why, begore, he'll come to the like sooner or later, mark my words if he don't. He's a drunkard now—at heart. Scores o' times I've reckoned to hear his throat split and crack when the drink dizzles down it."

A heavy flush rose to Rod's face. "And may it; the sooner the better," he said.

Thomas Rod's animosity to Dave appears to rest on Rod's own attraction to Phoebe. The older man leaves as Dave enters. Dave drinks a half-and-half at one gulp, and Rod tries to tempt him to drink more. At first Dave refuses, but when Rod asks him to "'drink me success to something I've set my mind on,'" Dave agrees when he hears it is something particular special, saying, "'may 'ee git wat 'ee want and more.'"

Thomas Rod's toast is "'To the damnation of Dave Vlint, body and soul!'" and he drains his glass and then throws it against the wall. He pretends to have only spoken in fun.

Walking through the woods, Dave comes upon Phoebe. She asks why he has avoided her for three weeks, and he says it is better that he "'bide away.'" She says he does not love her; he says he does; she can't understand him.

"Sweetheart, 'tis the drink I'm afeard of; 'twull have me wan day like did my vather and brothers afore me."

"But I bain't afeard."

"I might be cruel hard on 'ee, lass," he said, pressing her hands tight against his broad chest. "A man can't answer for hissulf when the drink's upon him."

Her dark grey eyes filled with tears. "But I bain't afeard, Dave," she reiterated. "I bain't afeard."

He looked at her with great tenderness. "I dursn't, dear heart; I dursn't," he said, and his voice shook.

"Ther wud ba the times atween whiles," she urged.

Turning from her, he caught hold of a tree-bough and steadied himself. "Lass, lass, don't put me in mind o' 'em."

She shows him that her beauty is still great, and breaks into tears as she accuses him of not even looking.

He let go of the branch of the tree, took her in his arms, and drew her close up against his breast. He put back her head with gentle force, and kissed her mouth and eyes, her throat and bosom. As they stood molten in one mould, there came down the wind the sound of children's laughter: hearing it, the man and woman fell trembling, then apart.

They stood staring at each other like two people guilty of a crime.

"There ba them that might ba born arter us," he said, hoarsely.

She watched the sudden hardening of his mouth. "Must us mind on 'em?" she pleaded—"must us mind on 'em?"

"I cud niver fo'ce no chile o' ours to bear wat I've bin fo'ced to bear," he answered; "twad ba devil's wark—I cudn't do it."

Her face grew white and hopeless. "I can't feel for the childer, I ain't no mother yet," she said, brokenly.

His desire for her is great, but with "an abrupt cry" he leaves her. He wanders long in the woods but at nightfall he returns to his cottage. Inside he finds that someone has put a bottle of spirits on the table, the cork withdrawn; "the air reeled with the smell of it." (No prizes to the reader for guessing whose wicked hand did that; Zack has given us enough to know that it must have been Thomas Rod.)

Clutching at his throat, striving to tear the thirst from it, he advanced—the bottle glistening in the moonlight, looking as if it were alive. He cast an agonised glance round the walls, seeking help from familiar things, and his eyes fell on his gun. A sob of relief broke from him: he took down the gun, loaded it hurriedly, the smell of the spirits dripping on to his lips, he licking it down.

He takes gun and bottle and goes deep into the woods where "no eye but God's could see his shame." He holds the bottle up.

> "So yer have got the best o' me at last," he said,—"yer have got the best o' me at last."
>
> The bottle glistened: he brought it nearer his lips, his thirst pressed for quenching, the thirst that he would slake before he shot himself.
>
> "Yer smiling devil," he burst out, with sudden fierceness, "yer reckon to catch me, do 'ee. No, by hell! yer don't; I'll die wi'out tasting 'ee," and he dashed the bottle into fragments at his feet. A moment later he had flung himself upon the ground, striving to lick up the spirits with his tongue.
>
> "Dog that I ba, dog that I ba," he sobbed. "No better than a dog—no better than a dog."
>
> Sick with shame and horror, he regained his feet: he took a piece of cord from his pocket, made a loop in it, attaching one end to the trigger of the gun. He pressed the cold steel barrel up against his hot beating heart, and placed his foot in the loop. "A dog's death for a dog," he muttered.
>
> The moonlight shone on him, on the gun, and on the broken bottle at his feet: the glistening glass attracted him and he stared at it, fresh thoughts crowding his brain. A tremor ran through him: raising his eyes, he fixed them on the moonlit heavens and grey wind-spun clouds. "Ther ba zommat in me a'zide the dog," he said, slowly. "Ay, begore, I'll live game, I'll zee it droo," and drawing himself together, he turned his face once more on life.

Thus ends this moving story, and the book.

Once again God has set a man a cruel dilemma. Dave has been born into a family with a strong predilection toward alcoholism. He has the same predilection. While he has not yet become a drunkard, the perceptive villager tells us that Dave is a drunkard "'at heart.'" The villager's colorful phrase is that he has "reckoned to hear his throat split and crack when the drink dizzles down it.'"

For Zack, life is a time of testing. We see that in all of *Life Is Life*, in all her books, and in this particular story of course as well. Different men and women are given different trials. What matters is how those trials are faced. Dave is a man of heroic character.

Even before his decision to "'live game,'" Dave has shown us the generosity of his spirit. Loving and desiring Phoebe with great intensity, he will not marry her, not only for her sake but also for the sake of unborn children. His somewhat immodest kissing of Phoebe is broken off when the wind brings the sound of children's laughter down to them. Reminded of the danger to any children born to them, his flagging resolve strengthens.

His heroism does not come easily. He bravely breaks the bottle rather than drink the strong drink, but immediately we are shocked to see Dave throw himself on the ground in an attempt to lick up the disappearing spirits. In shame he almost kills himself. Of course it would take a type of courage to pull the trigger, but he shows a greater courage: he will live game. He turns his face on life, determined to face life with courage.

We are not told whether he will continue to hold to his resolve not to marry Phoebe. My guess is that he will hold to that resolve. His love for her is far beyond romantic love, as delightful as romantic love is. His love for her and for the unborn children is agape love—the type of love that wants what is best for others. He doesn't want Phoebe to experience living with an alcoholic, and he doesn't want to bring children into the world with the same terrible temptation to drink which he has. That he also loves Phoebe with such a strong romantic love of course makes his renunciation of her all the more difficult and heroic. Dave himself is quite aware that his love for Phoebe, in renouncing her, is a greater love than when he pledged himself true to her "'down by the Wishing Well'" some weeks or months before. "'I didn't love 'ee then the zame as I do now by a deal.'" Phoebe can't "'fathom'" such a comment as that.

The beautiful Phoebe is given a different trial. She must be separated from the man she loves. Phoebe speaks one of the most memorable and insightful of Zack's sentences: "'Ther wud ba the times atween whiles.'" She accepts that Dave will be a drunkard and probably mistreat her when the drink is upon him, and yet she is willing to marry him for "'the times atween whiles.'" This simple phrase hangs in the memory. Zack has a gift for arresting phrases or sentences, and these few words spoken by Phoebe are among her most striking.

There is a possibility of course that when Dave turns "his face on life," that he will feel confident enough to marry Phoebe, with the determination not to give in to his temptation to drink. Zack gives us no definite answer as to what Dave's future life will involve. We know only that Dave is determined to live game and see life through.

Thomas Rod's appearance in the story is a brief one, but is filled with evil. Jealousy or envy make him hate and tempt Dave. Dave and Rod were "'thick anuff as boys,'" so that Rod's malice is poured out not just on someone who has forestalled him with Phoebe, but also on a boyhood friend. Thomas Rod raises a toast, and ironically causes Dave to drink also, to Dave's damnation. But the deeper irony is that Rod acts toward what could be his own damnation, while Dave chooses generous love, courage, and life.

"Dave" is one of Zack's finest stories.

Life Is Life is a remarkable book, and attracted considerable attention at its birth. Such attention was well deserved. It is still deserved.

An unnamed reviewer for the weekly journal "The Academy" had this to say:

> What she sees or says, she says and sees with implacable distinctness. . . . Yet her vision of life, though grim and unsparing, is not pitiless. It has the insight that irradiates rather than lays bare for dissection; and it irradiates strange places; hidden tendernesses in gnarled and twisted lives, set hard by time or native obduracy.[21]

W. L. Courtney made an insightful comment. In his review in the "Daily Telegraph," he indicated that force of personality rather than of art was the source of Zack's power.[22] I do not think that is even close to being entirely true. She is an artist. But it is also true that

---

[21]Unknown reviewer, "The Academy, '"Zack.,'" June 25, 1898, p. 689. The ellipsis is mine.

[22]The opinion of W. L. Courtney was given in the "Daily Telegraph," date unknown but no doubt sometime in 1898. I know of his opinion only because it is mentioned in a segment called Book Reviews Reviewed, with a subtitle of "Life Is Life," in "The Academy," July 23, 1898, p. 93.

her personality profoundly shapes her art. This may be true for every writer—but her personality is so strong and unique that some readers at least will be drawn to her instinctively partly because of that strong personality. It seems impossible to separate her personality from her art. But Courtney was on to something, however we might want to hedge about his comment with reservations.

A. T. Quiller-Couch, a name to be reckoned with in his day and no doubt still remembered by many, gave a longish review of *Life Is Life*.[23] (He followed it up with a respectful personal letter to Gwendoline Keats, asking that she contribute a story to the magazine he edited.[24]) The review as a whole is a very mixed bag, with some comments that seem rather wrongheaded. But one extremely long paragraph, of which I will quote only part, has an excellent insight into the nature of all short story writing. The application of his insight runs into his next paragraph. The ellipses and the bracketed portion are mine. He gives praise and criticism to her style, then goes on to say

> At the same time—and in short-story-telling, this is the root of the matter—all the tales are imaginative. Each one of them clothes, more or less effectively, an idea. And how important that is, we, from whose stories the idea has too often escaped, leaving only clothes and a few tawdry properties behind, may be allowed to know only too well. [He lists some of the cores of Zack's stories.] . . . all these are embodiments of ideas, and except as a presentation of an idea a short story is naught. . . . In short, the art of this particular form of story-telling consists in finding first an idea, and next a situation which impresses it sharply and almost at a blow. Or a situation may tease the author until at length he finds the idea which gives it meaning. But whether in conception it come first or last, in execution the idea must be present throughout. Ideas imaginatively clothed are the story-teller's final aim. They, and they only, make the difference between philosophical fiction and mere anecdotage.
>
> "Zack," then, has ideas, imagination and a philosophy of life.

---

[23] A. T. Quiller-Couch, "'Life Is Life,'" "Living Age," Aug. 27, 1898, pp. 619-621. This "Living Age" review apparently was reprinted from "The Speaker" where it originally appeared.

[24] A. T. Quiller-Couch letter to Gwendoline Keats, July 18th, 1898.

Quiller-Couch's theory in regard to short story writing is certainly worth pondering. In any case, it seems true that Zack, in this her first book of stories and in her subsequent books of stories, wrote stories that contained and clothed ideas. Probably she did this instinctively and unconsciously. She had something to say, knew she had something to say, and she said it. She had ideas, imagination, and a philosophy of life—at a relatively young age she had a "maturity of thought and life," as James MacArthur noticed.

Whenever I, pistol in hand, calmly and maturely try to persuade some innocent bystander to read something by Zack, invariably I recommend *Life Is Life* first of all. Yes, all of the first four books are excellent and could be reasonable starting places. But *Life Is Life* is the best place to start. This is the essential Zack, Zack at her best. But the book is not for everyone. Katharine Tynan Hinkson (1859?-1931), an incredibly diligent writer (perhaps 100 novels to her credit, leaving aside a considerable amount of poetry) and a close friend of Zack's close friend May Sinclair, said of *Life Is Life*, "'That book made me feel as though I must scream out.'" Mrs. Hinkson did not intend the comment as a compliment. But apparently she went on to read more of Zack's work, for she also wrote that she considered that Zack "'made a great jump in artistry after *Life is Life*.'"[25] I hope many new readers will try *Life Is Life*, and see whether, or at least how, they scream out.

---

[25]Theophilus E. M. Boll, *Miss May Sinclair: Novelist: A Biographical and Critical Introduction*, Rutherford, Madison, and Teaneck, New Jersey, Fairleigh Dickinson University Press, 1973, p. 67.

Having seen Mrs. Hinkson's comments in regard to *Life Is Life*, I made it a point to read at least one of her books. The only one of her approximate 100 novels which I have read is *The Great Captain: A Story of the Days of Sir Walter Raleigh*. According to Wikipedia she also wrote "five autobiographical volumes." I wonder if Zack is mentioned in any of those? Wikipedia has an article on Mrs. Hinkson, under her maiden name of Katharine Tynan. Patrick Braybrook lists her among Roman Catholic novelists, and the one book I have read by her supports that notion.

CHAPTER 2

On Trial

"To do right is mortal hard for the best o' us," she answered evasively.

"But you don't belave in me," he repeated. "You holds I bain't made o' the stuff that wins droo?"

She was silent a moment. "I believe in the Almighty," she said at last. "If I didn't, I shudn't believe in man, not if he was the greatest saint that ever walked the earth."

"Ay, God Almighty!" he answered with concentrated bitterness: "God Almighty don't help a man the zame ez you reckons He wud from reading the Bible and sich."

Then he went out and left her.

Zack, *On Trial*

I had a book with me, I remember, that was just the thing for my mood, Zack's *On Trial*, a magical thing, the kind of book that I should have liked to write had I genius, throbbing in every page with just that same passion for creating beauty that was also Harmer John's.

Hugh Walpole, *Harmer John*[26]

On Trial was published in serial form, five monthly segments, in "Blackwood's Magazine," from June through October of 1899. It came out in book form, published by Blackwood & Sons, in October of 1899, the month of Zack's 34th birthday (Oct. 4). It is a short novel running in the neighborhood of 39,000 words. The price was once again six shillings.

---

[26]Hugh Walpole, *Harmer John*, New York, George H. Doran Company, 1926, p. 405.

The book was widely reviewed, for the most part favorably. *On Trial* represents the high point in recognition for Gwendoline Keats/ Zack. Within a few months (Jan. 20, 1900) it would win a prize as the best novel of 1899, from "The Academy," a weekly journal. Her prize included 25 guineas—no doubt very welcome to Zack, who sometimes in her letters to May Sinclair described herself as "penniless."

It is fascinating to note the other prizewinners for that year. Of the five other winners, four are names still remembered and read today. In poetry: W. B. Yeats; in biography: Hilaire Belloc; in history: G. M. Trevelyan; in translation: Constance Garnett. Only H. G. Graham (miscellaneous) joins Zack in being unknown to the general reader of our time.

There is one other historical curiosity to the publication of *On Trial*. The final, October, segment of the novel appears in the same issue of "Blackwood's Magazine" (sometimes known as the Maga) in which the first segment of Joseph Conrad's *Lord Jim* appeared. The subject matter of the two books is similar, which did not escape the notice of Conrad himself. He wrote to William Blackwood, the publisher of "Blackwood's Magazine," on Oct. 27, 1899. The ellipsis is mine. Two editor's footnotes are omitted—one identifies who Zack was, the other describes the subject of both books as being "Dishonourable conduct."

> I think Zack may be congratulated on the novel. It is an advance on the short stories—a *promising* advance. I've just finished reading it having waited for the last inst: Of course I could argue vehemently (with the *Writer* not the *Lady*) about this and that par: this and that page; but the distinction is undeniable the vision at times most remarkably artistic. . . .
>
> Isn't it a funny coincidence me following Zack on essentially the same subject? I hope nobody will suspect Maga of having started a 'literary' competition for the best story on the State of Funk and that Zack and I rivalise for the possession of a nickel-plated chronometer or a lath-and-plaster palace, or whatever other 'literary' rewards are going now in the great world of democracy.[27]

---

[27]Joseph Conrad, *The Collected Letters of Joseph Conrad, Volume 2, 1898-1902*, edited by Frederick R. Karl and Laurence Davies, Cambridge, England, Cambridge University Press, 1986, pp. 213-214.

Of course *Lord Jim* is still widely read today. The reader will have to decide for himself whether or not *On Trial* deserves to be more widely known. I encourage you to read it for yourself.

It was Hugh Walpole's admiring reference to *On Trial*, as recorded in the second epigraph above, which first alerted me to the existence of the book and of Zack.

On Trial is a short novel concentrating on a small handful of characters and dealing with only a few incidents covering a brief time span. The main protagonist—his behavior does not really permit us to call him the hero—is young Dan Pigott. As the story opens, Dan has bought his discharge from the army rather than prepare for likely service in India; he has always hated soldiering anyway. He is returning to his home in Devonshire. The fifteen pounds his discharge cost him had been sent to him by his sweetheart Phoebe Hazeldene, and Dan wonders where she got so much money. Why she did it he understands.

> "After all," he concluded, "I'm none so bad looking, and there's more than one girl who would have been proud to have done the like: only maybe they wouldn't keep as quiet about it as Phoebe; her always knows what be due to a man's feelings."

On his walk from the railway station home, Dan meets the middle-aged pedlar Ben Tap. Ben informs him that Phoebe has gotten into trouble for stealing money at the farm of Dan's uncle where she worked as a servant. The two men encounter a man driving a dog-cart; he has been hired to remove Phoebe from the farm. Dan catches a ride with him. Dan now realizes that Phoebe stole the money for him. Dan

> remembered the letter he had written to Phoebe when first the regiment had been ordered abroad—a letter dilating on the unhealthfulness of the station, full of fears for his own safety, a cowardly letter; and deep down in his heart he knew he was a coward, and the knowledge was hateful to him. Lashing himself into a fury of repentance, he determined to go boldly forward and take his stand by Phoebe's side. "It be true," he would say, "that her stole the money, but 'twor for me her did it—if blame you must, blame me." Afterwards Phoebe and he

would marry, and live things down. The phrase "live things down" pleased him; there was something fine about the sound of it; he had a keen sense for the histrionic in a situation.

However, when he reaches his uncle's home, he strides across the moor rather than witness Phoebe being removed from his uncle's farm. Phoebe and her box are loaded into the dog-cart. Phoebe is "small and slight," and "she appeared in her defencelessness almost a child." As the cart pulls away, the pedlar Ben approaches and gently tells her, "'Things 'ull mend theirselves.'"

Dan walks blindly across the moor, full of bitter reproaches of Phoebe for bringing shame on the two of them. Since his uncle is childless, Dan is heir to his uncle's farm, and Phoebe's action spoils Dan's ability to take pride in his position.

> Phoebe was the daughter of the village carpenter, and from a worldly point of view had everything to gain by a marriage with Dan; and though he had refrained from pressing the fact upon her notice, he could not but be aware there was something generous on his part in thus abstaining. There were moments when he wondered if Phoebe quite saw the matter in the same light as he did; in some things she had proved herself strangely obtuse. His uncle had opposed the engagement, and now, lying on the moor, Dan recalled the afternoon when he had first broken the knowledge of this to Phoebe: he remembered the generous warmth with which he had exclaimed: "Come what will, sweetheart, I'll stick by you!" and the flatness with which her reply had fallen on him: "Ay, Dan, and I'll do the same by 'ee."

It had been Phoebe's inability to appreciate him enough which had driven Dan to enlist, hoping his absence would allow her to value him appropriately.

Now he meets the cart on which Phoebe is riding, on Exmoor. The driver had withdrawn himself as far as possible from the thief, and Phoebe, "realising his distaste, had crushed herself back into the corner of the cart."

> A wave of compassionate love rushed through Dan: springing to his feet, he went to meet her.
> "Phoebe!" he cried; "I've come back; you ain't alone!"

A great joy remodelled her face; instant, absolute, the metamorphosis was but one of those changes in her that Dan knew so well and found so illogical. It was if she had entered into a new heaven and a new earth; as if at sound of trump, a dead joy had sprung into life eternal.

The cart eventually takes her onward, leaving Dan.

"Her's so dependsome on me," he said; "and I have a sort o' feeling as if I should fail her."

The moon trod slowly out from behind the clouds; lifting his eyes, Dan sent winging through the great grey space a prayer to God.

"O God!" he exclaimed, "that I mayn't act cowardful this once."

It was the first prayer he had uttered since childhood: it comforted him.

Returning to the farm, Dan encounters his uncle, stern old Samuel Pigott, who accuses Dan of being at the bottom of Phoebe's thievery.

There was a long pause, during which Dan sought vainly to put the truth into words: it seemed to him that never had he striven harder to state the facts and nothing but the facts; and then, suddenly, as if in a dream he heard himself say, "I won the money on a horse."

He rubbed his sleeve across his forehead, a dazed wonderment taking possession of him. He had so desired to speak the truth, surely he could not be held responsible for a lie he had never meant to utter? There was time still to rectify the mistake: in a moment, he told himself, he would rectify it; but the minutes crept on and he did not speak, the words would not come.

Once again he tries to speak the truth, and again fails. His uncle mocks him.

There sprang up in Dan's heart a sudden hatred of this man, who seemed in some subtle fashion to force him to play a coward's part. Glancing hurriedly back on the long page of his boyhood, he saw the same *rôle* assigned to both, and a quick anger flamed up within him.

"I could curse you for making me the cur that I be," he exclaimed. For a brief moment his eyes met his uncle's on equal terms; then his anger died down, and he turned away with what sounded much like a rough sob.

We are surprised to hear Dan have the courage to speak out so violently to Farmer Pigott. But what he speaks has an element of truth to it, and his uncle does not take offense; for a moment the two meet on "equal terms." Near the end of the book the truth is repeated: Farmer Pigott's treatment of Dan, when Dan was a child, helped shape Dan's character in an unfortunate way. This is not to say that Farmer Pigott was unjust to Dan—only that Dan's nature, weak at birth, was not able to flourish under the farmer's stern treatment. Another child might have done very well raised by the same man.

A key question of the book is, how far are we responsible for our faults? Dan was made by God with a certain nature. Dan, we learn from the very start of the book, is cowardly. He doesn't want to be cowardly, but he is. Is it God's fault? Is it Dan's fault? How much blame do we attribute to Farmer Pigott, who is clearly a good man despite a somewhat stern nature? Dan, in his weakness and lack of objectivity, tries to see Phoebe (or circumstances) as largely to blame. The question of blame for Dan's character is examined from different angles throughout the book. Dan is weak and cowardly rather than intentionally trying to do wrong. There are even aspects of his character which we can respect. For one example, we learn in the latter half of the book that Dan has not taken advantage of his good looks to be a seducer.

Readers' attitudes to Dan may vary, depending upon their own circumstances in life. For those who have maintained a courageous behavior throughout life, it may be difficult to find any sympathy for Dan. For those of us who are forced to look back on our own cowardly or shameful behavior of one type or another, it may be natural to feel sympathy for Dan even as we acknowledge his wrong and even despicable behavior.

That evening Mrs. Pigott, a woman of "kindly face and plump person," tries to comfort Dan, testifying that Samuel Pigott is "'kind o' heart for all he be harsh o' tongue.'" He is upright and simple, but other folk are a "'closed book to him.'" Dan confesses, in general terms.

> "'I've acted black again,' he said, hoarsely, "and I would have given a deal to have played fair.'"
>
> She did not question him: she was used to Dan's confessions—his lapses from virtue—his crude fits of repentance. Her heart ached, but cherished no higher ideal for him. Suddenly, subtly, the knowledge of this came home to Dan.
>
> "Aunt," he exclaimed, and she noticed the note of fear in his voice, "you don't really reckon that I'll ever change—do you?"
>
> The question troubled her: Mrs. Pigott was a woman not given to analysing her feelings; but it required little to bring home the truth of what he said. Her natural kindness and veracity struggled the one against the other, the battle resulting in a draw.
>
> "You be only three-and-twenty, and youth's learning-time," she answered evasively, turning away.

Dan thinks his aunt has failed him just when he needed her most.

> For a moment he rebelled bitterly, then his mind, which unwatched by him had been gathering material for a startling question, propounded it.
>
> "What," it asked, "had he done that he should be trusted? Why should any one believe in him?"
>
> Deserted by man and by himself—face to face with the bitter need of an unearned character for rectitude—the utilitarian side of virtue was brought grimly home to Dan.

Zack's books are filled with many striking phrases. It seems to me that "the utilitarian side of virtue" is among the many. Acting virtuously does indeed lead to earning a character of rectitude—and failing to act virtuously makes it awfully difficult for people to see us as having rectitude! Dan's subconscious does well to ask him what he had done to be trusted. His aunt had not failed him; he had failed himself in his past actions.

The next day Dan's spirits revive considerably; he daydreams of his future happiness as owner of the farm. But then thought of Phoebe embitters him again. He rescues a sheep in distress, pleasing his uncle, and they have a partial reconciliation. Suddenly he realizes he has lost Phoebe's letter.

> "Uncle will find that letter; he'll turn me out: the farm 'ull never be mine."
> Then he cursed Phoebe for the thief that she was.

Phoebe, turned away from her father's home for being a thief, has gone to stay with her uncle, Captain Brattle, a retired seaman, and a man of generous heart. The captain's action in taking Phoebe in has angered his servant Hannah, sharp of tongue and of visage. She hates to see the wicked honored. Captain Brattle picks flowers for Phoebe's arrival, to Hannah's annoyance. She arranges the flowers grudgingly, but absolutely refuses to prepare scones. She speaks bitterly to herself about the captain's attitude. She hears wheels; Phoebe has arrived.

> She cast a quick scrutinising look down; the girl raising her head at the same moment, their eyes met in a long glance. The small face, on which the slight elusive bloom of childhood still lingered, disarmed Hannah by its air of extreme youth, and deep down in the woman's heart the desiccated germ of pity stirred into faint new life.
> "Maybe her would have acted different if her had been brought up different," she exclaimed.

The captain greets Phoebe tenderly, but she will give no reason for why she stole the money, saying "'I've brought disgrace upon 'ee all.'"

Many days pass, and Dan does not come to Phoebe. Phoebe hears her mother has given birth to a dead child, and is likely to follow the child into death. Phoebe immediately walks, sometimes running, the twelve miles to her parents' home. There she finds her mother dead. Her father blames Phoebe for killing her mother.

> "Look!" he exclaimed thickly—"look—her suffered—mark her face. Do 'ee see they lines?—death couldn't smooth 'em."
> Then with sudden cold rage he pushed the girl before him from the room, down the stairs, through the garden, out into the street.
> "Go!" he cried—"and my curse go with 'ee!"

Dan is also in town, at the inn, from where he sees Phoebe being cast out from her father's house. Dan has not courage enough to help her then, but follows her out of the village and tries to comfort her. He wants her to help him be a better man.

Returning to the stables at the inn, Dan finds his mare being eyed by the hostler, Silas Trustgore, the same man who had driven Phoebe from Samuel Pigott's farm. (Only late in the book do we find out that Silas Trustgore is aged sixty-five.) Trustgore has a sleazy proposal for Dan: a way to cheat Samuel Pigott out of fifteen pounds by convincing him the mare was worth less than its true value. It could be sold for £70, while Samuel thought it was sold for £55. Trustgore feels able to make this proposal because he has found the letter from Phoebe to Dan; he is blackmailing Dan. Dan lacks the courage to try to take the letter from Trustgore by force, and Dan rides off. Dan here lacks the courage to fight. Will he display a different form of courage by simply telling the truth to his uncle, and accepting the consequences?

Mary Anne Wort, "a tall severe-faced woman," a fifty-six or fifty-seven year old spinster, seeks the advice of Captain Brattle. She tells the captain that Silas Trustgore has proposed marriage to her: "'ha's been casting sheep's glances at my garden this long while; and then I keep me own pig.'" She is a little uncertain about Silas' character, but the idea of marriage appeals to her.

> "Not," she added, "that I hold with the allurecaciousness o' man ez man; he may tempt some, but he don't tempt me—still, 'tis human nater to like company; there be a lonesomeness in death that a body would gie a deal to keep out o' life: die alone I must, but there's a choice ez to living."
>
> She stopped speaking, and putting up her hands, smoothed her thin brown hair back under her bonnet. "I've took Silas Trustgore's fancy," she said, "that is, if you reckons the garden and the pig in."

The captain encourages her to marry Silas, which brings a "gleam of happiness" to Mary Anne's face.

Mary Anne Wort is one of Zack's most fascinating characters. She will have a lot to do with the unfolding of the plot. She is a plain woman not given to self-deception. She knows that Silas' fancy for her has much to do with her garden and her pig—and says so straight out.

On an August Sunday, Dan sees Silas Trustgore ride up to the farm. Silas talks with Samuel Pigott, terrifying Dan that the story of the letter is being revealed. Silas comes to Dan's room. He picks out and takes one of Dan's ties, saying he will be married in it. Silas says,

> "what call has a man to steal when he can come by all he needs honest?"
>
> "You be a sight wuss than a thief," Dan exclaimed, hotly.
>
> "Na, na," Silas answered. "Na, na. I walks wi'in the law." Then, turning on the young fellow with an abrupt change of voice: "What have 'ee done about thicky mare?" he demanded.

Dan accuses Silas of being "'mortal much a devil.'"

> The hostler made no immediate reply.
>
> "'Tworn't me but the Almighty that put evil into the world," he answered, after a pause. "Na doubt His puppus wor a good wan, and it don't become sich ez us to question it. All I does is to tarn the evil to my own ends; but—mark 'ee—I kapes mezulf unspotted."
>
> "Good gore, you unspotted!"
>
> Silas drew nearer and laid a shrivelled hand on the young fellow's shoulder: "Wor it I or the Almighty that made 'ee white-livered?" he asked. "Answer me that."
>
> Dan tried, without effect, to release himself from the hostler's grasp. "Hell 'ull have 'ee anyway," he answered, evasively.
>
> "Na," Silas replied, "I shall draw back in time; but there iddn't no call to draw back. I walks circumspect, and wi'in the law. 'Tiddn't like thic wi' 'ee, mind—you wor marked out for destruction from the day that your mother conceived 'ee."
>
> Dan whitened. "Why me more than you?" he gasped.
>
> The hostler released his grip from the young fellow's shoulder. "There be they," he answered, bringing the first two fingers of his right hand down on to the palm of his left, "that have a say in their own lives, and there be they that have none. I belongs to tha fust; you ta tha last."

Was Dan marked out for destruction from the day he was conceived? Has he no say in his own life? These are dark notions. To answer such questions we must each one decide how the world is put together, and take our chances on being right or wrong. Is the world created and run by God? Even if we say yes, by God, then we must ask what is His character and how does He deal with man? Simply to say that God is in control does not answer all our questions. We must plumb the depths of His character and actions, to determine the answers to such questions. Such answers are not served up on a platter for us. But it is good to struggle with such questions rather than just to live without asking.

This is a fascinating sentence: "'Na,' Silas replied, "I shall draw back in time; but there iddn't no call to draw back."' Zack has given us a wonderful example of self-deception, in one sentence. Silas begins by saying that he will draw back from sin in time to avoid hell, but before the sentence is even over he revises his evaluation of himself to say that he doesn't even need to draw back in time! He pictures himself as walking so circumspectly that he is not even sinning. Self-deception is one of the key attributes of mankind, and Silas has his full fair share.

Silas gives Dan a week to act in regard to the mare. Dan goes to the stable, and half-consciously plants a germ of uneasiness in his uncle concerning the mare's physical soundness. Walking dejectedly on the moor, Dan finds Phoebe, equally dejected.

> There came to him a sudden, living need of her; in silence he drew nearer, in silence their eyes met, and in silence love healed them of many things. Kneeling beside her, Dan raised her hands and placed them on his eyes.
>
> "I've been hungering for 'ee, dear heart," he said. She drew his face down till it rested on her breast. A sob rose in her throat, but she answered nothing. Her heart had hungered for him also.
>
> "Phoebe! Phoebe!" he burst out, "do 'ee reckon that some folk be damned right away from the fust? that they ain't got no chance the same as the rest? be 'em ever so wishful to go straight, they 'ull always end by going crooked?"
>
> In a flash she divined his trouble. "No, no," she answered, pressing him closer to her, "there be thic that be alles stronger than natur, and that be Love."

He confesses all his shame to Phoebe, concealing nothing,

and when she heard all, and realised yet again how deep had been the injury she had done him, there rose up in her a hatred of that which is crooked and evil.

"Oh, Dan!" she exclaimed, "us have had enough o' sich things; let us deal fair wi' folk."

He broke into a bitter laugh: "That be just like 'ee to reckon things can be altered all o' a minute," he said. "Do 'ee want me to be ruined?"

But she saw only his moral overthrow. "Dan, Dan," she pleaded, "don't let me be the cause o' yer ruin. I acted wrongful; be a fine lad in spite o' it."

"Ay," he said, "a fine lad! What would you have me do?"

"Up and speak the truth."

"Up and speak the truth?"

"Ess."

"And lose the farm?"

Her eyes followed the course of the stream, but they were filled with a vision of a glorified Dan. Her face glowed, a passion of well-doing was upon her.

"The truth be more vally than any varm," she exclaimed. He stared at her in dumfounded bewilderment. That truth, as Truth, had an abstract value was beyond his grasp.

"You must be mazed," he said.

She looked at him pityingly, but she did not understand how hard was the task she wished to impose on him.

"I bain't mazed, Dan," she answered. "I see there iddn't no other way out for 'ee; 'tiddn't no—but that."

"'The truth be more vally than any varm,' she exclaimed.' Truth has an abstract value, although Dan is not able to grasp that fact. In fact Truth deserves and gets a capital letter, in Zack's moral economy. We are reminded of the book of Proverbs, where wisdom is so ecstatically praised. Surely Truth must be one of the attributes of wisdom; both are attributes of God.

Phoebe blames herself for everything having gone wrong, but can think of no other help for Dan except that he speak the truth. "'Lad, what can I zay to 'ee?' she exclaimed in a broken voice, "'cept that wan way be right and wan be wrong.'" Dan angrily leaves her.

Silas visits Mary Anne on a Saturday night. After supper, he unveils his present to her: her old deceased cat Tom, whom Silas has dug up and stuffed. She is very happy at the gift, and Silas foresees their future domestic happiness.

> "'Tis a tidy little place you've got here," he remarked, in a pleased voice. "Us 'ull settle down comfortable wi' wat us 'ave laid by and wat us makes out o' vules and sich."

Just then one of such fools knocks on the door, and he and Silas go outdoors to speak alone. Mary Anne Wort, after a moment of indecision, secretly follows them. She hears Dan ask for time to earn the fifteen pounds by honest work, but when that fails he accuses Silas of wanting to ruin him.

> "Ruin 'ee? I don't want to ruin 'ee," Silas answered. "I uses 'ee for my own puppusses, that's wat I does; and if you valls to pieces in my hands that be your Maker's fault, not mine. Na, na; there iddn't no wan outside a man's zulf that can bring him to ruin, lest 'tis his Maker."

Silas is self-deceived in imagining that he himself is without fault in his dealings with Dan. But is he wrong or right, when he says that only two people can ruin a man, God or the man himself? Is God ruining Dan? Or is Dan ruining Dan? How much blame should fall on Silas?

Neither his pleas nor his anger do Dan any good with the implacable Silas. After Dan departs, Mary Anne Wort confronts Silas; she has heard every word of his conversation with Dan. They go inside to talk.

> The woman spoke first; her voice, though dry, was firm and even.
>
> "Us must part from this night," she said.
>
> "Ez yer wull."
>
> "I wud ha' made 'ee a good wife."
>
> "I knaws it."
>
> She put her puckered big-boned hand on his shoulder. "Silas," she said, solemnly, "s'posin' this lad testifies agin' ee on the day o' Jidgment?"
>
> "I ain't got no fear o' sich trash ez he."
>
> "Happen he's trash in our eyes, but who shall say if he be zo in the Almighty's?" she answered. "Oh, Silas," she continued,

By Noble Things She Stands

and her voice for the first time betrayed emotion, "I couldn't bear to see 'ee cast away when it comed to the last!"

"I walks circumspect," he answered; but he spoke without his usual glibness.

"That may save 'ee wi' man, but I fear sore it 'ull no save 'ee wi' God," she replied, turning from him with what sounded like a rough sob. He took up his cap and opened the door, halting a moment, his hand on the latch. "You be a good woman, Mary Anne Wort," he said; "I reckon, ez things go nowadays, us cud ha' made wan-nother comfortable." And he went out and left her.

She listened to his retreating steps in silence, and then her eyes fell on the stuffed cat. Sinking down on a chair, she covered her face with her hands, and between her red fingers the sparse tears of middle-age trickled slowly.

"Oh, Silas, Silas," she exclaimed, "what a varrigated thing human nater be!"

This conversation shows both Mary Anne and Silas at their best, although the quality of the "best" of course varies according to the quality of their characters. Mary Anne, now knowing the character of Silas, knows she should not and can not marry him. Silas accepts the decision without whining. When Mary Anne says she would have made him a good wife, Silas generously says that he knows that to be true. Mary Anne tries to warn Silas of the day of judgment. Silas claims to walk circumspectly, but has the decency to speak "without his usual glibness" as he makes that claim. She warns him again that God's judgment may be more strict than Silas anticipates. Silas speaks honorably in saying that Mary Anne is a good woman; he is indeed correct that the two of them might have been comfortable together as man and wife. (Of course it is his willingness to act in an evil manner which is what separates them from marrying, and keeps them from that comfort.) He leaves quietly, leaving Mary Anne to see the thoughtful gift he had made her. She weeps "the sparse tears of middle-age"—another striking phrase from Zack—as her chance at married companionship ends. Human nature is indeed variegated.

The next day, Sunday, Silas talks to Samuel Pigott in the presence of Dan. The flummery about the mare not being completely sound is continued, Dan not being able to bring himself to speak the truth when he sees a letter in Silas' hand. On Friday Dan sells the mare for seventy guineas, telling Farmer Pigott that he sold it for sixty. Dan gives ten pounds to Silas as his blackmail payment. But Silas had intended to make fifteen pounds. He says he will come some day for the remaining five pounds.

In September Captain Brattle dies suddenly. Phoebe and Hannah are both sorely distressed at the loss. Hannah's mother encourages her to leave her job, for she doesn't want Hannah serving a thief. Hannah, unconvinced of Phoebe's badness, reluctantly agrees.

Hannah has a very minor part in the book, but it is an interesting part. She begins by being angry that the thief Phoebe is being given refuge by the captain. Her heart is very far from being cruelly hard, however. Even her first sight of Phoebe inclines her toward mercy. As the days unfold, she warms toward Phoebe, and we see that she leaves Phoebe only reluctantly. We respect her ability to learn and change. Greatness of character eludes her, however. Had she reached greatness, she would not have let her mother's opinion cause her to leave Phoebe. Without disrespecting her mother, she might have bravely chosen to stay as a servant to Phoebe. This would have taken courage, but it would have shown a spiritual wisdom. Spiritual wisdom is not easily come by, of course! Or we all would have lots of it. Hannah leaves the story, but we know she is a person who can learn and grow, though she is not yet exactly where she needs to be.

After the funeral, Hannah leaves Phoebe, who chooses to remain totally alone in the house now belonging to her. The next morning, very early, Phoebe slips out of the house. On her walk she encounters the pedlar Ben. Instinctively the thoughts of both of them return to the day when Ben had told her that things would better themselves. But they haven't. Ben speaks to her at length about the beauty of the world, but Phoebe has other things on her mind. She asks him advice concerning speaking the truth.

> He looked down a moment into her blue eyes before answering. "Truth iddn't no smooth thing to handle most times," he replied.
> "No," she assented eagerly; "and the lad 'ud lose all he had if he spoke out. 'Twud be cruel, cruel to force the truth from

him. Oh, do 'ee reckon that punishment wud fall upon the lad for failing this wance?"

A smile, half sad, half pitying, crossed the pedlar's face as he realised that she was speaking of her lover, and that in her desolateness it was of him and not herself that she thought. "Lying," he said, "is a temptacious thing; 'tis always for halting at the next door but wan, and if you give the skiddick its head there ain't its ekal for leading 'ee into mischief."

"Oh," she cried, wringing her hands, "'tis o' thic that I be afeared. Where shall he stop?"

"There be only wan place to stop short wi' a lie," said the pedlar, "and that be afore 'ee tells it. And if it shud happen, maybe, that you have zlipped vrom the truth, wull, drive your heels inter the ground, and hang back wi' all the grit that be in 'ee—it gives 'ee a nasty jar, I'll allow; I knaws that, cuz I've lied mezulf in my time."

Instinctively the girl realised that her lover lacked the courage necessary to save himself in the way the pedlar advised. She sank her face in her hands. "Oh, Ben," she sobbed out, "I've brought ill to them I love—I've brought ill to them I love."

Ben tries to comfort her, and tells her that "'there ain't no wan outzide a man's zulf ez can wark him harm.'" It is fascinating to note that Silas made almost exactly the same point, as quoted a few pages previously. The mean-spirited Silas and the good-hearted Ben both say that we can only be worked harm by ourselves. It is an important point about the moral economy of the earth. But is it correct? Each reader will have to decide for himself. To me it seems the essence of Zack's attitude toward life—and it also seems correct. Granted, others can work us harm by doing bad things to us, but no one can force us to do wrong. It is a subtle and important point. In any case, Phoebe is not comforted, and feels that she has brought temptation close to Dan.

A few weeks later Samuel Pigott discovers, in Exeter, that Dan had sold the mare for seventy rather than sixty guineas. He confronts Dan, who tries to speak the truth, but fails to do so, and repeats the lie that he sold the mare for sixty guineas.

> For a moment the two men sat staring at each other, and the lie seemed as some living thing between them. Then the farmer pushed back his chair and left the room without a word.

Samuel Pigott discusses all this with his wife, and tells her he will throw Dan out the next time he catches him "'at his slack-twisted ways.'"

In October Mary Anne Wort falls ill, 'and the villagers, discussing the matter among themselves, shook their heads. "Her's got the lonesome-fret," they said, "and when folks git that they don't last long.'" Mary Anne eventually decides to be reconciled to Martha Stiggins, a woman she believes has wronged her in the past concerning bees and bloaters. (Bloaters are salted and smoked herring or mackerel.) She invites Mrs. Stiggins to her home. While Mary Anne remains in her sick room, Mrs. Stiggins dines on an excellent meal of tea and toast. After her meal, she goes to Mary Anne who is propped up in bed. They talk. Mary Anne makes it clear that she still believes Mrs. Stiggins was in the wrong.

> "I've told 'ee whiles enough what I thought o' sich goings on," she continued, "and there iddn't no call for repeating o' it now; but this I'll say, I made up my mind from the fust that when death took me I'd lay the matter afore the Almighty Hiszulf: 'tis a personable pleasure when you know you've been treated poor to hear the same from the lips of them you rispact."

Mary Anne has a fit of coughing, then says she knows it may not be long before the churchyard has her. She repeats that she has looked forward to hearing the Almighty's opinion on the old bee and bloater score.

> "Howsomever, not further back than the night afore last I wor lying here all by myself, the same as I do most nights. The blind wor up, and I cud see the moor there, stretched out that quiet I cud almost hear the silence tread across it. The moon had riz, 'twor new, and the poor little skiddick threaded its way droo the darkness kind o' insecure; but the stars reg'lar rang in the sky, they looked that bright and hard. Kaining up at 'em made me think o' the gates o' heaven flashing agin the darkness o' the night, and I kind o' figured to mezulf God on His great white throne and me laying my cause afore Him. Then all to a sudden it seemed a mortal tiddlewinkie cause to call to mind up there, and it kind o' made me hot all over to think o' axing the Almighty to listen to it. There comed to me they wuds from the Book, 'His ways are not our ways, nor His thoughts

our thoughts,' and I tarned my eyes away from the stars kind o' tiptoe, and I said to myself I'll make up that old bloater score here on earth. I'll not go into heaven smelling o' a chandler's shop!"

She asks Mrs. Stiggins' pardon for any ill-considered words, and extends her hand, which Mrs. Stiggins tentatively accepts. Mary Anne ends, "'if I gits well things shall be the same as they were afore. And now I wish 'ee 'good-day' and a pleasant walk home.'"

A few days later Phoebe visits the still-ailing Mary Anne, bringing her a shawl she has knitted for her, which Mary Anne receives with great pleasure. Phoebe speaks:

"I wor afeared maybe you'd look unfriendzome on it cuz 'twor my work; but you don't," she exclaimed gratefully.

Mary Anne Wort glanced down on the girl's bent head with its heavy coils of soft brown hair. "I wor niver wan for dragging the past into the present," she said. "There be alles zome dinky bit o' truth that you leaves behind."

Phoebe asks what is ailing Mary Anne.

"I can't fathom it," the sick woman answered, after a pause. "Happen 'tis cuz I've seen they I care for most act beneath theirzulves."

Phoebe looked up at her. "But you ain't brought 'em to it," she exclaimed passionately; "'tis thic that breaks the heart."

"No; I ain't brought 'em to it," the woman repeated; "but then I ain't stood by 'em when they fell. And how shall the weaksome rise if they that loves 'em best deserts em?"

"Oh, Anne!" said the girl. "What do 'ee reckon a woman shud do?"

There was a long silence, and Mary Anne Wort's face grew set and stern. "I knaws, but I ain't a-done it," she answered, "and maybe 'tis thic that's killing me. Her shud stand atween them and their sin, that's what her shud do, even if her brought suffering on 'em. 'Tis better to see they you love punished o' man than o' God. Do you mind they wuds in the Book, many's the time I've thought o' 'em lying here—'For what is a man profited if he shud gain the whole world and lose his own soul? Or what shall a man give in exchange for his soul?'"

Phoebe sank her head down upon the worn patchwork quilt. "'Tis hard, hard, hard to see they that you loves suffer," she sobbed.

One day Silas joins Dan on the moor. Dan, a good shot, is hunting successfully. Silas has come for the remaining five pounds. He suggests that Dan get Phoebe to give him the money; she is well-to-do since her uncle's death. As they talk, Silas changes his mind and decides he must have ten pounds instead of just five. Dan eventually defies Silas, who gives him until next Monday night, almost a week away, to deliver the money to him. Left to himself, Dan speaks aloud.

> "Let un do his wuss, I defy un," he muttered; but his heart sank, and keenly as he was conscious of his degradation, the dread lest he should be unable to rise above it proved keener.

Sunday Dan drives over to see Phoebe. He finds her at the cottage, alone.[28] He tells Phoebe he is ruined, eventually blaming her for everything.

> "Ay," he said, flinging himself back in his chair, "if on'y you hadn't took thic money. Every mortal thing has gone awry since."
>
> The words left her shivering like some wounded animal.
>
> "Oh, lad, I meant so well by 'ee," she protested. "I kind o' reckoned that if I acted unrightful the punishment 'ud vall on me alone; but it's valled on thee instead."
>
> Not generous enough to understand her suffering, he was silent, pondering on the hardness of his own fate, and, as with all weak natures, he held his circumstances and not himself responsible. Still smarting from the treatment that Silas had meted out to him, he found a certain melancholy pleasure in

---

[28] At this point we seem to have an editing error on Zack's part. She tells us that "Hannah, who never willingly missed a service, had trudged off alone to church." But we were told earlier that Hannah had left Phoebe's service shortly after Captain Brattle's death. Perhaps in her rough draft Zack intended Hannah to remain in Phoebe's service. Later she decided that Hannah would leave her job with Phoebe rather than stay after the captain's death, and perhaps neglected to make the necessary change to the text at this juncture.

tracing back the origin of his sufferings to the fount of Phoebe's misdoings.

"Ess," he said, "Silas Trustgore wud niver have had me in his power if it hadn't been for 'ee."

Dan mentions his need of ten pounds, but Phoebe wants him to refuse to give in to Silas.

"I know, lad, you won't be for believing me when I tell 'ee there be on'y wan way and that be to make a friend o' yer uncle," she replied at last. "Varmer Pigott belongs to they folk who'll forgie nigh on most things except lies."

"Ay, and I've lied to him over this from the fust."

"Well, go and tull him so to his vace and mark me if he don't forgie 'ee the vust a-cause o' the last. Can't 'ee zee, lad, that life 'ull be a deal happier for 'ee if yer makes up yer mind wance for all to ha' done wi' lies. Silas cudn't hurt 'ee then. 'Twud be worth a bigger risk than the losing o' the varm, to be done wi' sich scoundrels ez he; and then, Dan, what a vine upstanding thing the truth be, look at it which way yer wull, and how a man who tulls it is rispacted o' hiszulf and others. 'Tiddn't no light day's work to speak things out ez they be, special when they tells agin yerzulf; but lad, 'tis by the doing o' sich work that a man earns standing room to face life."

Dan, strongly moved by her words, vows to defy and even beat Silas. He will go straight to his uncle and speak the truth. He and Phoebe drive quickly toward the farm, but on the way they encounter Silas. Dan's resolve collapses at the sight of him. Driving away from Silas, he assumes Phoebe will give him the ten pounds. But she refuses.

"I won't have no hand in making a slave of 'ee," she said. "I'd rather zee 'ee turned out o' the varm. I'd rather see 'ee dead at my feet than in the power o' sich a man."

"But you must give me the money," he pleaded; and when she still persisted in her refusal, he turned on her and accused her of being the cause of his ruin. "'Twor you that brought me to this," he said; "and now you grudge the miserable ten pun that wud zee me a free man."

So they parted; and she crept across the moor homewards, and the rain fell in a blinding grey sheet between her and her lover.

Later that same day, Phoebe is visited at home by Ben the pedlar. He has come with a message from Hannah. The two talk. Phoebe's recent experiences with Dan evidently are on her mind.

> "Things zim simple; but they iddn't, they iddn't!" she exclaimed passionately. "Folks tull 'ee that 'tis a deal better to zee they you love perish o' hunger than that they shud sin agin God; but s'posing they be too weak to profit—what then? You wud on'y have added wan more ill to their load. 'Twor the Almighty that made 'em weak—must He alles, alles be punishing 'em acause o' it? Must wan be called upon to step in the zame ez the perlice and hand 'em over to the law, when wan knows all the while 'tiddn't punishment but jest a dinky bit o' time to find their better zulves agin that they be so sore in need of. Folk bain't alles the better for baing punished—there be zome that walks a deal nearer God prosperous than cast down."
>
> The pedlar listened to her appeal in silence.
>
> "A man must zee a sight furder than I can to answer questions the like o' they," he said, after a pause. "Good and bad lie turrible close wan to t'other, but 'twud be a poor thing to fear to do right a-cuz o' it."

Phoebe repeats the question about what to do in a situation in which someone is too weak to profit from his punishment from God.

> The pedlar's rugged face lit up with stern triumph; he knew she spoke of Dan, but for the moment he forgot him in the question at issue. "Who be us," he exclaimed, "that us shud play at wet-nurse wi' other folk's souls? Who be us that us shud zay to 'em, 'Come shelter agin our breast, you iddn't strong enough yit to meet the Almighty vace to vace. Wait awhile, us 'ull stand atween 'ee and God.' Lass," he continued more gently, "'tiddn't for the like o' sich ez you and I be to ha' the picking and choosing o' sich things. Us be poor machines, most o' us, and this life don't zim much more than a trial trip. Happen when it comes to the jidging 'twon't be condemnation that the Lord 'ull be for meting out, but jest readjustment."

Phoebe says she can see no further than that "'They that I love must zuffer.'"

A curious pang shot through him, almost as if his heart had been nailed back from beating. "What be there in women," he exclaimed with sudden anger, "that they shud alles love best thic that brings 'em the most zarrer!"

"What do 'ee knaw o' them I loves best?" she flared back at him, indignant. "You iddn't no right jidge o' sich ez they. You, who talks zo glib o' punishing."

Her words struck him like blows; but she had no mercy, turning on him with all the injustice of a defender of an unjust cause.

"I wish I had niver trusted 'ee," she said. "I might ha' knawed how 'twud be. I wud a deal liefer turn to a ripe back-slider for comfort than to wan o' yer just men—the vust knaws anyway what temptation be, and how turrible near folks can git to right wi'out doing o' ut."

The pedlar listened to her denunciation of him in silence. His heart was hammering out a message to his brain, while he himself, standing, as it seemed to him, behind heart and brain alike, fought with a desire to take the angry woman in his arms, and quell her misery and indignation in the mastery of his love. Then with a rush he remembered that she was not and never could be his. Putting out a hand, he steadied himself against the wall.

"I hadn't no speshil wish to speak unkind o' them you love, lass," he said; "God knows I wor niver wan for hasty jidging."

But she did not relent. "Jidging!" she repeated—"what call ha' sich es 'ee to come jidging? But if jidge you must, why don't 'ee take to jidging me? Ain't I tarned mezulf inter a thief?"

The expression on the girl's face as she trailed her name through the dirt in defence of her lover, was almost regal in its pride, and, watching it, Ben did her homage.

"You do wull to be angert," he said. "What do I knaw o' the rights o' things?"

Taking up his cap, he left the cottage.

Phoebe's strong words seem calculated to shrink the testicles of most men. Ben takes it as well as he can, and speaks respectfully and humbly as he leaves. Will Ben's romantic love for Phoebe be killed by her attack on him? We will see eventually.

When Phoebe asks, "'why don't 'ee take to jidging me?'" there seems to be an acknowledgement on her part that Ben is biased in her favor, that he is judging Phoebe more mercifully than he is judging Dan. This may be a hint that Phoebe understands Ben's attraction to her. If she does, she certainly doesn't grant him any mercy on account of it. She does indeed turn on him "with all the injustice of a defender of an unjust cause."

That night Phoebe visits Mary Anne Wort, but her welcome is not very friendly. Phoebe feels a difficulty in asking a favor of someone who is "'unfriendzome.'"

> "Who told 'ee I wor unfriendzome?"
> "You bain't the zame Anne that wor alles that mortal kind to me," the girl protested.
> A curious change passed over the sick woman's face. "Ay," she exclaimed harshly, "I bain't the zame—us can't bide by what us knaws is wrong and be the zame ez us wor when us strove to act uprightful."

Phoebe asks Mary Anne's help, wanting her to intercede with Silas and get the letter from him. Mary Anne figures out now that Phoebe had stolen the fifteen pounds for Dan's sake.

> "I suspicioned ez much from the vust. Vule, vule, ye reckoned to stave off harm from they you loved by acting unrightful yerzulf, and now you vinds you've on'y brought fresh evil upon 'em. Ess, vath, you ha' shielded 'em yesterday, maybe, but yer can't termarrer."

Mary Anne's opinion of Dan is that "'he's jest no more than nothing nailed togither to look like a man.'" Mary Anne finally admits that possibly she could have stepped in to help rescue Dan. Phoebe begs her to save him, but Anne says, "'Git ye gone!'"

Monday night Silas is waiting at his two-room cottage, for the arrival of Dan. But the knock at the door turns out to be instead Sarah Emmet, the hump-backed woman who lays out dead bodies for burial. They have a long conversation punctuated by Sarah's attacks on Silas' apple cider, reluctantly given by Silas. Among many things, we find out that Sarah Emmet holds a grudge against Phoebe. Silas is shaken by the entire encounter, and near the end he finds that the doctor has thrown over hope of Mary Anne's recovery. As he rides in the direction of Mary Anne's cottage, "the knowledge that he too must some day die was indescribably dreadful to Silas." He makes some plans for the future as he travels along.

> "I'll stay no longer in this here vullage," he said. "I'll not give thickey hook-backed toad the chance o' playing hanky-panky wi' my corpse. If 'tworn't for Dan Pigott I'd hike to furren parts termarrer; but there's money in the sniveying slack-twist. Wance I've done wi' he I'll let vules bide. I'm grawing old. Sin be a risky bisness when a man is gitting up along in years. I'll wring him dry, and then I take up my lot wi' the saved; I shan't caddle away my time when wance I gits to wark. Maybe I'll turn chapelite: they be alles a mort surer o' Heaven than yer church-folks, handling the Lord more boldacious."

A neighbor woman lets Silas into the house, telling him Mary Anne has been calling for him. He is reluctant to go to her, however.

> "Ez yer wull; but the poor soul is calling on 'ee painful."
> "Death be a creepacious thing—a creepacious thing," he exclaimed huskily. "I'd a deal liefer bide where I am." Impelled even as he spoke by some power other than his will, he began slowly to ascend the stairs. The voice of the dying woman rang against him, and he put up his hands, warding it back. "I'd liefer not come," he muttered; "I'd liefer not come."

But he finds himself standing in her presence, and tremblingly asks what she wants of him. The ellipses are Mary Anne's.

> "I be dying," she gasped—"dying; and there bain't no hope out there, none. There bain't no faces; the Almighty bain't there, nor the Lord Jesus; there bain't no path—nought but dark, stretching on and on and on. I can't hold back from it, do what I wull I'm foced forrard, foced forrard. In my ears, there be a chime o' a mort o' voices; but wan I hears above all the rest, and it sounds like Dan Pigott's voice . . . and there's a wail in it, the zame ez the wail o' a damned soul . . . and it witnesses continually afore God agin me and agin you . . ."
> The sweat poured down Silas' face as he listened. "Say a wud to the Lord for me," he begged; "'tis the eleventh hour, but 'tiddn't too late. You've lived upstanding, He'll hark to you. Tull Him about your good work, and how you ha' alles gone to

church come storm come fine. Plead for me, Anne. Don't let Him listen to the lad's prayers."

"'Tis dark, dark," she answered; "even the gert white throne has ceased to shine . . . I can't find me way to it droo the dimmet; but if I flung mezulf face down 'pon tap the staps what wud it profit? . . . The Almighty wudn't heed while that voice testifies on . . ."

"Speak for me, Anne; speak for me!" he pleaded, sinking on his knees beside the bed. "Tull Him I be reckoning to ha' done wi' evil ways and repent. Tull Him I have put by a tidy bit o' money, and shan't be uncharitable to them that goes in need o' it."

"'Tis dark . . . dark . . ." she repeated,—"I can't find the gert white throne, and what wud it profit if I flung mezulf face down 'pon tap the staps . . . the Almighty wudn't heed while that voice testified on . . ."

"But I'll be easier wi' the lad; I'll no ruin him," Silas cried in a terror-stricken voice. "Zee," he continued, fumbling with trembling fingers in the lining of his cap, "zee, here be the letter. I ain't never showed it to Varmer Pigott, though I've had a mort o' temptation. Take it, Anne, lay it afore the Almighty—the lad can't witness agin me then."

He pressed the letter into her hand and her fingers closed upon it with the stiff grip of death. Her eyes turned back in their sockets, leaving only the white exposed: she opened her lips—a curious sound, half gurgle, half rattle, forced itself between them, and she fell forward on her face—dead.

He bent over and shook the prostrate form. "Testify, testify!" he shrieked.

She paid no need to him.

Then he tried to take the letter from her: but she would neither give it up nor witness for him.

When Sarah Emmet is called in to lay out the body of Mary Anne, she discovers the letter and reads it. Phoebe enters the room, and Sarah vows aloud to show the letter to Farmer Pigott and thus ruin Phoebe's supposed scheme to get Dan Pigott to marry her. Pheobe begs her not to be so cruel, but Sarah says she will do her "'duty.'"

Sarah drives her cart across the moor, stopping to inform the pedlar Ben of her "'tasty'" bit of news.

"Oh! her's a brazen piece, a true darter o' Babylon; but her'll no profit: there wor niver a sinner yit that profited when it comed to the last."

"Her's a better woman than you be, and ez sich you shudn't take on yerzulf to jidge her," said the pedlar, raising his head and looking her full in the eyes.

"Better'n me! Be you market merry, Ben Tap, or off your chump, or what? Why, I have the proof of all I zay, writ by the maid's own hand." She drew out the letter and held it up. "Afore another day be out the parish shall jidge which be the better woman, her or me."

Sarah drives on. Ben is not surprised to hear that Phoebe had taken the money for the sake of Dan. Ben sees Phoebe walking and running toward the farm. Ben unlashes his pack and hides it. She is too distressed to understand his words, but he swings her up into the saddle of his horse and walks beside it, heading for Pigott's farm.

The girl sat straining forward, searching the horizon with her eyes, and, watching her, Ben's heart grew hot with pity. A vision of Dan's weak, handsome face rose before him, and the pity changed to bitterness. Why, he asked himself, did she love this man? Then, like a wave of blood, his own love and its implacable needs rushed over him.

By some subtle instinct the girl divined his feeling. "I won't need to trouble 'ee furder," she said, and before he could protest she had slipped down from the saddle and fled along the path that led to her lover's home.

Ben stood and watched till the moor, descending abruptly, hid her from view.

Meanwhile, Dan, not having been able to pay the ten pounds, "gave up the struggle and waited for fate to do its worst." Mrs. Pigott sees his misery and goes to his room. She tries to encourage him. Her sympathy moves him to tell her why Phoebe stole the fifteen pounds. He blames Phoebe for putting him in the mess he is in.

His aunt looked at him, but made no answer, and the shame which he was incapable of feeling reddened her face. A long, long silence ensued; little by little there came to Dan a faint, far-off perception of his own meanness.

Under Mrs. Pigott's guidance, he begins to understand Phoebe's suffering, and what he owes to her. Mrs. Pigott advises him to tell his uncle the whole story, and Dan promises to do so right away. She warns him not to "'hark back'" from his promise at the last, saying it is the kind of thing we all are tempted to do. Then follows the passage I have used as the first epigraph for the chapter, in which Dan bitterly says that God does not help a man as much as you might expect from reading the Bible.

Dan takes his gun with him as he goes, hoping to chance upon a rabbit. On his way to find Farmer Pigott, Dan encounters Silas, and tells him he doesn't have the money. Silas is disgusted with himself for having been so easily moved at Mary Anne's deathbed, but claims he never intended harm against Dan from the first, making lemonade out of a lemony situation. He also extorts five shillings, a lucky six pence, and a watch and chain—the best he can do for himself under the circumstance of no longer having the letter. Silas rides on.

Dan exults at his supposed release, then remembers that he still needs to tell the truth in order to clear Phoebe in his uncle's eyes: "his heart was pregnant with a nobler music, and from it the first hesitating note of self-sacrifice leapt heavenward."

> "I mustn't stap to think or 'twull be all over wi' me," he muttered. "Uncle," he continued breathlessly, halting in front of the old stern-faced man; "I've zommat to tull 'ee; it's bin lying on my mind this long while. You knaw Phoebe Hazeldene. You mind on they fifteen pun her took; you alles reckoned ez how I wor at the bottom o' ut. Wull, I—" he stopped short.
>
> "Wutt iver ba 'ee driving at now?" exclaimed the farmer, eyeing the young fellow's pale agitated face with evident distrust.
>
> "I wanted to tull 'ee," Dan persevered, but the words came hesitatingly, "that—" he stopped again.
>
> "That you've bin a domned blackguard all along."
>
> "Noo, noo; not that."
>
> "What, then?"
>
> "I wanted to tull 'ee that—that—"
>
> "Thic money wor stoled for 'ee?"
>
> Fear spattered to bits all that remained of Dan's new-found courage. "Noo, noo; I hadn't nought to do wi' ut. You alles held 'twor me from the vust; but 'twor't me, 'twor the maid."

The farmer looked at him with growing disfavour. "You banging gert sloppy spirut!" he said; "wutt do 'ee mean wi' coming to me wi' that tale at this time o' day? I shud ha' thought you'd bin content to latt the maid's name alone, jidging ez how you guv'd out that you wor sweet wan 'pon t'other."

In that moment of bitter self-revelation Dan was indifferent to any words of his uncle. "I bain't made of the stuff that wins droo," he exclaimed hopelessly. "I shall niver, niver, play the man."

Just then Sarah Emmet appears, and shows the letter to Farmer Pigott. He reads the letter, and sends Sarah on her way. Dan says that he had tried to tell his uncle, but his uncle is unmoved, and tells Dan to leave and never come back. "'You drashed me into baing afeard o' 'ee ez a lad,'" Dan begins, but doesn't finish speaking. He begins to walk slowly away. Farmer Pigott tells him to take the gun which is leaning against the tree, and put a bullet through himself. Dan takes the gun and walks out on the moor; "his heart was emptied of feeling." When the fog parts,

> he found himself face to face with Silas Trustgore. At the sight of his enemy, the need of revenge came to Dan, streaming down each tingling pulse into his empty heart. Laying the gun on the ground, he gripped the old man round the waist, lifted him from the saddle, and the fog closed in upon them both, so that each saw the other through a grey veil.
>
> Then Dan spoke, and his voice sounded soft and dull, so that he told himself that it was not he that spoke but some other man, or the mist, maybe.
>
> "Me and you," he said, "have a deal to zettle. Look to yerzulf, for either you kills me or I kills you." Then without further words he took his enemy by the throat, and dashed his fist into his face. Swaying back, Silas grasped at the gun, where it lay muzzle towards Dan on the ground: a spray of heather caught in the trigger, and in a moment the contents of both barrels were lodged in the young fellow's chest. With a half-uttered cry, he fell, rolled a few paces, and lay tearing at the soft turf, along which the blood began to trickle slowly. A brief moment the hostler stood and watched the red stream, then, mounting his pony, he rode away. Far below in the valley a breeze arose, parting the fog into long grey strips, which it caught again and rolled out of sight beyond the high

ridges of the moor. The winter sun gleamed coldly on the red farm-buildings, the great yellow stacks of corn; on the alder-hedge, the spinney of tall slender larch-trees. Raising himself, Dan looked for the last time at the farm that he loved so well, and for the possession of which he had played so poor a part.

"I wud dearly liked to ha' bin master o' ut wance," he murmured. Then the blood frothing up choked his utterance, and he fell back dead.

There the novel ends.

As is often the case with Zack's stories, there are loose ends, including what we might call spiritual loose ends—as is true with life in general. We don't know what will happen to the other characters. We can only guess, given their behavior which we have seen.

Silas, it seems to me, will keep silent concerning the episode, hoping that his presence at Dan's death will not be suspected. Very likely his hopes will be confirmed. No one has seen the fight. Moreover, there is an excellent chance that Dan's death will be assumed to be a suicide. Samuel Pigott himself told Dan to take his gun and put a bullet through himself. He may well guess that Dan has done exactly that. That will be a blow to the sturdy farmer. It is one thing to require his nephew to leave the farm forever, quite another to tell the young man to kill himself and to find that kill himself is exactly what he has done (supposedly). Farmer Pigott's trials, emotional and spiritual, may just be beginning. Samuel Pigott will not lie, however. He will speak up honestly and recount what his last words to Dan had been. That will encourage everyone to guess that Dan's death was indeed a suicide.

Silas has escaped death, narrowly. In a hand to hand battle with Dan, the older man may well have died, since Dan said that it was to be a fight to the death. Will Silas continue his self-deceiving ways in which he tries to consider himself as walking within the will of God? Or has he had the fright he needed to cause him to see his need for repentance? We can't be optimistic about his spiritual state, given what we know of his past. But we can't be certain what he will do.

My guess is that Ben's love for Phoebe Hazeldene will go unrewarded. He is a good man, even in some ways a very great man, but Phoebe has never given a sign that she could care for him in a romantic sense. Now that she is free from her attachment to Dan, she will be free to give her heart elsewhere, if she chooses to do so. One hopes that she will choose more wisely next time, but Zack has given us no reason to hope that Ben will be her choice. Ben will live out his honorable life alone, as he has done already into middle age. He may well die alone. Then he will face God. Here is a man who has a chance of hearing ""Well done, good and faithful slave"" (Matt. 25:21, 23). There are far, far worse fates! This life is for seventy or eighty years; eternity is forever. Ben is one of the numerous Zack characters who face life with courage and high principles and generosity of spirit. Phoebe, despite her sin of having stolen the fifteen pounds, is another one. But it seems unlikely that Phoebe will look to Ben for a companion for life.

The death of Dan will be difficult for Phoebe to absorb. She loved him with a generous love that saw his faults and went on loving. Her love for Dan may have been unwise, but it was deep. One can easily imagine Phoebe remaining unmarried the rest of her life, despite her great physical and moral attractiveness. It is difficult to imagine her loving again. But she is very young. She may recover and love again— hopefully choosing her man more wisely next time. If my advice were asked, I would nudge her in the general direction of Ben. But there is no foreshadowing of such an outcome for Phoebe.

For Dan, there is no loose end about this life: he is dead. But the spiritual loose ends are numerous. It seems to me that the reviewers missed the significance of the way Dan died. One said he "perishes miserably."[29] None of the reviewers seemed to see anything encouraging toward Dan in the way of his death.

But I find his manner of death to give us some reason to see that Dan has grown spiritually to a significant extent. For the first time he has the courage to grapple with his enemy. From the start of the story Dan has been afraid to fight Silas for the letter. Now, when it is too late for a fight to get the letter back, Dan is willing not only to fight, but to fight to the death. Now that he has lost all human hope for this world— he has been thrown off the farm, and has been reviled to his face by his

---

[29]Unknown reviewer, "The Spectator," October 7, 1899, p. 34.

uncle—he somehow gets the courage to fight the man who has been his nemesis and before whom he has acted in a cowardly manner numerous times. How? Is it possible that his prayer to God, early on in the book, has been answered? The prayer is answered belatedly, true. But God's ways are not our ways, His timing not the timing we would prefer. Near the end of the book Dan bitterly complains that God doesn't help a man as much as you might expect from reading the Bible. But God may have at last given Dan the courage to fight, to be in some way a man, to be willing to die rather than just walk away. Certainly Dan has the courage from somewhere. It is wrong to think that he "perishes miserably." He perishes fighting to the death, like a man should.

The irony of Dan's last words shows Zack's artistry at its best. Dan dies saying that he would have dearly loved to have been master of the farm once. It is a happy irony which Dan does not understand, that he has indeed been master of the farm one time—now in these last moments when he was master of his own spirit enough to fight his enemy. Dan has missed seeing that truth, and I think the reader may easily miss that truth as well, as the reviewers all seem to have done!

Still, there are more spiritual loose ends here for Dan. By what right does he challenge Silas to a fight to the death? Silas has acted dishonorably, and a good thrashing at the hands of Dan would seem to be just about what Silas should get. If Dan does not come out unscathed from such a fight, he would have no complaint. His behavior has earned a thrashing too—he would be better off receiving some lumps and bruises for his cowardly behavior in regard to the letter, than to come away from the fight unhurt. But does Silas deserve death for his behavior? Silas has neither murdered nor raped, has not done any crime for which the just (biblical) judgment is execution on this earth.

Dan, then, in challenging Silas to a fight to the death, is not acting completely right. Even as he finds some courage—at which we all cheer—he is threatening to beat a man to death for a crime which does not deserve the death penalty. He is in the wrong to want to fight to the death. For this Dan also must answer to God, when he stands before Him.

There are degrees of wrongness. Dan is not exactly murdering Silas. He could have murdered Silas by discharging the gun upon him.

Instead, he lays the gun on the ground. God providentially arranges the fight so that the gun is fired, but it is fired accidentally, and the victim is Dan, not Silas. Still, had Dan killed Silas in the fight, that would correctly be identified as murder. Giving Silas a sound beating in a fair fight is not murder. Beating Silas to death would be murder.

Dan will stand before God with many things to answer for. We can hope, with Ben, that when it comes to judging, it won't necessarily be condemnation that the Lord hands out, but rather readjustment. Certainly Dan has "played so poor a part" in his life, but his nature was against him. We are glad, at least, to see him stand up like a man at the last.

Zack has showed us Dan Pigott on trial. For the most part Dan has failed his trial, but there is a gleam of hope about him here and there in the story, and I think more than a gleam at the end.

But Dan was not the only person on trial in the book *On Trial*. For Zack, life is in its essence a moral test. Many of the characters are more or less on trial. Silas Trustgore, Phoebe Hazeldene, Captain Brattle, Mary Anne Wort, Ben Tap, Samuel Pigott, Mrs. Pigott, Hannah, Sarah Emmet—all face a moral trial in how they will behave. We could say the same of characters we meet only briefly, such as Mrs. Stiggins or Phoebe's father. They meet their trials with vastly differing degrees of success. For Zack, life is not just something that happens. It is a time of moral testing. Zack's moral wisdom allows her to see that we are all on trial.

Port Hill, the birthplace of Gwendoline Keats, is on the A386 road about 1/2 mile south of Northam, on the west side of the road. The front of the house faces south. The house is about 120 yards from the road. Port Hill is currently owned by Mr. and Mrs. Michael (Penny) Portman. Photo by Mrs. Michael (Penny) Portman; used by the kind permission of the Portmans.

A watercolor painting of Port Hill, by Tim Scott Bolton. His view is from the left front of the house. Painting used by the kind permission of Mr. Bolton, and of Mr. and Mrs. Portman.

William Rochfort Keats, father of Gwendoline. He died of tuberculosis at age 35, when Gwendoline was a month short of her seventh birthday. This photograph and the eighteen following are all used by the kind permission of Mr. and Mrs. Andy (Beverley) Keats.

Lucy Elizabeth Thorold Keats, mother of Gwendoline. She died, probably of cancer, at age 44 or 45, when Gwendoline was about 15 ½ years old.

Thorold Goodwin Keats, first born child of William and Lucy, and the oldest brother of Gwendoline. He was called Bob in the family.

Jessie Eliza Cumming Keats, wife of Thorold Goodwin Keats.

Three of the seven children of Thorold Goodwin and Jessie Keats:
Richard Goodwin (3rd), Thora Violet (2nd), Gladys Elizabeth Lucy (1st).
It was Gladys to whom Gwendoline gave the brooch (see Chapter 6).

Margaret Gwendoline, fourth child of T. G. and Jessie Keats. She would go on to attain a measure of fame as an Australian veterinarian, and was awarded an MBE (Member of the Most Excellent Order of the British Empire).

William Thorold, fifth child of T. G. and Jessie Keats. He
suffered from the effects of gassing in World War I.

Sybil Anne (6th) and John Francis (7th), the final
two children of T. G. and Jessie Keats.

Herbert Frederick Cyril Keats, second born child of William and Lucy,
and brother to Gwendoline. He was called Fred in the family.

A picture of Mary Cecilia (Cis) Cumming at a young age. She would grow up to marry Fred. She was a younger sister to Jessie, who married T. G. Keats.

Four of the five children of Fred and Cis Keats: Frederick Thorold (2nd), standing; he would be killed in action in World War I; John Rochfort (3rd), seated bottom left; he was wounded in World War I and also received the Military Cross; Lucy Cecilia Anne (1st), larger girl; Freda "Pauline" (4th).

Arthur Rochfort Keats, third born child of William
and Lucy, and brother to Gwendoline.

Eva Gollin. It is uncertain whether or not this photograph comes prior to or after her marriage to Arthur Keats. Apparently they had one child, Lucy Gwendoline.

Bertha Gwendoline Keats (taller), called Gwenda in the
family, fourth born child of William and Lucy, with her sister-
in-law Jessie Keats, in a photo taken in London.

Gwendoline Keats, in a photo taken in London.

Gwendoline Keats, in a photo taken in Dresden, Germany.

Gwendoline Keats, in another photo taken in Dresden.

Gwendoline Keats in her mid 20s, in a photograph taken in South Australia perhaps as early as 1887. All three of her brothers settled in Australia.

Painting of Gwendoline Keats by Friedrich Anton Otto
Prölss, made in Dresden in the early 1890s. The painting
remains in the possession of the Keats family.

CHAPTER 3

The White Cottage

"The Bible says," he muttered, "that the man who holds by the Almighty, the Almighty will hold by him. Well, I have led a clean life an' acted fair. The devil ain't never bested me yet, and what's more, he never shall." A curious muffled sound, like a subdued laugh, echoed across the water as the wind dropped round a point more east. Mark glanced about him uneasily. "One could most believe that he was on the listen. Well, let him listen. He can't work me no harm. I'm on the Lord's side."

Zack, The White Cottage

Zack's third book, *The White Cottage*, was published by Constable & Co. in April of 1901. It was her second and final novel. Like *On Trial*, *The White Cottage* is a short book, its total words somewhere around 40,000. In the U.S., the book was published by Charles Scribner's Sons, also in 1901.

The book was widely reviewed, for the most part favorably, although as usual there were critical comments even among those who admired the book. The book did not escape public recognition for excellence. In November of 1901, "The Academy" listed *The White Cottage* as being among the twelve best novels of the year.

One astonishing fact regarding the book comes out in one of Zack's letters to her writer friend May Sinclair. That is, prior to the book being published, Zack offered to return a significant portion of money to the publishing company. Her handwriting is sometimes hard to read, but in this case only one word is uncertain. Writing possibly in March, but certainly in 1901, and from the context just prior to the book coming out, Zack wrote, "I have just corrected the proofs of mine & felt so sick at its rottenness that I have written Mr. [Miss?] Constable offering them back £40 out of the £150 they gave me for it."[30] This from a woman who occasionally described herself as "penniless"!

I hope that Constable & Co. politely declined that offer.

At least one reviewer expected the book to live on in the reader's mind. The ellipsis is mine. The spelling of unforgettable is the reviewer's.

> There is no doubt that Gwendoline Keats, who writes under the *nom de guerre* of "Zack," is a power in the world of letters. What she says, she says with brevity, intensity, and dramatic force. The record of every page is burned in with such sharpness that even after twenty years one would say, "I once read a story—the name of it has escaped me—in which a Devonshire coast woman was loved by two men, one a fisher, the other the shiftless son of a poacher." . . .
>
> So would the mind travel on from one unforgetable detail to the next. It is the kind of story that one never forgets.[31]

The book opens with twenty-six year old fisherman Mark Tavy in his boat pulling in his lines off the coast of Devonshire, near the village of Bere-Upton. Seeing the small white-washed cottage at the top of the cliff, the cottage which gives the book its title, Mark vows to rent the place when he and Luce Myrtle are married. Then follow the words quoted in the epigraph above.

From the start we sense that things may not go as smoothly as Mark hopes. The "subdued laugh" makes even Mark uneasy. He lands, daydreaming of his future happiness with Luce. He knows Luce "'has never cared for me the same as I have for her,'" but fully intends to be a good husband to her.

Mark discovers that the cottage has already been rented to Ben Lupin, Mark's old enemy, back in Bere-Upton after five years' absence. Their interests had clashed before, and Mark had always come off the loser.

---

[30]Zack letter to May Sinclair, March?, 1901.
[31]C. S., "A Devonshire Love Story," "The Book Buyer," May 1901, p. 328.

Nothing, perhaps, would have astonished Ben Lupin more, had it been possible for him to realize it, than the strength of the resentment which he had aroused in Mark. Personally he bore no grudge against, neither had he ever wished to compete with, the young fisherman; he had rather a contempt for him than otherwise. Events that had left a rankling sore in Mark's heart, had passed by, making little or no impression on Lupin's: the fight, the struggle against too heavy odds, the ultimate inevitable failure, had fallen to Mark; success marched with Lupin, and he had not even heard the jarring of its wheels.

When Mark goes to call on Luce, he sees the cheerful but poor Ben Lupin outside the Myrtle home. Mark takes the unusually pale Luce on a walk, bitterly recounting what had happened.

"Lupin's taken our little cottage," he burst out; "the cottage where our children would have been born."

The girl drew nearer, leant upon the small gate and stared across at the cottage with a curious, tense gaze, as if it were not the cottage that she saw, but some vision which frightened and yet fascinated her.

Luce, desperate, begs Mark to hold her

"so that no wan, no matter who he be, can take me from 'ee."

He clasped her against his breast.

"Why is it," she said, "that I can't feel 'ee close? Why do 'ee stand so far away sort o' insecure?"

"But I am here, sweetheart; my arms be round 'ee."

"Your spirit iddn't here," she cried bitterly. "I don't feel it saying kinder masterful—'Luce, you be jest Mark's, and he'll up and do wi' 'ee what he reckons best.'"

"Why should I say that?" Mark expostulated. "You've got your rights the same as me."

Dropping her hands to her side she retreated a few paces from him. "'Tiddn't no use," she said; "a man can't be more'n hisself."

Luce hints that they may never marry. After more words discouraging to Mark's hopes, they separate.

Nearing home, Luce encounters Ben Lupin. She knows his reputation is a bad one. Years ago he had left the village after "a wild piece of work in which a woman's honour had fallen victim."

> Ben cared little for the abuse showered so liberally upon him; above all else he loved to hold life in a careless hand, tossing it now this way now that, indifferent to what befell, playing with the happiness of others, even as he played with his own. Fate had watched his career strangely complacent, letting him have his will with men and things, and Lupin hardened, scoffed at the idea of retribution. It seemed to him as if suffering could never fall to his lot, life containing nothing that he either loved or feared. Unknown to him he had long held sway over Luce Myrtle's imagination, fired by tales of his wild fantastic doings. Secretly she had wished for and again half dreaded the return of this ugly faced man, who had such a way with a maid, that all women perforce must love him; yet had she so shielded her longing in the privacy of her heart that it had been to her but a half-conscious need of some more subtle flavour in life and love than had hitherto fallen to her share. Up to the time of Lupin's return the fear that she might some day be tempted to be unfaithful to Mark had never troubled her; still she had been restless under her promise, much as a young filly strains at the bit, when the wrong pair of hands holds the reins; but with the meeting again of Lupin the veil of self-deception which had hidden the truth from her was torn aside, and she saw that it was he and not Mark whom she loved.

In this encounter, Ben easily masters the spirit of Luce, but his desire to fondle her body is frustrated—apparently by an unwilling respect for Luce, surprising even to Ben—and she escapes home. She tells her father, John Myrtle, that she prefers not to marry, and but to stay home with her parents. He does not fully understand her, but comforts her as he can. She is "tired out by emotion," and falls asleep on his breast. Her father carries the sleeping, frail young woman up to her bed. She is not much more than "'a sprig o' a chile'" as her father describes her to himself.

> Long afterwards she awoke with a start. Below, in the street, a man was whistling; the notes thrust themselves upon her, challenging her to heed.

She put out her hands imploringly.—"Don't call me, Ben; don't call me or I'll be fo'ced to valler," she cried.

In the next days Ben Lupin is uncharacteristically indecisive; Luce has confused him. On Sunday he slips into a part of the church where he can see without being seen. Mark is there, for the calling of the banns which indicate that he and Luce are to be married barring any legal impediment. This Sunday apparently marks the first of the three Sundays of the calling of the banns for Mark and Luce. Mark "was serenely happy, the memory of his many failures passed from him, he weltered in success as only he to whom it seldom falls, can." Zack's insight into human nature here seems, as is so often true, right on target. To Mark's disappointment, however, Luce has not come to church today. The rector, Rev. Baugh, will read their names out.

> the Rev. Benjamin Baugh had a way of reading the banns that made a man feel there was to be no drawing back, and villagers of a less decided turn of mind preferred on that account to be "put up by the currit."

(Once again Zack has inserted a family name into her fictional narrative. Her grandfather on her mother's side was Reverend Henry Baugh Thorold, rector at Grantham in Lincolnshire. Thanks to Mrs. Beverley Keats, we know there is a Dec. 1, 1882 letter from Rev. Henry Baugh Thorold to Fred Keats saying that Arthur and Gwenda were expected for Christmas; the reverend wondered how he was going to entertain Gwenda! Gwendoline [Gwenda] would have been age seventeen in 1882. Rev. Baugh has a small but honorable part in the novel. One wonders if Zack's grandfather had a similarly decisive way of reading the banns.)

When Lupin understands that Mark is to marry Luce, "A joyous elation possessed him; he knew his own mind at last, and saw straight as a shaft of light the way that led to his desire." He hurries to the Myrtle cottage, where he finds Luce outside. He goes to her, and finally sits down beside her. Neither speaks; she weeps; he leaves her.

The next morning Mark, while fishing for herring, is blown down the coast. He returns to Bere-Upton on the next Sunday. As he anchors his boat, he is met by Ben Lupin, who takes him to the White Cottage and sends him inside. There he finds Luce. She is tearlessly sobbing, but does not at first speak.

> It seemed to Mark standing there that his heart was being drawn from his breast, and peeled piece by piece as a boy peels a willow twig.
>
> "I wud ha' been true to 'ee," she exclaimed at last in a broken voice. "I wanted to be true to 'ee; but, lad, I just worn't."
>
> He turned away, the pain of her words was unbearable.
>
> "I reckoned," he said, "that you was the wan pussen in the whole world that sort o' understood things."

Outside, Lupin informs Mark that the two had been married by special license. Mark calls Ben a "'blackguardly thief,'" but Ben calls Mark a fool, and says, "'I didn't steal the maid; her was never yours.'" Mark draws his knife to murder Ben, but Ben stuns him with a blow from his fist, goes inside, and closes the door. When recovered, Mark goes off.

Mark decides to leave the village temporarily. He sells his boat and his nets. On his way out of town he is stopped by Luce's mother, who asks him to come inside. He unwillingly complies. She acknowledges that he would have made a dependable husband.

> His thin, emotional face flushed hotly. "You mustn't reckon I'm gwaying away beat," he said with sudden passion. "Lupin ain't seen the last of me yet by a long bit—there's zommat that tells me that if I hold myzulf to patience, the Almighty 'ull show me how to get quits wi' un."
>
> An expression of uneasiness came into the old woman's eyes.
>
> "I've no opinion o' the high falutin'," she answered. "That what a man can't get iddn't meant for him, and you'll be wise if you let Ben Lupin alone in the future."
>
> "Do you reckon the Almighty is gwaying to let 'un alone?" he burst out. "Do you reckon that God is always gwaying to zee the wicked flourish at the expense o' the well-doer? No, I tull 'ee, there be ill days in store for Ben Lupin, and when they are at hand I shan't be far from un."

Mark walks to the nearest seaport town, and sails for Nova Scotia, "brooding over his wrongs," and frequently rereading the words "'Vengeance is Mine; I will repay, saith the Lord'" from Romans 12:19. Zack incorrectly identifies this quote as coming from the eleventh chapter of Romans rather than the twelfth. It is an interesting error, it seems to me. It indicates, at least possibly, that she was quoting from memory. She got the words right, but was one chapter off as to the location of the quote. However, it is easy to make too much of this, because it is very easy to cite the wrong location for a verse, even with Bible in hand.

After several months Mark sails back to England, arriving at the end of winter and beginning of spring. He sees the White Cottage: "the thought of God's impending vengeance failed to comfort him; it seemed but of scant account compared with what he had lost."

He slips behind a bush close to a window and sees Ben and Luce together. The latter is crying, but Mark well understands that they are tears of happiness. At that moment Luce reveals to Ben that she is pregnant. Mark rushes away, the hills ringing with his derisive laughter. Apparently Mark now views his own hope for God's vengeance with derision: God has ignored Mark's hope for vengeance on Ben.

Mark wanders all night in the fields, and by morning is still tormented by what he had seen and heard.

> His virility rose in rebellion against the existence of this yet unborn child—the child that should have been his own, and was Lupin's. How often had he not dreamed of the child, felt its soft kisses upon his face in sleep, the tiny hands playing with his beard. It could not be that Luce should bear it to another, and that other his enemy. Yes, she would bear Lupin's son, she longed to bear him, for she loved Lupin. Mark raised his face wet with dew and tears to heaven. "O God," he said, "'tiddn't true her loves un. O God Almighty, not that, not that!"

At last he sleeps somewhere in a field, healing somewhat, and on waking finds his cousin Samuel Bompas standing over him with kindly concern. Bompas takes Mark into his home. "The big, unpretentious kitchen, with its air of homely comfort and hospitality, seemed to bid Mark welcome, and yet to make no undue fuss over his arrival." Mark finds himself hungry, and is invited to eat by the practical Bompas, who understands that food can encourage "'a man on to finding himself.'"

> The young fellow did as he was bid, surprised at the vigour with which he attacked the food, and the satisfaction that the mere act of eating gave to him. It seemed to him a paltry kind of comfort for an aching heart, and yet he felt less miserable than he had on entering. Well, if bacon and fried potatoes could cure him of his trouble, so much the better, and he pushed out his plate for a second help.

The meal over, Mark falls asleep, dreaming of a flower—clearly stated to be the vengeance of God—which wounds his hand when he tries to pick it. He awakes to find a woman, with a striking and sad face, standing in the doorway. She asks if a man named Lupin lives in the area. Mark instinctively feels "that she was no ordinary woman, but the chosen instrument of God's vengeance." But Samuel Bompas chases her away, and Mark does not follow her immediately. He wonders if the woman had been betrayed by Lupin as he, Mark, had been betrayed, and exults at the possibility of God's vengeance.

That same afternoon the woman encounters Ben Lupin. She is his wife, Hester Lupin. She tells him she is no longer a drunkard, having been dry three months. But he has already told her he has done with her, and he never goes back on his word. She pleads with him, but he is firm, and tells her he is married, adding that she can have her revenge by going to the law. But she wants him, not revenge. He is about to leave her, and she asks him to kiss her once before he goes.

> For a moment he stood and looked upon her face, which seemed as if all the sorrow of the world had been crushed into it, and a horror seized him of this woman capable of entertaining such suffering. He thrust her from him and hurried away into the gathering darkness.

That night Hester begins her return journey home, but loses herself in the country lanes. Mark has been searching for her all day, and now finds her. He tells her that she is God's appointed instrument of wrath, and invites her to bear witness against Ben Lupin. He guesses, without being certain, that she is Ben's wife. Hester will admit nothing, and refuses to enter a plot to punish Ben. She contemptuously calls Mark a fool.

> "I'll larn the truth in spite o' ee," he answered, shame sending the hot blood spurting across his brow. "I've acted fair all my life, and 'tiddn't to be believed that the Almighty is going to see me wronged."
>
> Hester Lupin, who had walked away a few paces, stopped short and turned her sad, tragic face towards him. "There be more wrongs in the world than just yours and mine," she answered. "S'pose the Almighty in righting 'em wor fo'ced to let ours bide?" Then, without further speech, she left him and pursued her way.

Hester makes the fifty-mile journey home. She stays sober another seven months, then one August morning takes the train to Bere-Upton. Outside the White Cottage, Luce finds her looking faint and tired, and invites her inside to rest. They talk of Luce's coming baby, Hester eventually warning Luce that life may not always run as smooth for her as it has thus far.

> "Haven't 'ee niver heard o' zarrer? Who be you and yours that you shud hope to escape it? Do 'ee think cuz the chile lies safe agin your heart now that the day 'ull niver come when he'll stray far from 'ee? Do 'ee count that the Ben you have larned to trust in the saft months o' courting 'ull be the zame droo life?"
>
> The younger woman drew away her arm and sank down on the nearest chair.
>
> "It scares me to hear 'ee talk zo," she protested. "What do mak' 'ee do it? Zee, I am all o' a trembly."
>
> "I don't want to scare 'ee," Hester answered in a sad voice. "I don't wish 'ee no harm, nay, more'n that, I cud find it in my heart to wish 'ee wull. To add to your zarrer 'ull take nought from the weight o' mine."

Ben hears part of their talk, and at last Hester sees him, but she leaves without revealing her secret, leaving Ben considerably shaken.

> True, his secret still remained undisclosed, but not till that moment had he realized how great was the gift he had been

willing to accept, and his manhood trembled beneath the weight of a craven gratitude. He had never analysed his love for Luce, nor understood how rapid had been its growth, or how closely his happiness had become bound up with hers. He had believed himself strong enough to do wrong and bear the punishment of his wrong-doing; but standing, a silent spectator of the scene between the two women, a novel sensation had come to him; for the first time in his life he had been afraid. His whole nature revolted against the harbouring of fear, but he could not thrust it from him, stronger than his pride was this strange new need of happiness. Unobserved by him it had sprung up in his heart, sheltered by the presence there of the one woman he had ever learned to love.

When Hester leaves the White Cottage, the curious Septimus Spong follows her and sees her faint. He helps her, and suggests "'a drop o' spirruts 'ud put fresh life into 'ee.'" They go into the inn, and Spong pours a glass of rum for her.

> She put out her hand and drew it closer, but did not drink. The smell of the spirits filled the room. Leaning back in her chair she closed her eyes; her hands, gripped tight together, were folded on her knee. From time to time her throat twitched as if she were swallowing. Suddenly she bent forward, thrust her lips to the glass, sucking up the liquid with a hideous sound of hurry. Spong watched her in dismay, but she had forgotten his presence.
>
> Seizing the bottle, she filled and refilled her glass with pure spirits. An unsexed expression came into her face, the wan cheeks seemed to cave together; it was as if some oubliette of the soul had opened through which her womanhood had sunk out of sight.
>
> The sweat began to gather on Spong's forehead; he wiped it off with his hand.

While drinking, Hester accidentally lets slip the fact that she is Ben Lupin's wife. When she falls into a drunken stupor, Spong flees. Spong, although by nature 'an "interfering man,"' is unsure how to act. He sleeps on his decision, and wakes still undecided but determined to tell Ben Lupin "what he thought of his behaviour." However, he sees Lupin hurrying away toward the village. Spong goes to the White

Cottage, where he finds Luce in labor pains. Spong says to himself, "'I cudn't find it in my heart to part 'em—things must jest bide ez they ba.'"

Spong keeps his secret three weeks, but one day lets slip to Mark a hint of the situation, and Mark tricks the truth out of him. Spong cautions Mark,

> "Tiddn't no matter to be lightly meddled with, and the man that takes it on hiszulf to interfere ull ez like ez not ha' the breaking o' Luce Myrtle's heart for his pains. You can't strip a maid sich ez her be o' decency and rispact and reckon to be thanked for your trouble."

Mark takes his boat out to sea, daydreaming of making an honest woman of Luce. He tries to convince himself that it is the right thing to do to reveal Lupin's bigamy, but is somewhat startled when he finds that he has a fixed purpose to speak out on the topic. He senses that part of his motivation may be unworthy, but accepts such a notion only tentatively, "for it was part of his faith that he was a good man and that his cause was just."

Meanwhile, Spong has entered the Widow Flutter's cottage, where once again he and Constable Garge are courting the widow. Annoyed at his rival, Spong magnifies himself by telling the widow of Lupin's bigamy while Garge sleeps.

Mark plans to reveal the secret of Lupin's bigamy to the Squire, who is a magistrate, at the Great House. On the way there, he sees Luce with her child outside the White Cottage. She tries to be friendly to him.

> "Lad," she said, putting her hand upon his arm, "do be friends wi' me, do, and then I do think I shall have nothing left to wish for."
>
> "Friends," he repeated, shaking himself free. "Who cares aught for sich ez thic?"
>
> An expression half sad, half tender, came into her face.
>
> "Us wor niver more'n friends, Mark," she answered gently; "but us have been friends iver since us wor childer."
>
> His heart rose in rebellion against her. It seemed to him that she was trying to cheapen his love, to class it out from being love at all.
>
> "'Tiz zommat a mort different from thic that I veel for 'ee, and you know it," he replied.

She turned from him to the open window. "Zims ez if you must be mistook, lad," she said softly.

He did not answer. The pity which filled him a few short moments back had departed, and in its place a dull anger burnt in his heart. For the first time the desire came to him to punish this woman who was so indifferent to his love, to teach her through suffering the lesson that kindness failed to instil.

"I must be gwaying," he exclaimed. "I've zommat to zay to the Squire up to the Great House. Maybe you and Lupin'll have cause to hear o' me again," and swinging round on his heel, he left the cottage.

However, as he enters the Great House grounds, Mark's anger dies. He becomes unsure of himself and hesitates. His conscience alerts him to the fact that he "was about to plant his foot on the wrong road."

Nevertheless, he goes forward, intending to turn in Ben, despite the urging of his conscience. In the presence of the Squire, a frank man generous of spirit but sparing of words, Mark's prepared speech deserts him,

and Mark—anger, jealousy, bitterness, the need of Luce's love and the fear of parting with self-respect making a strange turmoil in his heart—stood looking at this imperturbable old man, who, unmoved and critical, gazed back at him and seemed in some subtle way to represent Mark's own long dormant conscience. A craving for help came to Mark, and he stretched out his hand as one seeking support.

"Sir," he said thickly, "if a man had acted black to 'ee and you had it in your power to do the same by 'un, what wud 'ee do?"

Without naming names or specifics, Mark consults the Squire's opinion, asking him if he would force a woman to take shelter with him. After a long pause,

The Squire rose and came to where Mark was standing.

"My lad," he said, laying his hand on the young fellow's arm, "you have given me a tough question, but I think you and I are of the same opinion as to the answer."

"And what be thic, sir?" Mark asked breathlessly.

"To leave her where she felt most sheltered," replied the Squire in a low voice.

They speak a bit more, and Mark leaves without having revealed his secret. Mark is glad he had not "told his tale," "but his heart was sore because Luce could never know how much the silence had cost him."

But Spong's inability to keep silent has finally resulted in Constable Garge arresting Lupin. Garge allows Lupin liberty to break the news to Luce. He struggles to speak, and after a long time, tells her the truth, and says he will come back to her after his sentence is served. She first cries out in dismay, then as he holds her in his arms, "he felt the slow receding of her love from him as a great physical agony that could not be borne." She doesn't speak to him, and never comes to him during his trial; he is sentenced to five years' imprisonment.

Luce is first pitied by the villagers, then gradually comes to be seen as "willing accomplice after the act" in Lupin's bigamy. Luce's mother meets her trouble in a "genteel" fashion, but Luce's father John Myrtle is deeply grieved.

> Good birth—like murder—will out, and nothing at this point could afford a more striking contrast than the behaviour of John Myrtle and his wife; but then, all the world knew that he had been a work-'us lad with no parents to speak of. There was an unrestrained sincerity about his grief that made it, to the critical taste of the village, almost vulgar.
>
> He sat by the kitchen sink, unwashed, yet within reach of water, his great, hairy chest exposed, and shaken by tearless sobs. "'Twor a throw-back to his mother," the villagers said, who, to her shame, had been deceived and cast upon the streets.

The Rev. Benjamin Baugh is sincerely sorry for Luce, and tries to comfort her, but is uncomfortable before Luce's "sad, serious eyes," and retreats hastily. Her father is left in the cottage with Luce and her now illegitimate child.

> John Myrtle found a chair close to the cradle and sat down. A curious sensation came to him. It was much as if the child that lay there sleeping so unconcernedly were himself—for he too had been a child of shame: a like indifference had filled him in

those far-off days; he supped in life and waxed strong, knowing only that the breast that fed him was sweet, and not that it covered an aching heart. Thinking of it, pitying tears for the mother long since dead darkened his eyes; he half longed that she might live again so that he might give her now that which he had owed her then. The dusk of a long summer evening deepened into night, and Luce came from the inner room, and, sinking down beside her father, laid her head upon his knee. There, in the dim twilight, he became part bearer of her sorrow, suffering, and shame. He was not a clever man, John Myrtle, and the few times his mind had been set stirring it had been by emotion, not thought; but deep within, and unknown to himself, the mother he had long held dead still lived, enabling him to understand his daughter's grief.

Mark goes to Luce's mother, and asks if she thinks Luce will have him now. Mrs. Myrtle is somewhat comforted in her grief. As for Luce,

Some have found that to love was to enter again as a stranger into their own hearts, and many of those that hate have made a like journey. It might be that Luce was such a one, for though she was slow to realize all that had befallen her, and the truth took long to fit into the crevices of her heart and brain, yet, as bit by bit it forced a way in, pushing out before it all that hitherto she had held dear, a strong new self, bitter of thought and tongue, rose up and confronted her. It almost seemed as if the power to forgive was not hers, and her heart hardened under the lack of it; she felt that Lupin had done a deed for which there was no forgiveness, and that she was not called upon to forgive; and yet there were moments when she was seized with terror, lest in spite of all she might forgive him.

One evening Mark goes to Luce.

He looked nervous and ill at ease; self, partly scotched, had left him startled at its grossness, his victory over it had so near ended in a defeat, the thought that his hands had all but helped to draw tight the cords of shame round Luce, left him shuddering. Still, threads of elation ran through the woof of his feelings, though he himself was scarce conscious of their existence; but to Luce they were glaringly visible, jarring on her as some hideous colour till the fabric of the man became a thing of distaste to her.

He asks Luce to marry him, but she is only indignant. Mark wonders if Luce believes he has been the one who had betrayed Lupin, but before he can ask her, Mrs. Myrtle approaches the cottage. Mark leaves. Mrs. Myrtle tries to persuade Luce to marry Mark, but she refuses, and Luce and her mother part bitterly. Mark returns the next morning to tell Luce that it was not he who had reported Lupin, but she does not care, and slams the door on him.

Four months after Lupin's arrest, the fever-ridden Hester Lupin visits Luce at the White Cottage one winter night. "'I've come," she said, "to die in my husband's house.'" Luce lets her in, and they sit together.

> Colder and colder grew the night, and the two women cowering over the fire were forced to draw closer together, yet each looked upon the other as an intruder. Neither spoke, but their hearts fought for the possession of the same man; while from without the storm slashed in upon their combat, ripping open the silence with a fine cut and thrust.

Hester tells how she had visited Ben at Exeter prison. However, Ben had been hungering only for Luce, and when Ben realized his visitor was Hester rather than Luce,

> "He worn't angered the zame ez he wud ha' been wance, he wor jest starved wi' waiting. He didn't zay nought, but sort o' told me wi' his eyes that I cudn't be no help to 'un, zo arter a bit I tarned and went."

Luce is moved by Hester's story, muttering to herself, "'I dursn't forgi'e 'ee, Ben.'" Hester remains at the White Cottage that night and all the next day. That night the fever takes Hester more strongly, and only with difficulty is Luce able to keep the child from Hester's arms. In her delirium, Hester believes the child is her own. Eventually Luce is able to put Hester to bed. Luce knows Hester is dying, and goes for a doctor for her.

When Luce returns twenty minutes later, Hester and the child are both gone. The doctor arrives and sets men searching for the pair, but after many days they are still not found. Luce invests her few shillings on sewing gear, to be resold to support herself, and goes to search for her child.

Somewhat more than three and a half years later Luce returns one August evening, her quest to find the child having failed. Mark sees her coming up the road, and carries her bundle to the White Cottage, neither speaking.

> Drawing nearer she saw that smoke rose from the chimney and the door of the cottage stood open. She glanced questioningly at Mark.
>
> "I reckoned maybe you wud come back along home to-night," he explained.
>
> Her face fell. "What did make 'ee think I wud come to-night o' all nights?" she asked, after a pause, surprise fighting with disappointment in her voice.
>
> He turned away his head. "I didn't reckon speshil on 'ee coming to-night."
>
> "Have 'ee been and lit the fire afore to-night?"
>
> "Ess."
>
> "Many times afore?"
>
> "Ess, most nights."
>
> "Why it be nigh on four years agone that I wor here!"
>
> "I reckoned you might drop in any time."
>
> Luce sighed wearily. "I've been far," she said. "I shall be glad to bide still and rest."

Luce enters the White Cottage grounds and sits down on a seat under the porch. After hesitating a bit, Mark turns and walks away with "sudden determination."

Many weeks pass, and Mark stays away from Luce, to her surprise. One evening she sees him on the rocks by the seashore, and goes to him. She acts more warmly to him than she has in many years, and Mark is uncertain how to respond.

> The girl's unexpected friendliness troubled him. He did not wish again to raise false hopes, the laying of them cost too much. True, it was as well known to him as to the rest of the village that Luce's love for Lupin had turned to hatred. Deep down in the young fisherman's heart, however, there lurked a suspicion of such a sudden transformation; he felt that the rapidity of the change must entail a lack of thoroughness in the

process, which would leave the whole fabric of the thing open to the rot. In his opinion, Luce, like the rest of her sex, was fickle. Who, he asked himself, could depend on the constancy of either her love or hate?

But even while he pondered the matter his need of her increased, and he was fain to distrust his own judgment. Rough handling had not altered the man's nature much; it had grown a little softer, perhaps, a little stronger, and showed a certain meagre capacity for expansion. The spirit's growth is a subtle thing, not lightly to be measured.

When they reach the path that leads up the cliff to the White Cottage, Mark makes no effort to accompany her, and instead walks along the beach away from her.

Meanwhile, Ben Lupin's reputation rises and falls with the villagers. The rise comes when a letter for Lupin, from Australia, arrives at the village post office. The postmaster Septimus Spong talks himself and his cronies at The Fisherman's Desire pub into believing that duty requires the letter to be opened and read. To his dismay he discovers that both lenses of his glasses have fallen out. But rather than pass the letter to someone else to be read aloud, he invents a tale of a legacy of a thousand pounds coming to Lupin. After everyone but Spong leaves, the innkeeper reads the letter and sees that Spong's story is all fictional. However, the story of Lupin's supposed inheritance spreads through the village, raising his stock with the villagers.

The thousand pounds makes Mrs. Myrtle less interested in Mark as a possible son-in-law. Mark goes to the White Cottage, where he hears Luce sobbing. She has a bundle of clothes and a basket of food beside her.

He goes in to her. She says she is leaving, and at last tells him why.

> "Lad," she said, "us wor childer together, and I'll tull 'ee the truth—I be a-feared—I be a-feared o' zeeing 'un vace to vace. All these long years my heart has been hard agin 'un, and I reckoned maybe 'twud be all wan to me whether my eyes looked on 'un or no; but he be coming back, and I kind o' feel 'un near; tiddn't no furren lad zame ez I thought to meet, but jest the old Ben. I've been angered agin him all these long years, and now my anger is gone from me and I be a-feared."

Mark suggests that possibly Hester is dead, which they both know would leave Ben and Luce free to marry. They both agree that the law requires evidence of such a supposed death, and Luce says "'I will niver valler 'un to dishonour,'" and picks up her bundle to leave.

Mark asks her to stay as his wife. She is unenthusiastic at the idea, but promises to tell him yes or no the next day. In the night she takes her bundle and, weeping, walks away from the cottage. Unbeknownst to her, Mark follows her. However, she changes her mind about leaving, and retraces her steps to the White Cottage.

> Mark saw her reach the door, wrench open the lock, and enter.
> He broke into an unconscious sigh of relief.
> "Maybe her will let me work for her now," he said.
> When the morning came he knocked at the cottage, and she came out to him.
> "Be it 'ess, Luce?" he asked tremulously.
> She looked for a moment in his face, pale and worn as her own.
> "'Ess," she answered.

A few days later the villagers learn that Ben Lupin has been released three weeks early. By now the non-existence of the legacy is understood, and Lupin's reputation has fallen to a new low. Some resolve to "duck Ben in the horsepond the moment he was rash enough to set foot inside the village."

As for Luce,

> Her promise to marry Mark remained a secret, and she tried to thrust the memory of it between herself and the thought of Lupin; but it proved a feeble weapon of defence, which she had already come to regret having laid hands on. After all, it would have been better to have fled away alone; she had but added to her burden a double weight of responsibility. Courage to retract her promise failed her.

Mark has sold his boats to the first bidder, and has gone to a town ten miles down the coast, where Luce is to join him for a private marriage.

The interval of waiting seemed interminable to Luce, each day bringing the coming of Lupin nearer. There were moments in the long watches of the night when it was as if he had already come, recalling her imperiously to the duties of wifehood. Putting out her hands, she would try and thrust him from her, only to grasp the thin, intangible air; and yet she felt that he had conquered, and remembering her wounded honour, shrank back appalled from those nuptial embraces in which her spirit succumbed to his. It seemed to her strange and terrifying that her wrongs no longer served as a barrier between her and the man who had injured her; for close on five years she had leaned on it in fancied security, now it had fallen, and she knew not where to lay hands upon another.

Luce hears a tumult, and goes outside to see Ben Lupin, "bleeding, mud-bedraggled," finally escape the mob which has tormented him. He shakes a fist at the mob before entering the White Cottage,

and when the door closed behind him she turned on the crowd with a fury exceeding its own. Half satiated, but loth to let go of its prey, the mob faced her motionless, stubborn, ill at ease. Intent on protecting the man she loved, Luce had no words to throw at the hungry crowd, yet she held it at bay by sheer force of will. Driven to reflect the mob at once became ashamed, edging back from the woman, and she, with a quick glance of scorn, turned and entered the cottage.

Ben has dressed himself in clean clothes, and, ever courageous, takes a stick from the corner and prepares to go out to face the crowd. Luce even goes down to her knees to beg him not to go out to risk his life with the mob, but a change of emotion quickly comes to her.

She rose to her feet, a new wave of emotion sweeping over her as she remembered again all she that she had to fear from this man. "Go if you will," she said bitterly, "life iddn't everything arter all."

Ben halted, struck by her apparent indifference. "'Tis all the zame to 'ee, I s'pose, whether I be killed or no."

"You be nought to me now," she answered, turning away her head.

"'Ee say thic, Luce?"

"'Ess—arter what you've done."

"You'll no live wi' me again?"

"Do 'ee reckon I be so mortal fond o' dishonour?"

"You'll no live wi' me again?" he repeated, raising his voice.

"Haven't I told 'ee?"

"Luce," he exclaimed, drawing close and putting his arm round her, "'tiddn't nought but talk, thic?"

She pushed him from her. "I do mean what I say," she exclaimed feebly. "Me and Mark—" then she stopped short.

But Lupin paid no heed. "Where's the chile?" he exclaimed, looking round with a start. "Be 'un a-zlape in t'other room?"

She did not answer, and he rose and went to the bedroom in search of it.

Mark, meanwhile, hears of Lupin's return to Bere-Upton, and hurries back toward the village. He is unafraid that Luce will go back on her word, but "cursed himself for making her trials harder." On his walking journey he sees a mass of thrift, a type of flower that he knows Luce loves. He climbs down to pick some of the flowers for Luce. From the perspective of the thrift, he sees something that resembles part of a skeleton. He climbs further down the cliff to investigate, and discovers the skeletons of Hester Lupin and the baby she had stolen in her delirium long ago.

A wind rose and swept away the mists so that the sea looked bluer, the grass greener, and the bones whiter, and Mark stared down at them till he lost the power of seeing. One question circled continually in his brain. "Why had he been called upon to find the bones now? Why not five years ago? Why now?"

Night fell, and when darkness had hidden the skeletons he threaded his way up the cliff's face, turned once more in the direction of the village, and as he walked he muttered, "'Tiddn't to be expected that I shud tull."

The door of the White Cottage was open; the moon, rising, shone in on Mark and on a small piece of pink thrift that he still held in his hand. When he saw the flower he suddenly cried out as one possessed: "Luce, Luce! You be free to marry who you wull."

But she had not waited to be released; the cottage was empty, she had left it to follow Lupin.

This passage is followed by a blank space. Then comes the final paragraph of the book:

> Years passed; the White Cottage fell into disrepair, for the villagers held the house to be unlucky, and no one ventured to live there; but each year, with the coming round of summer, Mark would steal into the little garden, sit beneath the apple tree, and, closing his eyes, dream that the cottage was his home, Luce his wife, and the voices on the breeze those of his children.

Mark's love for Luce was defeated. She will never be his. And it seems he will live out his life without the children he so hoped one day to have—the voices on the breeze are those of his children. The ending gives us little hope that Mark will ever marry. He seems to have put all his eggs in one basket—it seems to have been Luce or nothing. This may not be wise on Mark's part, but then Mark has never been a model of wisdom.

He has, however, grown spiritually since we first met him. When we first meet Mark, he is convinced of his own righteousness. He is often self-deceived, and he is far too dependent on the opinions of others as to his standing in the community. When feeling cheated by Lupin of Luce's love, he tries to commit murder! He certainly has some virtues—is a hard worker and dependable, is without any vicious or immoral habits, and is determined to be a good husband to Luce.

The circumstances God puts Mark through in regard to his failed love for Luce, were not pleasant. But it seems those circumstances have helped Mark to become a far more mature adult. Some of his dross has been burned away. The change is subtle, however. Zack points out about Mark (and about all of us) that "The spirit's growth is a subtle thing." One of the subtle ways that Mark has changed for the better is that he is no longer as concerned about what the village thinks of him. As a happy irony, this change comes in tandem with the prospering of his material affairs, so that just as he cares less about the village's opinion, their opinion of him rises.

Mark was sorely tempted to reveal Lupin's bigamy, and escaped doing so only by the skin of his teeth. But he did do the right thing then, and knew it once he had acted. Almost five years later, he is once again tempted to do the wrong thing—keep silent about the death of Hester Lupin! But he does the honorable thing—speaks to inform Luce that she is free to marry whom she will. He is spared the effort of providing details, because Luce has already left with Lupin.

If we could give Mark advice, we would tell him to find another young lady to court and marry! There's more than one catfish in the sea. Luce was a beautiful girl with an interesting character, but should he remain unmarried simply because he can not have her as his wife? I don't think so. Mark has become a stronger, more self-reliant person. Let him mourn for a while, then move on. Zack, of course, gives us no hint that such a moving on will take place. We expect Mark to go on mourning.

One of the things that Zack understands, and shows very well, is that romantic love can't be forced. One can only love where it fits one's character and fate to love. Mark, in losing Luce to Ben Lupin, has not really been cheated by Ben. Ben's words to Mark that "'her was never yours'" hit the nail on the head exactly. Luce's personality is not suited to Mark. Luce is the type of woman who needs a masterful man, and Mark is not that sort. When Luce says "'there's sommat missing 'twix he [Mark] and me,'" we know she speaks the truth.

It is Luce's nature to love Ben Lupin's sort. This is a commonplace thing in real life: many women are attracted to men who are irresponsible and immoral. Luce fights against that attraction, but she fights unsuccessfully. She knows, as everyone knows, that Ben Lupin has acted dishonorably with one of the women of the village. Instead of rooting his image out of her heart, she has for years allowed her imagination to wander over his doings. Although rigorously chaste in behavior until the very end of the book, there is a sense in which she is "a rake at heart." One of Anthony Trollope's heroines, in *Ralph the Heir*, has a character similar to Luce's: "She was innocent, pure, unknowing in the ways of vice, simple in her tastes, conscientious in her duties, and yet she was a rake at heart."[32] Sorrow and disappointment eventually taught Trollope's heroine a hard lesson so that she avoided disaster, but the fate of Zack's Luce is different.

Luce says she will never follow Ben to dishonor, but when put to the test she is unable or unwilling to stick to her resolve. She leaves with

---

[32] Anthony Trollope, *Ralph the Heir*, New York, New York, Dover Publications, Inc., 1978 [original date of publication 1871], p. 354.

Ben, unmarried—willing to live outside the boundaries of Christian behavior. The sad irony is that if she had waited a few minutes, she would have found out that she and Ben were able to be legally married. It would have been unwise to marry a man who has shown himself to be an unprincipled man unwilling to live within the boundaries provided by God, but at least she would have been legally able to marry him. She and Ben would have had, as Hank Williams sings, "'a license to fight,'" but even that escapes her. It is a sad fall for her, but we can not be too surprised. When she allowed herself to be married to a man she knew to be immoral, she was setting herself up for worse to come. It came eventually.

Ben Lupin is portrayed consistently and fairly. He is a self-absorbed man who sins and lets the chips fall where they may without caring but also without complaint. He is courageous. When married to Luce, the best of her nature calls out the best of his nature. Though we know him to be an immoral man, he loves Luce with a sincere and tender love. In his selfishness, he has married Luce well knowing that such a marriage is bigamous. But once married to her, he treats her very well. The rules of Christian behavior are not made for men such as Ben Lupin. He sets his own rules. A brave man, and a man attractive to women, he can set his own rules and get away with it. Sort of, anyway. When civilized society imprisons him for bigamy, he pays the price of setting his own rules. When he stands in the presence of God, we will see if he really did get away with his behavior. As Mark obsessively noted, vengeance is God's. Mark was wrong to assume that Ben Lupin has cheated Mark of Luce, but he is not wrong that vengeance is God's. We will leave Ben Lupin to God.

Hester Lupin is a character with whom we can sympathize, but she seems fated to lose. She fights a sometimes losing battle with alcoholism. Her scene with Septimus Spong in which she falls to the temptation to drink is frightening, and puts sweat on the good man's brow: she is for the moment "unsexed," her womanhood sinking out of sight. Her love for Ben Lupin is firmly rejected; Ben has moved on from her, and the legal facts of his marriage mean nothing to Ben, who sets his own rules. When Hester knows she is dying, she goes to the White Cottage to die in her husband's house. Worse than just death at a young age awaits this woman, however. In delirium she steals Luce's child, and is the unintentional but very real cause of the child's death.

Many of the minor characters are superbly drawn. Samuel Bompas, Mark's cousin, we see only in one scene, but we get a good feeling for the man's simple, quiet, generous spirit—as well as for his distrust of women. "'The skin of a sex," he called them, "hastily made and ill-considered at that.'" It is completely typical of Zack that she never lets a man's unfavorable opinion of the female sex sour her on the man taken as a whole.

John Myrtle is a simple, quiet man of no very sparkling intelligence. He is the illegitimate child of a woman who had been seduced and deserted. When the news comes that Luce has unknowingly been married to a man already married, John mourns almost in sackcloth and ashes as might an Old Testament prophet over the sins of, or hard providential judgment on, God's people. Zack's portrayal of him as he mourns, cited earlier in this chapter, is remarkable in its sympathy and insight. There is a line regarding John Myrtle which gives us a large window onto the moral universe of Zack: "He was not a clever man, John Myrtle" we are told as part of a sentence. But for Zack, cleverness is of far less value than the desire to do right. John Myrtle may not be clever, but his moral compass is far more accurately pointed in the right direction than is that of his higher born, more naturally intelligent wife. When the "news" of Ben Lupin's supposed thousand pound inheritance gets about, Mrs. Myrtle begins to see Ben (convicted of bigamy) as a good potential candidate to marry Luce after all. John Myrtle is not fooled.

> Less alert of mind than his wife, John Myrtle failed to look at the matter in the same light. "He could not," he said, "see what the thousand pounds had to do with the matter," and no reason that his wife could adduce served to clear his mental vision.

The self-deception of the more clever Mrs. Myrtle doesn't destroy the ability of the slow thinking but biblically anchored John Myrtle to think things through accurately. Cleverness is of far less value than understanding and living God's law. "The unfolding of Thy words gives light;/It gives understanding to the simple" (Ps. 119:130). The simple John Myrtle understands more than his more clever wife does. Reading about John Myrtle we begin to get some small understanding of what western civilization has lost in mostly turning its back on the Christian faith. May heaven someday again send us millions more of men and women like John Myrtle, clever or not clever.

Mrs. Myrtle herself is another character consistently portrayed, in her weaknesses and strengths.

The Squire has one scene, but it is a fine one. We see his character revealed, and learn to admire him. His advice helps point Mark toward Mark's better nature.

The book is very good, and very Zackian. Being Zackian, it will not attract every reader, despite being good. There are coincidental meetings without number. There is no happy ending. The defeats of the main characters are real; the triumphs are subtle. The people are not highly educated. Most readers of serious literature are middle class, and how many middle class people are interested in people like Mark, Luce, and Ben, who come from a class below middle? A great many are, I think, but perhaps also a great many aren't. The use of dialect is very likely to put off some readers. Several reviewers, over the course of Zack's publishing career, pointed out that Zack is not a "big" novelist. I think this is a fair comment. Her novels are short, her characters few. This may hamper her acceptance as an important writer.

One reviewer read *The White Cottage*, and took a thoughtful measure of Zack.

> "Zack," we fear, will never be a "popular novelist." Her self-repression, her neat mind that will look only at the facts of life, and those not the brightest, her contempt for sentiment, her sympathy for the unlettered, are against that. But she is a writer who counts.[33]

I think the nameless reviewer is correct. He is correct in noting some of the elements which limit her appeal. He is also correct in his final sentence. *The White Cottage* is a book which shows why she is a writer who counts.

---

[33]Unknown reviewer, "Fiction. *The White Cottage*. By "Zack."," "The Academy," 18 May, 1901, p. 425.

CHAPTER 4

Tales of Dunstable Weir

"I reckon," he said, "that the lad be sort o' dreamin' jest now."

"That's it. He's dreaming, Eben. And we have all been content to let him dream."

"'Tis through our dreams us be made, Miss Bet."

She frowned and bit her lip. "That's no comfort. Why does he dream such stupid dreams?"

"Thic be the nature o' 'em. They be always a bit beyond us."

Zack, *Tales of Dunstable Weir*

Tales of Dunstable Weir first appeared in the fall of 1901. The English edition was put out by Methuen & Co. Charles C. Scribner's Sons again published the American edition, in the same year.

The White Cottage had been published just a few months previously, in April. So, in 1901, in little more than half a year, Zack published two books of great literary value. She had published four excellent books in four years. On October 4 of 1901 she marked just her 36th birthday! How many more superb books would she be able to write before she went the way of all flesh? We had a right to hope for many more.

However, only one more book followed, *The Roman Road* in 1903, and it marked, in my opinion and in that of others as well, a significant falling off in quality. After 1903, silence. We will discuss the reasons for the falling off in quality, and the subsequent silence, in the proper place.

But *Tales of Dunstable Weir* is still excellent work. One reviewer of *Tales* classed her with Guy de Maupassant, the French writer of stories. He says Zack "has so far worked only on a small canvas."

> But she need not fear comparison with any writer who is working in the same *genre* or on the same scale. Whether her Devonshire stories are quite equal to Maupassant's Normandy stories we will not decide on a first reading. We must wait awhile and see whether they wear as well. But, whether "Zack" be the equal of Maupassant or not, she is unquestionably in the same class with him, and is one of the few of the younger English writers of fiction from whom we confidently anticipate great things.[34]

My interest piqued by the comparison to the famed de Maupassant, recently I read a book containing 51 of his short stories. Does she really belong in a league with the French master? I have to admit I think she is better. No disrespect to de Maupassant—I'm glad I read the book—and I would be willing to read more of his stuff, but Zack is for me a more interesting writer. You will understand my prejudice in her favor and will receive my opinion with an industrial size grain of salt. But anyway it is encouraging to hear her compared to someone universally acknowledged as a great writer of stories.

Despite the high quality of the book, it seemed to garner somewhat less attention from reviewers than did her previous work. The reviews I have found are few in number and rather brief.

The book contains seven stories, of varying lengths.

Zack the author tried something a bit different this time. The narrator of every one of the stories is Zack the Devonshire villager. He is a male, a laborer of the working class. This is the same Zack who told the story "Widder Vlint" in *Life Is Life*. But that was the only story the villager Zack told in that book. Here he tells us all seven stories. That means seven more stories in which the narrator speaks (and writes) the Devonshire dialect.

I will deal with the stories in the order they appear in the book.

---

[34]Unknown reviewer, "Fiction. Zack.," "Literature," November 9, 1901, p. 446..

Since all these stories are written by Zack the villager, every subsequent reference in this chapter to Zack will be a reference to Zack the villager. When I refer to the ultimate author of these stories, I will speak of Gwendoline Keats.

"Benjamin Parrot's Fancy"

This is the second longest story in the book, checking in at 44 pages in my (excellent) Books For Libraries Press hardcover reprint from 1969.

Benjamin Parrot comes back from Australia, and promises to leave all his money to the first man who took his fancy. This got the attention of the people of Dunstable Weir, as well as the attention of many outsiders.

Meanwhile, Martin Fippard's wife Susan was sickening toward her death. Susan was painfully jealous of Belle Hart. There was controversy in the village about whether or not something was going on between Martin and Belle, but Zack the villager makes it pretty clear that nothing immoral was happening between the two. But, as we will see from subsequent events, there really was a mutual attraction between Martin and Belle. They had never acted on it in a dishonorable fashion, but it was there.

Martin was a plain man, usually almost painfully silent. On rare occasions he would speak up, however. Once when Zack was lamenting that outsiders had come "sniffing round after gold" in regard to Benjamin Parrot's promise, Martin came forth with a single sentence.

> "Mostlike they wud bring more money into the village than they'd ever succeed in taking out o' it." Zim'd a poor-spirited fashion o' looking at matters, but he wasn't no patriot, taking no interest in war or the grasping ways o' t'other nations, though there was not a child in the parish who couldn't have told him that if 'twasn't for England there would be little enough honesty left in the world, or religion either for the matter o' that.

Here we have a wonderful contrast between Zack the villager and Zack the writer (Gwendoline Keats). Zack the villager assumes it is clear even to children that England is honest and religious, while the other countries in the world are grasping. Gwendoline Keats gives us another perspective. She hints at how easy it is to become complacently sure that our own country is always right. There's a message we would all do well to take to heart in our own era! My own country the United States seems convinced that everything we do is right automatically. To disagree, and to see the U.S. as being as bad or worse than any other nation, is to risk being considered unpatriotic as Zack was willing to consider Martin. How typical of Gwendoline Keats to suggest the need for objectivity! She does so with humor; she lets Zack the villager's blindness make her point. It is passages like this that remind us what a strong-minded and honest person was Gwendoline Keats.

Martin's other moment of speaking up was also one sentence only. When the Squire had the villagers up to the Great House to dinner and encouraged them to

> "vote straight," Martin got up and said, "What was straight for one wasn't always straight for t'other," which the village held, for a silent man, was saying a deal too much. Farmer Burden was terrible put out, Martin being carter to he, and went so far as to ax if the Squire was wishful to have Martin turned away; but the Squire wouldn't hear o' it, and because o' that there be some who reckon the Squire's own politics iddn't sound.

Martin Fippard begins to take the fancy of Benjamin Parrot. Zack, who is a day laborer who works at various jobs throughout the book, is hired at sixpence an hour to haul around Benjamin, who is troubled by dropsy. Parrot hired the carpenter to build him a wheel chair. When they pass Belle Hart's cottage, Benjamin asks Zack if he thinks there is truth in the tales about her and Martin.

> "Well," I answered, scratching my head to ease out the words, "me and the village be one and the same mind in public, but when I gits by myself I has a single man's judgment."

There are certainly times when Zack is blind. But we underestimate him at our peril. He has moments of insight as well. He thinks for himself enough to doubt—correctly doubt, we can be sure—that anything immoral is going on between Martin and Belle.

During a winter cold spell, Zack drops in to see how Susan Fippard is doing. In fact she is on her deathbed, and knows it. Susan tries to persuade Martin to promise that he will not take up with Belle (although without naming her; they all know of whom she speaks) after her own death. But Martin resists making such a promise.

> "Martin," her cried, shrill-like, "you pramised to be faithful to me afore the altar."
> "And I have been true to 'ee, Susan."
> "But you and her will ha' killed me between 'ee."
> He sat stone quiet, and if he looked about for words, he didn't find 'em.
> All to-wance her held out her arms to un. "You iddn't glad o' it? You iddn't glad I be leaving 'ee—"
> He rose up and went to her and put his arms round her poor thin body terrible pitiful, but he didn't answer, and kaining across at 'em I saw sommat o' what it is to be wi'out the gift o' words. I reckon, though, her understood un better'n I did, for her seemed sort o' comforted.
> "You've been a good husband to me, Martin, in spite o' it all," she said.
> He gave a banging great sob, and the sound o' it seemed to take the life out o' her. "I'll no axe it o' 'ee. Marry her if you will"—and wi' that her face stiffened, and she fell back dead.
> Martin he stood a-looking down on her, then he took her hand in his and called me up to the bedside.
> "Zack," said he, "you be my witness that I promise never to marry t'other woman."
> "I wudn't pass my word on it if I was you," I answered, being no friend to rash promises. But he didn't pay no heed.
> "See," he said, taking me by the arm, "her's heard."
> Sure enough, her did look more content-like.

Zack goes to the Red Lion pub and tells, two or three times, what had happened. Eventually someone proposes that they step across to Belle Hart's cottage to get her response. They walk in on her without stopping to knock. Belle Hart treats them scornfully. Zack begins to understand that "us looked amazing foolish, standing gapnesting across at her." The story of Susan's death, and of Martin's promise, comes out gradually—Zack himself uneasily telling only of the death—and Belle dismisses them all quietly but firmly.

As the weather softens, Zack once again goes to work for Benjamin Parrot. Parrot is extremely interested in the story of Martin's promise. He says, "'I like a man that sticks to his promise, but—" and he'd stop short and end to hisself, "Fippard should ha' thought o' t'other woman.'"

With the coming of spring, Martin begins to visit Belle Hart openly. When Zack is out with Parrot in the wheel chair, he sees Martin in the woods they are traversing. Zack drives softly, Benjamin Parrot wakes up, and they see Belle Hart join Martin. The two, intent upon each other, do not see Zack and Benjamin.

> Martin and the maid was that took up one wi' t'other they didn't pay no heed to aught else. Her sat down 'pon tap a big log and Martin stood 'long side o' her. Not a word passed the lips o' either o' 'em, and I was jest thinking to myself that for sweethearts they made a terrible poor display, when all to-wance Martin fell to cursing. He cursed hiszulf and folks in general, and the maid; he cursed the tongue atween his teeth, which zimed proper enough considering the use he was putting it to—he cursed God Almighty—a thing I had never known no man in Dunstable Weir ha' the face to do afore. Belle Hart her sat there and listened, not a finger did her hold up to keep the words back from coming, though I cud zee her small white face grow sort o' smaller and whiter afore my eyes. All of a minute the wuds stopped o' theirzulves, and he flung his arm round the branch o' a tree and leaned his vace up agin it. Then 'twas that Belle riz and went over to 'un, but he flung her off becase, he said, that if the dead cud hear maybe they cud zee as well, and wi' that he fell to laughing in a fashion that was amazing disquietful for them that cudn't enter into the joke. The maid kained across at un rather pitying, and I reckoned arter a bit maybe her'd say sommat to make un give over sich show-sides, but her jest tarned and hiked off through the wood. I drawed the chair back tenderful the way us had come, for t'wasn't no manner o' use gapnesting at Martin.

It is shocking to read that Martin was cursing God Himself. At least it shocks me—an approximately orthodox Christian—whatever it may do for others.

The next day Zack is at Benjamin Parrot's home. Benjamin questions Zack as to the sort of man Martin Fippard is. Benjamin goes on to say that if Martin acts the way Benjamin wants him to act, Benjamin will give him all his money. The way he wants him to act is to marry Belle Hart.

> "Let un marry Belle Hart and the money's his."
>
> "Why, dom it," said I, "iddn't that what he's been arter doing all along?"
>
> "There's his promise to his dead wife."
>
> "When I drop un a word o' what you say I reckon 'twill be your promise, not hers, he'll be thinking upon."
>
> Benjamin Parrot zot up in the bed. "You'll keep what I tell 'ee to yourzulf," he tapped out sharp.
>
> "'Tiddn't possible; a janius couldn't be answerable for sich, much less ordinary folk zame ez I be."
>
> The old man let fly another o' they curious smiles o' his.
>
> "Oh, yes, Zack," he said, "you'll bide silent because"—and he stopped quat and fitted the tips o' his fingers terrible careful each to each—"because if Martin don't git the money maybe you will."
>
> "Lord help us," I answered, sinking down 'pon tap the bed, "there shall be no silenter man inside the village or out o' it than myzulf."
>
> "Ah," piped old Parrot, "I knowed I cud trust 'ee under the circumstances."

From that point on Zack begins to feel less kindly toward Martin Fippard: "'twas much as if he was a-trying to keep me out o' my own." As the two men watch over Martin's dying old black sow, their conversation turns to Benjamin Parrot. Martin tells Zack that Parrot has said that he would leave Martin all his money "'if I tarned out to be the man he took me for.'" Martin wonders if Parrot has heard of his promise to Susan. Martin speaks.

> "If so be I was to marry again," he said.
>
> My heart banged up agin my ribs, and then stopped quat—

"He wouldn't leave 'ee the money, I s'pose," I answered. The wuds slipped out unconscious, for I hadn't a mind to say aught sich.

Martin breathed a bit hard. "That's how I reckoned it out myself," he said.

Zack has deceived Martin about how Parrot would look on Martin marrying Belle Hart. Martin stays away from Belle Hart's cottage for three or four weeks. Belle is a milliner by trade, and just about now her business falls off dramatically, partly due to the village considering that there is too much talk about her for her to be as respectable as she should be. Belle sits by the window largely idle most days "Her seemed to be thinking a deal, which iddn't good for maids, they, pour souls, not being built for sich." Thus speaks Zack the villager, to our entertainment. His creator, Zack the writer (Gwendoline Keats) is a woman who was very much built for thinking.

It appears that Belle is being "'sold up,'" that is, put out of business. Zack continues to encourage Martin to believe that marrying Belle would cost him a chance at Benjamin Parrot's fortune, and Martin says he won't go near her.

Zack suddenly gets the idea to marry Belle Hart himself. We can guess, though he does not say so explicitly, that much of his motivation is to keep her from marrying Martin. We learn that the village has never held Zack to be good-looking, though he thinks that if he were taller, the maids would have been more attracted to him. He tells us that he is just under five foot tall. Zack thus is very well named, for it was the Bible's Zaccheus who was unable, because of his small stature, to see Jesus Christ, and who ran ahead to a sycamore tree to see the one who would become his Savior (Lk. 19:2-10). Zack smartens himself up and visits Belle Hart with the intention of asking her to marry him. But before he can do so, Belle reveals that she and Martin are married. She asks Zack to keep their secret.

Zack goes home, trying to convince himself that the Lord is on his side, but the wind speaks up in mocking words. Martin arrives at Zack's cottage, with the news that Benjamin Parrot is dying, and that Benjamin Parrot has sent for Martin. But Martin says what is the use of going to him, for he tells Zack that he and Belle were married two days ago.

"S'posing you don't tell," says I.

Martin gripped hold o' my arm thic hard I nigh hollered wi' the pain o' it.

"I've axed mezulf thic," he said.

My breath got that scart I was forced to zit down, for it zim'd to me that the devil wud ha' one or t'other o' us, and I prayed to God that it might be Martin.

"Zack," said he, "what wud it feel like to come by the money unhonest?"

I kind o' crept togither. "Why do 'ee ax me thic, *now?*" I answered. But he didn't pay no speshil heed, and the clock hammered out so loud "Wan or t'other o' 'ee will have to pay for this," that I was certain sure Martin would hear and take heed in time. Instead o' thic he put his hand deep down in his pocket and pulled out a big canvas bag. Untying the string round the neck o' it, he poured a power o' gold and siller into his hand.

"It's took me all my life to save 'ut," he said, "and 'tiddn't a penny more than seven-and-seventy pun."

The sight o' the money sort o' hardened me. "Not much put aside o' Benjamin Parrot's," I answered.

"But it's come by honest," said Martin.

"'Tis only thieves and sich that harp so on baing honest," I tumm'l'd out. I couldn't abide the sound o' the wud on his lips thic often.

"Maybe," Martin answered, "for 'tis only since I thought o' baing a thief I've took to saying it."

Wi' that there riz up in my heart a banging great desire that he, not me, should try and steal the money dishonest, and I hungered after zommat temptatious to zay which hadn't no lie in it.

"Who'd be the loser s'posing you didn't tell?" I axed. Then I laughed out short and sharp, for I could answer that question better than he.

The wuds made Martin start. "S'posing I was to have a son," he said.

"You should think o' that afore you drow away the money—"

"I niver much keered to have childer," he said, half to hiszulf. "They eats up more'n they brings in most days, and a man be lucky when he comes to die if he has got enough together to pay for his own funeral and his wife's arter him, but s'posing so be that Belle bore me a son, I shud like un to be honest. I couldn't a-bear to blacken aught that comed to me droo her."

I sort o' hated the man. "Iddn't Benjamin Parrot dying while 'ee stand there and prate so purty about baing honest," I burst out. "And don't 'ee reckon to git the money if so be he shud die not knowing that you and Belle be man and wife."

"By the Lord," cried Martin, "I'll tell un the truth afore it be too late."

Then I saw what a vool I'd been to tauntify un, and I caught hold o' his arm.

"Bide where you be, the wuds wasn't meant serious." He pushed me from un.

"I'll make no thief o' the child," he said.

The church bell sounds. At first it seems it could be the Passing Bell which would indicate Benjamin Parrot's death, but it turns out to be the church clock striking the hour, twelve.

And wi' the last stroke there fell such a zilence as will drop upon us, no doubt, at the last day when the Books be opened and us harks to hear how all that us have doed has looked in the eyes o' God Almighty Hiszulf.

Standing there all o' a-listen, I didn't pay no more heed to Martin, for it zim'd to me that I stud afore the Jidgment Seat o' God and He kained down into my heart. I drapped on my knees and hid my vace afore Un. How long I kneeled there I can't tell, but when I comed to mezulf I was alone.

A blank space precedes the last paragraph of the story. Then:

'Twas a week and a day arter thic Benjamin Parrot died. Then it came out that he hadn't left no money, and the furniture had to be sold to pay for his funeral. Zim's twadn't nought but an annuity he had, arter all. He kind o' played wi' folks. "Human nater," he said, "was built for experimentation, and twadn't to be supposed that the Almighty should have all the pulling o' the strings to Hiszulf."

Zack, in the penultimate paragraph, looks into his own heart, and knows he has been found wanting in the eyes of God. Even with Martin looking on, Zack drops to his feet, hiding his face from God. He has played a very poor part indeed. Like Jonah the grumpy prophet, he reports on his own shameful behavior, without pretending any more that he has done right.

Martin, by contrast, has been tempted to be dishonest, but has resolved to tell the truth to Benjamin Parrot, even though it will probably cost him the fortune. We are not told that he did in fact speak the truth to Parrot in the next day or so, however. I am not sure why. I have been tempted to think that this is an artistic mistake by Gwendoline Keats. However, it is probably not a mistake at all. Most likely, Gwendoline Keats expects us to understand that Zack the villager would have told us if Martin had gone back on his resolve to tell the truth to Parrot. I think we safely can assume that Martin fulfilled his resolve to be honest.

Martin is an interesting character. He should never have sworn to Susan that he would not marry Belle Hart—as Zack tried to warn him. But when we swear to foolish things, we should break our oath rather than fulfill the foolishness. Martin's dilemma reminds us of that of Herod the tetrarch. He promised with an oath to give the daughter of Herodias whatever she wanted, when her dancing pleased him. (Tradition, rather than Scripture, names the daughter as Salome.) Prompted by Herodias, she asked for the head of John the Baptist on a platter. Rather than break his oath, Herod had John executed, and indeed brought his head on a platter and gave it to the girl (Matt. 14:6-11). Herod would have done more wisely to break his oath. Martin shows better judgment: he breaks his foolish oath, and marries Belle Hart, as indeed he should have done.

Martin is indeed tempted to do the dishonest thing by not revealing his marriage to Benjamin Parrot, but correctly senses that if he wins the Parrot fortune by dishonest behavior, that he would bring dishonor on himself and even on Belle Hart and on their (not yet conceived) son. He is absolutely correct that his pitiful 77 pounds, painfully but honestly earned over a full lifetime, is worth far more than a fortune dishonestly gained. His is a profoundly Christian decision. "'By the Lord,' cried Martin, 'I'll tell un the truth afore it be too late.'" This, we remember, is a man who was even cursing God Himself earlier in the story! To read of that cursing we are reminded how flawed we human beings can be. To curse God was a foolish and wicked thing. But Martin apparently has not committed the unpardonable sin of blasphemy against the Holy

Spirit (Matt. 12:31-32). We can be extremely hopeful about this because his conscience definitely is not seared. "'By the Lord'" he resolves to tell the truth, even though he believes that speaking the truth will probably cost him a fortune.

Most of the writing of Gwendoline Keats features people put to a moral test. Here Benjamin Parrot is the person who sets the test in motion. He has indeed pulled some strings. He has put the entire area, and especially two men, to a moral test. We are reminded of Mark Twain's story "The Man That Corrupted Hadleyburg," where a similar test is recounted. It is at least possible that Zack had read that story, although we will probably never know for sure one way or another. Twain's story appeared in "Harper's Monthly" in December of 1899, and came out in a collection of stories in 1900. So it was mathematically possible for Gwendoline Keats to have read Twain's story, since "Benjamin Parrot's Fancy" was published in 1901. Most likely the similarity in theme was simply a coincidence, the way Zack's *On Trial* and Joseph Conrad's *Lord Jim* were similar in theme simply by coincidence.

In May of 1901 Gwendoline Keats wrote to her friend May Sinclair, and mentioned "Benjamin Parrot's Fancy" and actually called it "good."[35] She seldom mentions her individual stories in those letters, though she does occasionally, and she tends to speak very humbly. (It is worth remembering that she offered to return £40 of the advance for *The White Cottage* to her publishers because she doubted the quality of the book!) But she was right: "Benjamin Parrot's Fancy" is a good story.

- -

"The Hall and He"

"The Hall and He" is the second longest story Gwendoline Keats ever wrote, shorter only than her two novels and "Life Is Life." At about

---

[35]Zack letter to May Sinclair, postmarked May 12, 1901.

114 pages, it is almost as long as the title story of *Life Is Life*. It is one of her best stories.

Looking down the table of contents of the book *Tales of Dunstable Weir*, all seven stories seem to have large measures of sadness and human failure. There is considerable humor, there are occasional victories. But the victories tend to be subtle, the defeats obvious and crushing. "The Hall and He" is no exception. Yet it is a moving and in some ways profoundly encouraging story—despite the obvious defeats.

Dunstable Weir is a small, "tiddleliwinkie"—insignificant—village in Devon. The Hall, where the squire and his family live, is prosperous and big, and the Hall sits at the top of a hill and looks down upon the tiddleliwinkie village. Halfway between the Hall and the village sits the church, which is where "Miss Bet first clapped eyes on he."

He—who is never named—is about nine years old, and a newcomer to the church. Miss Bet is a child as well. Many in the church "marked how like the lad's face was to her own." He is sitting with the housekeeper and other servants in the row behind the squire and little Miss Bet (the squire's granddaughter). When Miss Bet gathers Bibles, climbs up on them to stare over the pew at the boy, then falls, she sobs, at which the boy immediately goes over the boards, apparently to her rescue. The squire unceremoniously throws the boy back over the pew.

That Sunday afternoon Zack and his mother go to the Hall to take tea in the housekeeper's room. This they can do because the housekeeper, Aunt Flint, is sister to Zack's mother. There they see Miss Elizabeth pacing in the garden. Miss Elizabeth is the daughter of the squire. Miss Bet shows up as well. Miss Bet is the daughter of Master Geoffry (son of the squire), who is away in India soldiering. Suddenly the young boy shows up. The two children stare at one another for a while, then Miss Bet turns away.

Zack's mother notices that the two children look alike. Aunt Flint is asking her to take the boy and treat him the same as little Zack.

> Aunt Flint pressed one black mittened hand 'pon top the other. "And isn't Zack your son?"
>
> "La, yes," my mother answered, "and familiar as such from a child."
>
> "Well, treat them same for same."

At that my mother fell silent for a bit. "Zack 'ull have to work for his living wi' his hands," she said.

"Ah!" answered Aunt Flint, slowly, "that's where blood tells."

Then the lad came in and my mother made ready to go, kaining across at him, half suspicious, half friendly to one. He must have been pillared and posted a deal in his bit of a life, for he took it all wonderful unconcerned, reckoning mayhap that one home was like to be as good as another.

Zack (who was about the same age as the boy) tells us that

He and the village never took to one another; this did not surprise my mother, but I think she was a bit put out at his not being friends with his book. Learn he either couldn't or wouldn't, and he and the cane got close acquainted. My mother used to argue wi' him sometimes when she bound up his hands in a bit of damp rag after a more than usual bad basting, but, though he was fonder o' her than of any, save one, she couldn't get him to mend his ways.

Every Sunday Zack's mother took both boys to the Hall. Zack was forced to stay by her and Aunt Flint, but the other boy was allowed to play in the rose garden in front of Miss Elizabeth's windows, and if Miss Bet happened to be with her aunt, "she would come scurrying down to him, for he and Miss Bet had always a deal to tell one another."

As he entered his fourteenth year, a "hurrying sickness" came upon the village. It struck down rich and poor with an equal hand, killing many. Aunt Flint comes to her sister's cottage to take the young boy up to the Hall to see the dying Miss Elizabeth. This frustrates the boy's mother by adoption. Zack, pretending to be asleep, hears the conversation of the two sisters.

"'Tis flinging the child's life after a dead one; for Miss Elizabeth is as good as parted," said my mother.

"The child's her child."

"More shame at the sacrifice."

"Come," exclaimed my aunt, sharply, "wake the lad; the sooner he is dressed the better."

"She has lived wi'out un, let her die wi'out un," my mother answered harshly.

"If she hadn't done the first, maybe she could have foregone the last," said my aunt, and at that mother gave in.

"Ay," she murmured, "if us had but strength to do right in this life, but us haven't; there's times when we must fail, every mother's son o' us. Oh, bodies and souls, bodies and souls, 'twud be well if we were all one or all t'other."

"Don't waste time blaspheming," Aunt Flint put in harshly. "Be thankful that, if mixed we are, the mixing was done by higher hands than ours."

"And they but 'prentice, with all reverence be it spoke," said my mother. At that, feeling perhaps that she had been a bit free, seeing who it was she had been criticising, she made haste to wake and dress the lad.

The boy having gone with Aunt Flint, her sister prays out loud a passionate prayer to God, leaving young Zack unsure whether she was praying for the boy's life or his (Zack's) life. The boy is back in his bed when Zack wakes in the morning. A week later Miss Elizabeth is buried during a falling rain. As the funeral procession is going forward,

the lad shot out from behind an elm, put himself straight behind the hearse and walked chief sorrower afore 'em all. Some were for stopping and laying a whip across his back, but most said: "Who be he? No one will mark sich for the rain." So they let him bide, and when the coffin was lowered, the earth thrown in, and the gentry shut tight and dry inside their carriages, he flung himself 'pon top the grave. I wondered why he sorrowed, seeing that she had never loved him.

The boy falls ill later, and young Zack is packed off to his Aunt Flax's home. He returns five weeks later, the boy having recovered and grown taller. Aunt Flint had also died in the "levelling sickness," so that there were no more trips to the Hall during Sunday tea times. Zack guesses "that the money for the lad's keep stopped quat wi' Miss Elizabeth's death." There begins to be talk of putting the lad to a trade, but his adoptive mother feels he should be let bide, and that his blood will put him forward eventually.

One day after church the boy follows the squire and Miss Bet out of the church building, instead of waiting for them to leave as was customary. The squire

> turned round, and the lad looked up in his face.
>
> "I want," he said, "to walk home wi' Bet."
>
> At that the squire's red face grew a bit redder and a grim kind o' smile came upon the same.
>
> "Well, Bet," he called out in his big voice, "what answer am I to make to your cavalier?"
>
> "I like him," said the little lady, for she was never one to desert a friend.
>
> "Then be off with you both," the squire answered.
>
> But the following day he rode down and said that such a thing must not happen a second time, and my father passed his word that it should not.

The squire doesn't wonder at "who the lad might be." To Zack, the boy seems to have gotten "the yokel's tread, and seemed to me nearer o' kin to us than he had first-along." In Zack's mother's eyes, however, "he was always Miss Elizabeth's son, a gentleman, and, maybe, though he never put tongue to the words, he saw at one with her in the matter."

On "the morning o' his seventeenth year," the lad and Zack are in the woods. The boy tries to jump the brook. He fails to make it and falls in the water. Just then Miss Bet shows up. She has "grown most 'mazing pleasant to look on." When the boy tries to pull himself up with a willow twig, it breaks, he gets another sousing, and Miss Bet laughs in response. In anger and shame the boy runs off.

He broods away from them all for days, and finally Zack follows him to see where he is going. He finds him at the spot of the boy's previous humiliation. This day Miss Bet shows up.

> At sight o' her the lad sprang to his feet and pulled off his cap.
>
> "Dear me, are you really dry again?" she called across.
>
> "'Tis naught o' a jump," he answered, the blood aflame in his face.
>
> "Indeed!"
>
> "Leastways, I could jump it to-day," he said.
>
> "Why to-day?"
>
> "I could jump it to-day," he repeated, stubbornful.

"Please don't try, you will only fall in, and I am sure you can't afford to spoil your clothes," she cried, seeing him run back a few steps; but wi' a rush and a spring he was over at her side.

"There," he said, "I knowed I could do it to-day."

"Why to-day,?" she asked, curious-like.

"Becase," he tummil'd out, speaking terrible broad—for, wi' all his blood, he had grown at one wi' us in speech—"becase you be over to here."

I reckon myself that Miss Bet was a bit taken aback at this speech o' the lad's, for she was silent a while, then she asked all-to-once, "Where's little Zack?"

Now, though I bain't as big, I be full as old as the lad hisself, so I wasn't altogether made up in being spoken of as "little Zack," but that is neither here nor there.

"I dunno," he answered.

"Perhaps he is at the fair?"

"Maybe."

"He works for Farmer Burden, doesn't he?"

"Ess."

"And you?"

"I don't go to work."

"Why not?"

"I dunno," he said, sullenful.

She looked him up and down. "But surely," she asked, "a big fellow like you are is not content to be idle all day?"

He didn't make no answer.

A bit of a smile crept into her face. "Perhaps you mean to earn a living by your head and not with your hands. That is what all you young men do nowadays, isn't it?" she asked.

He turned and walked a few paces from her. "I ain't larned," he said. At that she seemed a bit sorry to have spoke.

"Well," she said, going up to him and touching his arm, "I am glad to have seen you again. Do you remember we used to play together as children?"

He didn't answer her a word, but stood there terrible proud and downcast to one. The little lady looked at him a moment and then began to move slowly away.

"Good-bye," she said, stopping and kaining back at him, but he made as if he hadn't heard, so she walked on and left him. When there wasn't no sound o' her footsteps nor no sight o' her atween the trees, he flung hisself down 'pon top the earth and sobbed and sobbed. I couldn't mind that I had ever seen him do the like afore, and I wondered what 'twas that made un do it then.

The boy does not come home to supper that night, but is back on the scene quickly. The next few days he and his adoptive mother are both upset. Zack and his father return from Sunday's afternoon service to find "mother and the lad was sitting hand in hand before the fire." The four of them sit around the table, "each o' us silent, saving mother, who was painful silent." The boy leaves the house, and Zack's mother informs them that the boy is going away from them. He is going to earn his own living. "'The blood won't let un bide content; like to like.'"

Within a few days he is packed and ready to leave. He cries openly as he rides the cart through the village, to Zack's displeasure. They are not sure where he is going, but expect that he will not come back without having seen Exeter, a major city in Devon. Zack wonders if the young man will become educated, and if he'll become a gentleman "'again,'" but his mother says "'a gentleman he is and always will be,'" and believes a gentleman can do without education.

She yearns after her missing adopted son, and she reveals more of his story to young Zack. The boy had been born at the Hall, though only Aunt Flint knew that. Aunt Flint had carried the boy to Zack's father, Ebenezer. Ebenezer took the boy and was absent three days. Ebenezer was a man well capable of keeping a secret, and had never revealed where he took the newborn child.

The secret of the lad's father is finally revealed to Zack by Zack's mother. It was Black Mark Hay, the same young man the old squire threw down the Hall steps.

> "Ay; and 'tis told that Miss Elizabeth followed un out and gave herself to un thic same night."
> "And then?" I asked.
> "He shot himself. Reckoning to have a sure revenge on the squire. But the squire never larned the truth. No, nor ever will."

The boy himself, however, had learned at least some of the truth at the time of the levelling sickness. His mother, Miss Elizabeth, knowing she was dying, had requested that Aunt Flint bring the boy to her. She did so, as we already know. Miss Elizabeth spoke:

"'Come nearer,' she said; and he came nearer. 'Give me your hand,' she said; and he gave her his hand. 'Stoop down,' she said; and he stooped down. 'Lay your face on mine,' she said; and he did as she bade un, so that the tears that fell from her eyes fell 'pon him. Then he raised his head and looked her full in the face. 'Be you my mother?' he asked. And she answered, "Yes,' and wi' that she died.'"

They receive no letters from the young man during his year away. When he finally comes back, it is in the same clothes he went away in, and not looking at all like a gentleman. It slips out gradually that he had indeed been to Exeter, where he had found work—but not the sort of work a gentleman would be doing. "His hands were terrible rough and worn away, and when I asked how that had comed about, he said he had been hod-boy to a mason." A hod carrier mixes mortar, and carries the mortar and bricks or blocks, to the mason. This is very heavy and difficult physical labor, as I know from hard experience gained in my younger days! It was not the sort of work a gentleman would be doing, but it was the only job the young man had been able to get.

Later on the same day, Zack finds him keening across at the Hall. Zack feels a bit sorry for him, and they talk.

"Why don't 'ee larn to speak more like ginelfolks, seeing that you are quality?" I tummil'd out, for the clack o' his tongue always kind o' tarned me agin un.

He reddened up at that, and then he said, sort o' wistful, "Do 'ee reckon, Zack, Miss Bet would lay my speech agin me?"

"Miss Bet," I answered, "don't trouble her head over such, seeing that she holds you for naught above the hod-boy that you be."

The blood crept away from un, leaving his face white, but he didn't say naught, and I felt kind o' sorry for un again.

"If so be you was to tell her who by rights you are," I put in, after a bit, "she might help you back to yourself."

"I shan't niver get back to myself thic ways," he answered.

"Nor no ways," I said short; "for you ain't got it in 'ee."

A week later Zack and "he" encounter Miss Bet riding. She is, as always, friendly, but Zack carries all of the male side of the conversation, the other young man remaining silent.

One night as Ebenezer smokes on the porch, and Zack has his head on the table almost asleep,

> the lad turned his face up to my mother.
>
> "Mother," he said.
>
> "Well," her answered, soft-like.
>
> "Zack's asleep—iddn't he?"
>
> "Ay—I reckon he be."
>
> "Do 'ee love me, mother?" he asked.
>
> I kind o' smiled to myself, 'twas like the lad to be asking such—and I reckon mother thought the same, for she jest runned her fingers through his hair and didn't answer he at all.
>
> "Mother," he said again.
>
> "Well?" her answered.
>
> "'Twas but a poor thing I made o' it."
>
> "Us can't all succeed first-away," her answered.
>
> "I know what 'tis I'm after having, but when I try to get it, I'm all abroad," he said, sort o' helpless.
>
> "You be one o' the quality—and you want to take your place as such."
>
> He drew his breath sharp in between his teeth. "I be but a poor-witted lad, mother."
>
> "Wits iddn't everything."
>
> "They wud help me wi' a deal I can't fathom now."
>
> I reckon that my mother knowed well enough that the lad wasn't over and above bright, and it kind o' made her sore, though her wouldn't own to such, for her said, impatient-like, "You've got the blood anyways, there's no denying thic."
>
> He was silent a long while after that. "It don't bring me no nearer her," he said—more as if he was speaking to hisself.

Not long after that the young man left a second time. "He slipped away quietful, not so much as bidding good-bye to mother." With the lad going off like that, and them never hearing from him, his adopted mother falls ill and takes to her bed. Miss Bet hears of her illness, and one "dimmit"—twilight, she comes to visit her.

A long and powerful scene follows. I will resist the temptation to quote all of it, and will only give the latter part. To summarize the early part, Miss Bet is at the window when the young man comes back to his adopted mother. In the darkening twilight he doesn't see her there. He tells his mother that he has "'fathomed'" what he must do. He will go to Australia to colonize. "'A man can do a deal over to there.'" His mother tries to discourage this idea, fearing he will not come back to her. But he says he will come back to his mother, and also "'to her.'" When his mother leaves the room to fix him some food, he discovers that Miss Bet is present.

"I am afraid," she said, "I have let you make me partner to all your plans."

He came closer, but did not say aught.

"And so you intend to colonise?"

"Yes."

"Why?" she asked, looking curiously at him.

"Becase, becase," he tummil'd out, "there be sommat I can't reach noways else."

"Money?"

"No, 'tiddn't money, though I'll have need o' it."

"What, then?"

He opened and shut his hands nervous-like. "Maybe you would only laugh if I was to tell?"

"No, I should not laugh."

"But you hold my speach for queer," he said, edging nearer and kaining sort o' anxious down on her.

She half turned away. "I find nothing the matter with it."

"Tiddn't like speach o' yours."

"Well, perhaps not altogether," she answered, the corners of her mouth twisting up into a smile.

"I knowed well enough you couldn't but laugh at me," he said, drawing back.

"But I'm not laughing. Why should I be?"

He looked closely at her as if to make sure 'twas truth her was speaking.

"Well?" she said. "Well?"

And at that all-to-once the tears sprang to his eyes.

"'Tiddn't naught but that I want to be sort o' equal wi' the rest o' 'em."

She took his hand. "Equal to whom?" she asked, soft-like.

"To they I comed from."

"And they?"

"They was ginelfolks."

She smiled up at him, half-amused, half-sad to one.

"And will that be so great a business?" she asked.

"I reckon to fathom it," he answered, drawing himself up proudful.

"Then you must not be ashamed of being yourself."

"'Tiddn't that I be ashamed o' what be there." He stopped quat.

"Well?"

"A terrible deal iddn't there, and I don't know where to lay hands on it."

"It is like that with all of us."

"Not wi' 'ee," he muttered, soft-like, to hisself, though I reckon the words reached her, for she turned away half-smileful.

"I thought," she said, "that you were starving."

He didn't pay no heed to thic, but kained across the fields at the church, that stood terrible apart amid the graves. The moon rose and gapnested through the window at him and at her, and I thought as I looked at 'em that they was more'n usual like one t'other. He covered his face wi' his hands. "I shall never fathom it," he cried, bitter-like. "I feel I shall never fathom it."

A wonderful deal o' pity creeped into her eyes.

"Hush!" she said, "it is only the world that is so stupid." But I marked that when her had spoke the word her drawed herself a little apart as if her held there was quality and quality.

"Seems terrible far away all-to-once Australia," he said.

"But you will come back."

"Ess. I shall come back."

"Why," she said, smiling, "in four years I shall be of age. You must be back in time to wish me well."

And he said he would.

The young man does indeed leave for Australia—his third attempt to find what he is looking for in himself.

One Sunday another young man is sitting in the church pew with Miss Bet. Zack recognizes him at once to be "Quality." This eventually leads to a disputation with his mother about the missing lad, she of course defending him and young Zack quite dismissive. The new young man, Zack says, is "'brainful.'"

"Brainful," repeated my mother, laughing sort o' uneasy and contemptuous. "Hasn't the lad a head on his shoulders?"

"Vath yes, but 'tis the head o' a vool."

"Out on 'ee to call un such. He'll live yet to larn 'ee the need o' better manners."

"No," I answered stubbornly, "I shall feel contemptful o' un to the last."

"You dursn't say it."

"Yes, I dare. I can't abide quality that ain't quality."

"Quality," repeated my mother, disdaineous. "Your quality be all clothes and fine speech, but God Almighty would have 'em be sommat else aside that, I reckon."

"And what would He be after having 'em?"

"Tenderful for others, for wan."

I burst out laughing. "Hivers! I could be thic myself."

We learn that the "quality" young man is nephew and heir of Black Mark Hay who shot himself (and was the father of "he" by Miss Elizabeth). This young man is now the Squire of Chickenham Chase. While the squire of the Hall was totally opposed, almost twenty years ago, to Black Mark Hay courting his daughter Miss Elizabeth, we hear now that he favors this young man—and the estates adjoin.

A few days later Zack, working for Farmer Burden, is hoeing turnips in a field close to the river. He tells us, in one of those comments that tend to stay in the memory—at least in mine—that "I wasn't working pushful hard, knowing well enough that, if I lived long enough, I should have my fill o' it." He sees Miss Bet seated beneath a willow. She was "'mazing pleasant to look on," and Zack moves closer to her with his hoeing. He sees the young Squire of Chickenham Chase come close to her, albeit on the other side of the river. Their conversation establishes several facts. The young man really is her social equal: his speech and his behavior tell us this clearly. And he is smitten with her. And she, while humorously teasing of him, is certainly aware of his attraction to her, and quite possibly not uninterested in him.

After three months a packet arrives from "he." It includes, with a letter, the wings of a flying fish. After another long stretch of time the lad sends them a whip with a lash fourteen feet long.

Miss Bet heard tell so much o' the whip that she came down from the Hall on purpose to see the same, but mother put on a chariness and said it was put away in peppered paper for fear o' the moths, and it wasn't till the little lady had begged most particular that she was allowed to set eyes on the whip at all. Howsoever, when at last mother did bring it down, and stretched the lash out full length along the floor, Miss Bet stared down on the same 'mazing intent, though I have my doubts if her was seeing further than her thoughts.

"Who is he, Martha?" she asked all-to-once, and mother was so took aback that she picked up the whip and brought down a china dog and a text wi' the lash.

"Bodies and souls o' us!" she exclaimed, "but this whip was never made for company."

"Well, and who is he?" repeated the little lady.

"The lad?" said my mother, in a questionful voice, though she knew well enough that 'twas he Miss Bet meant.

"Yes."

"Oh," mother answered, kind o' unconsarned, "just a lad wi' blood in un."

The little lady stooped down and picked up the lash o' the whip, turning it over thoughtful-like in her hand. "But whose blood?" she asked.

I reckon, had mother dared, she would dearly o' liked to ha' spoken out. "Let his face speak for 'un," she said at last.

Miss Bet raised her head, and, catching sight o' her own face in a small glass over agin where she sat, the blood flared up to the brow o' her, and mother, half-flusticated, stood gapnesting down on the little china dog that was lying all to bits upon the floor.

"Well," exclaimed the little lady, jumping up and shaking her skirts as if the room and us had become mighty distasteful all-to-once, "I must be going. But that is a beautiful whip o' yours, Martha," she added, her eyes falling on my mother, who stood dejected-like, "and I am sure there will never be such another in Dunstable Weir." Then, nodding to us both, away she tripped before the red had scarce time to die out o' her face.

Another letter arrives from Australia, and it is clear that "he" is not prospering. Miss Bet hears of the letter, and the message from the Hall is that she would like to read it, but Martha didn't want the letter "laid afore the great folk." However, the following week Miss Bet brings her watch down for Ebenezer (called Eben by most) to clean. She pretends being casual in asking about the letter from Australia. At last Eben finds the letter and hands it to her.

She carried the letter over to the windy and read it through three times, first quick, then slower, then mortal slow. I marked that because I watched her, wonderful surprised.

"Well," said father, "'tis but middling he's doing, I fancy, Miss Bet."

"I'm afraid so."

The room was silent a while, and father picked up the spoon and began to set it. "He took a deal o' hope away wi' un."

"I wish," cried the little lady, "that he hadn't."

"A man's never more alive than when he's hoping, Miss Bet," father answered, sort o' smileful.

She came closer and looked into father's face. "Tell me, Eben, does he belong to those who had better not have been born?"

His face growed dreamful-like under the little lady's eyes. "Be there such?" he asked half o' her and half o' hisself.

"Yes, Eben, yes."

"I ha' my doubts o' it, Miss Bet."

"He can never be what he wants. And what can he be?"

"Thic that he was made for."

"Oh," she said, "I would like him to succeed in being what he wished—or never to have wished."

Father took off and wiped his spectacles terrible careful afore resettling 'em on his nose.

"I reckon," he said, "that the lad be sort o' dreamin' jest now."

"That's it. He's dreaming, Eben. And we have all been content to let him dream."

"'Tis through our dreams us be made, Miss Bet."

She frowned and bit her lip. "That's no comfort. Why does he dream such stupid dreams?"

"Thic be the nature o' 'em. They be always a bit beyond us."

"Well, I don't dream," said the little lady, decisionful. "Do you, Eben?"

"I've had 'em wi' the rest, Miss Bet."

Before she leaves, Miss Bet tells Eben a secret he says he will do his best to keep: she is engaged to Mark Hay. She very much wants to know what Eben is thinking of, after hearing that news.

"What are you thinking of, Eben?" she demanded, masterful-like.

"You'll make a handsome couple. There was never one o' your family, or his either, that failed in looks."

"That was not what you were thinking of."

"'Tis true for all o' thic."

She came closer. "Eben, how can you?" she said, codoodling-like. "When you and I are such friends, and I stole all those evil-smelling powders just for you to blow yourself up with."

"So you did, Miss Bet, so you did," father answered, softening.

"Well?"

"I was jest reckoning back on t'other lad."

She fell silent at that, the colour flared across her face. Her always seemed a bit ashamed o' un when he was mentioned sudden-like. "I hope he will get on," she said, sort o' kind o' contemptful to one, and, nodding to father, she tripped away out o' the shop.

Not too many weeks later, "mother got her last letter from the lad." It was short. Gold had been found close to where he was, and there was no reason why he should not find gold himself. Martha tells Zack to take the letter up to Miss Bet at the Hall. He does so. Miss Bet read the letter, then read it once again. In the next quote there seem to me to be two errors—both of which errors I think belong to Gwendoline Keats rather than to Zack the villager. I will discuss them after the quote. Miss Bet, thinking to herself and cutting three roses, speaks.

"Zack," she said, "why was it always in *this* garden, before these windies, that he played?"

"Hivers!" thought I, "shall I be after telling?"—and I reckoned I would, telling being pleasant work. Still, I was a bit afear'd—because I knew well enough that neither father nor mother nor the lad hisself would have had me bide silent.

"This be Miss Elizabeth's garden," I said.

"Yes."

"And they were Miss Elizabeth's rooms."

"Well?"

I stooped and picked up my cap, that had fallen from my fingers. "Thic was the reason," I answered. The flowers must have slipped from the little lady's hand, because when I raised my head the roses lay all o' a heap, the basket a-tilt beside them, and the little lady was walking, slow-paced, away.

"'Twasn't much o' a tell, after all," said I to myself. "I reckoned to ha' drawn it out more."

The first error is that Miss Bet would not have said windies. Throughout the entire story, Zack has always given the speech of the upper class people exactly as they spoke it. Miss Bet would have said windows, not windies. Here, one of our two Homers, Gwendoline Keats or Zack the villager, has nodded.

The second error is in the sentence in which Zack says he is afraid to tell the truth. The sentence seems to read as if father, mother, and the lad would *not* have him bide silent. From the context as well as from the personalities of the three people he mentions, we know that what he means is that they would have had him bide silent. He is afraid to tell precisely because he knows they would have him be silent. The phrasing of the sentence is wrong, or confused. The sentence should read something like this: "Still, I was a bit afeard—because I knew well enough that father and mother and the lad hisself would have had me bide silent." Again, Homer nods.

A few paragraphs onward, we learn something about the beliefs of Martha, and possibly about the beliefs of Gwendoline Keats. The father reports to the ailing Martha on the day's sermon, and says the parson was "'powerful plain on sin.'"

> "Sin!" mother 'ud repeat, contemptful-like; "'tis a queer, but I never was no overbold believer in sich."
> At that father wud wipe his spectacles against the sleeve o' his coat and nod across the room at me.
> "Unwisdom, then," he wud say, sort o' questioning.
> "Ay, us all fails o' wisdom," mother wud answer.

The orthodox Christian faith is "'powerful plain on sin.'" We need the Savior Jesus Christ precisely because we are all profoundly sinful. Here Martha is contemptful of the notion of sin. Our problem is that we fail in wisdom, she says. One can sympathize with her point of view to a certain extent. Certainly a major cause of our problems, whether we are Christians or non-Christians, is that we do not live with practical wisdom. It is completely true that "'us all fails o' wisdom.'" In fact, I would go further and say that the general failure of Christians to seek after wisdom is a large part of the reason that the faith advances so slowly in the world.[36] The wonderful book of Proverbs is a key biblical

---

[36]For more on the possible centrality of wisdom in a truly orthodox brand of Christianity, please see Carl Wells, *What Are God's Goals?*, Bloomington, Indiana, AuthorHouse, 2014.

source for showing in what high regard God holds wisdom. We have not echoed His high regard! So Martha is partly correct. Of course in a sense sin is always unwisdom! To do evil is to bring down bad consequences upon oneself, not just upon the people we are harming. Doing evil is not wise, and is not practical.

But to deny the power of sin seems to be an error. If this is an error Gwendoline Keats made in her personal view of how the world is put together, there may have been consequences for her ability to evaluate reality with complete accuracy. When our theology is flawed, there are always consequences, although we might not recognize the consequences. In fairness, we should remember that Gwendoline Keats is quite capable of portraying people who act with great evil. Dick Atter, Ben Tapp, and Thomas Rod come immediately to mind. Would she hold such men to be acting solely out of unwisdom, rather than out of sin? I don't know. Maybe we will be so fortunate to discuss these issues with Gwendoline Keats herself someday—when her thinking and ours will have been greatly improved on lots of things.

Martha, her health failing, yearns mightily for the lad. To Zack's surprise, one twilight night he is there.

> It didn't take more than one glance at the lad to see that 'twasn't gold he'd found.
> "Mother," he said. "Mother!"
> Seeing them standing there, the thought came over me that there were big things in the world beside gold, and then I minded what a terrible big thing gold was. Let that be as it may, certain enough he hadn't found it, and when, a bit later, he allowed that he had naught but the clothes he stood up in, and they were that poor that 'twas only hisself that held them together, I turned to him and said,—
> "You have gone away quiet and unbeknown before, and there be time between this and daylight to do the like again."
> He looked at me surprised-like. "Why, *don't* her come o' age to-morrow? Do you think I've forgot that? I reckon not."
> "You bain't thinking o' going in they clothes?"
> "The very same, unless, maybe, you can lend me a fit out."
> I held the speech for unfriendsome, because he had a foot to the good o' me in height. "So you will put Dunstable Weir to shame afore three villages," I burst out.
> What's Dunstable Weir to me?" he asked.

"Us be sommat, I hope."

He turned to mother and took her hand. "You'll put on your best bonnet and let me walk aside 'ee—aye, mother?" he asked.

And she said she would, though clothes were a deal to her.

The next day Zack continues to fret over his adopted brother's poverty-stricken appearance, and indeed the villagers of Dore Apple howl at the sight of the young man. His face is somewhat drained in color at the mockery, but he perseveres.

All-to-once the lad, who had been kaining about him considerable, clapped eyes on the little lady, and at that up he hopped up and away he went over the grass and through the big gates, for all the world as if the place belonged to him.

"Great God Almighty!" I said to mother, "if he bain't quality, he has the cheek o' such," and I made haste to get as close to the rails as I dared, to see what would befall, and mother, half crying wi' fear and pride, crept up beside me. The great folks, reckoning, no doubt, that the ragged gawkin was either mad or drunk, stepped back instinctive, leaving the little lady standing alone.

When she marked who 'twas coming so boldacious, she went a few steps to meet him and kained proud-like into his face, which had naught in it but the need o' seeing her, and 'twas easy telling that neither o' they two gave thought to who craned forward, curious as village-folk, to see their eyes-ful.

"I minded the day," he said.

"And the gold?" she asked.

"I never struck on that."

"Ah," she answered, sort o' slow.

"But I minded the day," he said again. "I minded it every hour I was awake."

The blood sort o' swept out o' her face, but she didn't answer a word, and young Squire Mark came forward and laid his hand upon her arm. First into his face and then into hers the lad kained questionful, then he turned and walked back the way he came.

A few minutes later the lad is devastated to hear that Miss Bet and Mark Hay are promised to one another as man and wife.

The lad is hired as carter to Farmer Burden. Martha, meanwhile, is nearing the end of her life. The lad and his adopted mother testify their love for one another. "'Life gived us one to t'other,' he said.' This reminds us of Dave's words to his mother in the story "Widder Vlint": "'God guved me thee.'"

The three men are at Martha's bedside on her last day. It is clear that Ebenezer, always held for "'an unseeing man,'" has always observed Martha much more closely than might have been expected. The two hold hands as she dies. After the funeral,

then there was a knock and the little lady came in. She talked to me quiet-like, and after a bit her asked for the lad.

I told her he was up to mother's room and asked if I should call him down.

But she answered she wouldn't have him worried. I said maybe 'twould be well if her stepped up to he. Her stood undecided-like, then her turned and went softly up the stairs and knocked at mother's door, and, no answer coming, her hiked in unbid. There was a loose board atween mother's room and mine, and, feeling curious-like, I pushed it one side and looked in. The lad was crying all to hisself terrible sore, his face pressed deep agin the pilly where mother's head used to rest, and the little lady kained down on him unmarked. When he had sobbed a while, she leaned forward and touched him, and he looked up.

His face growed still as if the sorrow had stiffened in it.

"Oh," she said, sort o' helpless, "what can one do against death?"

"'Tis just because one has such a deal that one misses," he answered.

"But that only makes it harder."

"Us can't have it both ways," he said.

She looked at him, half-pitying, half-afraid. "You won't lose courage?"

"Her wouldn't have me do thic."

"And your plans?" she asked, hesitating-like.

"Oh, they!"

"Yes."

He walked to the windy and stared past the three wind-twisted firs at the Hall, that stood so terrible prosperous big above him.

"I reckon, if I live honest it's about the size o' me."

The little lady turned away, and her face was full of the need o' helping, but she didn't say naught.

He waited till she had reached the door, then came terrible swift across to her.

"I be going away; I sha'n't niver come back." He stopped short. "But I shall always mind on the folks I knowed here," he ended, feeble-like.

Something in the words touched the speech in her. "You musn't go like that," she burst out, passionful, "wi' no one to help, no one to care whether you succeed or fail."

"I bain't bound up in no terrible big need this time," he said.

"But you must be," she insisted. "Your need must be just as big, bigger. I used to think you had no right to big needs, but now"—she stopped quat—"I think differently."

The lad smiled to hisself like. "You and mother be most one in that," he answered. "The mother I buried to-day, the mother who tended me that mortal untiring. 'Tis her son I be, and 'tis in her footsteps I'll follow, God helping."

She kained at him 'mazing full o' thought. "I'm glad your blood and mine be the same," she said.

Then she went out and left him.

I thought 'twas a poor show of words on both sides.

Thus ends this fascinating story.

"The Hall and He" reminds us of the long story "Life Is Life," discussed in Chapter 1. There, Humphrey was born of a gentlewoman and a man of lower class, but raised as the Squire's grandson. Humphrey became very much a gentleman in spirit. Here, "he" is born of upper class parents, but raised by working class people. He becomes working class in his speech and bearing, but he also knows his upper class roots, and strives to regain his position. This striving is complicated by his romantic love for his cousin Miss Bet. He hopes to become upper class so that he can be worthy of Miss Bet and win her love.

Reading this heartrending story for the first time, I wondered how it would turn out. Will the author give an honest, realistic, possible ending? The answer is yes. Root though the reader may for the young man, it is not going to be possible for him to become a suitable mate for Miss Bet. He remains lower class in his speech. He barely is able to earn a living—comes back from Australia so poverty-stricken that he has only the clothes on his back, and those so shabby that he is holding them together. The gloriously beautiful Miss Bet will wed another. What makes his defeat so much more poignant is that Miss Bet really is a wonderful person—loyal, kind, thoughtful, gracious.

So he is defeated. And yet, as always when reading Gwendoline Keats, we see victories as well. He shows admirable courage. He leaves his home three times, seeking financial success and seeking somehow to regain a footing in the upper class from which he sprang via his biological parents. He fails. He becomes a hod carrier the first time, works hard, and earns little. The second time he also fails. The third time he goes as far as Australia. Again, the courage involved is remarkable. After four long years, he returns to honor Miss Bet as she comes of age (as he promised her he would), and again the result is: financial failure, no apparent upper class bearing, and the young lady he loves will marry another.

He looks at his future, and foresees no likely success. Despite his upper class origins, he had never shown an interest in book learning. He will probably remain a day laborer of some sort, and seems to know it. "'I reckon, if I live honest it's about the size o' me.'" But while his position seems to indicate failure, is this not also success of a sort? To face the truth about ourselves is a victory. Most of us live in various stages of self-deception. "He" is now looking at his future without self-deception. His "dream" was to become an upper class man who could win Miss Bet's heart. It was a dream far beyond his capabilities of fulfilling. But as Eben wisely saw, we are made through our dreams. His dream drove him to acts of courage. He failed to attain his dream, but became a man worthy of respect in the attempt. What if all he does from here on out is to "'live honest'"? That, I submit, is very far from a small thing. How few people live honest! We most of us live in self-deception, and most of us are always looking for some way to vote our neighbor's property away from him so that we can have an extra chicken in our own pot—and, though we won't admit it to ourselves, a chicken less in the pot of our neighbor who actually raised the chicken. If "he" lives honest, he will be accomplishing a lot. By the end of the story he is very far from a fool, young though he is, and despite his lack of book learning. For another example of his practical wisdom, he understands that his great pain in missing his dead adopted mother is part of the price of loving her. He misses so much in losing her, which makes it harder to have her die, but "'Us can't have it both ways.'"

To fail to attain the hand of Miss Bet is certainly a failure. But this is the old, old story! How many million men in the history of the world have loved a woman unattainable, a worthy woman beyond their reach? But to have loved in such a manner is a sort of success. Miss Bet was worthy of such love. There is no disgrace in failing to win her love. There was much courageous character displayed in making the attempt. His "dream" was not "'stupid,'" as Miss Bet, in her inexperience, thought. It was noble.

Zack is scornful of the young man's attempt to be "quality." But Gwendoline Keats helps us think this through a little more deeply. Martha tells Zack her son that the Almighty would have the quality be tenderful for others. Zack scorns this notion, pointing out that he could be that himself. The irony is delicious, and thought-provoking. Yes, precisely, young Zack! You could. And so might we all, and thus move toward becoming upper class in the best sense. This is one of the mighty strengths of Gwendoline Keats. She points us toward the way we all, whatever our class of origin, can become aristocrats in the best sense. And, it is crucial to note that "he" is extremely loving toward his adopted mother. Young Zack never learns to act in that manner. This is not to say that Zack does not love his mother. We can be certain that he does. But he does not find it possible or necessary to express that love. "He" does express his love for his adopted mother, over and over. The tenderness between the two is a joy to witness. And he desires to honor her after her death, by the way he lives.

The character of the squire is interesting. In Gwendoline Keats' novels and stories, there are squires, and there are squires. In "Life Is Life" and in *The White Cottage*, the squires are admirable men—and they are capitalized as Squire. Here the squire is always the squire, not capitalized. Is this a coincidence, or a subtle indication that our squire here is a lesser man than the other squires? He certainly seems to be. He remains completely blind to the fact that "he" is the son of his own daughter. He never seems to be "'tenderful for others.'"

Miss Bet is a wonderful creation. There is always a lot to her character that is admirable. And yet she grows emotionally, to become even a finer person. While loyal to her young friend from her childhood on, we can also see her draw "herself a little apart" from him at times, conscious of the class difference between them. She had at one time thought the dreams of the lad to be "'stupid,'" and that he "'had no right to big needs,'" but by the end of the story she thinks very differently indeed. She tells him that she is glad that he and she come from the same blood. This is one very astonishing and gracious young lady. "He" showed a lot of practical wisdom in loving so remarkable a girl and woman. As we have discussed before, Gwendoline Keats, from her pictures, seems not to have been a woman of great physical beauty. If this is true, then we can guess that she was a person not given to envy, because she was always generous to those of her female characters who are physically beautiful, of whatever their social class. She has given us one of her most admirable and subtle creations in Miss Bet.

The other main characters are portrayed with consistency and insight. It is entertaining to follow young Zack as he tells us the story. The snooping, eavesdropping Zack sees and reports everything, sometimes with considerable insight, sometimes missing the point—and usually with a mixture of both. Zack may not understand everything, but he tells us enough so that the reader can understand everything, if we read closely. The ending of the story seems especially ironic. Zack hears the profoundly moving conversation between "he" and Miss Bet, and yet finds it to be "a poor show of words on both sides."

Martha and Eben are quite unique individuals. Eben is a bit of an absent-minded inventor, sometimes seemingly out of touch with what is going on around him. At times he provides comic relief. Yet he too is capable of insights, as his conversation with Miss Bet cited above will show. And his love for his wife is very strong. Martha is heroically committed to supporting "he," though her expectations of his potential prospects are too high. The love between Martha and her adopted son is very deep, and neither one is afraid to express that love in their actions toward one another.

"The Hall and He" is one of Gwendoline Keats' finest works. It, like "Life Is Life," points the way to an aristocracy of behavior which reconciles class differences. It is sad and moving and honest.

"The Right O' Way"

"The Right O' Way" is the second-shortest story in the collection, checking in at just slightly more than ten pages. It is a powerful story.

Zack tells us that Fig Tree Cottage is halfway between Dunstable Weir and Dore Apple.

> The door o' the house be fast shut most days, but that be neither here nor there, becase folks have a right to go droo, and no one can deny 'em entrance, for the old law holds good in Dunstable Weir Parish that the passing o' a corpse makes a free way for furren feet.

The "old law holds good . . . passing o' a corpse" etc. is a reference to the tradition reported on in *The Encyclopaedia of Superstitions* (1949) by the husband and wife team Edwin and Mona A. Radford (p. 83): "A very widespread belief, still far from extinct, is that if a corpse is carried over private land, its passage establishes a right of way forever." However, Zack reports that no one makes a point of trying to take advantage of this historical right in the case of Margarette Morse and Fig Tree Cottage, first because it is more "neighbourzome" not to attempt to go through the house, and secondly also because possibly they are a bit afraid of the old maid Margarette Morse, who lives in the house. It was through her that the right of way was established, however.

Margarette is old and homely now, but in her younger days "her was unusual personable," "most as persuasive looking as a flower." Noll Oliver, described as "foolish-faced Oliver—Rabbit Skins, folks called un, for selling the zame," was highly attracted to Margarette. He would enter the property each day on his rounds, to look upon Margarette. Margarette's brother Matthew Morse took offense at this, and one day gave Noll a beating with an ash stick.

After that "feeble-couraged" Noll never had the nerve to enter the property again, but he would come to the outside of the gate persistently.

He was always trying to contrive "how to diddle his cowardice and Matthew Morse to wan."

Rabbit Skins spoke not about this except to Zack's father. This was before Zack was born, when his father was still single. (He is called Tobin in this story; he was Eben in "The Hall and He.") Rabbit Skins says that he has the will to fight but not the power.

Then he would go off to the Fig Tree Cottage. Sometimes Tobin would follow him to see what the two would say to one another. Usually they were silent.

> Howzomever, my father tells that wance the maid looked across at un proudlike.
>
> "Why don't 'ee poke droo, Noll Oliver," her asked, "the zame as you've been wont to these five years and more?"
>
> At that the lad's body kind o' twitched forrard, and he put out his hands and clutched at the iron bars o' the gate, but made no move to lift the latch.
>
> Then her axed again, "Why don't 'ee poke droo, Noll Oliver, the zame as you've been wont these five years and more?"

However, Noll cannot find the courage to come onto the property, and Margarette goes back inside the house. Noll pitches forward on his face. Matthew Morse finds him there and throws him into the mud of the ditch.

After that Noll

> got more fetched in his head than iver, and many there was who thought he wud be safer inside the asylum, or leastways the jail; but, law, he baing naught but a poor man, no wan had the time to interfere, zeeing well that money 'ud have to be spent on the matter.

One market day when Matthew Morse was away to town, Noll Oliver takes the "blunderbus" belonging to Tobin. Tobin discovers this, and cautiously following Noll, sees him reach the gate of Fig Tree Cottage, and is afraid that Noll intends to shoot Margarette. Nothing of that sort happens. Tobin comes down the hill at a steady pace. The story ends as follows:

Thankful he was that no undue hurry possessed un, for jest as he came nigh the gate the gun went off, whether by accident or design the crowner or the Almighty be the best o' jidges, but 'tis sartin that in doing so it let fly a wonderful varrigated collection o' slugs, nails, and scraps o' old iron full in the broad o' Noll Oliver's chest. A banging big hole they tore out for theirzelves, and blood, my father zed, anuff to paint a good-sized field, welled from the zame. He and the maid togither carried un in and stretched un out under the fig tree, where he lay, his brown eyes wide stretched, looking terrible much a lad. Margarette her knelt azide he and took the hand o' un in hers.

"I knowed," her zed, "that you wadn't afear'd to come."

The blood and froth was oozing from his lips, so that he cudn't answer in wuds, but, for a man that had jest shot hiszulf, he zim'd wonderful plazed wi' the situation.

When Margarette Morse saw that the lad was past speech, her rose up and shook my father by the arm.

"Bear witness," her zed, "that he wadn't afear'd to come."

My father he stud there scratching his head, looking fust to wan and then to t'other, for well he knew that either he or they was mad. But law, Noll Oliver died even as her spoke, and the maid, zeeing for herzulf that he was past recall, put her two hands under un and beckoned to my father to do the likewise.

"Carry un droo the house," her zed. "In droo the front and out droo the back, and the passing o' his corpse shall make a free way for furren feet to tread."

My father did as her bade un, and that be the long and the short o' how there comed to be a right o' way droo Fig Tree Cottage—though folks say 'tis all o' a piece wi' Margarette Morse just to give and then to make the gift o' no account.

Once again we have a story in which tremendously sad things happen. Noll Oliver is not only weak of mind, but he is also "feeble-couraged." After his beating at the hands of Matthew Morse, he does not have the courage to enter the Morse property—despite the fact that Margarette is considerably encouraging to him. He becomes "more fetched in his head than iver." He ends up shooting himself—whether accidentally or on purpose only the coroner or God can say for sure—and quickly dies.

And yet, with all the sadness, there are things to triumph at. Noll does not have the courage to face Matthew Morse in a fight, but he does have the courage to kill himself. We can not be completely sure, but it seems to me almost certain that he killed himself and that the gun did not go off accidentally. It is crucial to note that it was on a market day when Matthew Morse was gone, that Noll took the blunderbus (Zack's spelling). He had no intention of threatening Matthew or doing him any harm; he knew Matthew was gone to market. Why, then, take the blunderbus to Fig Tree Cottage? It was to show his courage to die, to Margarette whom he loved as well as he could. Margarette, in turn, understood his action and praised his courage, which tribute Noll received with great satisfaction: "for a man that had jest shot hiszulf, he zim'd wonderful plazed wi' the situation."

Margarette is a most unusual person. Noll, Rabbit Skins as he is called, is weak of mind, half-crazy, and "feeble-couraged." But she, a comely young woman apparently far beyond him in mental abilities and in strength of character, nevertheless is able to care for him. When he shoots himself, she praises his courage. That is the one gift the dying man—"looking terrible much a lad"—needs in his last moments. He dies content. And she never marries, though she lives to be an old woman.

"Village Pump Fewins"

This is the shortest story in the collection, about 8 1/2 pages long. It concerns a very strange man, Village Pump Fewins. We are not told his Christian name. He is called Village Pump Fewins because he considers himself to be the village pump. Not only that—he also felt that he needed to be fed on eggs to keep going.

Zack tells us that Village Pump Fewins "wadn't zactly mad," but most readers are likely to quarrel with that statement! To make matters worse, Village Pump Fewins "had a big appetite for food, and none for work," and his was a poor family—no doubt largely because he had no appetite for work. He had a wife and four children. They did not complain about their father's lifestyle, however: "indeed, they had all in their time been proud to work for their father, holding there wadn't his like for style o' behaviour inside the parish or out." The latter part of that sentence is a statement with which the reader is unlikely to quarrel.

The youngest son, Poddy Peter, was ailing, but even in his illness he loved to count his father's egg shells.

> He counted 'em out, a round dozen they comed to, while his father stud azide the bed wi' wan arm twitched out straight ahind un, the zame as if 'twas the iron handle o' a pump.
>
> "Mother," the lad continnied, kaining up in the face o' Kitty, "do 'ee reckon I'll live over the day? becase as like as not father 'ull fancy his supper to-night."
>
> "Yes," Village Pump Fewins chimed in, "I shall fancy eggs to-night."
>
> At that Kitty whipped round on her man pretty sharp.
>
> "There be nigh on seven in the house," her zed, "if so be you *can* fancy 'em."
>
> "Bile the lot," he answered, and Poddy Peter sot up in bed and clapped his hands.
>
> They was jest on to the bile when the small lad died.

The death of Poddy Peter meant that all three sons were dead; only a daughter, Jane Elizabeth, remained. Within a few months Village Pump Fewins himself begins to ail. Zack stops by the house with three eggs, and Village Pump Fewins insists that all three be boiled. Kitty Fewins complies with her husband's request, but she sighs as she does so, for she was "wondering, no doubt, where the next lot o' eggs was to come from."

At the time Zack was working as under-gardener at the Hall. "The squire was a hard man and close." Going to work early one day in order to beat the rain, Zack sees Kitty Fewins coming out of the squire's henhouse with her hands full of eggs. The story ends as follows:

> Us stud and looked at won t'other, and I marked that her face was more proudful than shamed.
>
> "Good gore, Kitty!" I zed, "whativer be 'ee doing wi' they eggs?"
>
> "I've stole 'em," her answered.
>
> "Gosh!" I zed, "I always held 'ee for honest."
>
> "I always held mezulf for honest," her answered.
>
> A terrible lot o' minutes went by, then I axed,—
>
> "Be he dying?"
>
> "Yes."

"And he fancies eggs the zame as iver?"

"Yes."

"Ain't 'ee got no money to buy 'em?"

"No."

"Lord!" I zed, "I won't tell on 'ee."

Her smiled.

"I wud be better pleased for 'ee to tell," her answered. "There iddn't no call for 'ee not to be honest."

"No," I zed, "I won't tell. But maybe," I added, anxious-like, "you'll put 'em back where you took 'em from."

"I can't do thic," her answered.

My feet moved sort o' uneasy. "Well, leastways you'll take no more eggs arter this?" I zed.

"I can't promise thic," her answered.

"Good gore, Kitty!" I tumm'l'd out, "I always held 'ee for honest."

"Ay," her answered, "I always held mezulf for honest."

"What's this talk about being honest?" axed the squire, coming in upo' us unawares. "And what's the meaning o' my eggs in your hands, Kitty Fewins?" he added.

"I stole 'em, sir," her answered.

"There be only wan place for a thief, woman," he zed, "and that's the jail!"

"Ah," her breathed, sort o' slow.

"I never had pity on a dishonest person yet," he zed.

Five eggs her stole, and five weeks her got, a week's hard labour for each egg. There wadn't no one left to support Village Pump Fewins when her was gone, so he and Jane Elizabeth was taken acrass to the work'us. Law, he didn't live long as a bluegown. Skilly iddn't eggs, and when Kitty Fewins comed out o' jail, her husband was dead.

Her kind o' prided herzulf that naught but eggs cud keep un alive. Us niver had his like in Dunstable Weir again.

This squire—again no capital S—may be the same squire of "The Hall and He." He does seem a hard man. This is not to excuse Kitty's thievery of the eggs. But a biblical punishment would be restitution of some sort, the amount arrived at with the application of some sort of practical wisdom (Ex. 22:1-4, etc.). Had that been done, Kitty might have been put to work to pay the squire two or three times the value of the eggs, which of course she would not be permitted to take. Instead, she was given a punishment quite disproportionate to her crime—actually jailed for five weeks, during which time she also performed hard labor. It is a reminder to us of how wise God's punishments are, and how foolish are the punishments decided upon by men ignoring the teaching of the Bible.

And, because Kitty was taken away from her family, Village Pump Fewins and his daughter went to the workhouse, where he died before the five weeks were up.

Along with the strangeness of the title character, there is sadness. The three sons die, the only daughter loses her job and returns home unsuccessful before she is sent to the workhouse with her father, Kitty becomes a thief and is jailed for five weeks, and Village Pump Fewins dies. Gwendoline Keats has given us another story in which a lot of defeats take place.

The interplay between Zack and Kitty is interesting. Kitty knows she is doing wrong, but is more proud than ashamed. Perhaps, driven to the end of her tether by her need to obtain eggs for her eccentric (eggcentric?) husband, she has been able to tell herself that the end justifies the means. (Such ends justify the means morality is of course anti-biblical, as Romans 3:8 makes clear.) She does not even expect Zack not to tell, and in fact encourages him to do so! Zack, for his part, is put between a rock and a hard place. He doesn't want to get Kitty in trouble, but he also doesn't want the thieving to go on indefinitely. He would have winked at one episode of thievery, but the hint that Kitty might steal again makes him very uneasy. How quickly and easily most of us are put in compromising moral situations in which we are not sure quite what to do! He is relieved of his practical problems by the appearance of the squire, who takes a sledgehammer to a situation requiring kid gloves and perhaps a set of small screwdrivers.

Zack tells Kitty that he had always held her for honest, and she says she has always held herself for honest. A few paragraphs later on, the two repeat these sentiments almost word for word.. Zack is so shocked by Kitty's thievery that he can't fully get his mind around it, and instinctively says the same thing twice, Kitty echoing his comment each time. This is good writing on the part of Gwendoline Keats, showing her usual excellent insight into human nature. That is exactly how such a conversation might have unfolded.

That Village Pump Fewins could exist so many years without being institutionalized, and have some sort of family life, is amazing. The whole story is in some sense a testimony to the power and value of the family as an institution. The pride of his children in their father's uniqueness is both humorous and moving. Poddy Peter knows he is dying, but wonders if he will live long enough to see his father eat eggs that night. When his father replies that all the eggs in the household should be boiled for his supper, Poddy Peter sits up in bed and claps his hands in delight. This occurs while Poddy Peter knows very well that he himself is dying. Such self-forgetfulness is touching. With all their disadvantages, the Fewins family maintained some sort of coherence. Kitty, described early on as "hard-working," held the family together— as so many women hold their families together in our own era. If the family's village pump had developed his appetite for work to a degree similar to his appetite for eggs, this unusual family would have held together even better.

"Crooksie"

"Crooksie" is a story about 17 pages in length. In this story we learn a lot about Zack himself. A lot of what we learn is not very flattering to his character. But he tells the truth. He tells what happens and if that means the story he tells does not bring credit to himself, so be it.

> Crooksie wadn't no more than a small, hump-backed child wi' a wonderful fancy for aught that had a straight look to it. He lived 'long o' me, not that he was any child o' mine, though folks did give me credit for the fathering o' un.

That is how the story opens. We quickly learn more about the history of Crooksie. The mother used to go nutting with Zack when they were children. She gave birth to the child on Dunstable Heath, "wi' the grey mist for sheet, blanket and coverlet." A nameless man comes to Zack's door, and bids Zack to follow him, asking if he would have the maid die without having had speech with him. Zack takes his coat down from the peg to follow the man, who seems not to be the father of the child, although this point is left uncertain.

> "'Tiddn't to waste words that either o' us be standing here to-night," I answered.
>
> "No," he zed; "but the sight o' that squat little body o' your'n kind o' stirs a laugh in me every time I set eyes on it. 'Twadn't impidence that failed 'ee in holding yerzulf a fitting mate for the maid."
>
> "I wudn't ha' brought her to ruin and left her to die on Dunstable Heath," I tumm'l'd out.
>
> "Vule, who be you to judge your betters?" and wi' that he whipped round and hiked off, I vallering.

There is a lot of light on the heath, and Zack instinctively feels that there should be more shadow, seeing as how the maid lay dying. "Still, there was new ways ahead o' her, poor soul, and maybe her found the light more to her taste than I did." They find the young woman holding the newborn child.

> "Zack," her zed, "us sha'n't niver go nutting no more togither."
>
> "There's pramise o' a good season this year," I answered, though I thought to mezelf 'twas like the maid to talk o' outzide trash jest then. Maybe her knowed that time was getting scarce, for all-to-wance the tears pushed out o' her eyes and her tried, sort o' tremorful, to riz; but 'twas more'n her had the strength for, and her sank back upo' the green sod, much as if 'twas her grave and the Resurrection Trump hadn't but jest stirred her. The child gie'd a little tittering scrit, and her drawed un closer.
>
> "He ba a sma' and crooksie, Zack," her zed. "Sma' and crooksie."
>
> I put out a careful hand and touched un.
>
> "'Tiddn't to be expected that his father 'ull iver own to a crooksie chile," her continnied.
>
> There was more zilence than speech inside o' me.
>
> "You must take un in and do you best by un," her zed, and wi' that her closed her eyes and died, stiff and angered becase I had no wuds.

Zack, wanting the child to be with women folk as soon as possible, takes him to Widow Bartlett, who lived next door to him. She hints that she believes that the homely, misshapen child is Zack's—precisely because the child is homely—but he does not respond to this verbally. She predicts that nature will not overwork herself to straighten the child's back. This prediction turns out to be true: "crooksie he was born and crooksie he bided."

> I bain't altogether a hard man, nor wan to bear over and above heavy on the weakzome, but there was zommat in folks holding the chile for mine, because he was crooksie, that kind o' tarned me agin the crooksacious, and he knawed it from the vust and held back from me. Times there was I wud ha' dearly liked to ha' passed over that he wadn't straight-limbed, but he wud niver let me forget it, zim'd most as if he was fair glad that us cudn't be vriends, wan wi' t'other, becase o' the zame. I was hard and bitter in they days, and the chile drank o' it, arterwards thic which was sweet in life was niver sweet to he.

Zack only heard the child laugh once—at the sight of the rain falling straight down. Zack brings a kitten which he has found in the field when he was working.

> 'Twas a terrible mismanagement o' a critter, baing most as crooksacious in the make as Crooksie hiszulf. Afore I knowed what I was arter, I whipped out the lil' skiddick and pitched un down aside o' the lad.
>
> "Maybe you'll take to thic un," I zed. "You and he be much o' a make."
>
> A curious look, sort o' angered and shamed to wan, comed into his face, much as if he was axing hiszelf if 'twas true that he cut such a figure afore the world. Stooping down, he picked up an almighty big stone and made as if he wud ha' killed the poor misshapen critter, then he stapped quat and the stone slipped from un.

The cat pitches itself into Crooksie's arms, and lived with them from that day forward. The child does not mistreat the cat, but Zack senses Crooksie's eyes saying, "'Be I crooksie the zame ez thic un?'"

As the years unfold, the child is silent, which at first Zack takes to be the child's nature, but gradually Zack understands that the child would "talk a deal to the things around un, if 'twadn't no more than a terrible tall blade o' grass."

At their "end of the village there lived a good-for-naught poaching gawkin, Simeon Bag by name. He was tall and upstanding, and many's the time I had marked Crooksie kaining arter un." Zack wonders if the child would be more willing to speak with Bag, but he can't bring himself to invite the man in. One day, however, Simeon Bag walks in unbid and goes up to where the child lay beneath the apple tree. Zack eventually turns his head to see Simeon stretched out on his back beneath the apple tree. With "a curious pain," Zack understands that this is not the first time "they two had lay there, zide by zide," looking at the sky through the boughs. To Zack it seems almost as if Simeon Bag is trying to steal somewhat from him; Zack distrusts him.

Crooksie had always been an ailing child. One day as Zack is working, Doctor Budd pulls alongside him in the road and tells him he is going to lose the child. Zack doesn't even make an answer, but gathers up his tools and starts for home. Through the hedge he sees Crooksie and Simeon Bag stretched out under the apple tree, the cat three feet away.

> For a young un, Crooksie had always walked lonesome droo the world, and it zim'd wonderful poor to grudge un to the wan pursen who had tooked his fancy, but all-to-wance my life zim'd winnowed down to jest mezulf and my heart's desire, and aught that stud atween me and it took on an extry vally. Times and times I laid awake at night figuring how I cud stap Simeon Bag from coming and yet make on to Crooksie that the fellow had desarted un for furren folk, but I never comed to a settled mind on the matter, baing sort o' wishful to do well by mezulf and the lad to wan. All this while Crooksie was dying o' the galloping-fade, so that I had but to mark back the days to zee how he was slipping away from me, and he niver so much as noting that I was in the world 'longzide o' un. Folks have always held me for zlow, and when the village larned that Crooksie hadn't more'n a few weeks to live, they comed in wan by wan to tell me the tale, believing that I cudn't take such in for mezulf. I didn't pay no special heed to what they was letting up, and that made 'em more repeatful than iver, but the lad listened to their talk

terrible interasted. The last week Crooksie was wi' me, Simeon Bag was in and out continuous. It zim'd pushful o' un.

Zack rebukes Simeon, and the next day Simeon does not come near the house. Zack knows this for sure because he himself stays home from work to be with Crooksie.

> We had been unspeechful sich a terrible number o' years, and I knawed from the veel o' my own heart that there was a deal to zay and only a sma' snip o' time to zay it in, but for all thic, us was zilent the zame as iver. I thought back on the days us had been together, and, though I cud mind many a sharp word I had drawed at un, yit he had niver wanted for naught, and it zim'd as how he might ha' a smile for me jest at the last. The arternoon wore on. Crooksie lay wi' his eyes fixed on the door, watching and kaining, kaining and watching. I got sort o' desperate, for how was I to know whether Simeon Bag wudn't take up hiszulf to distarb us at any moment.
>
> I went up to the bed and touched the lad.
>
> "Zay zommat, Crooksie," I said.
>
> He drew away much as if he hadn't heard, so I tippy-toed back to the fire, and zat there kind o' guilty, for it comed over me that I was axing the chile for a bit o' love, and all the time I was holding back from un the wan pursen he hungered arter zeeing. Still, wadn't he as good as a son o' mine, and who shud he want to ha' wi' un at the last if it 'twadn't me?
>
> Night was long in coming, for summer was full on, but when the room was most nigh dimmet, I stole up to un agin.
>
> "Zay zommat, Crooksie," I zed.
>
> Then he riz right up straight in the bed and cried out as wan zore wounded,—
>
> "Why do 'ee bide away?"
>
> I went out and fetched Simeon Bag, and he took Crooksie up in his arms, and the lad stretched hiszulf out, tiredful, and died.
>
> They niver zed naught wan to t'other. I cud swear they niver said naught wan to t'other, leastways not in words.

Thus ends this sad and remarkable story.

Zack says of himself that he isn't "altogether a hard man," or one hard on the weak. This is no doubt true. But he falls prey to the first sin of most of us: pride. Wounded by the general opinion that because the child is deformed, the child must be Zack's child, Zack turns against the child from the start. How easily we fall prey to pride! And we see here that to love in the Christian, agape sense, is an act, not an emotion. Had Zack determined to love the child in the agape sense of loving, which is to act in a manner which is to the best for the child, he would have acted in a manner which in the long run would have allowed a genuine affection to build between the two of them. Crooksie correctly sensed that Zack had something against him. Zack understood that himself: "he knawed it from the vust and held back from me."

What a warning to us! To love as God would have us love can be hard work. But it is work that must be done, in simple fairness. Christ showed active love to us, in dying in the cross in our place—and we are all "crooksacious" with sin, one way or another. Who are we to refuse to show active love to others, beggars as we have been? However, it is very easy for us, in our wounded pride, to withhold love from where it should go. Zack is most of us here—except that he has, on looking back, the honesty to see and admit where he went wrong. We seldom come up to his level of honesty.

Simeon Bag is another warning to us! Zack describes him as good for nothing, and a poacher. We have no reason to doubt Zack's evaluation, for he always seems honest in what he says. Simeon Bag probably worked as little as possible, and poached as much as possible. He was not your garden-variety admirable Christian man. And yet this good for nothing poacher is not really good for nothing at all. For all his faults, which I believe were very real faults, he instinctively senses Crooksie's need, and answers that need in the best fashion possible. He spends time with Crooksie, stretching out his long straight length on the ground under the apple tree beside the boy. This is active love—and the result of this love is a genuine affection between Crooksie and Simeon Bag. Crooksie, silent and lonely and despised and ashamed of his deformed physical condition, yearns for the straight. And like all of us, no matter how hardened and cold we think ourselves to be, he needed human companionship with someone who respected him. Simeon Bag proved to be the ideal companion. We may feel frustrated that Simeon was "good-for-naught" and a poacher, and it is not wrong to be frustrated with the man's faults, but we are well advised to admire and emulate his behavior with Crooksie. We will leave God to judge his faults. Life is sometimes astonishingly complex. The more humility we can painstakingly gather, the better—we are likely to have great need of it when we stand (or tremble and fall) in the presence of God.

It is no shock to find that Zack's attitude and behavior toward the child come back to him in a sad and painful manner. He is "axing the chile for a bit o' love" as the child is getting ready to die, but when has he acted to deserve such affection from the child? By refusing to love Crooksie in an active fashion, he has in return earned being unloved by the child. He senses all this, of course, but it is too late. Again, what a warning to us. The kingdom of heaven is always right next door to us. Usually we refuse to open that door, and we remain in a hell of our own making. Zack might have had an adopted son he cared for and who cared for him. Instead—nine years of coldness on both sides. However, we rejoice to see Zack finally put aside his pride, and bring Simeon Bag to the boy. In his friend's arms, Crooksie makes himself as straight as he can—he "stretched hiszulf out"—and no doubt was filled with joy to be with Simeon in his last moments on earth.

Gwendoline Keats notices things. We are glad for her help. As Travelling Joe helped us see the wonder of ditches, Crooksie helps us see the wonder of the straight falling rain. Zack is unobserved as he hears Crooksie talking about or to the rain:

> "Iddn't 'ee jest a straight-fallie thing," he kept on zaying, and he clapped his hands and laughed the most fresh-spoken laugh I iver heard out o' a chile's lips.

As in all these stories, there is sadness and defeat. The fair maid is seduced and gives birth to a child which the father will never acknowledge. The maid dies after giving birth. The child is deformed, and knows it and is ashamed. He is unloved by his adopted father, and he dies at about age nine. Zack fails the test to love the child as he should. A cold silence grows up between Zack and Crooksie, and that endures for the child's entire life. There is enough sadness here in one short story to fill several novels. And yet there are triumphs in the midst of defeat. The flawed but generous-spirited Simeon Bag shows a most admirable love toward Crooksie. He and Crooksie form a wordless but deep friendship, and Crooksie is able to die in the arms of the friend he loves best. Zack, entirely defeated by his pride for nine years, puts it aside at the last in order to bring Simeon to the boy. The defeats are powerful, the victories few. But the victories are as real as the defeats.

"Mary Amelia Spot"

This is the third longest story in the collection, checking in at about 39 pages. This story once again tells us a lot about Zack himself.

Mary Amelia Spot was from Dore Apple, a fishing village about a mile and a half from Dunstable Weir. Dore Apple is very far from being entirely a made-up name. Wikipedia tells us that a village called Appledore is "A little over a mile away along the coast" from Northam. It was at the beautiful country home of Port Hill, Northam, that Gwendoline Keats was born. In the census of 2011 Appledore featured a population of 749. In the same census Northam weighed in with a more substantial 5,427 (ward population as reported by the Wikipedia article entitled Northam, Devon).

Zack tells us, "A plain-featured woman Mary Amelia was, and had niver, I reckon, tasted much o' the soft side o' a man's tongue till Job Tremmy comed a-courting her."

Job earned good wages when working, but was very much a drinker. Zack speculates that it was when he was drinking that Job became involved with Mary Amelia Spot. Job was not a man to go back on his word, however. One Sunday he comes to Zack's cottage and asks for help with the words in his courtship with Mary Amelia. Zack takes his hat and follows Job out the door. On top of the hill above Dore Apple, Job says to himself, "'Whativer will her be like by light o' sober sense?'"

They go to Mary Amelia's cottage and walk in.

> My wud, but her was plain! I kind o' drawed back, thinking maybe us had come to the wrong house; then I slipped a glance

acrass at Job and I saw un straighten up, though his face had a divered look, as if he sore doubted whether he had spunk to zee un droo wi' the job. "Crikes!" says I to myself, "God Almighty made women, 'tiddn't for us to complain."

Job, he took a step forrard, then he tarned to me. "Clean," he says. 'Twas her one good point, and he lighted on it wonderful straight.

Outside the cottage, Zack gives Job his advice.

"Run!" I says.
"Run?" says he.
"And niver come anigh Dore Apple again as long as you live," I says.
He struck his right fist into the palm of his left hand.
"Me and Mary Amelia Spot be pramised wan to t'other," says he.
"Vorgit it," I says.
At that he drowed me such a look, and, tarning, went back to the cottage wi'out another word.

The following Sunday their names were called in church. The lads in Dunstable Weir hiked down to Dore Apple to see what Mary Amelia was like, and "comed back again marvellous quiet, for they was young and didn't know but what they'd soon be marrying theirzulves." The wedding took place. Zack stood at the altar as best man to Job, "and as I cast an eye acrass at Mary Amelia Spot I didn't vorgit to thank the Almighty that her wadn't no bride o' mine."

Job's cottage was next door to Zack's, and Zack, as usual, was very observant. Moreover, there was something about the woman that drew him back to look at her again and again. Mary Amelia got through a "wonderful" amount of work. She took in washing for the gentry, and gave great satisfaction. "Zeeing that money was plentiful, and not being a competitive man, 'twadn't long afore Job left off gwaying to work; for what was the use o' two wearing theirzulves to the bone?"

In the course of time Mary Amelia gives birth to a daughter. Job himself is a good-looking man. Zack asks who the child favors. Job groans before answering: the child looks exactly like her mother. He names the child after her mother, then goes on a drinking spree at the Red Lion.

As soon as she could, Mary Amelia went back to work. The child was puny and ailing, and "what wi' wan thing and t'other, Job began to lose patience wi' life." He sits drinking at the Red Lion, his attitude soured, his faith in women in general seeming to be gone. "I thought to mezulf that 'twas curious the way things falled out, for I had growed to respact Mary Amelia out o' ordinary."

One night Zack hears a sharp cry. In the morning when he goes to work he sees an ugly black bruise on Mary Amelia's face. Zack doesn't think that Job is the kind of man to raise his hand against a woman, but before long it becomes apparent that Job has become like the men in Dore Apple, where "the men beat their wives regular." (We have to wonder if, in 1901, the living people in the real village of Appledore heard about their dishonorable fictional cousins in Dore Apple! And whether they deserved the report Zack gives of them.) Her husband's conduct doesn't seem to surprise Mary Amelia, and she never cries out again, although many times Zack would anxiously sit up in bed and listen, "for, baing single, I'd had no taste o' the aggravation o women." When the people in Dunstable Weir began to suspect what was going on at the Tremmy household, they were very sore about it and would have asked them to leave if they could be sure of the truth. Zack himself kept silence on the topic, since Mary Amelia herself kept silence. She continued to work very hard, to Zack's admiring eyes.

Three years pass by. One night Mary Amelia comes to Zack's cottage, and tells him the child is sick. Zack offers to go for the doctor, but that is not her concern. Without saying so directly, she makes it clear that her problem is that it is almost closing time at the Red Lion, and that when Job comes home his "distarbacious ways," as Zack says, will awake the child just after it has fallen asleep. Zack accompanies Mary Amelia back to her home, although he is unsure how he is to keep Job out of his own home.

When they get there, Job is already in the house. He is only "friendly drunk," and Zack hopes that with management things would settle down comfortably. However, Job insists that Mary Amelia start dancing. She dances in an ungainly fashion, and Job laughs. But perhaps he wasn't as drunk as Zack first suspected, for even in his merriment he was mostly silent, thus not disturbing the child. The child slept on. But all at once,

> tired, maybe, o' the antics o' this world, the little skiddick drapped back wance more on the pilly, buttoned up its little eyes, and jest died right there in front o' us all.
> 'Twas done so unostentatious-like that Mary Amelia didn't fathom first o' long what the child had been arter. When her did, she drapped down aside the cradle wonderful unnoiseful and laid her plainzome face agin the plainzome face o' her child. I went back home, for I cudn't do no good by biding.

Not long after this Job Tremmy falls out of the back of a cart and breaks his neck and dies. Mary Amelia honors her husband with a handsome tombstone.

Mary Amelia goes back to work, washing and starching harder than ever. Zack would sometimes drop in and watch her in the evening, and the thought begins to come over him that he would "like to zee they worn red hands o' hers idle for a while." He begins to consider the idea of marrying Mary Amelia. He is not in a hurry to do anything rash, and talks the matter over with Farmer Burden. They count no less that sixteen widows in Dunstable Weir parish who might have been willing to marry Zack. But he considers them mostly a fast lot who had worried their men into the grave, and would have liked to do the same by him. Mary Amelia was a different sort. She will learn, Zack says to himself, what it is to have a man who doesn't drink to fend for. So he goes to her cottage and asks her to marry him. She receives his offer without great enthusiasm, even criticizing his looks as compared to those of Job, but at last consents to marry him.

They are married on a Saturday, and Monday morning Zack takes his axe and splits Mary Amelia's wash tubs in to small pieces. He intends to work for her, rather than to have her work for him. However, when Mary Amelia finds out that her wash-tubs have been destroyed, she says she has been used to work her entire life, and walks back inside the house without another word. When Zack comes back from work that day, he finds her with eyes red and swollen "as if her had been crying past belief."

Months pass. One day Zack comes back from work and smells spirits in the air. Mary Amelia says the smell comes from her having mended an old suit of Job's clothes. Zack is not surprised, since Job had drunk so much in his time that "it might well be that his clothes still leaked o' the liquor." However, the weeks went by and the smell of spirits continued. Mary Amelia insists that the fresh air makes no impression on Job's clothes. Farmer Burden eventually tells Zack that there is a rumor that he has taken to drink. His wife has been to the Red Lion regularly to get alcohol for him. Zack says he will drink when and how he wants to. When he returns home that evening after work, there is more of the smell of spirits. However, Zack gives her his entire week's wages, and says he wants to see her comfortable. Previously she had never been given more than a part of his earnings, and the large amount seems to make her uneasy and resentful.

She says, "'Let me go back to wark, Zack," her said. "I was niver made for an idle woman.'" Zack had set his heart on Mary Amelia having an easy time, but says to himself that life is a queer concern, and tells her that she may do as it pleases her best. She is profoundly grateful at this. Within days new wash-tubs were duly bought, and the cottage began to smell of a hot iron rather than of Job Tremmy's spirit-soaked clothes.

However, it turns out that Mary Amelia's washing no longer gives the satisfaction it once gave. Her feel for the iron and starch wasn't as sure as it had been in the old days. Little by little the gentlefolk took their business elsewhere. "It zim'd cruel like that a few years' idleness shud wark sich a change in a woman's power, and I knaw'd well enough that in her heart o' hearts Mary Amelia laid the blame at my door."

Job Tremmy's "spiritous-smelling weskit" begins to make its appearance again. Once Farmer Burden drops in, sees the condition of the home, and tells Zack that the house was a long way from being clean. Zack tries to make excuses for her, but Farmer Burden is not fooled. From that day on, Zack no longer gave all of his earnings to Mary Amelia, but rather kept part to fall back on.

One morning he puts a new coat of whitewash on the walls, touches up the windowsills with paint, and even buys a row of china jugs from a "pedler." Mary Amelia wonders why these changes have been made. Zack tells her,

> "A good wife desarves a good home."
> But Mary Amelia wadn't no friend to mealy-mouthed folk.
> "I've niver been a good wife to 'ee," her rapped out sharp,
> "and, what's more, flummery won't make me wan."

Coming home from work that night, Zack, feeling pleased with how "vitty" he has the house looking, finds an excuse to ask Farmer Burden to drop by the house. When they get to the cottage, however, Job's waistcoat is in the middle of the path, "like a sign-post wi' BEWARE writ on it." However, Farmer Burden is inside the cottage before Zack can stop him. The house is smashed up. Zack blames a (nonexistent) cat.

> "I niver heard tell that you had a cat," said Varmer Burden.
> "Begore, and I cud wish the zame! I was vule anuff to buy wan into Bideford," I answered, terrible smart—but there, a lie is always a fluid thing.

With the help of a couple more lies, Farmer Burden is chased off, although not before he has seen a boot with a foot in it lying on the floor in the next room. Zack leaves the house and locks the door behind him. He gains two days leave from his work, and walks eleven or twelve miles to the vicinity of his birthplace. He tells us he has a brother, a cobbler, living close to the village of Little Dunstable. Unless this is "he," his adopted brother in "The Hall and He," we can see that Gwendoline Keats can give us a somewhat "fluid" account of the family of Zack, as she did in another story where Zack's father was Tobin rather than Eben. He contemplates speaking to his brother of his situation with his marriage to Mary Amelia, but instead says nothing. He stays into the second day, then walks home.

The outside of the cottage looks bedraggled, with even the gate off the hinges. Zack hurries inside.

> "Mary Amelia!" I hammered out.
> But there wadn't no Mary Amelia. Naught but the bare walls and boards. Her had gone, and took every stick o' the furniture 'long wi' her.

I niver vallered her up to try and git the things back, though I knawed that, according to the law, a married woman hadn't got no claim to more'n her gold ring and the bit o' bootlace her ties her hair wi'; but Varmer Burden told me he had catched sight o' her wance into Barnstaple, and he added zommat that has made bad blood atween he and me.

After some time which Zack does not make clear—possibly some years—Mary Amelia returns to Zack's home at Christmas. Zack hears a feeble knock, goes to the door, and although he can see nothing, he rightly guesses that it is his wife. At his request, she lights a match, "and us looked wan into t'other's vace. A shiver ran droo me, though maybe 'twas zommat more'n cold that gripped hold o' my heart jest then."

Mary Amelia coughs fiercely, slips and falls to the floor, and a stream of blood spreads across her lips. Zack lifts her on to the bed, and plans to fetch the doctor,

but her wadn't have me go.

"Tiddn't no manner o' use, Zack," her said. "I shud be dead afore he comed, and there's thic that I must tell 'ee."

Wi' that, her fell zilent for a terrible number o' minutes. I kept piling on all my spare clothes 'pon tap of her poor, trembly body, for, though I wud ha' gi'ed a deal to help her jest then, I never was wan to know the right thing to do when took by surprise.

A bit o' a smile comed into her vace; maybe her suspicioned I was wishful o' plazing her.

"You was always willun, Zack," her said.

"I be zlow to larn, Mary Amelia," I answered, taking her hand. She gripped it close; then her head falled back, and I thought that all was over wi' her, poor soul. But wance more her opened her eyes.

I stooped down and placed my ear close to her lips.

"You should ha' taken the stick to me, Zack," her murmured. "When iverything went agin me, I was rispacted *then.*"

"I rispact 'ee, Mary Amelia," I said. "I've always rispacted 'ee."

"'Twudn't be right to rispact me now," her answered; "for I be—"

Death took the wuds from her lips, and though I cried out arter her terrible loud, I doubt if she heard.

> No matter, the Almighty knaws that there be folks that
> rispact Mary Amelia Spot.

The story ends there.

There is failure for everyone in this story. Job Tremmy drinks more than he should, beats his wife, and dies at an early age. Mary Amelia is painfully homely, and gives birth to a painfully homely daughter. She is regularly beaten by her husband. The daughter dies at about age three. Zack marries Mary Amelia, and the marriage is a failure, at least partly and perhaps even mostly due to Zack's lack of practical wisdom as a husband. His wife becomes a secret drinker, eventually trashes his home, takes all his furniture, and runs off. Although this is not stated explicitly, the hints indicate that she probably becomes a prostitute. She returns to her husband only to die.

The victories are few. Job, despite being appalled at Mary Amelia's looks in sober daylight, sticks to his promise to marry her. Zack, who begins by advising Job to run out on his promise to marry Mary Amelia, ends by respecting her hard work, and even marries her with the intention of making her life better. He, despite the misery of his failed marriage, respects his wife to the end and beyond the end. Mary Amelia looks back on her sad life with some insight: she knows that when circumstances had most gone against her she had been hard working and worthy of respect. She even says Zack should have beaten her. (Here is an echo of the story "Life Is Life," where Joe's wife looks back on her own beatings at Joe's hands with astonishing objectivity.)

The last paragraph of the story is a reminder to us to be willing to let ultimate judgment of people be left in the hands of God. Of course these are fictional characters, but the questions their stories raise apply to every day real life. Mary Amelia dies, probably having lived as a prostitute. If we assume she is condemned to the eternal torment of hell, we are making assumptions about the nature of God and of hell which may or may not be warranted by the Bible's teaching. We need to be very careful here. Zack himself, greatly harmed by his wife's behavior to him, says that "the Almighty knaws that there be folks that rispact Mary Amelia Spot." Zack's respect for her continues, and he mentions that respect in the same sentence in which he mentions God. Does God also respect Mary Amelia Spot? Or does He torture her for eternity? Read the Bible for yourself, and think for yourself.[37]

One thing we learn from this story is the great necessity we all have to work in order to maintain our emotional balance. When Zack breaks up Mary Amelia's washtubs, the reader may cringe with a premonition that he is doing exactly the wrong thing—especially when we see with what uneasiness Mary Amelia responds to Zack's generous gesture. Zack is acting with honorable intent—he wants to give her an easier life after her hard labor as Job Tremmy's wife—but he is taking exactly the wrong path to do her good. Her willingness to work hard was the best of her character. To take her work away from her was to destroy her emotional stability. There were dozens of ways Zack could have treated Mary Amelia with kindness to make her life better. However, to take her work away from her was a very foolish and harmful action. This is one of the saddest aspects of the story, and is sadly ironic. In striving to be kind, Zack is being cruel, destroying his wife's life and greatly ruining his own life. When he belatedly gives her permission to go back to work, it is too late—the skill has gone out of her fingers, in her washing and starching.

This seems almost too hard a fate for her and for Zack. At the worst, could she not have found other work which would help her keep her self-respect? But she is not flexible enough to adjust to her new situation. She again retreats to alcohol, which leads soon enough to the destruction of her marriage and of her life. Yes, Zack was at fault for taking her work away from her, but Mary Amelia is at fault too. Her wrongdoing comes back upon her husband and also upon herself—we get a good sense of how wrong she has been when Zack first looks into her face when she returns and his heart is struck cold by what he sees there.

----

[37]For a beginning look at questions concerning hell and eternal torment, please see Carl Wells, *What Are God's Goals?*.

"The Sisters"

In the same letter to May Sinclair in which Gwendoline Keats called "Benjamin Parrot's Fancy" good, she called "The Sisters" an "almost wonderful short story." Gwendoline Keats was usually quite modest about her writings, so it is surprising to hear her say that about "The Sisters." But she was saying nothing less than the truth. The story is indeed "almost wonderful," and we could with justice drop the word almost. The story appeared in "The Pall Mall Magazine" for August, 1901. It was illustrated by A. S. Hartrick; Wikipedia tells us he "was a Scottish painter known for the quality of his lithographic work."

"The Sisters," the seventh and final story in the collection, is about 20 pages in length. Two sisters, Martha and Susan, live next door to each other, and are both married to men with the last name of Barnaby, although the two men are not related. Martha's husband has disappeared.

> There were no children in her house, though a little extry room had been walled up special for sich; but into Susan's was a snip o' a lad called Jerry for short, he being held over the font to the name o' Jerulam. The wall that parted the two cottages wadn't over thick, most could be heard through it, and folks say that it was the sound o' Jerry's first puling cry that hardened Martha's heart agin her sister. Be that as it may, her was a changed woman from that time on, and wud tarn from a child's face much as if it was thic o' the Evil Wan hiszulf.

Susan expects things to mend with time, but they don't. Martha becomes "more and more queer in the temper" until Jerry comes to his eighth birthday, in March. Susan gives to Jerry a basket with her husband John's dinner,

> and told the lad to take it acrass to where John Barnaby was felling trees a good mile up on the hither side o' the river. Her niver set eyes on the lad agin 'til the water washed un round the bend and into the shaller where her stood, ankle-deep, rinsing a roll o' linen afore laying it out in the sun to bleach. Her took the child up in her arm and carried un to the cottage. When her comed nigh the door, who should rush past her, dripping from

head to heel, but Martha. For a banging great minute the two sisters stud and looked each into t'other's eyes, then Martha let fly wan o' her mad-house laughs, and bust away back acrass the meadow, cackling as her went. There wadn't a pussen inside the village or out, saving, maybe, mezulf, but held that Martha had drowned the child.

The police don't move in the case, and when an inquest is held, nothing definite is decided about how the child had died. That night, the people of the village painted the word "'Murderess'" in red paint "acrass the staps o' Martha's door." John Barnaby runs to Zack's house to ask for a drop of turpentine to remove the word before Martha can see it. That night when Zack goes to the Red Lion for a glass of ale, John Barnaby beckons him out of the pub; they hike into the middle of one of the squire's woods before John speaks. There is one potential editing error, which I have indicated in the text.

> "I shall be fo'ced to tull," he tumm'led out.
> "The poor soul knaws well anuff her hadn't no hand in drowning the chile," I answered.
> "Susan don't knaw. I shall be fo'ced to tull her."
> I hadn't wuds to answer he, but I eyed un sort o' hasty, and, though the night was dark past zeeing aught, I kind o' suspicioned the look that was on the vace o' un. It started to rain, sofy vust along, than [sic? should it be then?] more willun. The draps comed slattering down as us stood there zilent, and it zim'd to me that he was axing agin and agin the zame question.
> "Must I tell her?" he zim'd to ask.
> But no zound comed from his lips, and I made as though I hadn't heard.

Zack pretends not to hear a question which isn't asked out loud! This seems to me to be excellent writing, completely in tune with human nature and with the silent communication between the two men

John Barnaby runs like a man possessed to his cottage, Zack following. John has Zack peek into the window to see what Susan is doing. She is moving around some, apparently trying to put a different look to the cottage. Zack says he will be getting along home. John dreads speaking to his wife, but says he must tell her. Zack says to go in and get it over with, but John turns on him fiercely and says that Zack should come in with him; possibly Zack "'can throw in an easying wud.'" Zack tries to beg off, but John insists, saying he (John) may not speak to the subject while Zack is there. But he does.

> He comed across to where her zot. "Susan," he tumm'led out all-to-wance, "'twad all along o' me that Jerry was drowned thic day."
>
> Her riz up wonderful slow, and then zot down, heap-like, but nary a wud crassed her lips.
>
> John Barnaby tarned his vace from her, and went on wi' his tale quick, as if he feared that wance stapped short in it he wud bide zilent to the crack o' doom.
>
> "'Twad jest above the willows he fell in; where folks zay the water don't come much over a man's waist. The stream slewed un round, and he held out his arms to me and gav' a little scrit o' a cry. I ran to the side and was minded to jump in, but zommat held me there watching, though I knowed if I wadn't smart the river 'ud snatch un away. 'Twadn't more'n a minute that I bided kind o' humped togither, ready to jump, then the river snatched un, and he slithied into midstream. For a bit his little white face lay 'pon tap the water, and I runned along the bank, bawling out that I wud save un yit; but I niver got nigh un, I was afear'd o' the water."
>
> He stopped quat and the room was painful zilent.
>
> I wud ha' up and hiked, but there was thic about the zilence that bound me back from the breaking o' it. No wan minded on me, they had zommat other to think on. John, he comed forward to where his wife zot.
>
> "I cud ha' saved un, but I was afear'd," he said. "I wadn't smart enough. God Almighty gi'ed me jest wan minute. I heard His voice plain as I be speaking to 'ee. 'John,' He zed, 'don't waste time. Jump,' He zed. I was minded to jump later. I niver was well plucked on the instant."

Susan eventually asks John what he will do now, and he says he will tell the village what had happened. She discourages him from telling the village that he as good as killed his own child, and asks why God did not call on her to save Jerry. John moves toward the door to tell the village what happened. More of the truth comes out.

> "Be 'ee stark mad that you shud tull 'em sich?"
> "Zack can tull 'em, he wor there—"

"Zack?"

"Ess, he saw the lad drown."

Her tarned to where I zot, and I riz up from my sate, for there was thic in her vace that wud ha' stirred the dead.

"You crawling toad on two legs!" her cried, "Do 'ee call yerzulf a man to stand and zee a chile drown afore 'ee eyes? The village shall know 'ee for the murderer you are. Don't 'ee reckon to escape, I'll denounce 'ee to the Law."

"Zack was t'other side o' the stream."

"And what difference does that make?" her answered, vacing round on her husband.

"He can't swim four strokes, the zame ez mezulf."

"Swim," her zed, "swim! A murderer hadn't no need for swimming, he can murder wi'out thic," and zot herzulf down 'pon tap the nearest chair, flung her apron over her head, and fell to crying painful to witness. I tippy-toed out. It zim'd a murderous thing to ha' watched a chile drown and niver so much as to ha' jumped in arter it, swim or no swimy.

Zack doesn't sleep very well that night, and is glad "when the dark had been rubbed out o' the sky." On his way to work beyond the Barnaby cottages, he hears John speaking to his sister-in-law Martha. Zack edges closer to hear their conversation. John says he had forgotten to tell Susan that Martha jumped in the water after Jerry. Now he is going to tell the village that he had let Jerry drown.

"They'll cast it at 'ee that you let your own child drown afore your eyes."

"Ess," he answered, "I let un drown. I cudn't ha' believed it agin mezulf if anywan was to ha' told me so afore it happened."

"Nor I that I shud ha' tried to save un. Us be different from what us thinks, all o' us," her zed.

"He's dead now, anyway."

"Many's the time I wished un so."

"I loved un, though it zims 'twas a poor sort o' love."

Her movetted a bit closer to John. "'Twadn't longer ago than last year that I was nigh on pushing Jerry into the river at the very identical spot that the water took un."

"And yit 'twas you, not me, that tried to save the lad."

"I wudn't worrit over it, John Barnaby," her answered sort o' solemn. "God Almighty knows our hearts better than us do ourzulves."

John says he is going now to tell the village what happened. Martha, as Susan had, discourages him from doing this, but he is determined to tell them, and hikes off to tell his story to the village. Martha says to herself, "'Us be all afear'd o' different things,'" and goes up the steps to her sister Susan's house. Susan greets her harshly, and accuses her of having hated the child. Susan asks Martha if she has come to gape at his empty chair and bed. No, she has not come for that. She speaks of how she noticed things about Jerry, though she tried not to see him.

"There was always evil in your heart agin the lad."
"My heart was empty and hate growed there."
"Now my heart is empty and I hate 'ee becase 'ee hated the lad."
"Do 'ee mind his eyes? They was gold as water that runs acrass the brown moor sods."
"Who be you to name the colour o' his eyes?"
"I kind o' marked 'em, though I tried not to mark 'em."
"The river brought un back to me, but his eyes was closed—"
"And the smile gone from 'em."
"You niver zee'd un smile, for he was afear'd o' 'ee."
"Yit I kind o' knowed o' the smile."
"I shall niver zee un smile now."
"'Tis hid behind they long lashes o' un."
"Who be you to tell me how he zlapes?"
"He zlapes sound, no mother cud rock un to zo sound a zlape."
"Wud that I could zlape azide un."
"'Twud be a sweet rasting-place. I cud wish mezulf no better."
"Who be you to lie bezide my Jerry?"
"I have hungered for a chile these years."

The two sisters fall silent. Zack turns instinctively and sees John Barnaby coming over the stile, "a power o'folk" following him. John hikes up the steps to his own door, the crowd on his heels, Zack himself at the back. The villagers crowd into the cottage.

Susan Barnaby riz up from her sate and stared at us most 'mazing astonished.

"Be 'ee off your chump, John Barnaby?" her axed, "that'ee shud come here wi' all the trash o' the village trapezing at your heels?"

"He zed 'twor he that murdered the chile," wan o' the crowd tumm'l'd out, sort o' uneasy.

"Gwaying from door to door tulling folk," put in another o' 'em.

Susan Barnaby sank back on her chair. "He'd tell up any tale, zarrer has tarned his head," she said, feeble-like.

"Us knawed all along 'twadn't more'n his fancy," the crowd answered.

"Zarrer has turned other heads azide his," Martha zed, half to herzulf.

But the crowd tarned on her, hungry-like. "You'd best bide quiet, Widdy Barnaby, or the rope 'ull 'ave 'ee yit."

"It has had many that desarved it less," her answered.

There the story ends, also ending Zack's seven tales of Dunstable Weir.

The child drowns. The father fails to act courageously to try to save his son from drowning. Zack, looking on, also fails to try to save the child. Both men will have to live with the reality of their failure to act with courage. Martha Barnaby is childless, painfully so, and enviously spends eight years hating the child of her sister. She lets her natural, and very good, desire to have her own child to care for, be twisted into something very bad. Susan loses her beloved son, and has the added astonishing pain of knowing that her husband had a chance to try to save him, but failed the test.

The consolations of the story are few, albeit real. John Barnaby refuses to let his wife believe an untruth about how the child has died. He also has the courage to tell the village the truth. As Martha says, "'Us be all afear'd o' different things.'" Also, we can guess that Martha is exactly correct in saying that God knows John Barnaby's heart. His love for the child was real, despite his lack of courage in the time of crisis.

The greatest triumph of the story is Martha's. She has enviously begrudged her sister her child. But when the crisis comes, she acts with courage and tries to save the child. A year ago she was tempted to murder the child at the same spot in the river. Now she risks her own life to try to save the child. Moreover, she sees herself as she is. She sees the depth of her own sin. "'My heart was empty and hate growed there.'" What a commentary on how we all tend to live! It is a phrase we should hang in the sky to warn us all. To love in the biblical, agape, fashion is an act, not an emotion. The emotion of warm affection may follow. But first of all we need to act correctly. It was Martha's duty to love her sister's child. She failed to comply with that duty. The result was that hate grew in her heart. The child even sensed this hate, and feared her. But Martha has come to self-knowledge. She has come belatedly, but she has come. Her final words demonstrate how greatly she has been humbled. When the crowd threatens to see her hung—clearly they have not yet learned that she acted heroically to try to save the child—she answers without anger and without words defending herself. The rope has had many who deserved it less, she simply says. She is honestly facing the greatness of her wickedness for her eight years of soul-twisting envy which led to hate.

Martha has been humbled. Humility is a necessity for us, if we are ever to learn how to live. Her future will be greatly different.

While the story stops there, we can see considerable hope for the future relations of the sisters. Susan has not yet been told about Martha's attempt to save Jerry. But we know that John will tell Susan. Susan will then begin to understand that her sister had been the one person to risk her own life for Jerry. This was active love. She will appreciate what her sister did. The sisters, estranged by Martha's envious behavior which has lasted eight long years, will have a wonderful chance to be reconciled one to another. Martha, by her act of love in trying to save Jerry, has earned the right to mourn him with affection just as his own mother will mourn him. Both will mourn the loss of Jerry, and they will be truly sisters again.

Tales of Dunstable Weir is a book worthy, and typical, of the talents of Gwendoline Keats. The stories are moving. The defeats of the characters are real and often crushing, the victories real but subtle. The humor is frequent but often dark. The dialect in which Zack writes can be difficult to understand, but at the same time there are countless phrasings that are colorful and memorable. (This reminds me a little bit of Huckleberry Finn's narrative of his adventures: Huckleberry's words are not the king's English, certainly, but are living and riveting—impossible to improve upon with something more grammatically correct. But Zack's Devonshire dialect is considerably more difficult to understand than Huck's Missouri dialect.) There are numerous superb insights into human nature. God is present in the book, and His character is good and wise and deep, but the reader will have to decide for himself if Zack's God (or Gwendoline Keats' God) is the God of orthodox Christianity or a God slightly different.

Taken as a whole, the stories seem to me perhaps a shade darker than those in *Life Is Life*. If that is true—and there is no guarantee that it is true, for *Life Is Life* was dark enough in many ways—it may be because Zack himself undergoes so many personal defeats. He compromises the truth in order to put himself in the way of winning Benjamin Parrot's (imaginary) fortune. The fair maid he loves fancies him not. She is seduced by some unknown man. He fails to love the child she leaves him in the way he should. He makes a botch of his marriage. He does not muster sufficient courage to try to rescue Jerry from the river. Through all this he tells us the truth, but the truth is often not pretty.

But the truth is so much better than lies. Even a painful truth is better than lies. Our dying civilization is dying largely because we won't speak the truth about anything. In our country we have reached the point that anyone trying to tell us an uncomfortable truth almost has to join the government Federal Witness Protection Program, be given a new name and social security number, and be moved to some quiet backwater to live out his days in obscurity and silence. We are dying for the lack of the willingness to speak the truth and take the consequences. Zack, with all his faults and failures, points us toward a better path.

Chapter 5

The Roman Road

"What is the book to be called?" the boy asked.

"The book's name," said Richard, "is 'The Magnificent Adventures of King Pain's Henchman.'"

"What is a Henchman?"

"When real kings wore real crowns a henchman led King Pain's horse. A henchman is a servitor."

"A Servitor?"

"Yes," said Richard, "we all wish to serve, but only the great are born to serve."

"The Balance," *The Roman Road*, Zack

"If I then, the Lord and the Teacher, washed your feet, you also ought to wash one another's feet."

John 13:14

The Roman Road is the fifth and final book published by Gwendoline Keats/Zack.

The book appeared in the spring of 1903, published in England by Constable. In the United States the book was published by Charles Scribner's Sons.

So far I have found four reviews, two of which are brief paragraphs, a third which is three fairly long paragraphs, and a fourth containing two paragraphs plus two lengthy quotes from the book. While one might certainly quarrel with a few of the reviewers' statements, taken as a whole the comments are intelligently insightful, mostly respectful—and not highly favorable to the book. And the reviewers are correct. This is not an excellent book. Gwendoline Keats had written four books which deserve to be read by any lover of good literature—four outstanding books. Her fifth book falls far short of the standard she had set in her previous work.

The nameless reviewer for "The Academy and Literature" titled his review of *The Roman Road* Shadowy Psychology. The three longish paragraphs are worth quoting at some length. The ellipses are mine.

> There was a time when Zack seemed set upon a kind of hard realism; in two of the three stories which make up this volume she has abandoned realism for psychology. It is a curious and rather unsatisfactory psychology, neither objective nor subjective, but mingling both to make an impression strong, indeed, but without much real human appeal. Only one character in "The Roman Road" is alive, and that is a minor character. . . . we can get no grip of the mother and the two sons . . . The mother, with her scruples of conscience and her angina pectoris, does not move us, neither does the favourite son who at first elects to keep his brother out of his own. . . . the author does not carry us with her. Her comments are on too high a note. . . .
>
> The second story, called "The Balance," is even more remote . . . The lurid evil which overhangs the man like a cloud is too phantasmal to stir the emotions, and as a consequence his relations with the woman of the story leave us unmoved. The dialogue in both these stories draws nothing from nature; it is rhetorical, hard, bitter, clever, but never instinct with human modulations.
>
> Yet "The Roman Road" is a book that dwells in the memory by reason of its unquestionable cleverness and moral earnestness. . . . with a reaching out after beauty . . . At the same time we believe that Miss Keats is a real and a sincere artist. . . . The author's equipment is far beyond the average; it only needs direction and a careful pruning.[38]

H. W. Boynton, writing in "The Atlantic Monthly," noted that the first two stories in the book were "sombre in tone." "The titular story is varied, but hardly enlivened, by certain touches of that chill educated humor which Mr. James and Mr. Howells have taught us to believe that

---

[38]Unknown reviewer, "**Fiction.** Shadowy Psychology.," "The Academy and Literature," 6 June, 1903, pp. 557-558.

we enjoy."[39] (There is humorous speculation enough for seven or eight doctoral dissertations in the latter half of that sentence.)

"The Outlook" says the title story (which it considered the least deserving of the three stories) is after the manner of Henry James "—and (in our opinion) a long way after. The personages of the story, at one breath dull and inconsequential, at the next amazingly clever and profound, seem to us unconvincing and altogether too subtle for the comprehension of the average student of human nature." The reviewer saw "The Balance" as fantastical and overdrawn but original, and considered the final shorter story, "Thoughty," to be "a deliciously humorous recital of childish adventure."[40]

"The Athenaeum" felt that the first two stories "possess little or no merit." The "background in each of them" is "vague and unreal." "Of these two tales it is difficult to make anything whatever." The third story is "much better. It is a delightful piece of children's make-believe." Even with this story, though, the reviewer becomes annoyed, and recommends to the author "A thorough cleansing of the imagination."[41]

In a letter postmarked May 27, 1903, Zack told her friend the writer May Sinclair that *The Roman Road* was coming out that week, or was already out, and asked her to tell her how the book struck her. May Sinclair must have read the book, then said something to Zack about *The Roman Road* which called into question the book's literary qualities. Zack responded. Then May Sinclair must have persisted, because Zack felt obliged to respond to her comments a second time. May Sinclair's letters are lost, but we have Zack's letters to her. While I am not certain, I am guessing that the first letter I quote was the first of the two on the topic. It is the lengthier of the two responses. The exact month and day are unclear from the photocopy I have, but the letter was postmarked 1903.[42]

---

[39]H. W. Boynton, in a segment of the magazine entitled *Books New and Old*, "The Atlantic Monthly," Aug. 1903, p. 280.

[40]Unknown reviewer, "The Outlook," 23 May, 1903, p. 246.

[41]Unknown reviewer, "The Athenaeum," No. 3957, Aug. 29, 1903, p. 283.

[42]Zack letter to May Sinclair, postmarked 1903.

Dear old May,

I haven't been reading Maeterlink or any of the symbolists, or even writers of stories about children—it is nothing but the effect of a blow in the eyes so that I can't see anything. I wrote the book last year, thought it too bad to publish, then found I could not write anything this year either & being quite penniless published the book.

Thats the whole truth. I got two hundred for it, American & English, but have spent every penny but twenty pounds already. So I have chucked the book I spoke to you about & have begun a peasant story as I can do that sort of work better & quicker.

Thats the whole truth. It will all get right in time.

Yours
Zack.

Maurice Maeterlinck—Zack misspells the name very slightly— was a Belgian playwright, poet, and essayist (1862-1949) who wrote in French. Wikipedia tells us his plays "form an important part of the Symbolist movement." He won the Nobel Prize in Literature in 1911. But in her letter Zack says it is not the Symbolists which had influenced how *The Roman Road* came out. She had taken a blow in the eyes and could not see well. This is not the first time Zack mentioned a blow to the eyes in her letters to May Sinclair. The year 1902 seems to have been a trying one for Zack in several ways. She tells May Sinclair late in the year that she had a "racking time this year," "another turn with the flu," her head feeling "like a rotten apple." Her dog was dreadfully ill, had fits, and drove her "nearly distracted." Late in the year she was "obliged to destroy my dog," which she said knocked her "pretty flat." In a letter in late 1902 she says, "One can't write when you've had such a blow in the eyes you can't see straight." In this same letter she writes something that raises the possibility that some problem is bothering her emotionally: "Indeed, now I am no company, I have thought so much about one thing that I feel as if I had worn a hole in my brain." To this "hole in the brain" comment, May Sinclair scholar Theophilus Boll responds with these words:

What calamity it was that made her feel so distraught, Zack never confessed in her letters. And this, the last that May

Sinclair kept, left the mystery unsolved. I have found no trace of any later residence, or of anything at all about this writer, whose writing has such an elemental, earth-rooted power. She could well be the model for Nina Lempriere in *The Creators*.[43]

So there may have been an emotional "calamity" which was bothering Zack, to go along with her other problems. It is difficult to read the date of the year on the postmark photocopy I have seen. This letter may have been written in late 1903, as Boll believed. The date looks more like 1902 to me, but I have seen the letters only in photocopies, whereas Boll saw them in person.

May Sinclair, who apparently felt able to speak the truth to her friend, must have said something more in dispraise of *The Roman Road*. Zack says, "It is only a makeshift book. I was so hard up, I was obliged to publish something." In this very brief letter, she also says that she has "almost an idea for a good book at last." As indicated above, the order of the two letters by Zack could possibly be reversed.

We hear no more of the "peasant story," nor do we hear any more of the "almost an idea for a good book." Gwendoline Keats' writing and publishing career was at an end. Her two letters to May Sinclair, which I have quoted above, may have been the last she ever wrote to her—or to anyone. A letter from her oldest brother, Thorold Goodwin Keats, to her second brother, Herbert Frederick Keats (Fred), explains at least part of the reason why. T. G. Keats is writing from Australia. To clarify, Cicy is the wife of Fred Keats, Jessie is the wife of T. G. Keats. Gwenda is the name by which Gwendoline Keats was called in the family; she sometimes signed her letters to May Sinclair as Gwenda Keats. The letter is dated January 29, 1904.[44] The ellipsis is mine.

> My dear Fred,
>   I enclose a dividend for you although small it is probably the first you have received for some time. Cicy wrote Jessie very bad accounts of Gwenda & it appears from her letter that her case is practically hopeless. You may have received I hope

---

[43]Boll, *Miss May Sinclair*, etc., p. 67.

[44]T. G. Keats letter to Fred Keats, dated January 29, 1904. This letter is a transcription kindly given to me by Mrs. Beverley Keats.

better news however we must consider what is best to be done, I myself feel that it would be almost a sin to put her in a public lunatic asylum but if a private one is to cost £250 per annum I don't see where the money is to come from unless you can give much more than I can. As you know I have practically nothing except my screw here which hardly keeps me much less anyone else but I think Jessie & myself would guarantee £50 and more if possible a year. I would like to have your views on the subject. . . .

Your affectionate Brother
T. G. Keats

The situation of Gwendoline Keats was now "practically hopeless." The two options were a public or a private lunatic asylum. So Zack's prediction that "It will all get right in time" turned out to be wrong. It didn't get right, at least on this side of the grave; within a few weeks or months of that letter she would be a "practically hopeless" case ready to be put in an asylum.

It is possible that the blow to the eyes of which Zack wrote, was ultimately responsible for her mental condition. Mrs. Beverley Keats married Andy Keats in 1974. Andy Keats is a grandson of Thorold Goodwin Keats, Zack's oldest brother. Mrs. Keats writes, "Gwenda liked driving a 6 horse carriage and racing it, and on one occasion was thrown out of the carriage, and suffered brain damage, and was eventually placed in a mental institution."[45] Mrs. Keats later reported having talked to a cousin of Andy's, who also had heard the story of Gwendoline having a mishap when driving a horse carriage.[46]

What happened next to Gwendoline Keats is unclear. She has at least two possible death dates! It is possible that she was committed to Brislington House, Keynsham, Somerset, England. Wikipedia tells us Brislington House was built as a private lunatic asylum, and "was one of the first purpose-built asylums in England." It is possible that the Keats family found a way to finance Gwendoline's admittance there. Thanks to the researches of Mrs. Keats, we know that a Gwendoline Keats, age 67, died at Brislington House on June 8th, 1934. On her death certificate, her age is listed as 67, which would be only one year off; Zack

---

[45]Email letter to me from Mrs. Beverley Keats, Mar. 27, 2013.
[46]Email letter to me from Mrs. Beverley Keats, Oct. 7, 2013.

would have been 68. She died of cancer of the stomach; there was no post mortem. She is listed as being "Of no fixed abode," and being a "Spinster No occupation."[47] Mrs. Keats is inclined to believe that this is our Gwendoline Keats. Of no fixed abode certainly fits our Zack. The return addresses on her letters to May Sinclair showed that she moved around constantly. Keats family tradition has 1934 as the date of death. In fact there is one family picture of Zack with the dates 1865-1934 super-imposed along the bottom.

The second possible date of death is 1910. The year 1910 was the one I always assumed was the correct date of death, until my correspondence with Mrs. Keats began in 2013. The Library of Congress catalog, for example, lists her date of death as 1910. One sees this same date of death repeated elsewhere, as for example in *A Guide to the Best Fiction* by Ernest A. Baker and James Packman. Of course, the possibility exists that various reference books simply repeat the mistake made by whoever got it wrong the first time.

The reference that gives me most encouragement to believe that 1910 is the correct date of death, is from the *New International Encyclopedia, Volume 13*. This was published by Dodd, Mead in 1915. In 1915, the encyclopedia believed Zack to have died five years ago, in 1910. The encyclopedia reference is very accurate, which tempts me to believe that they were also very accurate in their date of death. They were unsure of her date of birth, and indicated that lack of knowledge with a question mark. I quote the encyclopedia reference in its entirety.

> KEATS, Gwendoline (pen name, Zack) (?-1910). An English novelist, born in Devonshire. After publishing several short dialect stories in *Blackwood's Magazine*, she came before a wider public with *Life is Life* (1898), a series of 12 tales, displaying great power in depicting the hard side of life. They were succeeded in a similar vein by *On Trial* (1899), which won the prize of the London Academy; *The White Cottage* (1901); *Tales of Dunstable Weir* (1901); *The Roman Road* (1903).

---

[47]According to the copy of a death certificate kindly provided to me by Mrs. Keats, Gwendoline Keats died on the "Eighth June 1934" at Brislington House, Bristol. Under the category of Occupation, she was described as "Of no fixed abode" and "Spinster No occupation."

It is possible that wishful thinking inclines me to believe more in the 1910 death date than in 1934. I hate to think of Zack lingering in an asylum, hopelessly insane, for thirty long years. The year 1910 seems like a date of death which is more fitting to the narrative of her life. That, admittedly, is no proof whatsoever that 1910 really is the date of death.

Will we ever know for sure? We might not. But I think we will know some day. Mrs. Keats' further researches may answer the question for us. And maybe it is just my native optimism peeking through, but I hope that if the question is not answered by my generation, some younger researchers will arise and do the work necessary to settle this question definitively. (Perhaps DNA evidence could tell us if the lady buried near Brislington House—if she is buried near there!—was related to the living family of Gwendoline Keats.) The book you are reading is not the last word on Zack. There is plenty of work—job security—for younger readers of her work—if any such begin to exist. I hope and expect they will. Zack is too good a writer to be ignored forever.

This has been a long introduction to *The Roman Road*. But it may help you to understand why the book is not as excellent as her other four books. She had suffered a blow to the eyes which made it difficult to see (most likely in a smash up while racing a six-horse carriage); the year of the writing (1902) was a difficult one for her; she may have experienced an emotional "calamity"; she was months away from a mental breakdown from which she would never recover.

"The Roman Road"

The story "The Roman Road" is a long one, about 104 pages.

Groot Hall overlooks the village of Groot. The village has "rotting houses." In fact at least five times in the course of the story the village is described with some form of the word rot. The one distinctive and positive thing about the village is that a Roman Road (both words capitalized throughout the story) ran straight through it.

Straight through the heart of the village ran the Roman Road
and passed on. It seemed to image forth life triumphant over
disease and failure.

The village is owned by the Groots. Old Sir Theophilus Groot had
three sons, but they all have died, and now he has died as well. The
property has been left to his nephew Roland, the older of two brothers
who are the sons of Mrs. Emily Groot. The villagers of Groot are agreed
that Providence might have acted more wisely in having the younger
son of Mrs. Groot, Wantage, be born ahead of Roland, so that Wantage
would have inherited rather than Roland. Roland is 28, but already "was
in debt to the Jews."

Mrs. Groot, age 45, suffers from the incurable disease of "angina-
pectoris." She is not a woman given to introspection, but events are
pressing on her, and she has to make some important decisions. Her
niece Jean Morice is arriving later that day, and before that she plans to
have a necessary talk with her older son—a talk she had hoped never
to have.

Mrs. Groot laments to Roland that all three of his cousins had died.
Now the property comes to Roland, whom she criticizes to his face as
"'an idle, good-for-nothing spendthrift.'"

Mrs. Groot says she has heard that Roland plans to have the oaks
in the long walk felled. Roland shamefacedly admits that is true. It
is not plainly stated, but clearly he needs the money to pay his debts.
What, she asks, would happen if the property were Wantage's instead
of Roland's? This is an idle question, Roland says. But it isn't an idle
question. She seems to Roland to speak in riddles, but the truth comes
out quickly enough: Mrs. Groot's late husband was not Roland's father.
An unnamed man sired Roland. This shocks Roland, of course. Mrs.
Groot had hoped never to have to tell Roland the truth, but the fact
that the three sons all died had put her in a tight spot. She would have
to tell the truth and have Wantage receive the property as was his legal
due, or keep silent and let Roland (whom she had always loved better
than she loved Wantage) receive the inheritance unjustly. Right now
Wantage knows nothing of all this.

Mrs. Groot tells Roland that if he were more like Wantage, she
would want the property to remain with Roland. Roland understands

that even if he turned saint, it would not alter the fact that the property belonged to Wantage by right.

Jean Morice, only child of Mrs. Groot's brother John, arrives at Groot Hall. She is accompanied by her homely middle aged friend, Miss O'Rell. Roland meets both. Wantage sends a telegram saying he is coming, and soon arrives—poorly dressed as always.

Miss O'Rell, an artist of sorts, paints a scene of the bowling green which is quite riotous in appearance, and later plays the piano. Mrs. Groot is shocked at the picture of the green, but Roland, who has never felt any interest in plain women, finds himself wondering about her.

> Had life in a spirit of grim farce given the plain-faced woman a heart to love with, and had Spring whispered for her with the tread of coming lovers, coming lovers that never came?

Even in this lesser collection of stories, there are flashes of insight and good writing from Zack. The sentence above represents both. Homely people may have hearts to love, yet may never, in the providential orderings of God, find some one person to love them and to whom they can express love. Zack, with her typical honesty, knows that some people remain unloved, and says so. She may even have been thinking about herself. She was in her mid thirties as she wrote, and she may well have sensed that there would be no coming lover for her. Yet, reading her books, it is very easy to imagine that this generous-spirited woman may well have had "a heart to love with."

Mrs. Groot has a painful attack of her heart disease, and we learn that this somewhat shallow woman faces her pain with courage. This is a point Zack makes often in her books: very flawed people can have some very admirable qualities.

Roland and Jean converse, and while Jean is very beautiful, Roland finds himself attracted to her personality.

"Clean as thought from a wholesome mind came the echo of the axe from the Long Walk." (This is another lovely sentence.) Roland is persisting with his plan to cut the oaks, some of which have already fallen. Roland is very conscious that he is taking another man's property. Speaking hypothetically, he discusses these issues with Jean. She says that he would lose by spending another man's money, even if he spent it well. "'The money would not be yours and you could not make it yours.'" Eternal realities are inescapable, no matter what appearances may show. But Jean questions mankind's love of truth. She says, "'I don't think that any of us care much for truth.'" Zack does not expand on the question at length, but this is a profound insight into our human nature. How many of us love truth in a serious even if imperfect fashion? The number must be incredibly small. As a Christian, I can see that even most Christians have no real interest in truth—mostly we want just enough truth to get us "saved," and very little more.

Roland, looking into his own heart, knows that he intends dishonestly to keep Groot. He, Mrs. Groot, and Miss O'Rell meet a villager, an old man named Jakes. He is an honest, uncomplaining man, who says that villages in general (not just Groot) are places of illness, but nevertheless makes clear that it would be very helpful if all the houses were weather-tight and his own pig-sty patched. Mrs. Groot tells him that "'you poor people never know when you are well off.'" Jakes treats this comment with polite scorn, and moves on.

Later, talking with his mother, Roland surprises himself and his mother by saying that if he keeps the property it will be with the intention of marrying Jean. His mother says such an idea is preposterous; Jean is "'A girl without a farthing.'" He realizes that if Jean knew he was a thief, it would change her opinion of him; "'but then you see, mother, she will not know.'" He and his mother quarrel over what he will do for the village. He makes her no promises in that regard. That night he drinks whisky and the next morning a housemaid finds him drunk on the floor. He is a favorite among the servants, and so he is put to bed without the story of his drunken episode being told among his own family.

Mrs. Groot tries to get Jean to influence Roland to put the village in good repair, and even tells her (without permission to do so) that Roland loves her, but Jean refuses to interfere with Roland.

Wantage and his mother talk; she recommends that he dress better. He entertains the idea of using Roland's tailor. When she warns that the tailor is expensive, Wantage's response opens a surprising window on his personality. "'Supposing,'" he said, "that the man whistles for his money?'" Wantage thus shows a potential for dishonesty, since he is willing to consider not paying the tailor once he has his expensive clothes.

Roland and Jean meet outside and it seems that both are beginning to recognize a mutual attraction, although this is expressed in a sufficiently vague manner by Zack.

> That night Death advanced and laid sudden siege to Mrs. Groot. Generalled by Life, she retreated by a series of forced marches, Death occupying the abandoned territory, till at last Life and Death confronted each other across an invisible line.

After some hours she wakes to find herself still alive, and sends for Roland. Roland is filled with compassion for his mother. She tells him that she will die at peace if he promises to rebuild the village. "The grotesque inadequacy of such a garment to keep out shame made him smile." But he promises to do as she wishes, and this energizes Mrs. Groot wonderfully. She sends for Wantage, who arrives, Roland remaining in the room as well. She tells him that Roland intends to care for the village just as Wantage would have cared for it, but Wantage confesses to be "'rather full up of the village lately.'" He has other things on his mind. He has noticed, for instance, that his cousin Jean is very pretty. In fact, the truth gradually comes out that he is thinking of marrying Jean. This surprises both Roland and Mrs. Groot. Wantage says he could use a little money just then, but supposes he shall have to whistle for it.

> At that Roland clapped him hugely on the back. "Whistle for money," he exclaimed. "We can all fife that tune; but you, Wantage, shall fife loudest and *longest*."

Roland proceeds with plans for vast improvements in the village of Groot. He tries to interest Jean in these plans, but she refuses to become involved. He makes his love for her clear, but she doesn't respond in a way that is clearly encouraging. Away from her, he throws the architect's plans for Groot into the fire, "but Wantage was no nearer coming into his own."

That same day death approaches nearer to Mrs. Groot, and she knows it.

> In those last moments she was haunted by the vision of something that needs had to be revealed. In other days Mrs. Groot had pecked at the idea of a death-bed confession, urged to it maybe by a half-formed wish to have revenge on Roland, but, death at hand, it was not revenge she thought of; she was possessed by a vague notion that her one road to safety lay through a public disclosure of all that she had hitherto kept carefully hidden.

At her request, many people gather in her room. She includes not only Roland, Wantage, Jean, and Miss O'Rell, but also at least four people who are not family members. She speaks, expressing gratitude that they had come. Fairly quickly she gets to the heart of why she called them there.

> "Dear Roland, I have always loved him best, but I must be fair to all." The dying woman stopped short and beckoned Wantage to her. "Groot is yours, Wantage," she said, "and poor, erring, misguided Roland has no right even to the name. He has known this for a long time and that is why I have found it so difficult to tell you. Right, Wantage, is harder to do than most people credit, and it has been the struggle, the ceaseless struggle to do right, that has killed me. Be kind to Roland, Wantage, for though he has not helped me I should be glad to think that you will help him." The small voice twittered away into nothing, and the guests as so many dolls stared woodenly at their feet, and then as woodenly rose and marched out, leaving the room empty of all but Jean, Wantage, Roland and the dying woman. Quiet and still they stayed. Death might have claimed them also for his own.

Jean eventually leaves the room, and, after a rather thoughtless comment on his part, so does Wantage,

> leaving her alone with Roland. She tried to peer through the thickening darkness for Roland's figure, but could not see him.
> "Are you there, Roland?" she asked.
> He came to her.

"I have always loved you best, Roland," she murmured. He understood that she spoke the truth.

"Are you happier, mother?" he asked.

"I don't know," she answered feebly.

The setting sun sought the horizon, filling as it did so the room with a noble radiance. Mrs. Groot looked at it, first carelessly, then with increasing interest.

"What a lot of light," she said, and died.

After the funeral, Roland finds Jean standing close to the Roman Road. He tells her he has been kicked out, and says it is only fair that she have her kick with the rest. He tells her he loves her, and that he had hoped to tell her that with the Groot name and property at his back. She tells him she loves him. He tells her that she cannot be the wife of a thief. The story ends as follows:

> She took his hands and drew him towards the Roman Road. "We are but children, Roland, you and I," she said. "Let us run from all the mistakes that we have made and leave men and women to put away our broken toys and raze our castles."
>
> He grew more stubborn. "They shall not say my wife has a thief for a husband," he burst out.
>
> "Hush," she said softly, "we have played too long and grown too earnest. What is the past, Roland, that we should value it more than the present? Even to dwell on the past is to forfeit the future. Look at the Roman Road. See how triumphantly it presses on. Let us trust ourselves to the Roman Road."
>
> "Jean," he answered, and his harsh voice sounded harsher than ever before, "this is madness. I have not the money to support a wife."
>
> She laughed. "I have enough and to spare," she said. "We will lend ourselves sufficient to be happy on and if we need more we will work for it. See," and she pointed westward. "The sun has begun to sink; soon the night will be here when no man can work. Let us hasten, Roland, while there is yet time."
>
> Hand in hand, helpless as children, they fled down the Roman Road.

So, despite the fact that Roland has been revealed as a thief, Jean loves him and will marry him. Roland, revealed throughout the story to be a very flawed man, will have a wife far better than he deserves. As for money to support the pair? We were told in the middle part of the story, although Mrs. Groot and the others were not told, that Jean had an annual income of about three thousand pounds—quite a large amount. Jean, far from being the pauper Mrs. Groot had supposed, has plenty of money to support them both. She encourages optimism toward the future. They are to press on triumphantly in a straight-ahead manner, just as the Roman Road does, leaving mistakes behind, refusing to let those mistakes ruin the future. Her penultimate sentence is a partial quote from Jesus Christ, who said "'We must work the works of Him who sent Me, as long as it is day; night is coming, when no man can work'" (Jn. 9:4).

Their marriage will have a chance to be a good one. But the reader has a right to wonder if they can pull it off. Roland was willing, after all, to be a thief. He has been exposed, which he gives signs of being able to accept without whining. But can he be a different man in the future? And what man can maintain his self-respect in a marriage in which the woman supplies all the money? Unless Roland is willing to go to work to support his wife, it is difficult to imagine the marriage succeeding. It is not necessary that he earn an enormous salary. Jean is not a woman for whom an extravagant lifestyle is important. But my guess is that Roland will need to show the character to go to work and earn money for his wife, or disaster awaits them. The path down the Roman Road, whether Jean, Roland, or Zack know it, will have to include for Roland the straight-ahead willingness to get up in the morning and hump it in the workaday world. The reader may or may not have enough confidence in Roland's ability and willingness to understand that. Zack certainly has hope for the couple.

We learn nothing more of Wantage. He has shown himself to be a shallow person, without high integrity. Of Miss O'Rell we hear no more. She will no doubt continue to be an honorable woman.

Mrs. Groot is buried, "and with her as much of her shame as the grave can swallow in, which, after all, is not much." She is an interesting character, frequently shallow and self-absorbed, but courageous in the face of pain and possible death. She has committed a great crime against God and against her husband, in the adultery of her youth. But she has the courage to confess that crime—at first only to Roland. Later, nearing death, "she was possessed by a vague notion that her one road to safety lay through a public disclosure of all that she had hitherto kept carefully hidden." She duly follows through on that vague notion, announcing her sin not only to her family but also to the Skiffingtons and the Ragstocks. Zack hints that this flawed and erring woman found that safety at death: "'What a lot of light,' she said, and died.' Honesty before God and men puts us on a path toward redemption.

"The Roman Road" is not Zack at her best. There are certainly glimpses of her greatness here, isolated sentences or paragraphs that are memorable and insightful. Early on in the story, for one example, we are told, "Life, over-rich in much, is prodigal of isolation; there is always a strip over to wrap each man round and spread out in quietude at his feet." This reminds us how solitary we all often are, and does so in colorful language. Was Zack thinking of her own mostly solitary life? Perhaps. When Mrs. Groot tells Roland that God must know that she tries to do right, Roland, who is not even sure that God exists, answers, "'I expect our measure was taken long ago.'" That is, God knows our character, and we fool ourselves if we think we can fool Him.

But the conversations frequently fail to carry the reader along, as the reviewers noted. The characters sometimes speak in a manner "unconvincing and altogether too subtle for the average student of human nature," as previously quoted from "The Outlook." This statement fits the next story, "The Balance," as well.

"The Balance"

"The Balance" is another long story, checking in at 80 pages.

It opens in Naples. A man in a palace seems old and grey, but when a match is struck we see that he is "a youth with a tired face." A carrozza (carriage) rattles down the street, a young man flings a coin to the driver, jumps out, and enters the palace. Reaching the topmost story, he knocks on the massive door and calls out the name of Richard East. The door opens, and the young man, beginning to doubt the impulse which had brought him here from "the other end of the continent," enters into the room, into the presence of his friend Richard East, the youth with the tired face.

> The lean, brown face of Richard East did not lend itself well to description. If the man's reticent spirit was portrayed, it was portrayed veiled. There was nothing common or unclean in the face, much that was harsh and uncouth, much that was tender, delicate and beautiful.

Jeffrey, having difficulty in explaining why he had come, tells Richard of a fishing village in England. He speaks partial truths and even an outright lie, and after looking at his watch he says that he must be off; he wants to catch the night mail back. So he has come all the way from Paris, to speak a few confused sentences, and now wants to return immediately! He scribbles an address on a sheet of paper, says he has read Richard's most recent book, and tells Richard to come out of Naples into the fresh air. He leaves, apparently to return to Paris or perhaps to the fishing village in England.

The next scene is one of the two most memorable in the story. Jeffrey is by the seashore in England.

> Near a mass of green samphire on the cliff opposite lay a woman asleep. Her pale face was turned towards Jeffrey, and against the dead blackness of the rocks her black hair was lustrous. The body, carelessly outstretched, retained inviolate its air of guarded mystery; and the sun's rays playing on the sleeping form seemed but an iridescence of womanhood. Very lovely the woman looked lying there. A feeling of awe stole over Jeffrey; and while he yet stood watching, the woman, touched by some hidden sorrow, wept. Quietly the tears had gathered behind the closed lids; quietly they fell, and unmoved the dead black rock received them. Raising her poor hands in protest the woman wept on. What communing did the spirit have with that body thus to disturb the serene recess of sleep? Those hands, raised in mute entreaty, against what did they appeal? Stirred to the depths Jeffrey moved away, and left the sea—a white fire—to guard the woman with leaping flames. Long it thundered at the base of the cliff, then drew off, muttering in all its channels: and the woman, waking and conscious of no hidden grief, knew not that she had wept.

There are at least four passages in the Bible which portray a sleeper as feeling instructed or blessed—somehow encouraged—during sleep. "Indeed, my mind instructs me in the night" (Psalm 16:7b). "When you lie down, you will not be afraid;/When you lie down, your sleep will be sweet" (Prov. 3:24). "'I was asleep, but my heart was awake'" (Song of Solomon, 5:2a). "At this I awoke and looked, and my sleep was pleasant to me" (Jer. 31:26). These passages seem to me to reflect an experience which many of us may have felt, if rarely. Sometimes good things are going on in our minds and spirits while we sleep. We awake, conscious of blessing which has occurred as we slept. Here, we have Rachel Loraine undergoing an opposite experience. She weeps in her sleep. There is some sadness which she subconsciously bears. But she awakes unaware that she has wept.

Rachel is "more girl than woman," a "bare twenty summers old." Leaving the shore, she enters a forest and arrives at a cottage. She hears a low moan from within the cottage, then a child's sobbing. A gaunt middle-age woman sits near the door of the cottage, knitting.

> "There isn't nought to be done. The doctor says so," the woman announced. "He's got to die: the sooner the better." Her face was white, with blue lines about the eyes and mouth, but her voice was stolid to hardness.

Jeffrey is there looking down on the "withered, skinny, big-headed, wide-eyed child" who "lay twisted half under and half out of the sheets." Rachel and Jeffrey are both impotent to help the child. The following passage is the second of the story's great memorable scenes.

> While she knelt there, her tears mingling with the child's, Richard East entered the room. He came to the head of the bed, unstrapped the knapsack from his shoulders, and laid it with slow deliberation on the floor.
> The child, ceasing to cry, watched him.
> "Who are you?" said the child.
> "The friend of the butcher's dog," Richard answered, and the child accepted the introduction.
> "What do you do?" he asked.
> "I write stories."
> "What kind of stories?"

"Stories of men and boys and the fierce adventures of the spirit."

"Then," said the child, "you will write about me."

"I will get paper and pen," replied Richard, and took both from his knapsack. Intent on interesting the dying boy he did not appear to see either Rachel or his friend. Withdrawing to the window Rachel watched and listened, as might some less privileged child, who, allowed to look on, was yet neither to be seen nor heard. Jeffrey also was silent: vague misgiving filled him. A few short hours back and he would have been overjoyed at the sight of Richard; but now something had come between Richard and his welcome and Jeffrey felt that it was the presence of Rachel.

"What is the book to be called?" the boy asked.

"The book's name," said Richard, "is 'The Magnificent Adventures of King Pain's Henchman.'"

"What is a Henchman?"

"When real kings wore real crowns a henchman led King Pain's horse. A henchman is a servitor."

"A Servitor?"

"Yes," said Richard, "we all wish to serve, but only the great are born to serve."

The child, who had half risen, lay back once more on the bed. "Don't speak, please," he exclaimed, adding after a pause: "We shall want a big piece of paper."

"The biggest."

"Who will see the magnificent adventures?" asked the child.

"No one," said Richard authoritatively.

"No one!"

"Magnificent adventures are never witnessed or they would not be magnificent."

"Ah!" said the child, adding not without satisfaction, "I shall have to tell you or you could not write them down."

"I am 'No One,'" observed Richard.

"You must put that in the title too," said the child, and Richard took the paper and wrote down, "The Magnificent Adventures of King Pain's Henchman as told to No One." "Now we must fill the book."

"Well," said the child, "I was born. I meant to be like everybody else."

"I hope not," Richard put in, "for then it wouldn't have been worth while being born at all."

"I mean," corrected the child, "that I meant to have been able to run very fast, a little faster than the other boys, just enough to beat them."

"Ah!" exclaimed distracted Richard, "then you would never have been King Pain's henchman and the book would never have been written."

"I did not think of that till this minute," the child admitted and looked solemnly into Richard's face.

"Well," said Richard, "we must pass it over."

"Do you think King Pain will pass it over?"

"He is a great king and it is your first offence."

"I am glad it is my *first* offence," said the boy. "How," he asked, "can I have magnificent adventures?"

"How!" exclaimed Richard, surprised.

"In bed, I mean."

"Magnificent adventures," answered Richard, "are adventures of the spirit. Other adventures are merely adventures. No man counts those in at all."

"Ah!" said the boy and shut his eyes tight. Then suddenly his body twitched together and he uttered a sharp cry. Rachel and Jeffrey turned their eyes to Richard, as if asking how he would meet an emergency they found so baffling. Richard's face was calm, almost placid.

"King Pain speaks to you," he said softly.

"Is that how the king speaks?" the child asked, surprised into attention.

"Yes."

"What do you think he said?"

"He told you to forget him."

The child's white, shrunken face grew pink, as he strove to be a faithful henchman. Then, all unawaited by Richard, the boy smiled. "I am glad I serve a king," he murmured.

"It is a great honour to serve King Pain," Richard replied, kneeling down beside the bed.

"What do you think he said then?" the child asked feebly.

"He told you to sleep and when he called you were to acclaim him."

"Acclaim him?"

"All kings are acclaimed. You must cry—'The King! The King!'"

The boy's face lit up. "I am glad I serve a king," he repeated, and shutting his eyes dozed off to sleep.

"None but a child could learn that lesson in twenty minutes," said Richard softly to himself, and looking up he saw the woman standing by the bed.

> "'Tis the first natural sleep he's had these many days and nights," she remarked. Her face grew less hard. She went back to the kitchen, the others following. "I'll not let you go," she exclaimed with sudden fierceness, turning on Richard. "Leastways not till the lad is dead. You can please un better than I can: 'tis more a matter of hours than days."

Is Richard East correct, that "'we all wish to serve, but only the great are born to serve'"? Rather, it seems like we all wish to be served rather than to serve. Leave it to Zack to put a thought-provoking idea in front of us. Richard's comment seems ridiculous at first sight. Then we remember our Savior, who washed the dirty feet of His disciples (Jn. 13:3-15), and told us, "'let him who is the greatest among you become as the youngest, and the leader as the servant. For who is greater, the one who reclines at the table, or the one who serves? Is it not the one who reclines at the table? But I am among you as the one who serves'" (Lk. 22:26-27).

It certainly seems that we do not all wish to serve. Mostly we like to have others serve us. But that only the great are born to serve may be far more true than we are likely to realize at first glance. Jesus Christ, certainly the greatest man who ever lived (as well as being God Himself) was among us as one who served. And He told us that the greatest in the kingdom of heaven was the one who had the humility of a child (Matt. 18:1-4). Richard may have been exaggerating when he said we all wish to serve—would that we did!—but he seems to have been right on target in telling us that it is the great who are born to serve. If we would seek greatness, we should seek to serve other people and our God. The humble dying child learns at least part of that lesson in a few minutes; he will strive to serve King Pain with courage in his remaining days of life.

It is a moving passage. "'He is a great king and it is your first offence.'" This is a line worthy of the best of Zack.

Jeffrey is a loyal man by nature, and loves his friend Richard East. But Jeffrey "had no welcome in his heart for Richard" because he can quickly see that Richard has come between himself and Rachel. Jeffrey spends a sleepless night.

But in truth this world is so contrived that the man who is born
with a loyal nature pays as heavily in fruitless strivings after
an impossible loyalty, as ever does the disloyal man for those
weird inclinations of his towards treason. Man's ideal of justice
is but a poor affair placed beside this implacable rectitude of
ruling. Good and evil are after all but different rays of the same
spectrum, thrown out by the soul in its efforts to grow.

The last sentence seems an overly optimistic view of how good and
evil fit together! I doubt that when we do evil that our souls are seeking
to grow. Rather, when we do evil, our souls are putting our pathetic
selves at the center of the universe and trying to make everyone else,
including God, bow to our wishes without reference to what is just. We
seek to grow big, but we do not seek to grow toward good.

Rachel seems not to realize the depth of Jeffrey's attraction to her.

Richard has another conversation with the dying child, which Rachel
hears. Of Rachel we are told, "She was not clever, but her spirit turned
towards the truth, as does a flower to the sun." This is another line both
worthy of Zack, and typical of her outlook on life. Zack strives to be
strictly honest. Rachel is not clever. But she has something far better—a
spirit which turns toward the truth as does a flower to the sun. If all of us
had that sort of spirit, our lack of cleverness would not hamper us unduly.
Almost all of us have adequate brainpower even if we are not clever. Where
we go wrong is that our spirits do not love and turn toward the truth.
Rachel loves truth, and when Richard looks into her eyes, he is "refreshed."
Her beauty is also very great, and Richard is disturbed by her presence.

Jeffrey and Richard briefly meet outside, and part with mutual
dissatisfaction. It is unspoken, but clearly Rachel has come between
them. In the dark night, near the village, Richard plays a flute. Rachel
hears, is attracted to the music, and draws near. After a brief conversation
in which Rachel feels hurt at having apparently intruded on him
unwanted, they part. Richard "despised women," but he recognizes that
Rachel is very beautiful, and "every pulse in his body bade him follow
her." But he resolves to go to the boy and forget the woman.

The next day Jeffrey follows Rachel to the edge of the sea. Looking
on from a distance,

love was born in him. It came—a reticence, a shyness; and a passionate longing to protect the woman he loved,—and the woman he loved was Rachel.

Jeffrey goes to the cottage, and calls Richard outside. Jeffrey leads onward, walking a considerable distance until they come to a road. Jeffrey points to the road and tells his friend that Richard "'must go.'" Richard says he will not go. They separate. Richard is deeply hurt. "The love of Richard for Jeffrey was the purest and best passion his heart had ever known." Richard is a man whose spirit was "soiled and stained," a man who was lonely, "having companionship more with ideas than with men." We are told that "ruin and devastation" followed on his heels, but that his eyes somehow had "seen the Promised Land" and that beyond "lay always the victory, the conquest and the kingdom."

Richard goes to the cottage; night falls and the wind rises to a gale. The dying boy sleeps through the disturbance.

> Again and again the storm shook the cottage, as if angered that the child dallied over going. It seemed about to drive death willy-nilly in upon the lad.
>
> "Lord, have mercy upon us!" muttered the woman, stretching out her arms above her child.
>
> Richard looked at King Pain's Henchman, lying there so stalwartly unafraid, then at the terrified woman, while quietly through the turmoil broke the dawn. Opening his eyes, the boy sprang upright.
>
> "The King! The King!" he cried, and smiling fell back dead.

It is apparently the next day. Rachel is outside reading but also thinking of Richard. "His spirit she felt was made for war; he was a born Henchman of King Pain." Jeffrey sits near her. Of her book, we are told that "Jeffrey saw from the title that not only was it one of Richard's, but it was also one that was least worthy of the man." It hurts Jeffrey to see her read the book. "It was almost as if Richard had already put out a soiled hand and touched her." Rachel has already read the book once and is about to read it again, but says with a smile, "'Shall I confess that I don't understand the book in the least?'"

Some few spring days pass. Rachel climbs the hill to the cottage, which by now is "despoiled of roof and forsaken." Jeffrey stands near the deserted cottage. Richard has gone away, and Rachel admits she is sorry. Zack says of Jeffrey,

> He knew that Rachel did not love him; he knew that never in this world would she so much as stay and attentively regard him: but his love for her was planned on a big scale, and had in it something of the slow wheeling eternities, and he could afford to wait.

They separate, but later on Jeffrey finds her on the moor. Trying to answer her question about how the world is put together, Jeffrey tells her,

> "We love, and are not loved; or we love and are loved; the whole of life is contained in that," he said.
> His silence did not trouble her. She would have found it as reasonable to have taken lessons in dancing from a bear, as to have learned of life from Jeffrey.

While Rachel is unimpressed, Jeffrey's answer seems to me to have a great deal of good sense to it. A great deal of life, if not quite the whole, is summed up in Jeffrey's one sentence.

They walk to the inn, and find Richard blowing bubbles from a long clay pipe. Rachel goes eagerly up the steps toward him. We are told that "no wish to see her had brought him, only bravado and bitterness."

Another day, Richard and Rachel meet at the Wishing Well. "So young she looked, so innocent, so fresh; all his troubles were swallowed up in the joy that she lived." After an inconclusive conversation which hints at their mutual attraction, they part.

Richard upbraids himself with having come back; he had meant to keep away from the woman his friend Jeffrey loved. He doubts his own ability to change for the better.

> There is for the soul no darker hour, no chiller moment than the one which breeds the hideous suspicion that for her also an orbit is fixed; and that turn she ever so willingly she shall never come nearer to the sun. Such a moment almost dawned for

Richard then, almost, but for him at least it never quite dawned. If it had, his spirit would have gently powdered away into dust.

This is insightful on Zack's part. She is saying things about our human nature which we may have sensed but never quite isolated well enough to enunciate clearly to ourselves. Probably many of us have feared that our spiritual growth is dead—that what we are we will remain, or we fear that we will backslide and become even worse than we are. It is a reasonable fear! As Zack said late in *The White Cottage* in describing the difficulty with which Mark Tavy matured, "The spirit's growth is a subtle thing, not lightly to be measured." And growth toward goodness is never automatic; often we grow worse rather than better.

Richard has an encounter with a nameless woman of the working class. Their conversation, while cryptic at times as is much of the entire story and volume, is worth quoting in full.

A woman crept towards him, a mighty faggot of sticks upon her back. Aged she was, and bent, and worn with toil, she might have been Time himself. To look at her was to understand that soilure, repentance, tears, all things are passing away. Richard could hear her groaning beneath her load; her short, laboured breathing and her heavy sighs.

"Your son," he said, "has forgotten to carry your sticks," and he took the faggot from her.

"My son has been dead these twenty years," answered the woman, "and I could wish that he had lived to make old bones."

"What is old age like?" asked Richard.

"Old age is like a coat, and made by the man who wears it."

"I see myself," said Richard, "beggared and in rags."

"It goes so with some," replied the woman.

"What shall a man do who cannot trust himself?"

"He shall flee from others."

"Why should one man have a home if another is an outcast?"

The woman raised her wrinkled face and looked into Richard's.

"Answer me first, has a man power or not over the working of his own heart?" she said.

"None can answer that question; none know."

"Get you gone," she exclaimed fiercely. "You cannot find God because you will not."

"Let me but carry your faggot to your door."

> "Nay," said the woman, "I know your breed, with the same hand you would carry the stranger's sticks you would rob your heart's friend of his wife."
>
> The faggot slipped from Richard's shoulders on to the ground. "You speak the truth," he answered. "These hands have done both."

There is much here to provoke thought. It is a fascinating thought that all things, including "soilure, repentance, tears," are passing away. Even our soilure—the meanness of spirit which most of us exhibit in one way or another in our lives—even this is passing away. That seems a consoling notion, perhaps typical of Zack, who tends to take the long view.

Certainly typical of Zack is the notion that the individual is responsible for his actions. We ultimately have power over the working of our own hearts, despite Richard's belief that such a question cannot be decided. The aged woman tells him that "'You cannot find God because you will not.'" These few words sum up the life of all those who do not find God in this world. If we do not, it is because we will not. We prefer to rule our own lives without interference from God. If we are honest, we will see our need for God. If we don't find him, it is simply because we prefer not to do so—His rule of our lives would cancel our license to sin, and that license far too many of us prefer to keep renewed and active year by year.

The woman's final words strike straight into Richard's heart: he would rob his heart's friend of his wife. Richard honestly and to the woman acknowledges that she speaks the truth.

Richard, leaving her, looks back at his own life. His ponderings on his past may ring a bell with anyone who deals with words a lot. Richard was a writer, remember. So, of course, was Zack.

> Richard found that the words that he had said were quite worthy of being commended; but when he came to examine his own deeds they were of such bestial foulness that he stood shivering and abashed before them.

We can at least wonder if Zack applied such a sentence to herself. She was I believe a woman of essential humility. Now, late in her writing career—much later than she could probably know—with her remaining time of sanity to be measured in months rather than years, she may have felt abashed before her personal sinfulness. I suspect that she was guilty of little or nothing that the world would call "bestial foulness," but most of us, looking into our own hearts, will see plenty of that sort of thing even if the people around us do not suspect us of being particularly bad. Zack was a woman who in her writing strove toward an astonishing honesty. The Bible tells us, "'The heart is more deceitful than all else/And is desperately sick;/Who can understand it?'" (Jer. 17:9). Zack in her humility and honesty, may have looked into her own heart and found it wanting. It is also possible that her words apply only to her character Richard East, and that she had no particular "bestial foulness" of which to be ashamed. It is sometimes said that "We all have our demons," but this is only approximately true. There may be some among us whose demons are few or non-existent. Perhaps Zack was one of those.

Richard returns to the inn. He sees Jeffrey, who neither speaks nor stirs. Inside, Richard sees Rachel; they look at each other in the darkness. Jeffrey comes inside. Rachel's face is wet with tears.

> Richard did not see her: he saw himself,—a Judas; he saw the Potter's Field; he saw the forked tree; and turning he went out into the night.

Walking in the dark and gusty night, Richard seeks rest and doesn't find it. He quarrels with his soul, wandering until the break of day. At a homely cottage he cries out for admittance "'Open the door to the Spring.'" A woman lets him in. He tells her that he has been with devils the whole night, but she says they can't come near him there. He senses that she is the mother of the late child whom he had so buoyed with hope. He is tired, and she bids him sleep "'with the Lord for friend.'"

> And Richard slept.
> The woman drew the blind, letting the shadows rest on the tired face worn with conflict. Pity and joy filled her; King Pain it seemed had found in Richard another henchman, and the woman another son. For a while she watched him. He slept

with clenched fists as one who had fallen asleep fighting; but the muscles relaxed, the hands opened, and the woman smiling to herself went about her work. From time to time she came back to look at him, and her fierce old eyes were full of savage tenderness.

When he wakes, Richard passionately longs to "escape back to Rachel." He calls himself a drunkard, and Rachel is drink. But he stays and talks with the woman. She is almost inarticulate, but knows that two things life had given her are her man and her lad. Richard asks her if God had ever helped her. She says she has never found God, and doesn't expect to. As night draws on, she makes up a bed for Richard in a corner of the kitchen. She

> went to the door and looked up at the great heaven of stars, and for a brief moment there was given to her fine old countenance the power to express that unquenchable longing of the soul for God.
>
> "Who be we," she said, "that us should find God. In His very Presence we shall not see Him. Aye, though His garments sweep us to the healing yet shall we not behold God face to face."

The eighth and final chapter brings us to the coming of Spring—capitalized in Zack's story. Zack tells us that self-distrust and searching of heart are "the beginning of righteousness." Spring makes Richard eager to be once more on his journey. Rachel finds Richard at the cottage and enters. Zack clarifies for us that Rachel loves Richard. But Richard says that woman "'has brought man nothing but misfortune since the world began.'" Woman drags man down and causes his soul to rust. Rachel leaves, and comes eventually to the ruined cottage where she had first seen Richard and where he had helped the dying boy.

> And it was to her as if all the misfortunes that women have brought to men fell on her and bore her to the earth. Sinking down on the heart-shaped bed, she wept.

Thus ends "The Balance."

The same woman who had—unbeknownst to herself—wept as she slept early on in the story, now weeps with full consciousness.

There will be, it seems, no satisfying solution to this odd love triangle. While Richard loves her, he has rejected Rachel's love. Jeffrey too is out in the cold. Rachel has never valued him as the reader may feel he should be valued.

The best we can hope for seems to be that Richard is conscious of his own past sinfulness, and therefore has refused to become involved with the young, innocent, fresh, and beautiful Rachel. Perhaps that is a victory of sorts. But we remain unsure of his motivation. His character never becomes clear for us. He seems more an outline for a person, than a person. We never feel a strong sense of his personality. Perhaps we don't know enough of his past actions to get a feel for the man. Clearly he has strivings toward goodness and greatness. But the "bestial foulness" he sees in looking at his past actions, remains difficult for us to picture.

Zack, with considerable insight, knew that the characters in her story "Life Is Life" were alive, and knew that even the critical reader would subconsciously sense that the characters lived. How true! Humphrey, Dick Atter, Joe, Joe's wife, the Squire, Wilkie, Captain Thursby, the poor gentlewoman raped by Atter, and on and on through even the most minor characters, live before us. We would know them if we met them. Here in "The Balance"—and we can say the same for "The Roman Road"—the characters don't truly live in the same way. Too much can be made of this, I think. We might well recognize Roland, Wantage, Mrs. Groot, Jeffrey, Richard, and others if we met them. They are sharply enough drawn that we might know them if we met them. But their motivation for how they act remains opaque to us, whereas we know why Humphrey and his companions act as they do.

Both long stories have occasional excellent parts. I have quoted many thought-provoking paragraphs and sentences. The reader will find others. But taken as a whole, neither story grips the reader. For one example, I reread *The Roman Road* only a few short days before I began to write about it here. When it came to writing about "The Balance," despite the fact that I had reread it just days or weeks before, I could not even remember how it ended! I didn't know if Jeffrey got the girl, or

Richard. As I wrote this chapter, I kept hoping Jeffrey won out in the end. As it turns out, neither man ends up with Rachel. My failure to remember a story I read only a few weeks ago may be partly due to my own encroaching senility, or to my careless way of reading. But I think it is also partly due to the stories themselves. They don't strike home in the way her four other books do.

"Thoughty"

"Thoughty" is the shortest story of the three in *The Roman Road*. (Depending upon the edition, the title may also be given as "The Thoughty Ones.") It is about 38 pages long, and is quite different in tone from the previous two stories. It is a story devoted entirely to the adventures of four children, three brothers and a sister. This is an entertaining story, somewhat reminding us of the wonderful "The Failure of Flipperty" which formed part of *Life Is Life*. However, this story stays on a comic level (approximately) throughout, unlike the earlier story in which Flipperty must face the reality of her beloved brother's death. The final story (at least in order of placement in the book) which came from Zack's pen—unless she left some which are lost or buried—was a good one.

It is a story also which almost certainly must be to some extent autobiographical. The four children are of a well to do class. The two oldest are boys. The third child is a girl and the fourth child is a boy. Art is here imitating life. In Gwendoline Keats' well to do family, the two oldest children were boys (Thorold and Fred). The third child was Gwendoline, followed two years later by her brother Arthur. It adds interest to the story to understand these facts—which the ordinary reader of course could not be expected to know.

The story opens with the "A little girl" "looking down the side of a big sun-reddened hill." The little girl sings to herself, "'I am so happy when I am alone.'" (Was this the young Gwendoline Keats as a child—happy when she was alone? If so, does that partly explain the adult Gwendoline Keats as well—happy when she was alone?) The little girl climbs upward

> and at once she thought she was Moses on his way to talk with God. Fear fell on her; she dared not raise her head lest she should see God's face and die; and at last her awe and dread became so overpowering that she crept into a little hole in the side of the hill and hid herself. All this time a boy, younger and smaller and wiser than she, had been following her up the hill. He put his hand into the hole and pulled her hair. She thought she was dead.
> "Why are you scrabbled up in there like a frog, Doozle?" he asked.
> She was thankful to recognize her brother Pepper, and know that she was still alive.
> "I am Moses, talking with God," she answered in a choked voice.
> "That's not the way to play Moses," returned Pepper disgustedly. "You must break the tables of stone, and strike the rock. You had better be the golden calf, and I'll be Moses."
> "I shouldn't care to be the golden calf," said Doozle.
> "It's a girl's part, anyhow," remarked Pepper, "and you'll have to be it or nothing."

Yesterday Doozle had been put in the saw pit as Joseph, and had been left there all afternoon. Knowledge of the Bible must have been something Gwendoline Keats began to take in with her mother's milk. Her books are filled with biblical references.

The two children begin to follow their two older brothers, but they are warned away by Gimlet, despite Pepper's pleading to be included.

> Pepper fell into a deep dejection which had in it also a fine blend of viciousness. He turned on Doozle. "Get away!" he exclaimed coldly. "I won't be dogged wherever I go by a girl."

Pepper refuses to let Doozle come with him, and Doozle at once imagines herself as "Elisha when Elijah threw down his cloak."

The two taller Thoughty Ones are far away on a bleaker, lonelier hill by the sea, huddled near a ruined church which at one time had been used by smugglers. They see a ship, and imagine it to be run by smugglers waiting to sneak in to shore after dark. They discuss this for some time, the eldest (who unlike the other three is not given a nickname in the story) saying that the coast-guard officials have been bribed—although one of the officials is either honest or "'Devilish deep.'"

Rain begins to fall and the two boys slip into the church building through a broken window.

> Drawing forward the lid of a coffin, the Thoughty Ones sat down and waited. A life or death affair this waiting at the risk of a slit throat or shattered brain-pan; but the Thoughty Ones had faced the odds before, and would, if they lived, face them again; for the Thoughty Ones, like all good men and true, had their code of honour; and it was to play the game to the best of the light that was in them. A queer rush of a light, a fata morgana of a light, an ignis fatuus, but such as it was they followed it faithfully, and that was what God meant them to do, no more and no less. A fine thing this license to sin given to every free-born man; this permit to do wrong so long, and only so long, as he strives to do right. Evil,—what is it, but the pathway over which we must all travel to righteousness? And one could well believe that shall death unseal our eyes, and we look again on that which we have done, it will not be our so-called sins that will trouble us, but those showy acts which we so fondly name our good deeds.

Here again we find Zack with the optimistic notion that evil is a path we must follow to get to righteousness. She said something similar in "The Balance." I think there could be some truth to the idea. That is, when we do evil and the consequences are bad for us, we are sometimes able to learn from the consequences that maybe it was foolish to do evil. God often uses bad consequences to teach us. But if we get away with our evil, we tend to continue to wallow in our evil even more. It becomes a path *away* from righteousness, rather than toward it.

The notion that what we "fondly name our good deeds" will trouble us more than our "so-called sins" is questionable as well. It is quite true that some of our good deeds are done with questionable motives, and those good deeds may show up to be less pleasing to God than we "fondly" hope. No argument there. But our "so-called sins" are not just so-called. They are really sins. They will trouble us as well.

Any time we go awry in our thinking about how God has put the world together, we pay a price. God decides the price. He will decide justly. We need to think for ourselves about what is true. Zack was a thoughtful woman, but she could get some things wrong. In this, she is very much like any other person. For example, in the American Christian church as currently constituted, countless millions of converted people, adults who should know better, support evil wars that kill innocent people, and support torture. There is no biblical warrant for such positions, yet most Christians take those positions. Such Christians are idolaters of an evil nation, the United States. Most American Christians have acquiesced in evil to an astonishing extent. So by all means let us quarrel with Gwendoline Keats/Zack when she gets an idea wrong, or partly wrong, but let us not imagine that she is the only person who sometimes gets something wrong. If we take the beam out of our eye, we may be able to help her take the speck out of hers (Matt. 7:3-5).

All this is taking us far away from the Thoughty Ones, but it was at least partly they who led us astray, with their "code of honour" in which they follow "the best of the light that was in them" and sometimes end up in unusual places!

After some misadventures with the candle dying out, the boys leave the church vault, and head in the dark for the Felon's Tree on the far side of the hill. "Many a dead man had hung on that tree in chains; his poor ghost might still be met where the rotting, crow-pecked bones had fallen and lain unburied."

Here, however, the boys have a true surprise:

> Then they stopped short, and even their stout hearts quailed.
> For, lying stretched out beneath the tree, white as cardboard,
> stiff as a wooden doll, was the deadest looking dead man that
> ever ghost charaded with.

The corpse is a "dead old reprobate" known as "'Rabbit-Skins.'" While they are shaken, the boys decide the thing to do is to bury him right there. Apparently the sandy soil cooperates, and after considerable effort the boys complete the burial before bolting away, chased by the risen (in their imaginations) Rabbit-Skins.

Meanwhile, Pepper and Doozle have had their own adventures. Pepper had driven twenty-two geese into the dining room and left them to feed on the carpet. This had not gone over well with the authorities, and he had been soundly spanked. When he is in bed, Doozle brings him a meringue which he eats without audible gratitude. He continues to treat her coldly. He comes up with a plan to bottle lightning. Doozle helps him to the extent she can, but when it comes time to wave the looking-glass, she, though "'dreadfully sorry,'" won't do it. When asked why, she says, "'I'm afraid.'" (This reminds us of the adult Gwendoline Keats, for whom truth is always so sparkling a virtue in her books.) Doozle's reward is the single, italicized word "'*Girl!*'" from Pepper.

A clap of thunder drives Doozle under the bed-clothes, but the lightning is not bottled, for which Pepper blames Doozle because she had not done what he told her. Another flash of lightning comes, and when Pepper asks Doozle what she is doing under the bed-clothes, we read, "'Praying that the lightning mayn't be bottled,' she answered truthfully.' (More truth from Doozle!) Pepper tries to chase her out of the room. But "the sky caught fire and blew up with the most awful bang that two children were ever asked to listen to," and even Pepper begins to be more than a little shy of his bottling machine. Doozle says she is praying, but Pepper refuses to join her in that endeavor. Doozle begs him to pray before it is too late, but Pepper refuses. Frightened white, the boy

> sat down on a chair, his small brown feet and legs drawn up under him, and it would be hard to tell what took place in Pepper's heart just then: yet one cannot but think that there was something fine in that stern refusal of his to seek God's protection.

The storm gradually draws off, and the two children sleep. Gimlet and his older brother return and see them sleeping.

> The Thoughty Ones gazed down on the small, ignorant brother and sister with eyes new washed by experience. "Ignorant as kittens," they murmured.
> Two at least of the Thoughty Ones awoke the next morning in a state of mind that might best be described as bursting to

tell and bursting not to tell; a most painful predicament to be in with a lot of joy attached to it. At last they told Pepper, and Doozle came in for the fag end of a fact here and there,—just such scrappy bits of information as is thrown out by little boys for little girls to build up a new heaven and a new earth as best they may.

The "four children spent an enjoyable afternoon in making preparations to resist the police." This includes winding a rope around Doozle's legs so that if the others are captured and in prison she can visit them and allow them to make their escape by means of the rope. The rope is heavy, causes her to wobble, and makes her legs sore. Doozle asks for relief, but all three Thoughty ones shout "'Girl!'" at her. Finally, however, they agree that she can take off the rope until it is needed. She swears her oath to follow through on using the rope when necessary for their rescue, and though called a "'cry baby,'" is permitted to take the rope off for the moment.

They build a fort in the woods, but the gardener

raked down the fort; and as it had taken three days to build and had been held to be impregnable, its demolition came as a surprise to the Thoughty Ones, and like most surprises that overtook them, proved to be unpleasant.

The next day they send Pepper as a spy to the village, to see what measures the police were taking, and whether Rabbit-Skins was missed. Pepper returns with the information that no one has even missed the dead man, but his older brothers are unimpressed with his spying activities and consider that he either has been taken in or made a fool of himself. (This is actually quite unfair; Pepper seems to have done an excellent job of spying!) He is accused of being a girl, and told that he will have to go into the housemaid's cupboard. "It was etiquette among the Thoughty Ones to accept the inevitable with stoicism." Doozle wanders by at just the wrong time, and is thrust into the cupboard with Pepper, so that Pepper "might see for himself exactly what he was like"—that is, a girl. "Several years passed away" and eventually Doozle sneezes, which results in an enraged housemaid chasing them out of the cupboard.

The Thoughty Ones take Doozle captive as a witch.

> She was conducted to the horse pond that it might be ascertained whether she would sink or swim, Doozle alone of the party cherishing no illusion as to which of the two she would be found to do on trial.

However, she is spared that ordeal, as Pepper has seen the policeman Kelly in the road. (In passing we note the presence of the phrase "on trial" in the last portion quoted. It shows up at least one other place in her books, not counting its use as the title of one of them.) The three boys steal away to have a look at Kelly, who is behaving calmly enough. They decide that Kelly needs to be shadowed. The eldest Thoughty One decides to take on the responsibility for this delicate task. He returns an hour later, with no particular news. Gimlet suggests the idea of giving themselves up as murderers. This meets general approval, but working out the details proves difficult. Gimlet is uneasy at the idea of firing at Rabbit-Skins through the ground. They finally decide that they poisoned him with rats' poison. This might "'stick'" the policeman Kelly.

> They found Kelly having his tea. A small baby bubbling noisily was balanced on one of the man's big thighs, while opposite to him sat his wife. Sarah Kelly had been nurse to each of the Thoughty Ones in turn, and she loved them with a fervour which a wide knowledge of their shortcomings served rather to augment than diminish.

In the official records for the civil parish of Northam, Devon for 1871, the information for Port Hill, the home of the Keats family, all the Keats family are there including Gwendoline (as Bertha G., who would turn 6 years old on Oct. 4, 1871). The seven servants are listed by name. The oldest is one Sarah G. Kelly, age 30, nurse. She was listed as unmarried, and as having been born in Northam. This woman must have made an impression on Gwendoline Keats. Thirty years later she paid tribute to her by putting her in the story "Thoughty." Zack's description of her and Sarah's subsequent actions show her to be a very kindly lady with a vast affection for the children.

Sarah tempts the three boys with potato cake for tea.

Pepper and Gimlet glowed, but the eldest Thoughty One, though by no means indifferent to the attraction of potato cake, waved back the proferred dainty.

"I don't think, Sarah, that we ought to take it."

"Why not, for ever no, then?" said Sarah. "It's piping hot and a touch heavy, just to a turn how you like it best."

Pepper at once rose from his chair and helped himself to a big bit of cake; Gimlet looked uncomfortable, and the eldest Thoughty One determined.

"Thank you, Sarah," he said; "but I don't think any of us feel like cake just now," and he cast a vicious glance at Pepper as he spoke.

Sarah smiled as she put the cake back on the table. "La, and how like yourself you are in everything," she remarked. "You always was one for having your play out first no matter what it cost 'ee."

"It is likely to cost us a good deal this time," said the eldest Thoughty One, gloomily, for he had begun to believe that he had killed Rabbit-Skins.

"Why," exclaimed Sarah, "whatever have 'ee all done now?"

"Well—Pepper is not in it; there'll be one of us at any rate who'll escape the gallows."

"Gallows indeed!" repeated Sarah sharply. "Don't you tell up none o' such stuff. Thoughty you always was, and God help 'ee, always will be; but murder never."

The eldest Thoughty One confesses that they killed Rabbit-Skins, and buried him under the Felon's Tree. The other two boys back him up. Kelly begins to believe that he should at least investigate at the gravesite, if there is one, but Sarah remains unconvinced that anything at all has happened. The boys leave the house. The story ends as follows:

"Let us steal a boat and get out of this," said the eldest Thoughty One.

They did so, and shipped two days' provisions and the breech-loader on board, the stable-bucket for water-cask, and the cat as live stock. They tore up Doozle's black velvet frock for a flag and cut a skull and cross-bones out of the tail of Pepper's shirt, and then, just as the sun began to set, they sailed away.

"Oh, where are you going to?" cried Doozle, who was left behind to play the woman's part, and be ready waiting to hear all about things afterwards.

"Out beyond the other ships," said Pepper.

"Oh, tell me what it will be like?" cried Doozle.

"You couldn't understand if we told," said Pepper.

"Oh, please, please tell," cried Doozle.

"It is *the feeling*," said Pepper, and hoisting sail the Thoughty Ones sailed away, out beyond the other ships, just the Thoughty Ones, the boat, and the feeling and not a soul beside.

There is great humor in the story, but more than humor is going on here. The Thoughty Ones are out of touch with reality, but they also have a "code of honour" in which they strive toward some romantic vision according to the light that is in them.

The boys' treatment of Doozle is almost completely rotten. In fact, in these politically correct times, the boys might be in danger of being arrested and sentenced to at least psychiatric intervention. However, if we view their behavior from a long view, we can see that the boys want to be brave. For that we can respect them. Girl represents lack of courage in their vision. This is completely unfair, we might well think. In fact, Europe was less than a dozen years away from blowing its silly brains out beginning in 1914, largely because the men of Christ's church had not developed a vision of courage which was in touch with reality. The boys would have been better advised to develop a chivalrous attitude toward their sister, perhaps imitating the generous spirit of Buster to Flipperty.

So, there are consequences for thinking wrong, and acting wrong. Doozle deserves better, as the women of Europe deserved better from the supposedly "thoughty" male leaders of their countries.

In fact, World War I would have great personal significance for the Keats family. While Gwendoline Keats would not know it—she was either dead or insane—her family would pay a heavy price for Europe's suicidal war. Her oldest brother Thorold Goodwin Keats had seven children. The fifth child, William Thorold, "suffered from the effects of gassing in WW1," we are told by Mrs. Beverley Keats. This seems to have affected William far beyond the war years.

The family of Zack's second brother Fred (Gimlet?) paid an even higher price. Fred had five children. The third child and second son, John Rochfort Keats, joined the military while at Cambridge in England. He was wounded, but later returned to the front lines despite being offered the chance to go home for good. Eventually he was awarded the British Military Cross. The Military Cross was instituted late in 1914 as a means of recognizing "gallantry in the field" by junior officers. (Since 1993 the MC has been available to other ranks as well.)

But there is worse news to report. John Rochfort Keats' older brother, the second child and first son, Frederick Thorold Keats (named for his father and for his father's older brother) also was at Cambridge when the war broke out; he enlisted. He was killed in action May 25, 1916.

Doozle is a sort of odd girl out, in the company of her three brothers. She is a gentle young lady, not given to rebellious anger. She takes what they hand out, striving to fit into their male world. She is imaginative, and heroically honest. She is quite an interesting young lady indeed. We wonder how closely the young Doozle represents the young Gwendoline Keats. Was Gwenda too spurned as "'*Girl!*'"?

If so, her life was not ruined. She grew up to be one of the finest writers of her era, a writer who deserves to be read as long as the world endures. Perhaps her struggles to fit into her brothers' lives helped her develop courage and persistence in life.

There seems to be an irony here. And Zack herself may well have understood that irony, when looking back as an adult. The three boys intend to sail "'Out beyond the other ships,'" and they leave Doozle on the shore. Doozle supposedly cannot even understand what it will be like. And yet, in real life, Gwendoline Keats was the one who sailed out beyond the other ships. She has given us "'*the feeling*'" from where she sails out beyond the other ships, just Gwendoline, "the boat, and the feeling and not a soul beside."

The Roman Road is certainly the least significant of Zack's books. It has moments of greatness, paragraphs and lines which are striking. It has one really good story, and two much longer stories which are not close to being her best work. If this had been her only book, we might remember her only as a curious writer who showed promise but never fulfilled it. (If we remembered her at all, of course—which we haven't yet got around to doing.)

But we have seen the reasons for her faltering, and we won't whine too much that the book is not up to her usual mark. She fulfilled her promise, giving us four outstanding books in four years. We should be grateful for those books, and be glad that at least we can see gleams of greatness in her last one.

CHAPTER 6

By Noble Things She Stands

Strength and dignity are her clothing,
And she smiles at the future.
She opens her mouth in wisdom,
And the teaching of kindness is on her tongue.
She looks well to the ways of her household,
And does not eat the bread of idleness.
Her children rise up and bless her;
Her husband also, and he praises her, saying:
"Many daughters have done nobly,
But you excel them all."
Charm is deceitful and beauty is vain,
But a woman who fears the LORD, she shall be praised.
Give her the product of her hands,
And let her works praise her in the gates.

Proverbs 31:25-31

There is nobility to the character and writing of Gwendoline Keats/ Zack. That made it an easy choice for a title to this book. Chapter 32 of the book of Isaiah tells us about the "knaveries of the knave" (v. 7), and contrasts the knave's behavior with that of the noble person. "But he who is noble devises noble things,/and by noble things he stands" (Isa. 32:8). That sentence is the epigraph to the book as a whole.

Gwendoline Keats has devised noble things, and by noble things she stands.

Many of her stories are deeply moving. They reveal people at a testing point. We are all "on trial" in life. We often fail the trial, and so do many of her characters. But for Zack, failure is not necessarily the end. From failure we can pick ourselves up, and go forward with courage. Maybe, as Termater Bill tells us, we can find color across the Divide. But it is maybe—not definitely yes. Life is what it is, not what we wish it to be.

Zack was a woman who thought for herself. That puts her very much out of touch with the spirit of our age. We are collectivists, who reduce all of life to sordid lies about how civil governments should steal from productive people and give the substance to poor people (or to needy "too big to fail" incompetent banksters). She, on the other hand, was an individualist, who saw people as being free and responsible for their actions. This may be part of the reason she has been temporarily forgotten. But if it is, there may be good news for her. The age of collectivism is rapidly drawing to a close. (Well, maybe not as rapidly as I could wish!) Collectivism has proven to be a false god. It has made thieves and liars of us all, and it is close to bankrupting us as thoroughly in financial terms as we have been bankrupted in moral terms. The approaching collapse of the despicable welfare state may well herald the beginning of a new age of freedom and responsibility. In that new world, a writer like Zack may begin to be appreciated.

Our collectivist age assumes strikers are automatically right in what they do. Zack knows better. Humphrey is an individual, and will not follow a multitude to do evil (Ex. 23:2). It costs him his eyesight. We know this is not because Humphrey is wrong—it happens because horrible things really do happen in life, sad ironies really do occur.

Who would dare to put in a word defending the possible usefulness of wife-beating? Zack has one of her most admirable characters, a victim of her husband's blows in earlier parts of their marriage, speak that objective word. This does not mean Zack approved of wife-beating. (In fact in *Tales of Dunstable Weir* the villager Zack contrasts the behavior of his own village, Dunstable Weir, where they don't beat their wives, with the less honorable men of Dore Apple, where they beat their wives regularly.) What it does mean is that Zack knows life is strange and subtle.

How many people, even today after a hundred years of disaster, have figured out that public education is not really a proper duty of a civil government? But we have reason to hope Zack figured it out, late in the 19th century.

It is difficult to believe that there is another writer on this planet—leaving out of the competition the Scripture writers who were guided by the Holy Spirit Himself—who has done more to point out for us the way toward the reconciliation of the classes. She wrote often of people of the poorer classes. They are always individuals with characters good and bad, responsible for their actions. The book of Proverbs tells us what Zack instinctively understood: "The rich and the poor have a common bond,/The LORD is the maker of them all" (Prov. 22:2). Since we all are made in the image of God (Gen. 1:27; 5:1-2), we all must answer to God for what we make of this great but challenging gift to us.

Nobility of behavior, Zack sensed or actively understood, is how the classes can meet one another on common ground. Joe's wife/widow is definitely a woman of a lower class origin; she is an aristocrat in her thoughts and principles. It is no accident that Humphrey, the son of a lower class man and of a (raped) poor gentlewoman but raised as part of the gentry and himself a gentleman in spirit, so readily calls Joe's widow "'mother.'" It is very fitting.

There is nothing sentimental or dishonest in Zack's vision of how we all become upper class. It will happen through hard work and humble action, or it won't happen. The mother of young Zack in "The Hall and He" wants to see the "'quality'" become "'Tenderful for others,'" and young Zack in his spiritual blindness laughs at such a notion. Why, "'I could be thic myself,'" young Zack says. Precisely. Young Zack misses the point—and so does the squire in that story, who fails to be tenderful for others.

Gwendoline Keats came from a class of very well to do people. Her grandfather was an admiral, her father a captain of rifle volunteers and a gentleman farmer. When young she lived in a beautiful house with seven servants. Once she began publishing stories as an adult her friends and acquaintances were the intellectual elite of her time. But from earliest consciousness she must have been very aware of the individual personalities of the poorer people around her. Thirty years after she was a child, she put her childhood nurse, by name, into her last published story—and Sarah Kelly is an admirable character in that story, and someone with a distinct personality.

I think it is fair to say that novelists notice things. That is part of what makes them novelists. Young Gwendoline noticed that poor people who were uneducated or slightly educated were individuals with moral dimensions equal to those of people of higher social class. When she grew up to write she noticed it better perhaps than any other writer who ever lived.

She noticed a lot more than that, however. Her stories are filled with wise insights into human nature.

We are enslaved to debt, as nations and as individual people. Zack proclaimed the foolishness of debt, over a century ago.

Zack's vision of how the world was put together was shaped by the Bible and by Christianity. This too puts her out of tune with the spirit of our age, for in our sophisticated wisdom we have turned our backs on the Bible and on the Christian faith—and our civilization lies in ruins around us as a result. Which is another sign that Zack's time of appreciation may yet come. When we humble ourselves and turn back to God, we may be able to appreciate a vision of how reality is put together which centers on God, His Christ, and His Bible.

We have come through a time in which people of revolutionary temperament rejected the truths of the Bible. And now, ironically, we are in a time in which the most radical intellectual and moral stance one can take is to stand uncompromisingly with the God of the Bible. It is not politically correct to do so, of course. But it is the brave and principled thing to do.

This is not to say that we can speak with certainty about Zack's personal religious faith. Her writing was instinctively shaped by the Bible, however. She was very alert to the fact that good is good, and evil is evil. God's views on which is which, shaped her views. If there were times she went wrong in her theology, then she paid a price, as we always do when we go wrong. If she was a believer—and I am not ready to move definitively beyond the word if—it may have been as a believer with some odd crotchets in her theology. If I had to guess, I think she was in some sense a Christian. I can't prove this, however. Maybe because I have such love and respect for her books and for her character, I want her to share my own religious faith and so have allowed myself to be self-deceived about her own faith.

She must have been temperamentally more in tune with the Church of England than with dissenters. At least three times in her writings she pokes gentle fun at the chapelites.

She wrote with great humor. Her humor is varied, sometimes but not always dark. The writer that comes to mind when ones thinks of dark humor is Fyoder Dostoyevsky. She is a worthy sister to that great novelist, in her humor.

A great part of her writing is in the dialect of her original Devonshire home. (One entire book is written in the Devon dialect by the villager Zack.) This too may have contributed to her becoming forgotten. Reading the dialect takes a bit of work. We are not always completely sure what is being said. Mankind usually loves to take the easy path, and reading the dialect is not always easy. But doing the work is well repaid, and at times the characters speak Devon dialect phrases which are wonderfully lovely and memorable.

She was a master of colorful phrases. Countless lines of her writing seem excellent candidates for long-term fame—once the world knows about them.

Above all the strength of her writing is in the willingness to look the truth squarely in the eyes and not blink. It is quite appropriate that the very title of her first book indicates her heroic commitment to honesty. *Life Is Life* is the book's title, and the phrase says a great deal about her outlook on how we should live: "'when a thing *is*, what does us gain by saying it isn't?'" as Joe's widow tells us. It may seem an obvious truth, but it is far from obvious that we understand that truth and take it to heart. We can easily spend most of our lives mired in self-deception. Self-deception seems easier. Zack points us toward honesty.

Of her personal life we know too little. We have evidence enough to pick up on a few things, however.

Apparently she could act in a hasty manner which led her to problems. Act hastily now, and repent at leisure, seems to sum up her behavior at times. We have at least five pieces of evidence that she could act recklessly.

The first is the very fact that she was driving six-horse carriages at warp speed! This was dangerous. It might be characterized as brave, but more accurately can be called foolhardy. It cost her a devastating spill which hampered at least her ability to see well. It is possible that the blow to her head also led to brain damage which ultimately cost her her sanity.

The second piece of evidence is in one of her letters to May Sinclair. In about the thirteenth of her letters to May, her last sentence before the closing reads, "I am so sorry that I said or thought hard things about you."[48] That's all. We can only guess at what went before. But Zack felt the need to apologize, so she must have said or written something that would have been better left unsaid.

Another later letter to May Sinclair provides us with our third indication of hastiness. Zack writes,

> Thinking over the Outlook, I felt miserable that I had been capable of believing there had been any spite in their criticism—after all, they only said exactly the same as the British Weekly & many others.
>
> Please write & tell me that you will forget every word that I said on the subject, & never mention it to a living soul.
>
> Why, why, <u>why</u> should not the Outlook be free to dislike my work the same as other folk.[49]

That represents almost all of the letter. There is one other sentence at the beginning, the salutation, the closing, and the return address. But most of the letter was devoted to her sorrow at having expressed what on looking back Zack felt was an unjust opinion. Write or speak in haste, repent at leisure.

Many of Zack's letters to May Sinclair are short, with closings in some form of "Great haste" or "Yours in haste." She seems to have felt hurried, often. That is our fourth hint that Zack could act perhaps too hurriedly.

We come now to the fifth evidence of Zack's occasional hastiness of behavior. It is by far the most serious proof of all. The letter is from her oldest brother, Thorold Goodwin Keats. He was writing from his home is Australia. His wife is the Jessie mentioned. The letter was dated Dec. 15th, 1899, and addressed to Miss Keats, 31 Sloane Square, London,

---

[48]Zack letter to May Sinclair, July 8, 1898.
[49]Zack letter to May Sinclair, Sept. 5, 1898.

S.W.. The letter is a transcription. There may have been some unreadable words. (I have at many places struggled to read Zack's handwriting in her letters to May Sinclair, and her brother's handwriting may have been similarly difficult to read.) Also, we sense that T. G. Keats may have been writing quickly, if for the most part calmly. Whatever uncertainty we might have about a word or phrase here and there, the meaning of the letter comes through crystal clear.

My dear Gwenda,

Jessie has received a letter from you dated (postmark) Nov 3rd 99, with reference to your Jewellery. I do not think it is necessary for me to tell you that it was one of the most offensive epistles it has ever been my misfortune to read & I cannot believe that you could have written it seriously thinking of what you were saying, I am answering it myself as Jessie refuses to do so, & quite rightly. As regards your Jewellery. When you left England in 1891, you were not there & I placed your Jewellery with my plate at the Bank of Australasia London, with a letter enumerating the various articles, so as in the event of anything happening to me there would be no difficulty in your getting your own. There are however a few trinkets of no particular intrinsic value in a safe with some things of mine stored at Dymonds Bideford. I enclose an order to my Bankers in London to deliver to you, on the necessary receipts for same all the Jewellery stored with them as anything there (not plate) is yours & G. Thorold will give you that stored at Dymonds. Now you could have obtained all this without writing such a letter which practically accuses my wife of retaining your goods & as you are kind enough to with the idea that you could not sell them & thus at some remote date they would be lost to my children, & you also emphasise this by saying "(that unless you tell me where my Jewellery is so that I may obtain it at once I will leave every bit of Jewellery away from the children)" such an insinuation is simply beneath contempt. You gave (as perhaps you may remember) a turquoise brooch to Gladys some years ago, in order to avoid any future unpleasantness I am returning as no doubt you will write & say in time stolen it.

You letter shows a very curious frame of mind. In the first place you practically accuse Jessie of obtaining your jewellery for the reason given on preceding page, in the next line you hope that it won't raise any ill-feeling between you. You must have by this time sufficient knowledge of the world to know that when you accuse an innocent person of practically being a thief & that for the most sordid of purposes they are not likely to return the other cheek for you to smite. However you will receive by this mail the necessary order to obtain your Jewellery which has simply been taken care of at your own request & in your best interests & I hope you will feel that you have acted very rashly & without any though of other peoples feelings.

I cannot believe that you would have written such a letter otherwise than on the spur of the moment, if you had only written asking for the articles you would have got them at once, but now you have deeply offended Jessie for no reason whatever.

Your aff. Brother

T.G.Keats

P.S. I enclose the original letter written by me at Halsdon re your effects so as you can see for yourself the ... ...[unreadable portion?] of the whole transaction.[50]

A brief note to a slightly different address for Gwendoline, possibly from a later date or possibly from the same date, gives further instructions in regard to obtaining the jewelry from the bank and from Dymonds in Bideford. Bideford is a town in Devon very close to Northam. Gwendoline Keats was born at her family's home, Port Hill, outside of Northam.

Receiving such a letter must have been, for Gwendoline Keats, like receiving a blow to the stomach which takes your breath away. She must have known instantly that she had done wrong in writing her own letter to Jessie Keats. We can only wonder at what prompted her to write a letter accusing her sister-in-law of having stolen her jewelry. Had there been some friction between the two, so that Gwendoline felt no great affection for Jessie and instinctively jumped at the chance to say something insulting?

T. G. Keats is correct in pointing out the "curious frame of mind" which allowed Gwendoline to accuse her sister-in-law of theft, while in the next line hoping it won't cause any ill feeling between them. And this from a woman who had already published two books which sometimes show a very subtle understanding of human nature! But we none of us are always consistently at our best.

---

[50] T. G. Keats letter to Gwendoline Keats, Dec. 15, 1899.

The tone of T. G. Keats is worthy of mention. He writes in a straightforward manner, but without bitter anger. He explains how Gwendoline can readily get her jewelry, which had been placed in safekeeping for her, at the Australasia Bank and at Dymonds. He defends his wife forthrightly, as he well should have done, and doesn't pull any punches about how offensive he finds his sister's letter. He returns the brooch which Gwendoline had given to his daughter Gladys, to forestall the possibility that one day Gwendoline will say the brooch had been stolen. (We wonder in passing how this was explained to Gladys, who was age 13 by that time. Gladys must have been sad and confused to have the turquoise brooch which had been given to her by her Aunt Gwenda, taken from her.) But he calls her "My dear Gwenda" and closes as "Your aff. Brother," and he says that Gwendoline could not seriously have been thinking what she was saying, and must have written on the spur of the moment. It seems to me a letter showing a good deal of emotional maturity in T. G. Keats. The oldest "Thoughty One" must have loved his sister—he and Jessie had named one of their children partly after Gwendoline (Margaret Gwendoline, born 1895)—and must have wanted to maintain fellowship with her despite her wrongheaded letter.

Occasional hasty behavior, then, must have been part of the character of Gwendoline Keats. Write or speak in haste, repent at leisure, must have been her mode of operation at various times. We can only hope that she mended her relationship with her brother and his wife. We know that a bit over four years later T. G. Keats was hoping to come up with 50 pounds a year—no small sum in the days before inflation destroyed much of the value of the pound—or possibly even more, to help provide for Gwendoline's keep at a private lunatic asylum rather than a public one.

Another aspect of the character of Gwendoline Keats is her restlessness. She never settled down to live in one place for very long. We know that as a young woman she visited Germany, Italy, and of course Australia. Once she began to publish her stories, she moved around constantly. In 1898 alone—it is the first year for which we have her letters to May Sinclair—we find her moving around in a most astonishing fashion. Not all the letters have return addresses. Of those that do, she stayed in 15 different places during the course of the year. Three letters came from the same location in Florence, Italy. In some cases she stayed in one place, moved away, and came back to the previous place—a good sign that she was paying her bills each time, since she was welcomed back.

There were fewer letters in 1899, but she still managed to live in eight different places, including Italy and Ireland. There are only two letters from 1900—from two different places, one of which was a replay of a previous location. (Again, evidence that she paid her bills.)

Another letter, for which I am unable to find a date, she writes from Scotland.

The year 1901 finds her living the longest in one place—eight letters over half a year or so came from the same address in Carlow, Ireland. She also spent time in Derbyshire, and by the end of the year was in Buckinghamshire.

Her mobility seems to reduce in the final two years for which we have letters. She stayed in Buckinghamshire shire during 1902, albeit in two different locations, first in the village of Loudwater, then later in Amersham. And her only three letters in 1903 also come from the town of Amersham in Buckinghamshire. Perhaps her restlessness was wearing out, as was her body, mind, and spirit.

Only one of the letters was written from Devon. Her second and final letter of 1902 has a return address of The Villa, Westward Ho!, Bideford. Bideford is near Northam and Port Hill, her parents' home and her place of birth.

Her emotional roots are in Devon. She was profoundly tied to Devonshire—to its dialect, its people, and probably to her memory of her home life. Some of her home life memories must have been very sad. Her sister Augusta Julia was born, lived about ten days, and died, when Gwendoline was five years old. Her father died when she was a month short of her seventh birthday. Her mother remarried, but died when Gwendoline was 15 ½ years old. When Gwendoline left Devon, she seems to have returned only rarely. But Devon flowed in her veins the rest of her life. Devon is part of what makes her writing so unique.

We may wonder how Zack managed to move around a lot, and still pay her bills. Yes, she had income from her writing, but it does not seem to have been huge. In her letters to May Sinclair, she occasionally describes herself as penniless. We have a hint to the possible answer, in a letter Zack wrote from Dresden to her sister-in-law Jessie Keats. The letter is undated, but it must have been well before the time when Zack was insulting Jessie and being rebuked by her brother in return. We know that Zack was in Dresden in 1892, the year that artist Friedrich Anton Otto Prölss painted her portrait. (T. G. Keats' letter, quoted above, mentions that Gwenda left England in 1891.) Her salutation is to "My dear old Jess," and she says later in the brief letter, "I have got so awfully fond of you—what an abominable time it will be when all the family take itself off to foreign climes." Foreign climes means especially Australia, where Zack's three brothers spent most of their adult lives.

Zack writes, "Respecting the £10, will you allow me to pay you from my next allowance in November, as I have had rather a lot to pay lately." So it seems quite possible that Zack continued to receive an allowance all her life. Her family had been well to do. Zack was born at the lovely country home Port Hill, where the family was waited on by seven servants. When her parents died, there may have been considerable wealth which eventually came to the children. Their mother had remarried, but the second husband, Admiral Edward Charlewood, did not inherit Port Hill. We know that the admiral had to vacate the home when Thorold Goodwin Keats reached age 21. (It seems that T. G. Keats was not fond of his stepfather.)

Thanks to the researches of Mrs. Beverley Keats, we now know the extent of the Port Hill property, and its very significant value. Thanks to information provided by Mrs. Keats, I was able to track down on the Internet, where it appears printed in full, the 1883 (4th edition) of *Great Landowners of Great Britain*. On page 247, T. G. Keats of Port Hill, Devon, is recorded as owning 2,664 acres with a gross annual value of £3,030. Clearly this was a very valuable property. T. G. Keats reached his majority, age 21, on Jan. 29, 1882.

Mrs. Keats says that her researches in family history lead her to believe that it was "the tendency for the eldest son to inherit." This, however, does not necessarily leave Gwendoline out in the cold. I think the probability is that T. G. Keats would have been expected to share the income with his three siblings, and I think that is exactly what happened. The "next allowance" of which Gwendoline wrote in her letter to Jessie Keats, must have come from money proceeding directly or indirectly from the valuable Port Hill property. From where else could the money have come?

Whether T. G. Keats sold the property eventually, or managed it, either way the income involved would be fairly large. Enormous wealth was not in question. The gross annual value of £3,030 does not mean that so much money came in every year. There would have been taxes. There were four siblings to receive a part. If T. G. Keats tried to manage the property from Australia, that would have been very difficult. If on the other hand he sold the property and received interest, the amount probably would have been fairly large, but again, not enormous. These details aside, still we can see that there was a potential for Gwendoline to have received an allowance her entire adult life.

We remember also that in the same letter in which T. G. discussed with Fred Gwendoline's insanity, he told his brother "I enclose a dividend for you although small it is probably the first you have received for some time." So apparently the money was still coming in from Port Hill one way or another, but the amount may have been small and dropping gradually, and perhaps coming in irregularly. And the sentence clearly shows that T. G. was sharing with his brother and it is fair to assume that Gwendoline had been receiving money right along as well. The amounts may have been small—we remember that Gwendoline sometimes described herself as "penniless" to May Sinclair—but we can assume that, when added to income from her books and stories, the allowance money was very important in permitting her to live and to travel extensively, and to pay her bills.

Very probably she often had to count her pennies carefully—witness the fact that she asks to delay repaying her sister-in-law £10—but until we have more complete information about her daily life we can at least guess that an allowance from the family treasure is what gave Zack the leisure to write books. She didn't have to go out and find a job. So when Zack called herself penniless in writing to May Sinclair, she was no doubt exercising hyperbole. She meant that she didn't have a lot of money. She seems to have been in no danger of figuring out where her next meal was coming from.

There is another possible source of income mentioned in the same letter. Zack says she has received permission "to translate Seidel's last novel." Seidel may mean German engineer, poet, and writer Heinrich Seidel (1842-1906), chiefly known for his children's stories and fairy tales. Apparently she did this translation with a partner, because she says "we have nearly finished it." She says she hopes "to make a little tin" by the experience (or experiment) and adds "at any rate there is no harm in these pauper times in trying to earn an honest penny."[51] So it is at least possible that she earned money doing occasional translating, at least in her young adulthood. That she had enough confidence in her skill in German to translate something for publication into English, shows that she must have had an excellent head for the foreign language. Did she begin her study back at Port Hill as a child or young woman, or only after she began living in Dresden? We don't know.

She seems to have been active physically. Along with the driving of six-horse carriages, which eventually led to such drastic results, we know that she was a bicyclist. In one letter she thanks May Sinclair for having sent her a bicycle.[52] (So she had money enough to pay for the purchase and shipping of a bicycle.) A month and a half later she is hoping to join May at Hampstead (the part of London in which May lived) to "go for a long bicycle ride someday."[53] Another letter indicates what seems to have been part of her routine at the time—she was "out all day bicycling."[54] (In the same letter she writes that "I never see the ghost of a paper here." Much of her life was spent in similar places. She was a town and country mouse rather than a city mouse. We may be reminded of Doozle singing to herself, "'I am so happy when I am alone.'")

The epigraph to this chapter quotes part of Proverbs 31, famous in biblical circles for describing the ideal virtuous wife and mother. Zack was neither wife nor mother, of course, but at least part of the

---

[51]Zack letter to Jessie Keats (her sister-in-law), undated (probably early 1890s), written from Räcknitz Strasse, Dresden, Germany. Her closing reads "Your affec Sister, Gwenda Keats."
[52]Zack letter to May Sinclair, Sept. 13, 1899.
[53]Zack letter to May Sinclair, Oct. 28, 1899.
[54]Zack letter to May Sinclair, Oct. 4, 1898.

description seems to apply to her. Let's look at some of the sentences, and see if they fit.

"Strength and dignity are her clothing,/And she smiles at the future." Zack was a strong woman indeed. She wrote what she wanted to write, and didn't worry too much about what other people had to say in response. She sensed, and sensed correctly, that she had to follow her own vision for what she should write. She knew it was what she could honestly do, and that would have to be good enough. There is of course strength and dignity in such a notion—at least there is if the writing is good, which it certainly was.

Does she smile at the future? Many of her stories are about human failure. There is much sadness. Death, quick or lingering, is commonplace. (This of course mirrors her experience in losing her family members early in her life.) Many of her characters act wrongly, and pay a price. But I think at bottom there is an optimism to her outlook. It is not an easy optimism, certainly! Failure and sin are constant. But honesty and courage permit her characters to face the future. Dave knows there is something beside the dog in his character, and so rather than kill himself as he had planned, he turns his face, not his back, on life.

"She opens her mouth in wisdom,/And the teaching of kindness is on her tongue." Many parts of her writing show great wisdom. Was she kind? Her books show a generosity of spirit toward people which must somehow be related to kindness. Hasty she could sometimes be, but at the core of her character there was a desire to be fair to all people. Most of her wicked, erring, or foolish characters need not worry that she will forget their good or admirable qualities. For one example among many, Mrs. Groot, guilty of adultery in her young adulthood, and rather a shallow person in her middle age, is given full credit for her virtue of courage in the face of approaching death.

Her kindness seems to be demonstrated in her relationship with May Sinclair. May Sinclair is a writer who is today much better known than Zack. She has attracted two relatively recent book length scholarly studies. Both scholars acknowledge Zack's role in encouraging Sinclair. Theophilus Boll tells us, 'A new friend who was to be of great importance to May Sinclair in raising her often drooping morale was "Zack," really

Gwendoline Keats, short story writer and novelist of Devon.'[55] Boll goes on to cite quite a few instances of Zack's encouraging words to her friend. He is quite accurate—all these comments are in Zack's letters. Among other things, she tells May that May's "work is good"[56] (is underlined once, good underlined twice), that May will "one day make a great name"[57] for herself, that it is absolutely certain that May will succeed in the long run, and in the same letter that May is one of "the real big 'uns" who "always have to face hell first of all."[58] These are just a few of many comments with which Zack encouraged May. Suzanne Rait's book on May Sinclair speaks of Zack's "loyal support" of her friend.[59]

There is a certain irony here. May Sinclair is fairly well known in our day, and has attracted book length attention from two scholars. There is a May Sinclair Society website on the Internet, for those people especially interested in her books. In contrast, *By Noble Things She Stands* seems to be the first lengthy attempt in over a hundred years to direct readers to the almost completely forgotten Zack. There have been a few (very few) brief and respectful mentions of Zack by scholars along the way, and we will come to them later in the chapter, but compared to May Sinclair she is vastly unknown. I think Zack would be disappointed to know that her own work has been forgotten, as any writer would be! But I don't think she would have begrudged May Sinclair her measure of fame. Zack was a generous-spirited person not given to envy. It is no stretch to describe her as having "the teaching of kindness" on her tongue.

"She looks well to the ways of her household,/And does not eat the bread of idleness." Zack's only household was herself. From hints in

---

[55] Boll, *Miss May Sinclair*, etc. p. 56.

[56] Zack letter to May Sinclair. The month and year of this letter are pretty certain. It was written in July of 1899, from Ireland. Boll believes the letter was written on July 14, 1899. It might have been July 5. Boll had the advantage of having seen the letters in their original form; I have seen them only as photocopies. In some cases I am unsure which envelopes go with which letters, etc.

[57] Zack letter to May Sinclair, Feb. 16, 1899.

[58] Zack letter to May Sinclair, Oct. 12, 1899.

[59] Suzanne Rait, *May Sinclair: A Modern Victorian*, New York, New York and Oxford, England, Oxford University Press, Inc., 2000, p. 81.

her letters, it does seem that she paid her bills. That is no small thing, it seems to me, and if you've ever been cheated by people who don't pay their bills, you might agree.

It is difficult to say how diligently she used her time. But we know that she worked diligently enough to publish five books in six years. They are short books, granted, but four of them are excellent books. I think most writers would feel like they had accomplished something to write so many excellent books in such a period of time, even though the books were short. Their relative lack of length does not stop them from being complete works of art.

'Her children rise up and bless her;/Her husband also, and he praises her, saying:/"Many daughters have done nobly,/But you excel them all."' Zack had neither husband nor children. Unless we say: her husband was her muse, and the five books she brought forth were her children. They are legitimate children, and possess an honorable character. The readers of her children have been few, but time has not yet come to a stop. Perhaps more than one or two will eventually arise to bless Zack. We are reminded of the Ethiopian eunuch. He had no wife and no children, in physical terms. But he has had many spiritual offspring down through the centuries, among people who have been taught and moved by his story (Acts 8:26-39; compare the eunuch Ebed-melech of Jeremiah 38:6-13; 39:15-18).

Does she excel them all? Well, one husband praised his wife in Proverbs 31. Another husband might argue and say, "No, *my* wife excels them all." The fact is that there can be a million, ten million, one hundred million, or a billion wives who are wonderfully outstanding. Perhaps not even God Himself would venture to rate such people from 1 to 1 billion! When it comes to writers, we have fewer numbers about which to quarrel. On the female side of the ledger alone, we have writers like Jane Austen, Anne Brontë, Elizabeth Gaskell, Charlotte Brontë, George Eliot, and Fanny Burney. We might argue about the relative greatness or importance of all these and more, but surely there is room for all of them in any listing of excellent writers. No one would claim that Zack excels all other writers absolutely, of course. But she excels, and what she could do supremely well perhaps no other writer in history, man or woman, can match. She could not do what Jane Austen did. But then Jane Austen could not do what she did. Thank heaven we have them both.

"Charm is deceitful and beauty is vain,/But a woman who fears the LORD, she shall be praised." As I have tried to make clear, I think it is necessary to be cautious regarding the religious faith of Gwendoline Keats. If she was a believer in some orthodox sense, it may have been with odd crotchets which cost her some ability to evaluate everything about reality with complete correctness. My experience of orthodox believers, among whom I consider myself one, is that we are all more or less confused and inconsistent, and that as the great English Baptist preacher Charles Spurgeon said in two or three of his sermons, we will all be saved "by the skin of our teeth." I hope she was in some sense an orthodox believer, but I can't be sure.

But whether or not she was a believer, Gwendoline Keats wrote from a position in which a biblical view of life bulked very large. Christian ideas moved her profoundly, whether or not she was an approximately orthodox believer. A Christian can move comfortably in her world. The moral furniture is recognizable. The moral challenges and difficulties Zack's characters face, will be understandable to a Christian.

This, of course, means that some non-Christians and anti-Christians may be repulsed by her work. For example, when Travelling Joe sees the ditches of heaven as he dies, the Christian reader may glory in the greatness of God and in His love for Joe. Some Christians at least will note God's flexibility and personal love toward Joe, which allows Joe at the point of his death to see the ditches the crippled boy yearns to jump. This story deepens our understanding of the nature of our God. The anti-Christian reader may be offended at such supernatural goings-on, consider Zack to have written sentimental (dishonest) garbage, and may reject the story as ridiculous. Each reader will have to decide for himself what he thinks of such an ending. Zack, with her steady view of what she could and should be writing, might say, "'What I have written I have written'" (Jn. 19:19-22).

As for her personal appearance, I don't think Zack would be considered a great beauty. But great beauty is not the only thing that makes an attractive woman. As Scripture tells us, character counts. Most of us can easily name several female type persons who are not exactly beautiful as Hollywood might count beauty, but who nevertheless are attractive. Zack may have fit into this category.

What we do know is that she wrote of women of all degrees of physical beauty. In the story "Life Is Life," Joe's wife/widow is "ugly enough," but has "a heart to love with," and is a morally attractive woman—to a very high degree indeed. And when Zack writes of women who were beautiful, she does so without any sort of hint that because someone is beautiful she is necessarily less intelligent or less moral. Some of her greatest heroines are beautiful. Zack, I think, was a woman for whom envy was never a problem. She was a generous-spirited person.

I think, at some central core of her being, Zack simply loved beauty—which is a good thing to love. God makes a lot of beauty, both in the physical world and in some of His human creatures, and Zack instinctively responded to that beauty with approbation. Rab Finch tells us: "'hares ba vantysheeny [Showy, handsome—Zack) baistesses.'" He noticed, because his creator Zack noticed first. We are reminded of the comment by one of Hugh Walpole's characters concerning Zack's *On Trial*. The book was "throbbing in every page with" a "passion for creating beauty."

"Give her the product of her hands,/And let her works praise her in the gates." Truer words were never spoken, concerning Zack. All we have to do is spread out her works—her books—and say, "Here." Her works praise her. The proof is in the pudding: four outstanding books (and one seriously flawed but interesting book).

The books will stand on their own, or they will not stand. Of praise by humans, Zack has had very little since 1901. She received a considerable amount of praise—and some criticism—from critics at the publication of her first four books. She gained a measure of fame, albeit a slight one. But since 1901 she has received mostly silence. I doubt if many people who consider themselves readers have ever heard of her.

There are a few mentions of her along the way. In his book *A Century of the English Novel*, published in 1925, the American scholar Cornelius Weygandt devoted about three and a half pages to Zack. He considered her to be a follower of Thomas Hardy—which I think is incorrect. But his comments on Zack in general are thoughtful and worth summarizing. He discusses her in the portion of the book devoted to "The Lesser late Victorians."

He contrasts the fate of A. E. Housman with that of Zack. Housman published his book of poetry *A Shropshire Lad* in 1896. Zack's stories began to appear in the same year, 1896. "*A Shropshire Lad* was acknowledged at once as poetry of power. *Life is Life* was acknowledged at once as fiction of power." But Weygandt points out how things have gone on from there. Housman continued in 1925 to be famous, his poetry gaining in influence. (And he is famous in 2015—quite deservedly so. I am not much of a reader of poetry, but I have read *A Shropshire Lad* twice, and even seemed to understand it—and appreciate it—at the time.) Weygandt said in 1925, 'Today the stories of "Zack" are known only to the few.' We could add in 2015—to the fewer still.

He does not think the difference in fate should be "charged to a difference in genius." The ellipsis is mine.

> Gwendoline Keats was acknowledged at once because of the sheer power of the personality that spoke in her stories. Working in old material, the west country life already widely familiar to readers in Blackmore and Baring-Gould, she struck a note that had not been struck before. Her disciplined restraint in the utterance of emotion gave a new quality to her dramatic moments. Her acceptance of the strange ways of providence had in it no protest, no echo of the old, old plea for poetic justice. Her style was her own. There was freshness in her humor, too, though it was of the sort traditional from Elizabethan times. . . .
>
> Her weakness lay in the selection of incident and in the architechtonics of story-telling. She liked to restrict her writing to moments of intensity, and she failed to connect those moments logically and to arrange them in patterns that would give balance and beauty of form to her stories.

(He was not the first writer to note that the sheer power of her personality was a factor in her early recognition; it was an insightful comment.)

He continues his comments by saying that he believes lapses of form are only a part of the reason the stories are neglected, since lapses of form are not all that uncommon in the English novel. He thinks that despite the books' "many excellences, they are lesser achievements in" "the Hardian story of country life" and because "they are not quite full scope novels." He adds,

> Whatever the reason, it is true that "Zack" is all but forgotten. I doubt if, even from her first recognition, she had ever the public that she deserved. She presents no gloomier reading of life than that of A. E. Housman, but people reading novels will not put up with unhappiness of an unsentimental kind as will people reading poetry. Though "Zack" was published in America as well as in England, and though her books were reviewed at length here, I have never known her to be the topic of conversation when the talk turned to books. Such a failure to hear about "Zack" may be chance, or it may be, as I must believe it to be, an indication that she has not been much read in America. All I have heard of her has been in print, or in letters in response to queries I have made.
>
> If lovers of literature have not read "Zack" they have missed some good writing.

He describes the "gruesome and haunting" scene of Mary Anne Wort's death in *On Trial*. He quotes part of *Life Is Life*. He mentions her "lyric description" in *The White Cottage*. He quotes part of that book, ending with Luce's words in which she reported her inability to remain true to Mark Tavy. "Those words of Luce have a poignancy and truth to life not unworthy the art of the great masters."[60] Weygandt was not the first person to use some form of the word poignant in describing Zack's work. An unnamed reviewer for "The Spectator" noticed in three separate reviews her gift of poignancy.[61]

A year after Weygandt's book appeared, we have, in 1926, a quote from Hugh Walpole's *Harmer John*, which I have cited previously in the chapter concerning On Trial; the same reviewer concerning The White

---

[60]Cornelius Weygandt, *A Century of the English Novel: Being a Consideration of the place in English Literature of the Long Story; together with an estimate of its Writers from the heyday of Scott to the death of Conrad.*, New York, New York, The Century Co., 1925, pp. 282-286.

[61]Unknown reviewer, "The Spectator," July 9, 1898, p. 49, concerning *Life Is Life*; the same unknown reviewer, "The Spectator," Oct. 7, 1899, p. 34, concerning *On Trial*; the same unknown reviewer, "The Spectator," May 4, 1901, p.661, concerning *The White Cottage.*

Cottage, "The Spectator," May 4, 1901, p. 661. It is worth citing again here. One of Walpole's characters says,

> I had a book with me, I remember, that was just the thing for my mood, Zack's *On Trial*, a magical thing, the kind of book that I should have liked to write had I genius, throbbing in every page with just that same passion for creating beauty that was also Harmer John's.

As mentioned previously, it was this passage that first alerted me to the existence of a writer named Zack. Walpole was not the first to use the word genius in connection with Zack. Early reviewers employed the word several times.

In his 10-volume work, *The History of the English Novel*, English author Ernest A. Baker gives the title of Volume 9 as *The Day before Yesterday* (with no capital for before on the title page). Volume 9 was published in 1936. In a segment subtitled in the margin as *Hardy's imitators*, Baker devotes part of a paragraph to Zack. Baker, like Weygandt, sees Zack as a follower of Hardy. I quote the passage in its modest entirety.

> On a higher level, and nearer in spirit to Hardy, was the lady, Miss Gwendoline Keats, who signed her novels with the pseudonym "Zack." The title-story in *Life is Life, and other tales and episodes* (1901), is of people in Australia, and the philosophy implied in a tale of calamity following on calamity is summed up in the pithy sayings of the patient old woman, who hammers it in that life is life. *On Trial* (1899) and *Tales of Dunstable Weir* (1901) are about Devonshire country folk; *The White Cottage* (1901) and *The Roman Road* (1903) are also stories of fishermen and country people and the dramas that hinge upon a guilty conscience. Zack was a not unworthy disciple of the Wessex master.[62]

He has an incorrect date of publication for *Life Is Life*. *The Roman Road* was not really about fishermen and country folk. He is similarly inaccurate in believing Zack to be a disciple of Thomas Hardy. I

---

[62]Ernest A. Baker, *The History of the English Novel, Volume IX, The Day before Yesterday*, New York, New York, Barnes & Noble, Inc., 1936, p. 95

remember reading one of Hardy's books and thinking how dismissively he treated the poor people. The contrast with Zack is startling. One of her strongest characteristics is her understanding that poor people are people. They may not be educated, but they inhabit the same world of good and evil as do middle class and upper class people.

In his 1973 book on May Sinclair, Theophilus E. M. Boll has several references to Zack which are not all strictly limited to Zack's friendship with May. He mentions the episode which I discussed in Chapter 3, in which Zack offered back £40 of the £150 she had been given for *The White Cottage*, and says "She neurotically underrated her powerful, if morbid, novel."[63]

Later Boll mentions his difficulty in knowing what happened to Zack after her correspondence with May ended in 1903. "I have found no trace of any later residence, or of anything at all about this writer, whose writing has such an elemental, earth-rooted power. She could well be the model for Nina Lempriere in *The Creators*."[64] We are only slightly better informed about what happened to Zack. We know that she lost her mind, but we do not know the details of her last years.

The reference to Zack possibly being the model for Nina Lempriere in May Sinclair's *The Creators*, of course led me to read the book. I am not sure if May Sinclair intended Nina Lempriere to be modeled on Gwendoline Keats, but it is at least possible. *The Creators: A Comedy* was published in 1910. May would have known that her friend had gone insane in late 1903 or early 1904—and that there had been no return to mental health. In *The Creators* there is no clear hint that I can see that Nina Lempriere is going to go insane, but there is a comment that Nina has a "face foredoomed to disaster," which could conceivably be a reference to the disaster of Zack losing her sanity.

There certainly are correspondences between Nina and Zack. Both are writers. Nina is described as an uncompromising genius with a powerful personality. She earns money from her writing, but is not largely popular among the reading public. (There are four uncompromising genius writers in *The Creators*. They all struggle to find a large audience.

---

[63]Boll, *Miss May Sinclair*, etc. p. 63.
[64]Boll, *Miss May Sinclair*, etc., p. 67.

Two of them eventually do so, but two do not. Nina is one who does not.)

Nina has published a book entitled *Tales of the Marches*. Zack published a book entitled *Tales of Dunstable Weir*.

An editor of a magazine (Mr. Brodrick) wants to publish one of Nina's stories, but another man with power in the running of the magazine complains that the story was gruesome. We are told that "Nina's tales usually were gruesome." We know that Zack's stories were often considered over the top in terms of subject matter. The novelist Mrs. Hinkson, we remember, wanted to scream at *Life Is Life*. However, we are glad to report that Mr. Brodrick stands his ground, and publishes the story. He would have felt "eternally disgraced" if he didn't publish it: the story might be gruesome, but it was also magnificent, says Mr. Brodrick.

Physically, Nina is tall with hooded eyes. Our few photographs of Zack indicate both descriptions might apply to her. Nina is impatient, called by another character "'The fiery lady.'" Zack we know often acted hastily.

Late in the book Nina's face is described:

> Sun-burnt, coarsened a little by the wind, with the short, virile, jutting bridge of the nose, the hot eyes, the mouth's ironic twist, it was the face not of a woman but a man, or rather of a temperament, a face foredoomed to disaster. She accentuated its effect by the masculine fashion of her clothes and the way she swept back her hair sidelong from her forehead.

The word virile probably is one which no woman wants to have applied to her! But we remember that a mostly admiring review of *Life Is Life* in "The Academy" for 24 December, 1898, said that "'Zack" is more aggressively, more fiercely, virile even than Mr. Kipling.' Nor would a woman want to have a face considered to be manly! But some of her photographs show her with a "masculine fashion of her clothes" and with swept back hair. We, knowing that Zack lost her sanity (as May knew also), may consider that "foredoomed to disaster" is not too strong a phrase for describing Zack.

A description of Nina from early on in the book gives us a different view of her looks and personality. George Tanqueray is one of the book's four geniuses. He asks himself why

> he had not been in love with Nina? Nina had shown signs. Yes, very unmistakably she had shown signs. He could recall a time when there had lurked a betraying tenderness about her ironic mouth; when her queer eyes, as they looked at him, took on a certain softness and surrender. It had not touched him. To his mind there had always been something a little murky about Nina. It was the fault, no doubt, of her complexion. Not but what Nina had a certain beauty, a tempestuous, haggard, Roman eagle kind of beauty. She looked the thing she was, a creature of high courage and prodigious energy. Besides, she had a devil. Without it, he doubted whether even her genius (he acknowledged, a little grudgingly, her genius) could have done all it did.
>
> It had entered Tanqueray's head (though not his heart) to be in love with Jane. But never, even by way of fantasy, had it entered it to be in love with Nina; though it was to Nina that he looked when he wanted the highest excitement in his intellectual seraglio. He could not conceive any man being in love with her, to the extent, that is to say, of trying to marry her. Nina had the thing called temperament, more temperament and murkier than he altogether cared for; but, as for marrying, you might as well try to marry some bird of storm on the wing, or a flash of lightning on its career through heaven. Nina—career and all—was pre-eminently unfit. (Chapter VII)

Some of this at least might possibly apply to Zack's looks and personality. Words or phrases such as "Roman eagle kind of beauty," "a creature of high courage and prodigious energy," "she had a devil," "her genius," "intellectual," "temperament," "bird of storm on the wing" and perhaps others might well fit with what we know of Gwendoline Keats/Zack.

In fact, Nina had fallen for Tanqueray, but it came to nothing. Later on, she falls, like a rock, for another genius, Owen Prothero, but that too comes to nothing.

Nina says some things about creators, which I find profoundly interesting. "'For any one who creates," said Nina, "nothing's important outside his blessed creation.'" Zack might well have felt something similar. She took her writings seriously. The reader might love or hate her stories, but we all can see that she put her heart into them. And: "'Creators are a brutal crew, Mr. Nicholson. We're all the same. You needn't be sorry for us.'" A brutal crew? Perhaps, at least in some sense. Such people are certainly not "all the same" in their personalities, but there may be a sense in which they are all the same in their determined driving forward to create. The word brutal might never be applied, for example, to Jane Austen, Anne Brontë, Elizabeth Gaskell, but if I were armed with a desire to try to come between them and the exercise of their creative gift, I wouldn't want to meet any one of them in a dark alley! And Nina is probably right that there is no need to feel sorry for them. A creator has consolations, even if the rest of us may not be able always to see them. Of the creator, we can say, "For he on honey-dew hath fed,/And drunk the milk of Paradise" ("Kubla Khan," Samuel Taylor Coleridge). We might feel a spot of sadness for Zack that her books attained only minor fame and since have been forgotten, but she had consolations. She had supped on honey-dew. No need to feel sorry for her.

We will never know with certainty, on this side of the grave, whether or not May Sinclair based Nina Lempriere on her friend Gwendoline Keats. Theophilus Boll's suggestion is at least plausible.

Boll's central interest is of course with May Sinclair. But near the end of his book he lists Zack with several other authors whom he describes as "serious writers" "who have not yet been given a sure place."[65] This is true on both counts. She is a serious writer. And she certainly has not been given a sure place in the list of writers who deserve to be read. In fact she is currently almost completely forgotten. I think she deserves a sure place, but she doesn't have it yet.

What exactly is the place she deserves? I hope the reader of this book will try to figure that out for himself. To do that he will have actually to read some of the books of Zack. Then, I think, Zack will gradually begin to find her true place as a writer who deserves to be read. Word of mouth will inform "lovers of literature" that there is

---

[65]Boll, *Miss May Sinclair*, etc., p. 314.

some "good writing" to be found in the books of Zack, as Cornelius Weygandt says.

As was noticed early on in her career, there is no bigness in Zack. She doesn't write long novels with numerous characters moving through plots and sub-plots. She wrote a lot of short stories. Her two full-length novels are both short. She doesn't write long. She is not Charles Dickens, Anthony Trollope, Thomas Hardy, or any other of the famous writers who wrote many books of considerable length. When recently rereading Dickens' *The Old Curiosity Shop*, it occurred to me that it would be an interesting exercise to count the approximate words in the book, and see how Zack's output matches up.

These figures are of course approximate, but they should be fairly accurate. *Life Is Life* is about 46,240 words. *On Trial* is about 38,766 words. *The White Cottage* checks in at 40,482 words. *Tales of Dunstable Weir*: 44,678 words. *The Roman Road* is 38,448 words. That's a total of 208,614 words for Zack's total published works.

The Old Curiosity Shop is about 233,408 words. So one book by Charles Dickens is about 25,000 words longer than the total output of Zack. And *The Old Curiosity Shop* is very far from being Dickens' longest book. He wrote many books, and quite a few of them are longer than *TOCS*.

If length were the sole criterion for evaluating books, we can dismiss Zack as obviously unimportant. But it is not the sole criterion. She writes books that challenge and move the reader. Some of her stories are among the best that have ever been written. She is a unique talent worthy of great respect. She will not replace Jane Austen or Charles Dickens or Fyoder Dostoyevsky. But she supplements them, and people who love good writing need to know about her and try her. She helps us understand life, as all good writers do.

In writing about the English Puritan pastor and theologian John Owen, J. I. Packer says somewhere that when God gives the church a writer/thinker with the talents of John Owen, the gift is for all time. That is, John Owen's value was not just for his era. He is for all of us, and for people in the future as well. The church needs John Owen forever.

I think something similar should be said about Gwendoline Keats/ Zack. It is sad, but not devastating, that she is currently forgotten. That error can be quickly remedied, as soon as people who love good writing discover that she exists, and those people begin to read her books. She will not be to the taste of everyone. But there should be a niche for her somewhere in the hearts of at least part of the book reading public. Maybe it's just my native and naïve postmillennial optimism showing through, but I think she will find her niche. Gwendoline Keats/Zack has been given to us for all time.

APPENDIX I

A Prayer

> When you come bring the cloak which I left at Troas with Carpus, and the books, especially the parchments.
>
> 2 Timothy 4:13

God, thank you that Gwendoline Keats lived and wrote such remarkable books. Thank you that you providentially arranged things so I could hear about and could read her books.

I ask that you permit her to attain the number of readers, and the measure of fame, which you know to be just—neither more nor less. If she is as valuable a writer as I believe her to be, please don't let the world's awareness of her dissipate into nothing. Use her books to delight and challenge endless generations of readers. In the near or distant future, please raise up one or several scholars who will be able to teach us more about her life and work.

God, I pray that Gwendoline Keats found salvation in Jesus Christ, on this side of the grave or on the other. Forgive any flaws in her understanding of you, or in her obedience to you, for His sake. Have mercy on her, and put her to work building your kingdom throughout eternity.

As I hope for mercy for Gwendoline Keats, I hope for mercy for myself through the world's one Savior, Jesus Christ.

If possible, Lord, let me meet her someday under the shadow of your wing—perhaps some place with ditches.

In Christ's name, amen.

APPENDIX II

Some Reviews

> And the king said, "This is a good man and comes with good news."
>
> 2 Samuel 18:27

Not all of the reviewers came with good news in their reviews of Zack's books! But she was widely reviewed, especially early on in her publishing career. Zack did not slip under the radar of the reviewers, despite the complicating fact that radar had to wait another generation to be invented. She was immediately recognized as a distinct voice—often admired, although not always. Very insightful comments were balanced by comments that missed the point entirely—sometimes in the same review. This I would guess is a constant of the reviewing art, in any age.

A handful of reviewers clearly put their heart into their work. Gwendoline Keats/Zack made a large impression on them, and they responded from the heart and gut. I will try to note those reviews which are especially lengthy and insightful.

These are the reviews I have been able to find so far. Most of the reviews I found when doing my library researching over 30 years ago. No doubt there are others I haven't found yet. The age of the Internet makes more resources available, and I am continuing to find new things now and then. If we ask Google the right questions, we may find a good deal more eventually.

The reviews are listed in approximate order of publication. Where there is a question mark, it means I did a poor job of recording something when I photocopied the reviews three decades ago (or did a poor job more recently). I have given a few comments on each review I was able to find. I have assumed—perhaps incorrectly—that unnamed reviewers are he rather than she. A few reviews I know exist, but I was not able to read them. They are listed as well, for the benefit of future researchers.

I have tried to quote with as much accuracy as possible. Some headings will look strange to modern eyes. So for example, where we would give a heading of FICTION, in many of the reviews of the day the style was to print FICTION., that is the word FICTION with a period after it. So I have tried to quote even the periods, which are used in many of the headings of that era.

Let me give an example, so that the reader understands how I am proceeding through all the reviews. In the first review cited below, from "The Academy," the magazine printed the heading of their review as "ZACK." with a period at the end, and with the word ZACK in quotes. So in my review I have listed the heading as "ZACK." but without further quotes. So I did not list it as "'ZACK.'" but rather simply as "ZACK." without the further single quote marks. My comma after "ZACK." was not in the original magazine review, of course. This is probably far more information than you need or want, but at least the reader will understand that I am trying to be consistent and accurate.

The last two entries refer to evaluations of Zack found in books by two scholars devoted to studying the English novel. They are discussed at greater length in Chapter 6 of this book.

"The Academy," June 25, 1898, two long columns entitled "ZACK.," p. 689, no author given. A review of *Life Is Life*. The author incorrectly identifies some of the scenes as taking place in Cornwall rather than Devon. (Cornwall is right next to Devon, to the southeast.) There are many appreciative and insightful comments. The reviewer quotes "Rab Vinch's Wife" at considerable length, and in response says, "This mixture of realism based on close observation with the symbol-making imagination is very like the quality that we call genius."

"The Academy," July 9, 1898, p. 39, no author given. This is one medium-sized paragraph commenting on the theory of Claudius Clear as revealed in his "British Weekly" review (see below) that the first 241 pages of *Life Is Life* were written with a collaborator (since they are so inferior to the final 80 pages). "The Academy" says 'Miss Keats replies: "I have no collaborator, and am as responsible for the 241 pages that he condemns as for the eighty pages that he praises."'

"The Spectator," July 9, 1898, about one and a half long columns entitled A NEW STORYTELLER. [with an asterisk after it, directing the reader to details about the book's publication], pp. 49-50, no author given. This is a mostly admiring review of *Life Is Life*, but the author considers all the stories to be depressing. He finds the dialect to be "highly irritating," and says it makes many of the "pages look as though written in a foreign tongue." He misses the point of "Travelling Joe." Zack is described as having the "gift of poignancy."

"The Speaker," July 16, 1898. Under a segment entitled A LITERARY CAUSERIE., with a subheading "LIFE IS LIFE.," pp. 81-82, the book is reviewed by A. T. Q. C. That we know is the well-known author A. T. Quiller-Couch. He devotes about 1 1/2 pages to the review. He admires in part, but has complaints as well. He ends by commending Zack's "genuine sense of life." This review was reprinted in "Living Age," Aug. 27, 1898, where it takes up about two and a quarter pages, pp. 619-621, and where A. T. Quiller-Couch's full name is given.

Quiller-Couch wrote a personal letter to Gwendoline Keats on July 18, 1898. Speaking of his "Speaker" review, he hopes she will forgive him "for not having echoed other peoples' compliments, well as you have deserved them: & I trust that a genuine admiration is there, to be read between the lines." "I hope you will let me have a story before long, & that you will kindly name your price for it: as I am at least a sufficiently bad editor to think that an author has the first voice in these matters."

"British Weekly" has a review of *Life Is Life*, 1898. Unseen by me, but "The Academy" for July 23, 1898 (see below) quotes part of the review, which is generally dismissive of the first part of the book. This review seems to have been written by Claudius Clear (see "The Academy," July 9, 1898, above). He didn't like the first 241 pages, but says of the final 80 pages of the book that they are "'great pages, notable pages, unforgettable pages, pages sufficient to give the writer a reputation.'" "'I should pity anyone who could read those stories unmoved. They are to be classed with Tennyson's 'Rizpah,' and there is not much to go along with them in English literature, not much with the same terrible, tearing, tearless passion.'"

"The Daily Telegraph" has a review of *Life Is Life*, 1898, by Mr. W. L Courtney. Unseen by me, but again "The Academy" summarizes Courtney's review and quotes part. Courtney sees his own age as pessimistic, and Zack's book reveal a "'despairing spirit. But as contrasted with the wails of impotent and mawkish hopelessness, there is in Miss Keats's volume an indomitable strength, an unshrinking courage, a masterful calm." Zack "'meets destiny like a man.'" He adds that the force of personality rather than of art is the secret of Zack's power.

"The Outlook," July 16, 1898. Under a segment entitled TO ZACK—"FROM A TRUE FRIEND," with a subheading including title, author, and publishing information, p. 762, *Life Is Life* is reviewed by an unknown author. This is the English magazine; there was an American magazine with the same title, which is cited below. There is one very long paragraph, and one very short one. This is a mostly very unfavorable review, written in a tone which is arrogant, patronizing, and insulting. The reviewer may consider himself to be a "true friend," but with friends like that, who needs enemies? The title is described as possessing "singular inanity." The early stories "contain no spark of merit," with "nothing in them that resembles life." Zack is a "neophyte." The last six stories, however, are given grudging, mixed praise. There is hope for Zack, but apparently only if she is "'a beginner.'" Zack "'seems to understand Devonshire peasant life, more or less.'"

This is a review which we know caused Zack to speak out with apparent vehemence to her friend May Sinclair. I found this review only very late in my writing on Zack. (Thanks to Mr. Google for helping me finally find this review.) It seems to me that the wonder is not that Zack was vehement in speaking about the review. The wonder is that she did not find out who the author was and shoot him. Maybe she did, and just covered her tracks well. However, if she had been indicted for murder, no jury would have convicted—it would have been seen as justifiable homicide.

In a letter postmarked Sept. 5, 1898, Zack devoted about three-quarters of her words to her regret for having accused "The Outlook" of spite in their review. She should be commended for having eventually worked her way to so much objectivity on the topic. This letter is quoted at length in the first part of Chapter 6.

"The Pall Mall Gazette," has a review of *Life Is Life*, 1898. While this review is unseen by me, "The Academy," July 23, 1898, quotes "TPMG": "'There is something more than promise in 'Zack's' greatest failures.'"

"The Academy," July 23, 1898, almost two full columns entitled BOOK REVIEWS REVIEWED., with the words "LIFE IS LIFE." in smaller capitals, pp. 93-94, no author given. This is a summary of reviews of *Life Is Life*. Six recent reviews are cited and partly quoted; "The Academy's own June 25, 1898 review is not mentioned.

"Literature," July 30, 1898, devotes almost one full longish column to a review of *Life Is Life*, pp. 85-86, no author given. The reviewer joins some others in vastly preferring the Devonshire stories to the other stories in the book. His favorite is "Widder Vlint": "the art rises to such a degree of perfection that it almost ceases to be art." He quotes "Widder Vlint" at some length (and not with entire accuracy). That story and three others "display the same grasp of truth that is universal, the same vividness of presentation, which, whether due to intuition and insight or to actual experience, are the life-stuff out of which great novels are created."

"The Critic," July 1898, slightly more than one and a half pages entitled **A New Story Writer**, pp. 70-71, no author given. This is a review of *Life Is Life*. 'The most recent literary reputation in England is that of Miss Gwendoline Keats, who prefers to be known by the pen-name of "Zack."' "She may not be the greatest story-writer that has appeared within the present decade, but she is one of the most original and forceful." Almost two-thirds of the review is a one page quote from "The Storm."

"The Bookman," (apparently an English "The Bookman"; there is an American "The Bookman" quoted below), August 1898, three paragraphs entitled LIFE IS LIFE. [with an asterisk after it, directing the reader to details of the book's publication], p. 132, with the initials of the reviewer given: J. E. H. W. The early stories in the book he finds powerful, but "there is something indefinably, subtly repulsive in their brutality." Like me, he sees "Travelling Joe" as especially distinguished. The latter part of the book contains "pages of exquisite tenderness and beauty, pages that no one could read unmoved. There are pages which stand unrivalled in contemporary literature." 'The author of such a story as "Travelling Joe" is not to be numbered among the crowd.'

"The Independent," August 25, 1898. In the pages devoted to Literature, the unnamed reviewer of "The Independent" gives one short paragraph to a review of *Life Is Life* on p. 563. The review is mixed. "The dramatic touch is genuine, and the characters are made almost startlingly real." The reviewer fails to sympathize with the characters. "As a writer Miss Keats attracts and holds; as a story-teller she fascinates; but as an artist she chooses models whose peculiarities, perversities and (sometimes) deformities make it impossible for her to satisfy natural, healthy taste, no matter how well she writes or how faithfully she tells her story."

"The Outlook," 20 August 1898, less than one full paragraph, p. 984. This is the American magazine by that title; for the review of the English magazine called "The Outlook," see above. This is a brief review (four sentences along with additional publishing information also; less than one medium-sized paragraph total) of *Life Is Life*. The unnamed reviewer acknowledges the stories' "quality of force," but is clearly put off by the "unadulterated misery."

"The Bookman," (New York), Sept. 1898, four full pages entitled THE LIGHT THAT BURNS UPWARD. [with an asterisk after it, directing readers to details of the book's publication], pp. 44-47, by James MacArthur. This is a review of *Life Is Life*. It is largely admiring. Clearly his reading of the book has profoundly moved MacArthur, who responds with a long and heartfelt evaluation containing many insights. "For a first book, one is also struck with the maturity of thought and life which marks these pages." "The unstrained feeling, too, which she is able to give to words that bring a lump into the throat is one of her rare gifts." It is in the latter (Devon) stories of the book "that Zack has shown a mastery which entitles her to rank with the best short story-writers in the language. She is a genuine daughter of Devonshire, and in depicting the life of the soil in which she has her roots, she has surely found her true place." He joins some of the rest of us in admiring "Travelling Joe" most of all.

"The Nation," Oct. 20, 1898, most of one long paragraph under a segment entitled RECENT FICTION. in which five books are reviewed, p. 299, no author given. This is a review of *Life Is Life*. The reviewer is clearly frustrated by the book. Zack's feminine temperament "extracts pain from everything, and declares that the sob of breaking hearts is the dominant note of human existence." The book is "perfectly fitted to extinguish hope."

"The Academy," 24 December, 1898, slightly more than one long column entitled "Zack.," pp. 520-521, no author given. A picture of Gwendoline Keats accompanies the review. One way or another "The Academy" had now mentioned *Life Is Life* at least four times in its pages. This review is partly admiring. "'Zack" is more aggressively, more fiercely, virile even than Mr. Kipling.' In two of her stories, "imagination is based upon the closest observation; but the essence of her work is and always will be imagination. The best of her work is very good indeed." "Travelling Joe" comes in for special commendation.

"The American Monthly Review of Reviews," Dec. 1898, p. 723. The article as a whole is entitled FICTION, POETRY, AND THE LIGHTER NOTE IN THE SEASON'S BOOKS., but the segment in which the review of *Life Is Life* appears is subtitled **FICTION, GOOD AND BAD**. RUDYARD KIPLING AND "ZACK.". A picture of Zack accompanies the review. The author is Henry Wysham Lanier. Lanier devotes one moderately long paragraph to Zack's book. He praises the title story, also "The Storm" and "Rab Vinch's Wife," but says "The remaining number are decidedly inferior." '"Zack" may safely be set down as one of the writers worth remembering and reading.'

"The Living Age," Nov. 5, 1898 p. 401. This contains two short paragraphs commenting on *Life Is Life*, by an American publication. We are told that "The Living Age" had reprinted three of Zack's tales in 1897. Her book contains "rather gloomy tales." The second paragraph is an unfavorable quote from the famous Andrew Lang, who wrote: 'People seem to like their novels muddy now, judging by the praise bestowed on "Zack's" book, "Life is Life." The stories run strong, I admit—very strong—and "flasker about" on the water (as a MS. note in an old fishing book of 1680 puts it); but the flavor, I think, is muddy, and, for one, I don't like them muddy.'

"The Athenaeum," Oct. 7, 1899. *On Trial* is reviewed under a segment entitled NEW NOVELS., p. 487, no author given. One short paragraph. "There is genuine art in the telling of this simple story of life and love on the edge of Exmoor."

"The Spectator," October 7, 1899. *On Trial* is reviewed under a segment entitled NOVELS OF THE WEEK. [with an asterisk after it, directing the reader to publication information for all the novels discussed], p. 34. No author is given, but it is the same person who reviewed *Life Is Life* for "The Spectator" of July 9, 1898. One very long paragraph is devoted to the book. 'The quality of poignancy, which we noted in "Zack's' earlier work, is present with redoubled force in this engrossing tragedy.' Yet he finds Dan Pigott "an impossible creature," and says "so hysterical a coward could never have survived three years of barrack life" even on home service.

"The Academy," 21 October, 1899. *On Trial* is reviewed under a segment entitled FICTION., p. 455, no author given. A subheading gives the title, author, and publication information. One and a half long columns are devoted to the book. This is a mostly admiring review, with some reservations. 'If "Zack" is not yet a master, she is on the way to become such. She has the magic, inexplicable gifts of vision and song, and she has them in full.' A "quasi-fault" of the book is that "*On Trial* is scarcely a novel. It is a short story elongated, and elongated a trifle too much." "Yet there is enough stuff in this short story for half-a-dozen six-shilling novels."

"Literature," November 4, 1899. *On Trial* is reviewed under a segment labeled in bold print **FICTION.**, pp. 447-448, no author given for the one medium length paragraph. This is a gently admiring review. The story is "strong in its simplicity." The reviewer adds that "comedy and tragedy jostle each other as they do in everyday experience." "The character of Phoebe is in itself a beautiful conception."

"Blackwood's Magazine," Nov., 1899. It was "Blackwood's Magazine" which first published *On Trial* in serial form in five monthly segments, June through October of 1899, and it was Blackwood and Sons which published the book in hardcover form in 1899. Here *On Trial* is reviewed under a segment entitled *Under the Beard of Buchanan.*, pp. 710-711, no author given. This mostly admiring review takes up most of two full pages. The reviewer's chief reservation is that a novel demands a "large canvas," which is not provided by Zack in *On Trial*. "To ascribe genius to Zack requires no critical courage: to believe that she will write in the near future a really great novel is not an exercise of faith but a well-grounded conviction." "When we close the book we are conscious of only one impression, that we have seen into the very soul of a coward as lit up for us by the light of genius." "The most striking quality of her work is the impression it conveys of an immense reserve of power."

"Cambridge Chronicle," 16 December, 1899. This is from Cambridge, Massachusetts, in the U.S. *On Trial* is reviewed very briefly, in a segment entitled SOME LEADING HOLIDAY BOOKS., in which the title, author, price, publisher, etc. are given. This is one short paragraph, p. 10, which mostly quotes part of the admiring review by "The Academy." No author is given. "English appreciation" of the book "is generous in the extreme."

"The Nation," Jan. 4, 1900. *On Trial* is reviewed in one fairly long paragraph, p. 17. The unnamed reviewer, who probably is the same person who reviewed *Life Is Life* for "The Nation" in 1898, has nothing good to say about either the novel or Zack. Her first book "proclaimed her depressing views of life," and she now appears "to have sunk into deep despair. 'On Trial' is a most discouraging work." "Such fiction as 'On Trial' is neither useful nor beautiful, but it has a sort of hysterical idealism which is at once responded to by sentimental, emotional readers, and thus gets a reputation for truth to life, even for literary skill, which is not deserved."

"Public Opinion," Thursday, 9 May, 1901. *The White Cottage* is reviewed under a segment entitled BOOK REVIEWS, p. 599. Under that, the title of the book is listed, and immediately after that we have the title again, the author, description of the book (cloth, number of pages, cost), place of publication (New York), and publisher. No author is given for the one very long paragraph taking up about 1 1/2 columns, which amounts to approximately one half a page. There is an accompanying picture of Gwendoline Keats. This is a very favorable review. "Miss Keats has laid bare every phase of life with that passion for pitiless, relentless truth which characterized her earlier work." "Human nature is here stripped of all pretensions and self-deceptions."

"The Academy," 18 May, 1901. *The White Cottage* is reviewed in slightly more than one long column, under a segment entitled Fiction., with details about the book just below, pp. 424-425, no author given. This is a mostly favorable review in which some reservations are expressed. The final summation: '"Zack," we fear, will never be a "popular novelist." Her self-repression, her neat mind that will look only at the facts of life, and those not the brightest, her contempt for sentiment, her sympathy for the unlettered, are against that. But she is a writer who counts.'

"Literature," May 18, 1901?. *The White Cottage* is reviewed in one long paragraph in a segment entitled in bold print **FICTION.**, with a subheading, also in bold print, **Zack's Latest.**, p. 418, no author given. This is an admiring review. "It was argued in our columns a few weeks ago that, though all long novels were not great, all great novels were long. The advocates of the contrary opinion will be entitled to quote the case of THE WHITE COTTAGE, by Zack (Constable, 6s.), which is short and amazingly good." "Tears and laughter are close together in the book, and the pathos is as admirable as the humour."

"The Book Buyer," May 1901. *The White Cottage* is reviewed in slightly less than one full page in a segment entitled A DEVONSHIRE LOVE-STORY, pp. 328-329. The author's initials are given, in italics, as *C. S.* This is an admiring review. 'There is no doubt that Gwendoline Keats, who writes under the *nom de guerre* of "Zack," is a power in the world of letters. What she says, she says with brevity, intensity, and dramatic force." "It is the kind of story that one never forgets." "The color is there without any apparent effort from the author."

"The Brooklyn Daily Eagle," Tuesday, June 4, 1901, p. 6. Under a segment entitled A Bright Young Author., we have a picture of Gwendoline Keats as well as the text. There is no author given for the three brief paragraphs, which mention the recent publication of *The White Cottage*, but make no attempt to review the book. The writer may not have read the book; he may have been working from something handed out by the American publisher Scribner's. Her first book "won recognition on both sides of the Atlantic." "Her ability to get at the heart of humanity was the dominant note of praise."

"The Bryan Times," June 20, 1901. Four short paragraphs are an appreciation of Zack's career rather than a review of a specific book, p. 3. The heading reads Gwendoline Keats, with a subheading saying English Girl Who Won World-Wide Recognition in Two Years. No author is given; my guess is that the author may not even have read any of Zack's books. The article mentions that *The White Cottage* has just been published. She is said to be a grandniece of the poet John Keats. This is an error that also appears in "The Booklovers Bulletin" review listed below. The writer may have been working from something handed out by her American publisher Scribner's, or may have been quoting from "The Brooklyn Daily Eagle" cited just above. At least two of the comments in the articles are the same almost word for word. Her first book "won instant recognition on both sides of the Atlantic." "Her ability to get at the very heart of humanity was the dominant note of praise." *On Trial* "set her place in literature once for all."

"The Bookman," June 1901. This is the English "The Bookman." *The White Cottage* is reviewed in a segment entitled **NOVEL NOTES.**, with a subsection listing the book's title, author, price, and publisher, p. 93. The reviewer is unnamed for this single long paragraph. This is a mostly favorable review, with a few complaints about construction and theme. The reviewer had his heart touched by the "forceful, rugged" and "good work" done in *Life Is Life*, which he remembers with "approbation." The reviewer ends, "we still wait with confidence to see her handle a really great story. She has the power, we know; and it is because of this knowledge that we dare to carp when she does not exercise it to the full."

"The Spectator," May 4, 1901. *The White Cottage* is reviewed as the lead book in a segment entitled NOVELS OF THE WEEK. [with an asterisk after it, directing the reader to publication information for all the novels discussed], p. 661. No author is given for this favorable review, which is one long paragraph in length. However, we know this is the same "Spectator" reviewer who discussed her previous two books, for he points out: "The distinguishing quality of her work, as we have remarked before, is its poignancy." "With a setting as bare and simple as that of the Elizabethan Stage Society's performances, she plucks out the core of elemental passion, and sets it before her readers with a directness and simplicity that go straight to the mark."

"The Bookman," July, 1901. Under a section titled Six Books of Some Importance, *The White Cottage* is reviewed in a segment entitled IV. ZACK'S "THE WHITE COTTAGE." [with an asterisk after it, directing the reader to publication information for the book], pp. 456-458. (This seems to be an American publication, whereas "The Bookman" mentioned two paragraphs above is British. The June review mentions the English publisher; the July review mentions the American publisher. The pages are laid out in different formats in the two publications.) Here the reviewer is Alice Katharine Fallows, and clearly the book made a strong impression on her. This review runs slightly more than two full pages, and is very favorable. "*The White Cottage* is the work of an artist—of an artist in whom the creative impulse would not be denied." The book "is an artist's expression of life—vigorous, strong, intense—a thing to be cherished in these practical days."

"The Athenaeum," No. 3848, July 27, 1901. *The White Cottage* is reviewed in a segment which includes the title, author, and publisher, p. 120. [This issue of "The Athenaeum" runs from p. 109 through p. 140.] No author is given for the one moderately long paragraph. "Zack's skill is evident," but the reviewer has several reservations and criticisms. This review might be characterized as only moderately favorable.

"The Sewanee Review," Oct., 1901. *The White Cottage* is reviewed in a segment which includes the title, author, place of publication, and publisher, pp. 498-499. The review by E. H. S. contains one long and one short paragraph, and is gently favorable. The story is "well-told." "The style is good and the action quick. The end of the story has a decided dramatic touch and a stern pathos."

"Booklovers Bulletin," unknown date, probably sometime in 1901. In the print on demand copy of *The White Cottage* which I have, a quote from "Booklovers Bulletin" gives one medium length paragraph on the book. No author is given. It is a favorable review. The book is "an exceptionally able piece of work." We are told, incorrectly, that Gwendoline Keats "is a grandniece of the poet Keats."

"The Academy" shares its magazine title with several pages labeled Fiction Supplement, 9 November, 1901. *Tales of Dunstable Weir* is reviewed under a segment entitled New Novels., with a subheading in which the book title, author, publisher, and price are listed, p. 431. The review is one long and one short paragraph, with no author given. The review is mixed. The reviewer questions the wisdom of having the narrator Zack be a man "with a rough and untutored tongue." On the positive side, 'The tales are very meritorious—restrained in manner, "strong without rage," calm without being flaccid, generally witty in the vein of pawkiness, and often humorous.' The "'strong without rage'" quote apparently comes from Sir John Denham's poem, "Cooper's Hill," in which the poet (1615-1669) praises the Thames as "Strong without rage; without o'erflowing, full" (line 189).

"The Academy," in the same issue, 9 November, 1901, has a good deal more about Zack's books. Once again the magazine's title at the top of the page shares space with the words Fiction Supplement. Two packed pages are entitled Ten Months of Fiction., pp. 429-430, no author given. The reviewer lists three writers as especially preeminent, but two have mostly ceased to produce (George Meredith and Thomas Hardy) and the third is recently dead (R. D. Blackmore of *Lorna Doone* fame). For "serious effort in the art of fiction," he lists, in alphabetical order (his choice), these eleven writers: Joseph Conrad, George Gissing, Maurice Hewlett, "John Oliver Hobbes" (pen-name of Pearl Mary Teresa Craigie), W. W. Jacobs, Rudyard Kipling, George Moore, Eden Phillpotts, Mrs. Humphry Ward, H. G. Wells, and "Zack." The modern reader will recognize many of those names, some of whom continue in fame, others of whom lurk on the outskirts of same.

The reviewer then lists the twelve best English novels of the year, in order of his preference. *Kim* by Rudyard Kipling is listed first. Books by George Moore, George Gissing, and "John Oliver Hobbes" come next, followed in fifth place by Zack's *The White Cottage*. "To these we must add a small, but rather unusual, group of short stories," in which

Zack's *Tales of Dunstable Weir* is listed fourth of four (after books by Jacobs, Phillpotts, and Hewlett). "There is, by the way, far more humour in these four volumes than in all the twelve novels." He proceeds with brief comments indicating the limitations of some of the books. "*The White Cottage* has no bigness."

Among American books of the year, he praises *The Octopus* by Frank Norris and *Sister Carrie* by Theodore Dreiser, with added praise going to books by Henry James and Stephen Crane.

"The Academy" had taken a vote of its readers for the twelve best books of the year. Kipling's *Kim* finished on top, with 80 votes. The twelfth place finisher received 29 votes. Twenty books received enough votes (7 or more) to be listed among readers' honorable mention. *The White Cottage* received third honorable mention (thus fifteenth overall) with 15 votes from readers.

"Literature," November 9, 1901. *Tales of Dunstable Weir* is reviewed under a segment entitled in bold print **FICTION.**, with a subheading also in bold print **Zack.**, p. 446. The reviewer's name is not given for the one moderately long paragraph. This is a highly favorable review. "Zack's West Country Stories are the real thing." "Her stories seem to flow from her pen as naturally as water from a fountain." Her stories may or may not wear as well as Guy de Maupassant's Normandy stories, but "she is unquestionably in the same class with him, and is one of the few of the younger English writers of fiction from whom we confidently anticipate great things."

"The Spectator," 2 November, 1901. *Tales of Dunstable Weir* is reviewed under a segment entitled in italics and in bold print ***OTHER NOVELS.***, with a subheading in which the title, author, description of frontispiece, publisher, and cost are listed, pp. 667-668. No author is given for the one medium length paragraph. This is a favorable review. 'Most beautiful but most melancholy are the "tales of Dunstable Weir" "Zack" gives us in a very fascinating little volume.' The dialect is mistakenly described as from Somersetshire, but is "so managed that it reads easily." (Somersetshire is just to the northeast of Devon.) In each story "some core of tragedy, more or less inarticulate, is seized and brought home to us." We are told "the relief of humour is never wanting."

"The Critic," Feb., 1902. *Tales of Dunstable Weir* is reviewed in tandem with Eden Phillpotts' *The Striking Hours*, p. 152. The review is signed J. B. G., which we know was Joseph Benson Gilder (1858-1936), joint editor of "The Critic" with his sister Jeannette Leonard Gilder. This one long paragraph is favorable to both books, but Gilder reserves his stronger praise for Phillpotts. "Both are accomplished artists," but of Zack he says "while one is impressed by her cleverness and admires the deftness of her touch, he feels that her talent has its well-defined limits."

"The Academy and Literature," 6 June, 1903. The magazine that was formerly "The Academy" merged with the periodical "Literature," in 1902, and took the name "The Academy and Literature." (The publication reverted to the name "The Academy" in 1905.) *The Roman Road* is reviewed under a segment entitled in bold print **Fiction.**, with a subheading entitled Shadowy Psychology., and with a line devoted to the title, author, publisher, and price, pp. 557-558. No author is given for this review, which is three fairly long paragraphs. This is in general an unfavorable review, with some praise mixed in. The characters are types which fail to live for the reader. The dialogue in two of the stories is "rhetorical, hard, bitter, clever, but never instinct with human modulations." Of the title story he writes, "Much of the work in the story is technically excellent, and it is charged with the writer's personality, but as art related to life it fails." 'Yet "The Roman Road" is a book that dwells in the memory by reason of its unquestionable cleverness and moral earnestness.' "The author's equipment is far beyond the average; it only needs direction and a careful pruning."

"The Outlook," 23 May, 1903. *The Roman Road* is reviewed in a segment entitled Books of the Week, p. 246. The book is introduced by its title (in bold print), along with author, publisher, place of publication, and further information about the book's size, number of pages, and cost. This is the American magazine "The Outlook," rather than the English magazine with the same title. No reviewer is named for the one short paragraph. The reviewer disliked the story entitled "The Roman Road," and thought "The Balance" "somewhat fantastical and overdrawn" but "certainly original." He found "Thoughty" to be "a deliciously humorous recital of childish adventure."

"The Atlantic Monthly," Aug., 1903. *The Roman Road* is reviewed in a segment entitled BOOKS NEW AND OLD. and subtitled SOME FICTION, MAINLY SERIOUS., with the segment containing the review of the book further divided into a section labeled II., pp. 280-281. The reviewer is H. W. Boynton. This is not a favorable review, but also not highly unfavorable. The review is slightly more than one full page in length. The reviewer chose to devote approximately 80% of the review to two long quotes, one from the title story and one from "The Balance." This may have reduced his own workload, but also had the advantage of letting the reader see of what kind of stuff *The Roman Road* consisted. "The titular story is varied, but hardly enlivened, by certain touches of that chill educated humor which Mr. James and Mr. Howells have taught us to believe that we enjoy."

"The Athenaeum," No. 3957, Aug. 29, 1903. *The Roman Road* is reviewed under a segment entitled SHORT STORIES., p. 283. No reviewer is named for the one medium length paragraph of this mostly unfavorable review. The first two stories "possess little or no merit," but "'The Thoughty Ones'" (the title of the story was given as "The Thoughty Ones" in one edition, as "Thoughty" in another) is "a delightful piece of children's make-believe." But "even here something fantastic and inexplicable intrudes and annoys the reader." The reviewer recommends to Zack a "thorough cleansing of the imagination."

A Century of the English Novel, by Cornelius Weygandt, published in 1925, has a section entitled "The Lesser Late Victorians." Within that section there is a segment entitled "Zack," which is 3 1/2 pages in length, pp. 282-286. Weygandt offers up many insightful comments in his mostly admiring evaluation of Zack's books.

Even as early as 1925, Zack was "all but forgotten. I doubt if, even from her first recognition, she had ever the public that she deserved."

She had apparently not been much read in America, despite having been published there. He speculates that "people reading novels will not put up with unhappiness of an unsentimental kind."

Her "sheer power" of personality had led her to be recognized at once, when she was first published. Weygandt speaks of her "disciplined restraint in the utterance of emotion." "Her acceptance of the strange ways of providence had in it no protest." "Her style was her own. There was freshness in her humor, too."

Her novels, in length, "are not quite full scope novels."

'If lovers of literature have not read "Zack" they have missed some good writing.' He quotes a passage from *The White Cottage* in which Luce acknowledges her failure to have been true to Mark, and says, "Those words of Luce have a poignancy and truth to life not unworthy the art of the great masters."

The History of the English Novel: Volume IX: The Day before Yesterday, Ernest A. Baker, first published in 1936. On page 95, about 11 1/2 lines are devoted to Zack. Baker sees her as "a not unworthy disciple of the Wessex master" Thomas Hardy.

APPENDIX **III**

How This Book Came to Be Written

> I had a book with me, I remember, that was just the thing for
> my mood, Zack's *On Trial*, a magical thing, the kind of book
> that I should have liked to write had I genius, throbbing in
> every page with just that same passion for creating beauty that
> was also Harmer John's.
>
> Hugh Walpole, Harmer John

The above quote, read by me 35 plus years ago, is what led me to
try to find one of the books of Gwendoline Keats/Zack. I read quite a
bit, and sometimes I am on the lookout for good writers who might be
forgotten or mostly forgotten.

I keep a record of my reading. My notes tell me that I read Walpole's
brief evaluation of *On Trial* on Tuesday, July 10, 1979. (Technically,
this is the evaluation of Walpole's narrator, but I think we can safely
say the narrator speaks for Walpole.) I had never heard of Zack.
In early August I went to the superb world class library at Indiana
University in Bloomington, Indiana, about forty miles away from my
home. I couldn't find *On Trial*, but three other of Zack's books were
right there on the shelves. I checked out *Life Is Life: And Other Tales
and Episodes*, Zack's first book. I was not a student, but as an Indiana
resident I was readily able to borrow books there. Although I did not
know it yet, a fourth Zack book was also in the library, in its original
magazine publication.

I read *Life Is Life* over about an eight-week period—not particularly
quickly, obviously. I remember dealing with the strangeness of the
dialect, and I remember that I was struck by the political incorrectness

of part of the book. I was and am politically incorrect myself, so that at least appealed to me.

It was almost a year before I read the second of the I. U. library's Zack books. That was *The White Cottage*, a novel. I read it in two days, in July of 1980.

Two and a half weeks later I began to read *Tales of Dunstable Weir*, which I finished over a two-week period in September of 1980.

A year later I reread *Life Is Life*, in three days in September of 1981.

In the winter of 1981-82, I discovered that three of Zack's books were still in print. They included *Life Is Life, Tales of Dunstable Weir*, and *The Roman Road* (previously unread by me). My mother bought them for me as a belated Christmas present.

In early May of 1982, I read *The Roman Road* over a four-day period.

By the summer of 1982, I had begun writing letters to libraries, and to Zack's publishers. I will spare you the details. I had mixed success.

My notes tell me that I made the basic decision to go to England to find out more about Gwendoline Keats/Zack, and to do my best for her, on November 20, 1982. My plans were to go in early 1984.

One publisher's letter told me that Zack's *On Trial*—the book which had so impressed Hugh Walpole—had been published in "Blackwells Magazine." In early January of 1983, I traveled to the I. U. library to see if I could find the "Blackwells" issue or issues which contained *On Trial*.

No success. But instinct, or perhaps a gracious providential shove, sent me to Blackwood's in the card catalog. And there it was. I. U. had the copies of the 1898 "Blackwood's Magazine" issues in which the short novel resided in serial form. I read half the book that day, stayed in Bloomington to attend worship at the church at which I was an adherent on Sunday, and finished reading *On Trial* that Sunday afternoon.

Later that month I traveled back to Bloomington. I found several old reviews of Zack's books. One of them contained the first picture I had ever seen of Zack.

More finding and photocopying of reviews took place in the following months. I was writing letters to and fro. I began gradually to zero in on the place where Zack was born and lived. I wrote up a lot of notes on her books.

In the spring of 1984 I traveled to England. I am not a particularly good researcher, but I found out a few things. I have a copy of her birth certificate. I saw the stately country home of her birth, Port Hill, very near Northam, Devon. I found out quite a few family details which confirm the relatively high social status of Gwendoline Keats. (Please see Appendix IV for more on her family.)

I found out that Devonshire had no more memory of their talented daughter than did the rest of the world! She and her books were forgotten. There were no copies of her books in the public library at Northam, a very short distance from Port Hill where she was born. So even her hometown had no memory of her.

Back to the colonies. My writing diary begins Jan. 1, 1985, and seems to have no reference to any writing done on Gwendoline Keats/Zack. So it must have been in 1984 (at least partly while I was still in England) that I wrote the somewhat numerous pages on the books of Zack which I compiled. I wrote about 31,000 words, breaking off after dealing with her third book, *The White Cottage*.

There things remained for almost three decades. I reread Zack's books occasionally. (By now I have read each of the books four or more typically five times.) I did some writing, off and on, on topics not directly connected with Gwendoline Keats, but had close to zero success in getting published. By the time I got to my mid-50s it was clear that if I were going to publish anything, it would have to be the self-publication route. Encroaching old age concentrated the mind. I began publishing books in 2008. Once I did that, there was little doubt that I would get back to Gwendoline Keats eventually.

In fact, it may be disgraceful that I have put off the writing of this book for so long. It was presumptuous of me to assume that I would live as long as I have. To die without having written a book on Gwendoline Keats would have been an act of ingratitude.

She is a writer who has meant a great deal to me, both for her books and for her personality. Because she is so forgotten, it took a special arrangement of circumstances for me even to know that such a writer existed. I think—rightly or wrongly think, as Bertie Wooster would say—that God directed me to her books. He knew that I would appreciate them. But that also put a very reasonable burden on me, to do what I could to see that Gwendoline Keats/Zack is not completely lost to history. "'And from everyone who has been given much shall much be required; and to whom they entrusted much, of him they will ask all the more'" (Lk. 12:48). In being given the books of Gwendoline Keats, I was given much. It is a basic act of justice that I try to alert the world to the value of her works.

I began preparing this book in mid-February of 2013. My first Internet researches in 2009—I am what might be called a late adopter, having come to the Internet only in early 2009—had told me that a Margaret Gwendoline Keats (1895-1970) had been a veterinarian in Australia. The job description fit the social class of my Gwendoline Keats. The name Keats, the spelling of Gwendoline, the location Australia, the date of birth, all gave me great hope that Margaret Gwendoline Keats was the niece of Zack. M. G. Keats, I felt, might be the daughter of one of Zack's three brothers. However, I put off trying to do more research until 2013. I wasn't ready to begin work on this book yet; I was publishing other things.

I began to try to do more research early in 2013. Thanks to the magic of the Internet, and after a few questioning emails, I began to get good results. I was referred to Mrs. Beverley Keats, and was given her email address. Bullseye. Mrs. Keats was the wife of Andy Keats who is the grandson of Thorold Goodwin Keats—the oldest brother of Gwendoline Keats. Margaret Gwendoline was indeed one of T. G. Keats' children, and thus Gwendoline's niece as I had hoped. I was in connection with the family.

Without the assistance of Mrs. Beverley Keats, this book would bear little resemblance to its final form. She gave me an incredible amount of information which I could never have found out on my own.

That included transcription of letters, family lore regarding Zack, family history, and photographs. For one spectacular example of the information she provided, consider only the letter of T. G. Keats to his brother Fred, in which T. G. discusses Gwendoline's hopeless mental condition and the options for putting her in an insane asylum. (See Chapter 5.) I could never have found out any of that, without Mrs. Keats' help.

Writing this book has been a challenge, but enjoyable. I was able to use some of what I had written in 1984. However, I am also glad I did not try to finish and publish the book then. Clearly, I was not ready emotionally and intellectually to write this book in 1984. I might have been ready to write this book ten years ago, but not thirty. I am grateful that I had the persistence to find out what I could about Zack and write about her, in 1979-1984, and I thank my younger, more adventurous self for doing work I would not have the energy or spirit to take on now. But I am glad the attempt at publication was delayed until I was older. I think it is a better book because I waited.

I want this to be a good book, of course. But if an angel had told me, "If you publish this book, it will be on the list as one of The Ten Worst Books Ever Written; you can back out now, before you disgrace yourself"—if an angel had told me that, I would have gone ahead with publication anyway. Gwendoline Keats is so forgotten right now, that she is in the position that even bad publicity is helpful to her. So while I have tried to make this as good a book as I can, the most important thing is that the name(s) of Gwendoline Keats/Zack come before the public for the first time in a long time. I owe her a lot. She is a writer worth reading, and a person with a fascinating character.

APPENDIX IV

The Family and Birthplace
of Gwendoline Keats

The approach to Northam from the Bideford road is highly
picturesque, on account of the numerous villas and country
houses scattered over the hilly grounds; among these the
principal are Port Hill, the seat of Vice-Admiral Charlewood
JP;

Kelly's Directory of Devonshire & Cornwall 1883

Gwendoline Keats was born into a family of some considerable
social status. Her birth certificate tells us that she was born at Port Hill,
Northam, Devonshire, England on Fourth October 1865.

Port Hill was the name of her family's home. Port Hill was built in
1760 by August Saltren Willet. Apparently he was the original owner.
Port Hill is about ½ mile south of Northam, and about 1.8 miles north
of Bideford. It sits on the west side of the A386 road, about 120 yards
from the road. The front of the house faces south. This stately home
is currently owned by Michael and Penny Portman. By the date of
Gwendoline Keats' birth the house was already 105 years old.

The birth was registered by her father on Nov. 13, 1865. (We should
note here that sometimes the name Port Hill is given as Porthill. But it
was Port Hill on the birth certificate.)

Her name was Bertha Gwendoline Keats. Her father's name was
William Rochfort Keats, and his occupation was given as "Captain
Rifle Voolunteers." The signature of the registrar was by John Mill.
(The misspelling of volunteers is either that of John Mill or of William
Keats.) The handwriting of William Keats and John Mill look exactly

the same to me. Did John Mill fill in all the blanks, in the presence of William Keats? Or vice versa? I don't know for sure. Box number 9 required the "Signature of registrar," so that would incline me to believe that John Mill filled in all the blanks. On the other hand, box number 7 is supposed to include the signature of the informant. Did Mr. Keats, perhaps holding his infant daughter in his arms so that signing the birth certificate would be inconvenient, simply say to John Mill, "Oh, John, you can sign for me."?

We are unlikely ever to know for sure. We do have the following further piece of evidence. Mrs. Beverley Keats supplied me with a handwriting sample (from 1841) of William Rochfort Keats, which included his signature. While I am certainly no expert in reading handwriting, it does seem to me that William Rochfort Keats did *not* do the writing on the birth certificate. This of course is strictly a guess on my part.

As we saw when discussing the story "The Red-Haired Man," Zack used the name Roch as the name of one of her important characters. Roch of course is taken from her father's middle name Rochfort. And her younger brother Arthur's middle name was also Rochfort.

The mother's name, with her maiden name at the end, was given as Lucy Elizabeth Keats formerly Thorold. Her maiden name of Thorold provided the Christian name of her firstborn child, a son, Thorold Goodwin Keats.

Bertha Gwendoline's paternal grandfather was William Abraham Keats, an admiral. He was a widower (twice) living with the family in 1871, but it may be more correct to say that the family was living with him, since Port Hill had been purchased by the admiral. Admiral Keats died in May of 1874, when Gwendoline was about 8 ½ years old.

Mrs. Keats reports that some articles on the Internet claim that the uncle of Admiral Keats was the first Keats family member to own Port Hill. This would be another admiral, Admiral Sir Richard Goodwin Keats. William served with Sir Richard in the earlier part of William's naval career. Mrs. Keats inclines to the belief, however, that Admiral William Keats was the first Keats to own the property.

The first wife of Admiral William Keats died by drowning, just after their marriage. His second wife, Augusta Lyford Keats, the mother of

William Rochfort Keats, gives Zack an astonishing connection to Jane Austen. Augusta Lyford was daughter of Giles King Lyford, a well-regarded doctor who treated Jane Austen in the last days of her life. So Zack's grandmother on her father's side was the daughter of Jane Austen's doctor! No need for "six degrees of separation" here between two remarkable writers; call it one or two degrees. Augusta Lyford Keats died in 1867, when Gwendoline was not quite 2 years old.

William Keats and Lucy Elizabeth Thorold were married on Feb. 19, 1862. Their union produced five children, of whom four lived to adulthood.

The oldest was Thorold Goodwin (called Bob in the family). He was born on Jan. 29, 1863.

Herbert Frederick Cyril (Fred to his family members) was born on Apr. 9, 1864.

Bertha Gwendoline was the third child born to William and Lucy Keats. Gwendoline (called Gwenda by her family) was born on Oct. 4, 1865.

Approximately two years later (in 1867) a fourth child, another son, was born--Arthur Rochfort.

A fifth child, a daughter, Augusta Julia, was born in early 1871. Mrs. Keats alerted me to the existence of a website called Genuki. There we learn that Augusta Julia's gravesite features an upright small stone cross in the form of logs. The inscription reads: Augusta Julia Keats/ Infant Daughter Of/W. Rochfort Keats And Lucy E. Keats/Of Porthill In This Parish/Died Febry 3rd 1871, Aged 10 Days/"Of Such Is The Kingdom of Heaven." The quote is a reference to Matthew 19:14. The disciples had been rebuking people for bringing children to Jesus to put His hands on and to pray over, 'But Jesus said, "Suffer little children, and forbid them not, to come unto me: for of such is the kingdom of heaven'" (KJV; compare Luke 18:16, which is similar). Given the words on the gravestone, we can estimate Augusta Julia's date of birth as Jan. 25, 1871. Gwendoline would have been about 5 1/3 years old when her newborn sister was taken from her. This early death probably made quite an impression on young Gwenda. The early deaths of children are frequent in her books.

Findmypast.com reports that all five of the children--even Augusta Julia, who lived just ten days--were baptized in the year of their birth, into the Anglican denomination, the baptism place being listed as "Northam & Appledore."

Death would come calling again soon, for the Keats family. William, the father of Thorold, Frederick, Gwendoline, Arthur, and the late Augusta, died at age 35 of tuberculosis when Gwendoline was about a month short of her seventh birthday. He is buried close to Augusta Julia. More on his burial site in a bit.

Mrs. Keats remarried within a couple years, in 1874, to the widower and retired vice-admiral Edward Phillips Charlewood. He was a justice of the peace for Devon. He was considerably older than his bride. He was in his early 60s, Mrs. Keats in her mid to late 30s. This marriage also proved fruitful. A son was born, Charles Aubrey Charlewood, then two years later a daughter, Nora E. Charlewood. Admiral Charlewood had ten children by his first marriage. We know that his unmarried daughter Alice F. Charlewood, age 31, was living at Port Hill in 1881. We also know that another of his daughters, Sarah Catharine, was married to the brother of Lucy Elizabeth Thorold Keats, mother of Thorold, Frederick, Gwendoline, Arthur, and Augusta.

Mrs. Lucy Elizabeth Thorold Keats Charlewood did not live to raise her six living children to adulthood. She died, probably of cancer, on May 19, 1881, when Gwenda was about 15 ½ years old. So, by her mid teens, Gwenda had seen her sister, father, grandfather, and mother die.

Mrs. Charlewood was still a young woman--about 45--when she died. Despite her marriage to Edward Charlewood, she was buried beside her first husband, close beside Augusta Julia. Genuki tells us that their tombstone is an upright large marble cross in the form of logs, on a marble base in the form of rocks with ivy. A footstone is similar but contains no cross. The inscription for the two of them reads: William Rochfort Keats/Died Died September 1st 1872 Aged 35/Also Lucy Elizabeth Charlewood/Died 19th May 1881. According to Genuki, the footstone reads: I Am The Resurrection/And The Light. At John 11:25, Jesus said, "'I am the resurrection, and the life: he that believeth in me, though he were dead, yet shall he live'" (KJV). One wonders if the footstone really says Light, or if that is a transcribing error by whoever put the information on the Internet.

Family legend has it that Thorold Goodwin did not like his stepfather. When Thorold reached his majority, Admiral Charlewood was forced to vacate Port Hill. Mrs. Beverley Keats reports that Admiral Charlewood was upset at having to vacate Port Hill. Apparently Admiral Charlewood went to France to live; he died at Biarritz, France, in 1894, at the age of 80. The fact that Admiral Charlewood vacated the property is a clear indication that the disposition of the valuable Port Hill property was at the disposal of the Keats children rather than at the disposal of their stepfather.

We have other incredibly strong evidence that the property remained in the Keats family rather than in that of Admiral Charlewood. Thanks to the indefatigable researches of Mrs. Beverley Keats, an extremely valuable piece of information about the Keats' Devon property reached me only in January of 2015. Mrs. Keats unearthed the fact that in 1883, Thorold Goodwin Keats owned 2,664 acres in Devon, the land having a gross annual value of £3,030. This information comes in a book published in 1883.

The book is *Great Landowners of Great Britain and Ireland,* by John Bateman, F. R. G. S., the 4th edition, published by Harrison, in London, England. On the title page a great deal of information also appears. I will quote it here, but leaving out italics and too many capitals: "A list of all owners of three thousand acres and upwards, worth £3,000 a year; also, one thousand three hundred owners of two thousand acres and upwards, in England, Scotland, Ireland, & Wales, their acreage and income from land, culled from The Modern Domesday Book; also their colleges, clubs, and services. Corrected in the vast majority of the cases by the owners themselves." The information regarding T. G. Keats, Porthill, comes on page 247. While T. G. Keats did not make the 3,000-acre mark, his 2,664 acres were well above 2,000 acres, and the gross annual value of £3,030 was obviously very large. The book is an astonishing fund of information. Anyone can visit it on the Internet. Needless to say, I would never have found it except for the help of Mrs. Keats, who I begin to believe is somehow related to Mr. Sherlock Holmes.

In the same letter in which Mrs. Keats showed the extent and value of the Keats property in Devon, she told me that her family research leads her to believe that in the Keats family "the tendency was for the eldest son to inherit."[66] The property being listed in the name of T. G. Keats in *Great Landowners of Great Britain and Ireland* would indicate confirmation of that tendency having been followed to the benefit of T. G. Keats.

Here, however, I want to exercise my imagination, and to indicate my belief that T. G. Keats felt a moral obligation to use the income from the property to the benefit of his siblings as well as himself. We remember that Gwendoline when living in Germany was receiving a family financial subsidy of some sort. Where could the money come from except from the proceeds from the Devon property? There is no contradiction here. Yes, T. G. Keats, the eldest son, inherited. But the expectation in the family--an expectation probably drilled into T. G. Keats from very early in life by his grandfather and by his parents-- would have been that he look out for his brothers and his sister as he inherited. My guess is that he did so, and that he did so well. Now that we know the extent and value of the Devon property, we can understand how it was that Gwendoline could afford to travel around England and Europe. Mrs. Keats has indeed given us a very valuable piece of information concerning the Keats family, their financial and social status, and how all this might relate to Gwendoline's ability to finance a life traveling from place to place and writing books.

After the death of their young sister Augusta Julia, the other four Keats children lived to adulthood. Thorold Goodwin died Oct. 12, 1928, at age 65. Fred died Nov. 28, 1916, at the age of 52. Arthur died July 29, 1927, at age 59 or 60. The three brothers lived all (or most) of their adult lives in Australia.

Their stepbrother Charles eventually served in the Boer War, and married Johanna Benjamina Vorster on July 18, 1906 at Ladysmith, Natal, South Africa. He settled in South Africa. Charles Oliver, uncle of the current owner of Port Hill, did some research on Port Hill, and concluded that Nora E. Charlewood grew up to marry a Mr. James of Hallsannery. She may ultimately have died in France.

---

[66]Email letter to me from Mrs. Beverley Keats, Jan. 26, 2015.

Thorold and Fred married sisters. Thorold married Jessie Eliza Cumming. Fred married Jessie's younger sister Mary Cecilia (Cis) Cumming. Both marriages turned out to be very fruitful.

Thorold was a farmer. Thorold and Jessie had seven children. Thanks to the researches of Mrs. Beverley Keats, we have considerable basic information about their lives, deaths, and families.

The firstborn child was Gladys Elizabeth (b. Oct. 14, 1886--d. Feb. 24, 1941). It was Gladys who was given a brooch by her Aunt Gwenda, only to have that brooch taken from her by her parents and returned to Aunt Gwenda! (See Chapter 6.) Gladys married Percy Bryer and they had three children. Elizabeth Anne and John Richard are deceased. Mrs. Keats believes the third child, a son, was still living in 2014.

Thora Violet (b. Nov. 2, 1887--d. October 1976) was the second child. Eventually she would keep the books for her father. Thora married Robert Hannah; they had one son who is believed still to be alive. Mrs. Beverley Keats met in person only two nieces and one nephew of Gwendoline Keats. Mrs. Keats has a vague memory of seeing Thora once in a nursing home.

Richard Goodwin (b. Apr. 14, 1890--d. Feb. 13, 1982) lived to be almost 92. This was the only nephew of Zack met in person by Mrs. Beverley Keats. Richard (Dick) married and had two daughters and one son. The family lived in Queensland in the northeast corner of Australia from the early 1900s. Two of their children had issue, at least one of whom may be alive.

Margaret Gwendoline (b. Aug. 14, 1895--d. Apr. 5 or 6, 1970) never married. There is more about her below.

William Thorold (b. Sept. 12, 1897--d. June 12, 1963) also went to Queensland and had property there. He married and had two sons and two daughters, all of whom married. At least one of the children (a daughter) was still alive in 2014. William suffered from the effects of gassing in World War I.

Sybil Anne (b. Nov. 6, 1898--d. July 17, 1967) remained unmarried. She spent considerable time in England during World War II, as she could not get back to Australia while the war raged. She died while visiting her brother Dick in Queensland. Mrs. Keats tells us that Sybil Anne Keats was interested in family history and gave her relations copies of the research she had accomplished. Those papers which went to Queensland sat on a verandah and were devoured by white ants! However, other copies survived, and Mrs. Keats subsequently has added to that research.

John Francis (b. July 3, 1901--d. Sept. 26, 1962) married and had one son, John Andrew, and one daughter, Jill April Christina. Jill married a man named Sutherland, and they had two children, a son and a daughter. Jill Keats Sutherland followed in the footsteps of her great-aunt Gwendoline Keats in becoming an author. She published, in 2000, a lengthy (750 pages) book entitled *Murrabit, Our Murrabit: The History of Why We're How We Are.* Murrabit is a small town in northeast Victoria, Australia. Wikipedia tells us that in the 2006 census, "Murrabit and the surrounding area had a population of 408." So Mrs. Sutherland wrote a very big book about a very small town! She died in 2012. The other child of John Francis, John Andrew, married Beverley. He was 81 in 2014. They have one son, John.

Readers of this book owe a special debt of gratitude to Margaret Gwendoline and to John Francis. Margaret's middle name was Gwendoline--clearly she was named after her aunt. Margaret gained a measure of fame in Australia. She was "the first woman to qualify as a veterinarian with University training in Australia."[67] She seems to have been a woman of extraordinary character--skilled, humble, gracious, and determined. She began her veterinary practice late in 1922, and continued until her death on April 5 or 6, 1970. Family legend tells us that originally she began her veterinary course with the idea of being better able to look after her father's animals on the farm, but she soon was responsible for veterinary service of a "massive area" of Victoria and New South Wales. She was awarded an MBE (Member of the Most Excellent Order of the British Empire). There is a Miss Keats Picnic Area in her honor in Murrabit, Victoria. And in March of 2008, thirty-eight years after her death, she was added to the Victorian Honour Roll of Women.

When in early 2009 I googled Gwendoline Keats along with the word Australia, I was alerted to the existence of Margaret Gwendoline

---

[67]Robin Giesecke, "Margaret Keats MBE BVSc: Australia's first University-trained woman veterinarian," an article available on the Internet.

Keats. I did not follow up the lead at that time, but did so in 2013, which led me eventually to Mrs. Beverley Keats--without whom this book would be vastly worse. The debt to John Francis comes about because it was his son John Andrew (Andy), who married Beverley.

Fred was a broker on the stock exchange in Melbourne, and also owned a property called Cobramunga. Fred and Cis had five children. Cis Cumming Keats was born July 23, 1865 at Darlington, Victoria, Australia.

We ("we" is a euphemism for Mrs. Beverley Keats) have good information on the births and deaths of most of the five children.

The firstborn child was Lucy Cecilia Anne (b. June 22, 1891--d. Aug. 27, 1978). She died in Melbourne at the age of 87. This was the second niece of Zack met in person by Mrs. Beverley Keats. She met Lucy Cecilia Anne Keats "on a few occasions."[68] Mrs. Keats has a fascinating memory of one of her meetings with Lucy: see the following paragraph for that.

Frederick Thorold (b. Aug. 20, 1892--d. May 25, 1916). He was at Cambridge when the world war broke out, and enlisted in England. He was killed in action. Mrs. Keats says that when she and Andy Keats had their son, Lucy Keats said the child was "the spitting image of her brother Fred."[69]

Frederick Thorold Keats, cut down at age 23, was a budding poet. About twelve of his poems, written prior to the war in 1910/11, survive in the family. Ernestina (Nesta) McKellar was the daughter of Grace Violet Cumming McKellar. Grace was a sister to Jessie and Cecilia, who married Keats brothers. The rumor in the family was Nesta and Freddy were going to marry. World War I, which ruined so many lives, put paid to that plan. Nesta never married. The poems, which may never have been published, were among Nesta's possessions. Gwendoline Keats, incidentally, encouraged Nesta to write. All this we know, of course, thanks to information provided by Mrs. Keats.

John Rochfort (b. Apr. 16, 1894--d. Dec. 17, 1964). He too was at Cambridge when the First World War broke out. He joined the military. He was wounded in the leg. When told he could go home,

---

[68]Email letter to me from Mrs. Beverley Keats, Jan. 7, 2015.
[69]Email letter to me from Mrs. Beverley Keats, Mar. 26, 2014.

he replied that if he was well enough to go home, he was well enough to continue to fight. He was awarded the Military Cross, and survived the war to live to age 70. Within the family he was knows as Roch. However, within his local Australian community of Murrabit, he was called Captain--very likely as a result of his World War I service.

Freda "Pauline" (b. May 23, 1897--d. Dec. 7, 1921). Freda married Alexander Thompson Heller, who was a fighter pilot in World War I. There is a fair amount of unverified family lore concerning this man. He may have flown under the London Bridge. Years later, he went missing after falling into the Murray River at Cobramunga (Australia). Apparently his body was never found and some people claimed to have seen him later in Melbourne. In any case, Freda and Alexander had a daughter named Pamela Pauline, who was born only a few weeks prior to her mother's death. Her mother Freda died at the young age of 24. Pamela was born Sept. 20, 1921, and died either the 8th or 9th of October, 1990. She had married a man named Moreland; the marriage produced no children. She died an alcoholic and a hermit.

The fifth and final child of the union of Fred and Cis Keats was Darby Ernest "Blythe." He was born March 2, 1902. He was cast off from the family because he stole from the estate, and also because he "married the publican's daughter."[70] He and his wife had a daughter.

Arthur Keats, like his stepbrother Charles Charlewood, served in the Boer War. Arthur married Eva Sarah Gollin, from a well-known Jewish family of South Australia. This union apparently produced only one child, a daughter named Lucy Gwendoline. (So for the second time Gwendoline Keats/Zack had a niece partly named after her, by a brother. Two of the Thoughty Ones picked a lovely way to honor their sister.) Mrs. Keats reports that Lucy "always said she was a Christian."[71] She lived in Perth. Lucy married and had two male children. There were many grandchildren and great-grandchildren from this branch of the family.

Arthur Keats married again after the death of his wife Eva Sarah. His second wife was named Elizabeth. Arthur died in Townsville, Queensland, Australia, on July 29 of 1927.

---

[70]Email letter to me from Mrs. Beverley Keats, Mar. 26, 2014.

[71]Email letter to me from Mrs. Beverley Keats, Apr. 2, 2014.

Mrs. Keats believes that only a few of the living Keats family know much about Zack. Her books are little remembered or read among them. This, I would submit, is very much in accord with what we would expect of human nature. Zack is not famous enough to prompt family members to much curiosity about her. Her books are not lying about everywhere; an effort is needed to find them. Moreover, she has been dead at least 81 years, and perhaps 105 years. We most of us are content to live in our own time, and to let the dead bury their dead.

I hope the publication of this book will encourage Keats family members to take a longer look at their distinguished relative Gwendoline Keats/Zack.

APPENDIX V

Zack's Letters to May Sinclair

> Why are you so downhearted dear Beggar. Your work is good
> & that is all that really matters in the long run.

Zack to May Sinclair, July 5, 1899

May Sinclair (1863-1946) wrote about 40 books in her long life, including approximately two dozen novels. Due to illness, she was mostly silent the last fifteen years of her life.

While she is not wildly famous today, she is far better remembered and far more frequently read than Zack. She has attracted recently scholarly books by Theophilus T. M. Boll (1973) and Suzanne Raitt (2000). There is a new (began 2013) May Sinclair Society active on the Internet.

The friendship of May Sinclair and Zack began when they were both in the early stages of their writing careers. May's letters to Zack are lost, so we can only reconstruct events from Zack's letters and from guesswork.

Reading Zack's letters, it seems likely that May Sinclair read something by Zack, admired it greatly, and wrote Zack. Zack welcomed the correspondence, read and liked May's work, and encouraged her. (See Chapter 6.) The two occasionally spent time together, although likely not a lot.

The surviving letters, Zack to May, are collected at the Rare Book and Manuscript Library at the University of Pennsylvania in Philadelphia, Pennsylvania, U.S.A. Some few of the letters are undated and difficult to place in time, at least for me. (I have seen only photocopies, and it might help to see the originals, which include many envelopes.)

The 70 letters range over six years, 1898-1903. We now know why the correspondence stopped completely after 1903—Zack apparently was institutionalized in a lunatic asylum, or at least was no longer sane. The letters are distributed like this: 1898—34 letters; 1899—14 letters; 1900—2 letters; 1901—10 letters; 1902—7 letters; 1903—3 letters. This distribution might need to be adjusted slightly, as there are a few letters difficult to place. (Zack could have done a better job of helping out people like me figure out when she was writing, and exactly from where!) While obviously the correspondence was most frequent in its first year, by a lot, it continued to be steady except for 1900. Is it possible that some letters from 1900 are lost? From the context, the last letter from 1899 for which we have an approximate date was probably written in November. The next letter is from Oct. 26 of 1900. It seems a large gap, and the tone of the letters doesn't hint at any quarrel between the two friends.

The salutations of Zack's letters are interesting. The salutations of the first five letters are very formal, with the words Dear Miss Sinclair. The sixth letter introduces Dear Beggar. There is no explanation for this, but we can at least make a guess. May Sinclair may have written a letter including something like, "I know my writing will be a failure. I'll probably end up a beggar on the streets." Perhaps Zack then responded with the humorous salutation. It easily led the way in number of uses among the salutations. A few more Dear Miss Sinclairs followed, but from then on Dear Beggar led the way.

There was a tremendous variety in the salutations, however. (Warning: it is difficult sometimes to read Zack's handwriting. What I took to be Dear Drifter, Theophilus Boll believed was Dear Duffer. He could well be correct.) In their order of first appearance, here are the salutations: Dear Miss Sinclair—10; Dear Beggar—27; Dear Drifter—2; [no salutation]—6; Dear Brainy One—1; Dear Stoic—1; Dear old Beggar—2; [missing word due to torn paper (Dear?)] Friend—1; Dear old Friend—1; My Dear Beggar—1; Dear old Drifter—1; My dear Brother-in-Arms—1; My dear May—3; Dear old May—3; My poor dear old Beggar [on responding to the death of May's mother]—1;

Dear May—6; Dearest May—1. We can see that near the end of the correspondence Zack was most commonly using some form of Dear May. The feisty, cheerful, ironic tone of Dear Beggar was giving way to the quieter Dear May. Perhaps Zack was worn out emotionally. But I may be reading too much into this, probably because I know that she was only months or weeks away from losing her sanity forever.

The closings contain even greater variety. She used a total of 77 closings (that is, counting none as a closing) in the 70 letters. So in several cases she used two closing phrases. In their order of first appearance, here are the closings: Great haste—9; Yours sincerely—16; Yours very truly—4; Yours in haste—7; Goodbye dear Beggar—1; Yours with many thanks—1; [none]—10; Great haste dear old Beggar—1; Yours—9; Very truly yours—1; Sincerely yours—3; Yours in great haste—5; Yours with every good wish—1; Your affec friend—1; Yours affecly—2; Great haste dear Beggar—1; Yours with much kindly feeling—1; Your affct friend—1; Yours great haste—1; Yours with much that is rubbishy in it—1; Affecly yours—1.

Gwendoline Keats/Zack signed her name six different ways in the 70 letters. In their order of first appearance, here are the six versions: Gwendoline Keats—24; Zack—34; Gwenda Keats—3; Gwenda—6; G. K.—2; Z—1. Gwenda was how she was most commonly known in her own family, and she used that version of her name nine times when communicating with May as well.

Some writers put a lot of time and thought into their correspondence. This is not the case with Zack. I think it is fair to say that she poured the best of her artistry and intellect into her books. The letters are dashed off quickly, and are mostly short or shorter. Her closings include the word haste 24 times.

Her handwriting, as I said above, is not easy to read. (Again, not helping out future researchers!) I was able to decipher most of it, but not all. Usually in these cases her meaning is clear from the context. Misspellings are fairly common, but rather mild, such as any well-educated person in a hurry might make. The punctuation follows a logic of its own—original if eccentric. For example, she sometimes has a colon followed by a dash. Or, alternatively, a dash followed by a colon. Some of this type of thing seems to show up in her books as well.

With the help of Google and Wikipedia, I was able to see that many of Zack's friends and acquaintances were part of the intellectual elite of her day. Here are a few examples.

"Mr. Courtney wrote to me on behalf of Chapman & Hall asking to publish my next book." William Leonard Courtney was the chief dramatic critic and literary editor of "The Daily Telegraph."

"Mr. Colvin told me." Sidney Colvin was a literary and art critic, a friend of Robert Louis Stevenson. Colvin married Fanny Sitwell, RLS's friend, in either 1901 or 1903. His name turns up often in Zack's letters. In a later letter Zack mentions a conversation with Mrs. Sitwell (in 1898, before her marriage to Colvin).

"Awfully pleased to hear Miss Hogarth thinks well of the book." Janet Hogarth was a writer and encyclopedia editor, who married W. L. Courtney in 1911. In a later letter Zack says she would (underlined) like to meet Miss Hogarth, "but expect I am too desperately shy ever to do so." In another letter she says that she is sure Miss Hogarth will think her a great fool if they meet—"my shyness driving away the few wits I have at any time." However, she did eventually meet with Miss Hogarth. A letter probably from late 1901 mentions Zack's pleasure in Miss Hogarth visiting her.

"Thank Miss Zimmern." Helen Zimmern was a German/English writer and translator.

"Quiller Couch has written me a letter full of praise." Sir Arthur Quiller-Couch was a poet, novelist, and critic who sometimes published under the pen name of Q.

"I am going to set an irrepressible girl called Gertrude Godden on your book." Gertrude Godden was an anthropologist and folklorist, eventually a winner of the Order of the British Empire.

"Mrs. W. K. Clifford came to see me yesterday; I told her about your book." Mrs. Clifford was a novelist and journalist.

The examples above are enough to indicate that Zack was moving in high intellectual circles. Here's just one more. I gave this following quote earlier in the book, but it bears repeating here. It is from September 13, 1899. "Had afternoon tea with George Meredith last Monday, it was awfully interesting but rather nervous work—he asked me to come again." George Meredith was of course a very famous novelist of the day.

As discussed in Chapter 6, the letters show the astonishing mobility—probably restlessness—of Gwendoline Keats/Zack. She moved about constantly. She had spent time in Germany, Italy, and Australia in her early adult years. During the course of the six years of the letters she visited Italy twice, and spent time in Scotland, Ireland, North Wales, and at about 20 locations in England. Incidentally, the letter written from Scotland is one for which I had to make an estimate as to its date, which I hopefully guessed as 1899.

The letters give many hints as to the circumstances and personality of Gwendoline Keats.

At least three times she calls herself penniless. The first time is when she says about *Life Is Life* that "I am practically penniless & it is important for me that the book shld sell." When discussing the possibility of publication of her next book (*On Trial*) she says in the summer of 1898 "I am so desperately penniless I really must make old B. pay a little more if he does take it." Old B. was the publisher of "Blackwood's Magazine" and also a book publisher. She already had an offer from Methuen, which she misspells as Metheun. A third time she uses the word penniless is in her next to the last letter to May. Zack thought *The Roman Road* "too bad to publish, then found I could not write anything this year either & being quite penniless published the book." In her final letter to May in 1903, she says concerning the "makeshift" *The Roman Road*, that "I was so hard up, I was obliged to publish something." In January of 1901 she included a one-paragraph sentence with just the words: "Beastly hard up."

We sense "penniless" to be hyperbole, and thus far from being strictly true. She had income from her books and from sales of short stories, and apparently she had a periodic allowance from whatever wealth her parents left. But while she may not have been absolutely penniless, she probably had to manage a small income carefully. On this (probably) small income she managed to travel a lot! Someone with a more cautious personality probably would have settled down in one spot, to be able to husband her resources more readily. But then she did not have a cautious personality. This I think shows up in her writing, as well as in her adventurous driving of six-horse carriages at race speed.

It seems she could be shy—witness the comments above regarding the possibility of meeting Miss Hogarth.

She may have been prickly at times. This would relate to the hastiness she demonstrated as discussed in Chapter 6. In a letter possibly from August of 1899, writing from Dorchester, she says, "What terrible people they are for calling on one—have been awfully rude, can't really stand facing strangers." Shyness, hastiness, prickliness may have made a bad combination on occasion. We can only hope that her "awfully rude" was at least to some extent exaggeration. In April of 1899 she says, "Got an invite to the Women's Writers dinner for June—but refused."

The letters give us good hints that she was physically active. As mentioned in Chapter 6, she speaks several times of bicycling; once she speaks of possibly bicycling with May, and once she has May send her a bicycle. (There was the racing of six-horse carriages, of course, although I don't remember that kind of thing being mentioned in her letters to May.)

Animals were part of her life. Once she mentions having bought a parrot, and in the same letter she says she has taken up showing terriers, at which she had won three second places. And as described in Chapter 6, the problems of her very ill dog had been a large contributing factor to making 1902 a difficult year.

She mentions several times having tried to write a play, and also mentions the possibility of writing a play with May, but it seems certain that no play of hers was ever produced. In a letter probably from early October of 1898 she writes, "Mr. Colvin thinks the play I wrote at Alfoxden too crude & terrible—so that's no go except as far as practice may be concerned." It is at least possible that "crude & terrible" did not mean crude and terrible in the sense of horrible writing, but rather crude and terrible in the sense of dealing with crude and terrible incidents. A reading of *Life Is Life* will quickly give a sense of what a play in 1898 by Zack was inclined to be like. It probably would not be for playgoers who were faint of heart! It is a pity that the play has not come down to us—even if it was "crude & terrible" in the most pejorative sense.

Theophilus T. M. Boll mentions how frequently Zack depended on May Sinclair to run errands for her. This is true. It may or may not have been a one-sided situation. It may have been that Zack was asking too much of May. Or it may have been that Zack was also running an occasional errand for May. And we need to remember that May was in or around London, the center of England and almost of the world, whereas Zack was mostly out in the countryside.

We know that Zack was doing what she could to further May's acceptance as a writer. The letters show her encouraging May constantly, and also doing what she could among her friends and acquaintances to recommend May's books to their attention. She was certainly generous-spirited in her support of May's books.

As with most writers—perhaps 100% of them, or a slightly higher percentage—she was pained by adverse criticism. But she struggled to be objective, and could sometimes agree that some unfavorable comments had hit their mark. I think she was helped along to objectivity by a genuine strain of humility in her character. She was not always trying to make much of herself and of her work. Two other factors of her personality helped her cope with unfair or thoughtless criticism. One, she seems to have been a brave person, well constituted to accept the slings and arrows of the literary life without undue misery. Two, she seems to have had a confidence in her own writing path. She knew what she could do, and she knew it was worth doing. (She was correct.) So if humility and confidence logically can fit together—and I think they can—they fit together in the personality of Gwendoline Keats.

Early on in her publishing career, "The Bookman" asked her to contribute a picture of herself. Here is her comment to May in a letter of July 8, 1898. The quote will also give some of the flavor of her slightly eccentric punctuation.

> The Bookman wrote & asked for my likeness to appear at the same time as their review of my book—: I didn't send it: I felt that for an absolutely unknown writer to allow her photo to be published would smack of something worse than ill taste—: also I hate the whole modern spirit of self advertisement.

Nine days later she writes on the same topic again.

> The Bookman wrote again for my photo, & today the Sketch—however, I refused:—for some things I regretted refusing—my brothers are not literary & they would have thought much of that kind of sucess [one c seems to be missing in her spelling of success].
>
> Still I like my old erractic [probably she means erratic] hole in the corner life best. I should hate to think of myself grinning away in some fool of a paper.
>
> Again I suppose having ones photo in the Sketch would help the sale of the book—however can't be helped. Chingaringo. [apparently an exclamatory word of some sort]

In late July she writes that she suspects that not giving her photo led "that mean Sketch" to dock her review in consequence.

However, apparently she did not stick to her resolve concerning her photograph appearing in the magazines. By no later than December of 1898, her picture began to appear occasionally. "The Academy" and "Review of Reviews" both printed photographs of her in that month. She doesn't explain her change of mind. Perhaps a magazine publisher, or May, was able to present her with cogent arguments—which can easily be made—as to why there was nothing dishonorable in having her photograph given to the public.

It is touching to hear Zack say that her brothers are not literary and would have thought much of that kind of success. Quite understandably she wanted her brothers to be proud of their sister, and she regretted not having her picture in the magazines, for their sake. When her picture did begin to appear in magazines, did she send copies along to her brothers? Or did she send along an occasional review which was very favorable to her work, even though no picture accompanied such a review? We can hope and expect and guess that the Thoughty Ones were appropriately proud of their sister, who had begun to make her mark on English literature despite being a "'Girl!'"

The sense of humor which is constant in her books, shows up in her letters often as well. For one example, she wrote a long sentence (possibly the first letter to May, or at least one of the first) about May's relationship with Mr. Blackwood. Her next paragraph is one sentence:

"There's a long sentence, minus punctuation & grammar for you!!" When she asks May to buy and send her a christening robe for the coachman's little baby, she adds, "Don't know how such things run—suppose dearer than the babies themselves."

She took her writing seriously, no matter how dismissive of it she could be in her letters to May. One of her comments regarding writing will ring true for all writers, for all time. She was trying to encourage the often discouraged May. "Your work is good, & that is all that really matters in the long run." (The word "is" is underlined once, but "good" is underlined twice.) This is a very insightful comment about what really matters in the long run. Writing success is all very well, and every writer is glad to sell as many copies as he can. Zack was no doubt pleased when she found out that *On Trial* was going into a second edition after a first edition run of 2,000 copies (from a letter possibly written in November of 1899). (I'd kill to sell 2,000 copies of one of my books. No, I'd kill to sell even 200 copies of one of them. Twenty? Probably.) But the most important thing is to do good work.

To do good work is exactly what Zack attempted to do. I think she succeeded. Her current forgotten status hints otherwise! Perhaps God alone is fit to make an exactly correct judgment. Until I am convinced otherwise—not likely—I will continue to bet on Zack. She did good work, and hopefully the day will come when that good work is recognized and appreciated by a large handful of people.

In any case, we are fortunate to have the letters of Zack to May Sinclair. They give us a window into the character of a fascinating woman.

APPENDIX VI

Finding Zack's Books

> "Or what woman, if she has ten silver coins and loses one coin, does not light a lamp and sweep the house and search carefully until she finds it? And when she has found it, she calls together her friends and neighbors, saying, 'Rejoice with me, for I have found the coin which I had lost!'"

> Luke 15:8-9

Zack's books are no longer difficult to obtain, despite the fact that she is currently unread and forgotten. The clue to this paradox is quickly found: print on demand publication permits the photocopying of out of print books at relatively inexpensive cost. Don't ask me to explain how they do it. I just know that it works.

The five Zack books I bought in this way worked out extremely well. One sometimes hears of people who have received incomplete books when ordering such print on demand photocopies—not any of Zack's books, as far as I know—so there can be problems. But I have had nothing but success, except for minor problems as noted below. With one exception, the prices were not low, but they also were not exorbitantly high.

Since Zack published her books 1898-1903, there is no longer a copyright on them. Anyone can print Zack's books.

All I did was go to Amazon.com and check out the options: Zack's books can be obtained. This process may not work for all authors, but it works for Zack.

Here are the five print on demand books I have purchased successfully. All are paperbacks.

Life Is Life. In April of 2014 I purchased this book from Nevido Books for $15.47 plus $3.99 shipping, for a total cost of $19.46. The size is 5" by 8". The print is dark, but it seems to me that it could have been larger. In the last story of the book, the text is lower down on the page than it should be. And on the final page of the book, the words retreat to a still smaller size. So this was not ideal, but it was certainly not a horrible edition.

On Trial was put out by BiblioLife, LLC. Their edition is from the 1899 Charles Scribner's Sons book published in New York. The print is large, dark, and clear, in a book 5" by 8". Their advertisement in the back of the book tells us that they feature larger than average typeface. The company can be found on the Internet at bibliolife.com. They have a mailing address also: BiblioLife, PO Box 21206, Charleston, SC 29413, USA. In August of 2013 I purchased this book from Nevido Books, for $13.99 plus $3.99 shipping, for a total cost of $17.98. So Nevido Books did better on this book than they did on *Life Is Life.*

The White Cottage is a reprint from the collections of the University of California Libraries. Their edition is from the 1901 Charles Scribner's Sons book published in New York. The print is not particularly dark, but it is plenty clear enough for reading. This book is also 5" by 8". More information can be found on the Internet at hathitrust.org and at bookprep.com. In August of 2013 I purchased this book for $18.04, with free shipping.

Tales of Dunstable Weir is a facsimile of the 1901 Scribner's Sons New York edition put out by Forgotten Books (forgottenbooks.org). It features very large, dark print, in a 6" by 9" book (larger than the previous three listed). The book from which they made their copy is stamped The Property of the New York Society Library. I got this book for a very low price: just $8.27 with free shipping, through Amazon. I purchased it in late June of 2014.

Astonishingly, in April of 2014 I was also able to purchase a used hardcover copy of *Tales of Dunstable Weir*—the Books For Libraries Press reprint mentioned below—from Full Paper Jacket, for $.01 plus $3.99 shipping, for a total of $4.00. This book had been withdrawn from

Ramaker Library of Northwestern College, Orange City, Iowa. The book had never been checked out and was in pristine condition. If you keep an eye open you may be able to find such bargain prices for others of Zack's books. Such opportunities no doubt are rare, but they occur.

In late June of 2014 I purchased a facsimile edition of *The Roman Road*. It is a Nabu Public Domain Reprint. It is a big but not unwieldy book, 7 1/2" by 9 3/4", and the print is big and dark. Their copy comes from the 1903 Scribner's Sons New York edition. Nabu made their copy of *The Roman Road* from a book in the Harvard College Library. Stamped into the original was information that this book was a Nov. 16, 1926 gift of Albert Bushnell Hart to the Harvard Library. The book cost me $16.13 plus $3.99 shipping for a total cost of $20.12.

Books For Libraries Press, Freeport, New York, published hardcover reprints of three of Zack's books a generation ago. They published *Life Is Life* in 1969, *Tales of Dunstable Weir* in 1969, and *The Roman Road* in 1971. I own one copy of each of these—now two of *Tales*—and they are very nice 5" by 8" hardcover books. They have no dust covers. There is no accompanying comment on Zack or on the books—just the original text of the books. You might be able to find these for sale as used books on Amazon.com, as I did with *Tales of Dunstable Weir*.

You can read all five of Zack's books for free on the Internet!

Ms. Suzanne Raitt, author of *May Sinclair: A Modern Victorian*, kindly has alerted me to the fact that *Life Is Life* is available at the website hathitrust.org.

At the website openlibrary.org, I found *On Trial*, *The White Cottage*, and *Tales of Dunstable Weir*.

At the website archive.org I found *The Roman Road*.

Here is a perfect way to sample some of Zack's work without having to invest money. The pages turned easily by pushing on the arrow, and the size of the print could be increased if necessary, at least on most of these.

The copy of *On Trial* which openlibrary.org used gives us some fascinating information on the popularity (and lack thereof) of the novel. This copy of *On Trial* belonged to The Boston-Library Society. A record of how many times the book was checked out is given. In 1899, the year the book became available, the book was checked out seven times in the last 3 1/2 months of the year. In 1900 the book was checked out 13 times through mid-October. After that, the book was checked out only once more, in 1914. So the book had a brief flurry of popularity, being checked out 20 times in thirteen months. After that, the book was instantly forgotten and ignored. This seems symbolic of Zack's career as a whole—a brief flash of interest and fame, then completely forgotten. Well, not completely, since the books are still available for those who take the trouble to search them out.

APPENDIX **VII**

Ten Writers for a Desert Island

> Finally, brethren, whatever is true, whatever is honorable, whatever is right, whatever is pure, whatever is lovely, whatever is of good repute, if there is any excellence and if anything worthy of praise, let your mind dwell on these things.
>
> Philippians 4:8

Here are the rules. You are going to be stranded for the rest of your life on a desert island. However, a beneficent Providence permits you to take along the complete works of ten fiction writers—and ten only—to read as often as you want.

If the writer wrote anything other than fiction, all of that too could be taken along. (These are my rules, and I'll make them come out the way I want them.)

An exercise like this concentrates the mind. One discovers the writers who really are most important to him.

What does this have to do with Zack? Well, if readers look over my list and see several writers who would make their own list, then it might encourage them to consider that Zack might be a writer worth trying. Of course, if you are in sympathy with none of the nine well-known writers on my list, you might not be attracted to Zack's books either.

In alphabetical order, here are the ten writers whose complete works I will take along when exiled to a desert island.

1/Jane Austen
2/Charles Dickens

3/Fyoder Dostoyevsky
4/W. W. Jacobs
5/C. S. Lewis
6/Aleksandr Solzhenitsyn
7/Anthony Trollope
8/Mark Twain
9/P. G. Wodehouse
10/Zack/Gwendoline Keats

For the most part, I found it surprisingly easy to pick my ten. These are almost entirely clear-cut choices. My list of honorable mentions had some distinguished names: Anne Brontë, Franz Kafka, J. D. Salinger, Leo Tolstoy. (No doubt P. G. Wodehouse would be delighted to find that he edged out Leo Tolstoy. I just couldn't give up the Wooster/Jeeves books.)

Zack makes my list.

For those keeping track, I came up with seven English writers, two Russians (in English translations), and one from the United States.

This is a fun exercise. Make up your own list, tell me mine is ridiculous—and think about at least trying one of the books of Zack/Gwendoline Keats.

Appendix VIII

Zack's Future

> Termater Bill cleared his throat and spat into the open grave. "Life," he said, "was a jumpt-up quare thing: there wa' they who bottomed payable dirt (*Bottom payable dirt*=find sufficient gold to pay working expenses.—Zack) fust go off, an' thar wa' they who—didn't." He was silent for a moment, and rubbed his face with his sleeve. "But," he continued, "maybe out thar," and he pointed vaguely towards a patch of sunset sky, "across the Divide, they finds colour." (*Find colour*=find gold.—Zack)
>
> Zack, "The Busted Blue Doll" in *Life Is Life*

It is difficult to know whether Zack will ever find a spot among those writers who are remembered and read.

The epigraph above might be applied to Zack's prospects. She "'bottomed payable dirt'"—which her footnote to the story tells us means to "find sufficient gold to pay working expenses"—immediately in her writing career. She gained a significant measure of respect and fame among the reading public. Then, very quickly, she was among "'they who—didn't.'" She was forgotten very quickly.

But as Termater Bill tells us, things don't necessarily always stay the same. Zack has gone across the Divide. Maybe she was one who "'finds colour'"—which her footnote to the story tells us means to "find gold"—when she came into the presence of God. And maybe she will again find color—find an appreciative reading audience—on the earth. I think she deserves it.

I hope someday to submit an article on her to Wikipedia. I don't know whether or not I will succeed at getting that placed.

Eventually I hope to start a website or blog devoted to Gwendoline Keats/Zack. If you read the books of Gwendoline Keats/Zack, and put up your own website or blog devoted to her, fantastic. The mare the moorier, or however that phrase goes.

I will be delighted to hear from anyone on the topic of Zack. My mailing address and email address are both listed in Other Books By the Author. Don't put off writing too long; I am closing in on Methuselah in terms of age, so I may not be around a lot longer.

A very grateful thank you to John G. Keats, the son of Andy and Beverley Keats, who kindly has granted permission for his email address and mailing address to be printed in this book in case future readers become interested in Gwendoline Keats/Zack. His email address is john@evanskeats.com, and his mailing address is:

John G. Keats
31 Cobden Street
South Melbourne
Victoria 32 05
Australia

I hope that someday, and the sooner the better, several Zack scholars will exist. Can that really happen? Well, read *Life Is Life*. Then, if you liked it, read the other Zack books. You may find yourself hearing the words of Nathan echoing in your ears: "Thou art the man" (2 Sam. 12:7, KJV). Or, to be politically correct, "Thou art the man or woman."

ACKNOWLEDGMENTS

He knelt down aside her. "Mother," he said, "do 'ee love me?"
"Ay, lad."
"It be a deal to me. Be it aught to you, mother?"
"Ay, lad, a deal."
"Life gived us one to t'other," he said.

Zack, "The Hall and He" in *Tales of Dunstable Weir*

Four people especially deserve special acknowledgment in making *By Noble Things She Stands* possible.

First, a grateful thank you to Hugh Walpole, who spoke up in generous praise of another author, in his novel *Harmer John* (1926). His praise of Zack's *On Trial* piqued my interest, and led me to search for the books of an author totally unknown to me.

Second, Mrs. Beverley Keats of Australia has been incredibly helpful in providing information about Gwendoline Keats/Zack. She has provided family lore, genealogies, transcriptions of letters, and Internet references. For just one example of how important she was to this book, I could have known nothing about Zack's descent into madness, without the transcription of Thorold Goodwin Keats' letter concerning Gwendoline, written to their brother Fred. Without the input of Mrs. Beverley Keats, this book would be a faint shadow of itself. I thank you, and anyone who ever becomes interested in the books and life of Gwendoline Keats, will have reason to thank you as well.

Third, I want to thank God for allowing me to find out that Gwendoline Keats/Zack existed and wrote astonishing books. I think He had to make a special effort to alert me to her existence. I think He did so because He knew I would appreciate her. And possibly also because He doesn't want her books to be forgotten, and He knew I would (eventually) do what I could to bring her name before the public. Thank you for creating Gwendoline Keats, for the great writing gift you bestowed upon her, for fostering her brave and unique character, for making sure I discovered her books, and for letting me live long enough to write about her.

Fourth and finally, thank you to Gwendoline Keats/Zack. You were given a talent, and you didn't hide it away under a bushel. You exercised that talent, and gave the world remarkable books which deserve to be read as long as the world exists and perhaps beyond. I hope you will be patient with *By Noble Things She Stands*. I think you will be. If I have read your character correctly, I think there was always a strain of humility and good humor in you which would have caused you to be willing to make the best of things without complaining too much. Now that you have entered the afterlife, I suspect and hope that your humility and good humor are only increasing. This book no doubt has flaws and weaknesses, but as you well know, such things are commonplace in our world. Life is life.

OTHER BOOKS BY THE AUTHOR

The following books are all paperback, and all are published by AuthorHouse in Bloomington, Indiana:

The Army of God: The Church, 165 pp., 2008, $16.00.
Financing the Vast Expanse of the Kingdom of God, 87 pp., 2009, $13.00.
The Christian Betrayal of the United States, 235 pp., 2010, $18.00.
Christianity for Rich People, 94 pp., 2011, $13.00.
Inconvenient Opinions, 246 pp., 2011, $18.00.
Nameless Heroes of the Bible, 372 pp., 2012, $22.00.
Is Slavery Christian?, 124 pp., 2012, $13.00.
Will War Survive Until 2084?, 378 pp., 2013, $22.00.
What Are God's Goals?, 216 pp. 2014, $18.00

The following three books, The Chronicles of Jupiter, were written and originally published on Jupiter, and have been translated and edited by me. Although they are by different authors, they are considered a trilogy. They were best sellers on Jupiter. They are paperback, and published by AuthorHouse:

War On Jupiter, by Lieutenant Nublander, 417 pp., 2008, $22.00.
Brains Ought Not to Be Overworked, by Wrinklebonk, 299 pp., 2009, $19.00.
Final War On Jupiter, by Sagwind IV, Emperor of Ramosan, 323 pp., 2010, $21.00.

Shipping costs in the United States are completely free. Handling costs, however . . . oh, what the heck--I'll throw in handling costs as well.

For shipping costs outside the United States, please write me. They'll be small.

The books are also sold on the Internet by the usual suspects, as paper copies or as ebooks.

If you order from me, here's my address.

Carl Wells
723 1/2 E. Walnut Street
Brownstown, IN 47220-1518
carlwells@pyramid.org

Additional copies of *By Noble Things She Stands* are $22.00, again with no shipping costs in the United States.

Lightning Source UK Ltd.
Milton Keynes UK
UKOW02f1827031115

262031UK00001B/115/P